When The Clock Struck in 1916
CLOSE-QUARTER COMBAT IN THE EASTER RISING

DEREK MOLYNEUX and **DARREN KELLY** are close friends sharing a passionate interest in Irish and military history. Derek lives in Westmeath and Darren in Essex. They manage the popular Facebook page 'Dublin 1916 Then and Now'. Derek has an intimate knowledge of Dublin's streets, based on many years as a motorcycle courier, and how the same streets and people have preserved so much history from when the clock struck on 24 April 1916. Darren, originally from Drumcondra in Dublin, has built up an in-depth understanding of Dublin's revolutionary period over many years. His initial interest in the 1916 Rising was sparked at the age of ten.

Follow the authors on Facebook: Dublin 1916 Then & Now

To our wives and children, for your endless patience, love and inspiration

When The Clock Struck in 1916
CLOSE-QUARTER COMBAT IN THE EASTER RISING

DEREK MOLYNEUX & DARREN KELLY

The Collins Press

FIRST PUBLISHED IN 2015 BY
The Collins Press
West Link Park
Doughcloyne
Wilton
Cork

A CIP record for this book is available from the British Library.

Paperback ISBN: 978-1-84889-213-2
PDF eBook ISBN: 978-1-84889-877-6
EPUB eBook ISBN: 978-1-84889-878-3
Kindle ISBN: 978-1-84889-879-0

Design and typesetting by Carrigboy Typesetting Services
Typeset in Garamond Premier Pro

Printed in Poland by HussarBooks

Contents

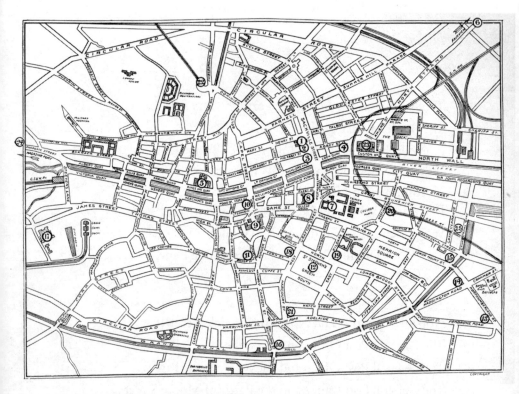

Map of Dublin City *c.* 1916 outlining the principal Volunteer and Citizen Army engagement areas. NATIONAL LIBRARY OF IRELAND.

Introduction

'Well, I've helped to wind up the clock – I might as well hear it strike.'

Michael Joseph O'Rahilly[1]

The Easter Rising of 1916 was a seminal moment in Ireland's turbulent history. Its justification has been hotly debated ever since. Those who were there found themselves in the midst of a no-holds-barred clash of opposing forces, one of which was the battle-hardened army of an empire, and the other a highly motivated and well-drilled force of volunteers, most of whom did not expect to survive the engagement. The vast majority of the fighting took place within a built-up city, the most feared combat zone of any soldier, and it is precisely there that we begin our story.

Volumes of books and articles have been published on both the causes and the long-term effects of the 1916 Rising, most from a predominantly academic standpoint. What this book sets out to achieve, however, is to present to the reader the dramatic story of Easter Week, from the perspective of the fighting that took place, and to convey its utter ferocity. For this we make use of subjective interpretation and licence. Everything you will read in the following pages is based on fact. All of the characters and events are real. Where we aim to differ from the vast bulk of previously written text is in presenting the sequence of events in as vivid a manner as possible. To this end we have employed some use of creative non-fiction.

The principal sources of our information are the numerous witness statements that are now widely available online, coupled with our own general but extensive knowledge of the subject matter, and backed up by the highly commendable works of several other authors. We combine this knowledge with an imagining of what the fighting actually felt, smelt, sounded, looked and even tasted like. How did the hungry, terrified and vastly outnumbered insurgents feel when confronted with thousands of enemy soldiers? How did the young English infantrymen cope with being placed into a streetscape for which they had received little or no training, only to be faced with seemingly fanatical rebels, many of whom felt they had nothing to lose? How did the civilians deal with the unleashing of an event very few saw coming, and the terrible consequences that accompanied and followed the cataclysm that claimed the lives of so many innocents?

It is only by placing the reader in the midst of the cauldron that was central Dublin during Easter Week 1916 that we feel we can do justice to the memories of those who found themselves there, whether by choice or otherwise. This is our aim. We will let you be the judge as to whether or not that aim has succeeded.

It was said by many of the British uniformed troops who engaged the Irish Volunteers and the Irish Citizen Army on the streets of what was considered to be Britain's second city that it was as dangerous a battlefield as any they had encountered before or afterwards. To the Republican forces it was a shattering experience, being vastly outnumbered and outgunned. Their skilful use of street-fighting tactics and their dogged tenacity in the face of overwhelming odds, however, was commended afterwards from the most unlikely of quarters, one of which, aston-ishingly, was the then British Prime Minister, Herbert Asquith.

Whatever one's opinions of the politics behind the event, its drama is undeniable. Both sides fought with great determination and, with some notable exceptions, great distinction. The casualty figures bear testament to this.

To Dublin's civilian population, the Rising was both tragic and bewildering, not to mention ironic. Many of their fathers, sons, husbands, brothers and cousins were fighting in the very same uniform of those the insurgents sought to kill in the name of the Irish Republic. The vast majority of these at the time were stationed throughout the far-flung corners of the Middle East and Western Europe but nonetheless, a great deal of those who fought against the men and women under Commandants Pearse and Connolly spoke with Irish accents themselves.

The reminders of the struggle are to be found today in just about every corner of Dublin's city centre. From the numerous bullet holes throughout the buildings along Northumberland Road and O'Connell Street, to the imposing facade of the Four Courts, there is much evidence of what the city endured, and what its people were faced with. It is also a reminder of what these same people overcame.

Dublin was a divided city in 1916. Its population was split between loyalty to the British Empire and fervent nationalism. Huge divisions also existed between the rich and poor. Regardless of their varying allegiances, its inhabitants were united in suffering through an event that resounded throughout the world at the time, and still does to this day. The story of such a relatively small number of men and women taking on the world's biggest empire in its own back yard stirred the imagination of both young and old everywhere.

It has been a truly humbling experience putting this work together. We have studied earnestly and, in doing so, have developed great empathy for the characters featured. We hope their experiences will leap from these pages and leave an emotional imprint on your mind. We do not set out to do this in order to manipulate or to suggest any particular opinion or ideology. We do it instead because it is our history, and it is rich. It is also more likely to be understood and remembered if presented in the compelling manner it deserves.

We have dealt with each of the Republican garrison areas separately in our work. This, we feel, will make it easier for the reader to break the Rising down and understand it piece by piece, or battle by battle, as it were. Having each confrontation presented as something of a set piece will hopefully facilitate this. We deliberately avoid bestowing laborious judgements upon the strategies employed by either side. Hindsight allows one to be analytical in depth, but it is not our aim here.

Some of the scenes we have presented may prove difficult to read for some, owing to their extremely graphic and bloody nature. We deliberately sought to present what street fighting was and is. We do this not to offend but instead to lay bare the very nature of combat. Sanitised descriptions of fighting do little justice to the unfortunate individuals who were ordered to kill and die in the name of the King, or the Irish Republic.

It is to the fighting men and women on both sides of this struggle, and the civilians caught between that we now dedicate this work. It is also to their descendants, the ordinary people who through their stories will never allow our history to be forgotten. Finally, it is to the woman whose witty comment quoted below inspired the decades of interest that eventually resulted in this book.

> *'Their bombs would barely singe the wallpaper ... but they held for a week.'*[2]

Derek Molyneux & Darren Kelly

Prologue

'I know you'll come through, but I won't.'

WITNESS STATEMENT

Bureau of Military History, 1913-1921

Statement by Witness

Document Number WS 157

Witness: Joseph O'Connor

Identity: Lieut. A/Coy. 3rd Bn. Dublin Bde. 1914-1915
          V/Comdt. 3rd Bn. Easter Week 1916

At a meeting of the Battalion Council in 144 Great
Brunswick Street on Good Friday night the following, I
am nearly certain, were present:-

   Commandant de Valera

   Captain Begley

   Lieutenant Byrne

   Lieutenant Charlie Murphy

   Volunteer Michael Hayes - on Adjutant's staff.

I represented "A" Company, Sean McMahon; "B" Company,
Eddie Byrne and Michael Malone; "C" Company; Captain
Begley, "D" Company. "E" Company was not represented,
nor was "F" Company.

We were given precise orders as to the positions we were
to occupy on Sunday and informed as to the quantity of

stores we would have at our disposal. A large quantity of provisions had been purchased and in addition each Company using their Company funds plus the £25 had accumulated an amount of stores. Each Company was to be responsible for the collection of such stores and for having them transported to the area in which his Company would operate.

The Commandant went over the plan in very great detail. In fact, he was able to tell each Company Captain where he would enter on to his area and what he would find to his advantage or disadvantage when he got there. The thing that concerned the meeting to a very great extent was the firm belief that enemy action would be taken before we had occupied positions, and it was with a view to having an alternative plan that an amount of the discussion resolved itself into.

The positions to be occupied over the area were given in detail.

"A" Company was to occupy the railway line between Grand Canal Quay to Dún Laoghaire. They were to occupy all the level crossings and assist in dominating Beggars Bush Barracks front and rere. They were to hold the railway workshops in Upper Grand Canal-Street and generally help other units coming within their range of fire.

"B" Company were to take over Westland Row Railway Station. They were to send a party up to Tara Street and link up with the 2nd Battalion who would be in charge of the Amiens Street section of the railway. They were on the other side to connect up with "A" Company on the railway at Grand Canal Quay.

"C" Company were to occupy Bolands Bakery and the Dispensary building at Grand Canal Street. They were to occupy Roberts builders' yard on the corner of the canal and Grand Canal Street. They were to barricade the canal bridge connecting Upper and Lower Grand Canal Street. They were to occupy Clanwilliam House, the schools and parochial hall on Northumberland Road and No. 25 Northumberland Road. "C" Company were also to have controlled the canal bridges at Upper Mount Street, Baggot Street and Leeson Street and join up with the 4th Battalion or the Irish Citizen Army.

"D" Company were to connect with "A" Company at the level crossing at Merrion. They were to hold a line from

Merrion to the Liffey along the coast including a boom which would be defended from land positions. This boom was to be at the end of the South Wall extending from south to north of the river. Their base was to have been Bolands Mills or the Distillery immediately adjoining which they were to have garrisoned. These were the instructions they got to occupy Bolands Mills.

"E" Company were not present and we were informed that they had a task to perform. This, we later heard, was to form part of the garrison of the G.P.O.

"F" Company was to connect with "A" Company at Dún Laoghaire Railway Station and to maintain the Railway Station and landing pier in the harbour.

On a calculation we all were certain that we would have eight to ten hundred men at our disposal.

After a very lengthy discussion as to the co-ordination of our forces Lieutenant Michael Malone of "C" Company, who had been detailed to occupy 25 Northumberland Road, walked over to where I was after the meeting had finished, and said, "Well, Joe, It's pretty close to hand. I know you'll come through, but I won't."

One of the main factors in the position was the railway line connecting Dublin and Dún Laoghaire. This was a main route of supply from Britain and it was very important that the enemy should be denied its use as it entered the very heart of the city.

I was amazed at the amount of information our Commandant had accumulated and how thoroughly he understood about the position each Company was to occupy. He was able to discuss every detail even to the places where it would be possible to procure an alternative water supply, where we could definitely find tools for such things as loopholing walls and making communications. I am positively certain that he had spent months reconnoitring that entire area and in our discussions, particularly that one of Good Friday night when we really got down to the task put before us, I cannot remember a query put to him that he was not able to answer immediately, and there was not a solitary suggestion to improve the dispositions made. De Valera certainly showed that he had given his full attention to the task ahead and that if anything did go wrong it certainly would not be his fault. This was all very encouraging to us.

As to how much our officers and men knew, I cannot say. I knew that there was to be a rising, and with outside help I thought it could be successful; I thought that every man would rush in to help.

The ordinary conditions of the national life had become so bad that it was nearly impossible to see a difference between Ireland and England. The little the Gaelic League did was largely undone by the Great War, and something big should happen to reawaken the country to her sense of importance.

1

The Assault on the Magazine Fort, Phoenix Park

'Wake up, wake up, Tim. It starts at noon.'

O n Sunday morning 16 April 1916, 27-year-old Irish Volunteer
Paddy Daly entered Clontarf Town Hall, which was situated at the
seafront 2 miles to the north-east of Dublin's city centre. Once inside,
he was greeted by Seán McDermott, one of the three Irish Republican
Brotherhood (IRB) members who were holding a meeting there.
McDermott then introduced Daly to his two fellow members saying:
'Paddy has some great ideas about the Magazine Fort and I would like
you to hear what he has to say.'[1]

Daly subsequently laid down his plan for the proposed attack to
destroy the British Army High Explosive and Ammunition Reserve held
in the Magazine Fort in the Phoenix Park.

The Fort dated from 1734, and presented a daunting yet tantalising
objective. It was a granite walled structure whose 12-foot-high and
4-foot-thick walls were protected by a deep ditch and ringed with several
turrets into which firing slits had been placed. The surrounding area was
heavily wooded and contained numerous small hills and depressions,
but to use these features to conceal the approach of an assault force
would be impossible. Its designers had ensured that the immediately
surrounding ground was clear of any such potential sources of advantage
to an attacker. To reach the Fort required a steep ascent on foot over

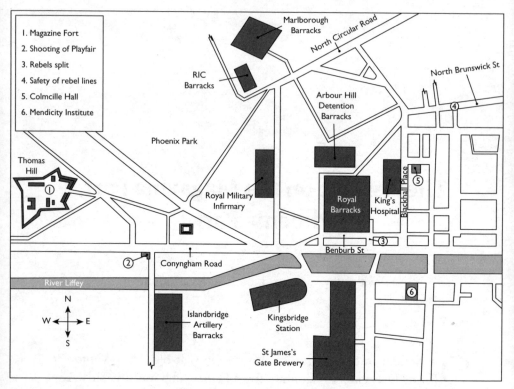

The Magazine Fort and the area from where the insurgents attacked and escaped.

several hundred yards of open ground, to where it dominated the entire southern area of the Phoenix Park, 2 miles to the north-west of the city. It commanded a relatively unobstructed view of both sides of the River Liffey, and several army barracks were located close by, the nearest being less than a mile away at Islandbridge, while another two sat within 15 minutes' marching distance. Daly then explained that the attack would have to be made during daytime, as any movement at night of a large force of men towards the structure would be seen as suspicious by its guards.

At first glance, the mission's potential pitfalls seemed insurmountable, but the ever-inventive Daly was only too happy to offer his solution. He worked inside the Magazine Fort as a carpenter, and possessed an in-depth knowledge of its day-to-day running and, more importantly, the strength of its guard. This knowledge would be combined with the imaginative employment of tactics used since the Trojan War: deception and guile.

Daly explained to the three men that during the daytime it was not uncommon for large groups of footballers to pass the Fort heading towards the nearby Fifteen Acres playing fields. The assault force could simply disguise itself as such a group until its men were close enough to its main gate to mount an attack. When asked by Thomas Clarke, the 59-year-old Republican veteran who stood next to McDermott, if there was a large quantity of high explosive still in the Fort, his reply was that in spite of the bulk having been removed to England for use on the Western Front, there was still more than enough to make a large bang.

Clarke nodded and the decision was made to go ahead with the attack, and to use its huge explosion, which would no doubt be heard throughout the city, as a signal to all that the Rising had begun. Clarke then asked Daly how many men the mission would need. 'About thirty,' was the reply, before he added that they would all need to be young Volunteers and preferably Na Fianna members.[2]

Thomas MacDonagh, the third of the upcoming insurrection's leaders present, entered the conversation by informing Daly that he would need to be promoted, so that he could assume overall command of the mission, and presented him there and then with his lieutenant's commission. As Lieutenant Daly prepared to leave, McDermott issued him with the orders: 'Take the Fort. Blow it up, but no loss of life if possible.'

The following day, Lieutenant Daly had a meeting with 24-year-old Eamon Martin, Commandant of the Dublin Brigade of Na Fianna, about the upcoming attack. He then held another meeting with two brothers from the same organisation, 21-year-old Garry and 19-year-old Patrick Holohan, during which he informed them also of the plan, and explained additionally that he needed them to recruit thirty men as part of a special force for the assault. The three then parted company temporarily before the enthusiastic siblings returned just over an hour later with the requested list. It bore their own names at the top.

Three days later, on Thursday 20 April, Lieutenant Daly, Eamon Martin and the Holohan brothers met with Commandant MacDonagh, and made their final selection for their unit. They then gathered the men they had selected, and the plan was laid out. Each Volunteer was told of his specific role in the attack, which was set to follow the force's assembly at the Holohan brothers' small bungalow at 8 Rutland Cottages, close to Summerhill in the city centre, at the appropriate time on Easter Sunday.

Contingency plans were then put together, and any potential mishaps were played out. There would be little or no room for error.

On Easter Saturday, the day before the Rising was due to commence, Garry Holohan found himself sitting in his bedroom staring at his haversack. His Martini-Henry rifle lay just across from it. With the rebellion just hours away, his nerves were starting to get to him, so to keep his mind occupied he checked his backpack over and over. It contained 24 hours' rations, consisting primarily of dry biscuits, cheese and some jam; there were also 100 rounds for his rifle, his bayonet, first-aid kit, water canteen and entrenching tool. Everything was there, but to his frustration he knew that his tortured mind would inevitably insist that he check it all again. He entered Pat's room, and when he explained his predicament, his brother laughed and replied that he was having the same trouble. They chatted for a few hours, before Garry left the cottage and went to Eamon Martin's house on Shelbourne Road in Ballsbridge, where he spent the night.

The following morning, on what should have been the day of days for the young Na Fianna men, Eamon Martin and Garry Holohan arrived suddenly in Pat's bedroom and flung that day's *Independent* newspaper onto his bed. He rubbed the sleep from his eyes and glanced over its headlines, a look of horror spreading across his face. He looked initially to Martin, and then to his brother, who explained to him that Eoin MacNeill had issued a countermand order, and that the whole thing could be off.

Soon afterwards, a somewhat agitated and breathless Lieutenant Daly arrived at the cottage, carrying information that was no less confusing. He brought word from Commandant MacDonagh that in spite of the day's unexpected newspaper alert, the job was merely to be postponed for 24 hours. He explained all he knew about the increasingly uncertain situation and then left, telling them he would return at the same time the following day.

Eamon Martin soon got up to leave, saying that he was going to see James Connolly to find out what was happening. He arrived back several hours later, this time accompanied by a pair of teenage Na Fianna members. He confirmed Lieutenant Daly's instructions and assured both Holohan brothers that the job was definitely on for the following day, Easter Monday.

(L–r): Eamon Martin and Garry Holohan, both of whom helped to spearhead the assault on the Magazine Fort on Easter Monday, photographed in 1916.
EAMON MURPHY

The three immediately began to write dispatches to send to their other squad members, ordering them to report to Rutland Cottages by early afternoon the following day. The two recently arrived Na Fianna teenagers were dispatched with the orders, before Garry Holohan set about collecting the 24 revolvers and semi-automatic handguns that had been hidden in the cottage for when the time came. With little else to occupy their time while they waited, the three sat down and began cleaning the weapons, methodically stripping each to its component parts while they talked about what might become of their planned insurrection.

At 10 a.m. on Easter Monday, an out-of-breath Lieutenant Daly banged on the Holohan brothers' front door. As Garry opened it, Daly barged past and exclaimed in great alarm, 'It starts at twelve, not half three! How many men do we have so far?'

'None at the moment,' was the somewhat startled reply from Holohan. This was immediately followed by more disturbing news for the young rebels, when the two Na Fianna runners sent out the previous day arrived back with word that most of the squad members they had been sent to contact had gone camping for the weekend, believing the job to have been postponed indefinitely.

The same two youngsters were ordered to proceed urgently to the houses of the individual squad members who were still at home, with instructions for them to report at once to Rutland Cottages. Garry Holohan rushed outside and jumped on one of several bicycles that had been leaning against the neighbouring wall, and pedalled at full speed to Tim Roche's house, which was in nearby Seville Place. He stormed through the front door and ran towards the bedroom, shouting, 'Wake up, wake up, Tim. It starts at noon! You need to get a van and be outside the Magazine Fort by half eleven!' Roche rushed to dress himself, while Holohan returned in haste to Rutland Cottages.

When he arrived back, he noticed that Seán Ford had arrived with the mission's supply of canister bombs, meaning that they now had the means, if not the men, to carry out their attack. A decision was rapidly made: Ford would stay there and guard the bombs while the others would go to Liberty Hall to see what help they could get there. Lieutenant Daly, the Holohan brothers and Eamon Martin cycled off at full speed to Liberty Hall in Dublin's Beresford Place, roughly half a mile from the cottage.

They arrived at 10.40 a.m. and were spotted by Irish Citizen Army Captain Seán Connolly. He asked what they were doing there and they promptly outlined their precarious manpower situation. They were immediately ushered into the office of the Commandant General of the Irish Volunteer Forces, where James Connolly, the 47-year-old veteran socialist, ordered a memo to be typed and delivered with speed to the four Volunteer battalions preparing to launch their uprising, stating that each was to donate six or seven men to the 'special force'.

The four then remounted their bicycles and set off, pedalling furiously in their various directions to the relevant parts of the city, where each rebel battalion was preparing. Garry Holohan's bones shook as he sped across the cobblestones that led to Commandant Éamonn Ceannt's house in Dolphin's Barn. As he was about to knock on the 4th Battalion's Commander's front door, 20-year-old Volunteer Barney Mellows walked out and told him to hurry inside. Ceannt quickly read Holohan's dispatch, but replied that he could not spare any men as he was already seriously undermanned. Holohan asked if he could take

Mellows. 'Yes', was the reply from the sombre-looking Ceannt, who also suggested that he show the order to Captain Con Colbert, whose Company was assembling in Emerald Square.

Holohan jumped on the bicycle and caught up with Mellows. He told him to go straight to Rutland Cottages, explaining hurriedly that he was needed for a job. He then pedalled to Emerald Square in the Coombe area of Dublin, where he was met by his good friend Con Colbert of F Company who was gathering his group of Volunteers. He handed him the order, adding that he needed men without uniforms. Colbert called out six men and passed them into the command of his comrade. Holohan told the Captain he would see him when it was all over. 'Sure you will,' was Colbert's confident reply.

Holohan quickly saw his six new charges onto another tram, pausing momentarily to ponder the contrast between himself and the blissfully carefree passengers, before cycling back to Rutland Cottages. On his way, he noticed the men of Commandant MacDonagh's 2nd Battalion gathering for their march on Jacob's biscuit factory. He sensed great urgency and increased his speed, hoping that Lieutenant Daly had managed to muster some men from the same assembling Battalion.

When Holohan eventually arrived back at the cottage it was full to the brim with men, while others continued to arrive either on foot or by bicycle. It seemed as though the walls of the small building would burst with all the movement inside, while the cache of handguns was distributed to those who had arrived unarmed. Then, with a rough map of the target, Lieutenant Daly laid out the plan to all and made sure every Volunteer knew his precise position and role in the upcoming attack. Fragmentary orders were given to the attentive sections of men, outlining precisely how each individual move was to be played out by their particular squad or group. Daly then asked if everything was clear, and looked around for any doubtful-looking faces. It was imperative that everyone, down to the last man, knew exactly what he was to do. The men, however, appeared satisfied. As they began to filter out, Daly issued a final word, that once the job was done, they were to try and make it back to their various battalion areas.

Tim Roche had no trouble starting the van he had selected for the job, albeit without the permission of its owner, and as he sped down Queen Street towards the quays he glanced at his wristwatch. He reckoned he should be just in time for the 11.30 a.m. rendezvous. Suddenly, out of

(L–r): Pat and Garry Holohan with Na Fianna comrades Michael Lonergan, Pádraig Ó Riain and Con Colbert. NATIONAL LIBRARY OF IRELAND

nowhere, a dog darted across the road in front of him. Roche swerved to avoid the animal, but crashed into a lamp post. The impact temporarily dazed him, and as he did his best to pull himself together, the few locals who had seen the crash began to gather around the vehicle.

They were dumbfounded when Roche leapt out and ran away. He sprinted towards the lower end of Queen Street where he noticed a horse-drawn cab with its driver, or jarvey, on board parked up at the roadside, waiting for a fare. He jumped in, asking the driver to take him to the Phoenix Park. The jarvey, pleased with his first fare of the day, then shouted 'Gee up!' and they set off. When the cabbie made a comment about the beautiful spring weather, Roche looked briefly up at the sky, but felt he had more pressing matters to discuss with his new-found accomplice. He checked that he still had his revolver and leaned back in the seat and told him he would have to wait when they got there as they would be picking up some more people. The driver smiled broadly, hardly able to believe his luck at getting what could possibly be the best fare of the day so early on a bank holiday.

Back at Rutland Cottages the assault force was leaving in small groups, some on bicycles, and others on foot, but with the intention of catching a tram. They planned to regroup near the Magazine Fort. When they had all departed, Daly, Martin and the two Holohan brothers set off on their bikes towards the Phoenix Park, making sure to stop at Whelan's shop on Ormond Quay, a known Volunteer meeting point, to procure a football.

When they arrived there, Séamus Whelan was sitting behind the counter of his shop. He looked up and nodded at Garry Holohan and Lieutenant Daly as they stepped inside, before the latter approached the counter explaining that they needed a ball, but didn't have any money. The proprietor laughed, but reached under the counter and produced a leather football. 'Will this do?' he asked as he handed it over. They thanked him and left to rejoin their comrades outside, before continuing to the Fort.

They entered the Phoenix Park via its Islandbridge Gate, where Garry Holohan scanned the wooded and hilly area nearby for Tim Roche and his van, concerned at their apparent absence. They eventually passed the parked cab, at which point Roche jumped down next to Holohan and explained to his surprised comrade the events which had led to him sitting in a horse-drawn cab. Holohan glanced at the driver and then asked Roche if he thought he suspected anything. 'Not a thing' was the reply. Holohan told him to ensure the driver did not bolt once it started, then dropped his bike and ran to catch up with Lieutenant Daly, who was now walking towards a group of men who had their eyes firmly fixed on the mission's leader. By the time he reached his side, Daly had thrown the football into the centre of the group. Their 'kick about' on the grass started and they began to edge towards the Fort.

The sentry at Magazine Fort's main gate cursed the monotony of his two-hour beat as he watched the bank-holiday footballers making the most of the midday sunshine. Most of his comrades were by now enjoying the Fairyhouse Races some 15 miles away in County Meath, and being stuck on sentry duty was not a chore that any private soldier relished. He kept his eye on the footballers as they drew ever closer. A game of soccer would have been the perfect antidote to his boredom.

The 'footballers' began to form into three sections. Paddy Boland shadowed the Volunteer carrying the ball, all the while keeping an eye on the sentry, who was now paying them his utmost attention.

'We're late,' muttered Garry Holohan to Barney Mellows. He looked at his wristwatch: it read 12.20 p.m. They both then glanced up into the air, as the ball arched up and over the Fort's wall. The game was on.

They asked the sentry if they could have their ball back, to which the answer, 'of course', came from the trusting young soldier. Paddy Boland drew level with the ball's kicker, priming himself for what was to come. He then pounced forward as the sentry turned, having opened the gate. As the sentry bent down to pick up the ball, he found himself suddenly dragged to the ground, where he crumpled unceremoniously under the weight of Boland's unexpected assault. He feared the worst momentarily as he felt the cold steel of a pistol barrel pressing into the nape of his neck, but the sharply uttered words, 'don't move and you'll be fine', provided welcome relief while he weighed up his options. The clatter of leather boots trampling close by his head as the rebels rushed past him convinced him that such options were few. He offered no resistance. The special force was in.

Daly's section stormed into the guardroom, having been the first to pass the grounded sentry. They overpowered the guards there before any of them had a chance to react. Holohan and Mellows then rushed past its door, keeping an ear out for any shooting from behind as they raced down the long corridor. The lack of gunfire to their rear reassured them that their backs were satisfactorily covered in order to allow them to capture another sentry, who was positioned on the parapet of the large quadrangle at the Fort's centre, before he could raise the alarm.

They burst through the door at the end of the corridor and into the bright sunlight, shielding their eyes as they scanned the parapet, but saw nothing. 'Where is he?' muttered Holohan, then he suddenly spotted the tip of a bayonet sticking out by one of the machine-gun huts scattered along the structure. He rushed to the steps nearest him, while Mellows ran to the set furthest away, thereby surrounding the sentry, before they mounted the steps onto the parapet and shouted 'Surrender!' while Holohan covered the sentry with his pistol.

The sentry un-shouldered his rifle to shoot, but his face suddenly twisted in pain as a shot rang out. Holohan had fired and hit him in the leg. He fell to the floor of the parapet, screaming. The pair of rebels scanned their surroundings for danger.

As the reverberations of the pistol shot faded, a pair of Volunteers went to knock on the door of the residence next to the Fort's guardhouse.

Mrs Isabel Playfair, 46 years old, went to open the door to the two, who expected her to assume the shot had been a 'negligent discharge' and hoped that she would want to give the Fort's commander, her husband, a right earful over the troop's lack of discipline. However, she drew back with a look of shock as she opened the door to the two armed men who then ordered her to 'gather the children and come with us, and no one will be harmed'.

Tim Roche, standing by the horse-drawn cab, noticed the section of Volunteers who had remained outside the Fort manoeuvering into covering positions. They looked from side to side as they moved, and scanning the small, narrow roadway that led east and west from the Fort. Roche walked slowly towards the horse, and patted it gently on the head. He assured the driver that it would not be much longer. The reply suggested that there was no hurry. Roche smiled back at him.

Daly and his section soon managed to enter the Small Arms Room, where they started smashing open the many ammunition boxes situated just inside. They were unable, however, to find the keys to the High Explosives Room. They decided to improvise, piling the broken ammunition crates against the wall, which they then covered in paraffin, drums of which were wheeled in from outside. Seán Ford unpacked the many canister bombs while Eamon Martin and Pat Holohan methodically placed them throughout the explosive cocktail. They hoped the ensuing blast would blow through the wall and ignite whatever high explosives were inside.

Back on the parapet, Garry Holohan and Barney Mellows were tending to the soldier whom Holohan had shot. Unable to get him upright, and not wanting to leave him there helplessly in the midst of what they hoped would be an earth-shattering explosion, Mellows did his best to reassure him. He stemmed the flow of blood from the sentry, getting his hands and clothing covered in blood. Both he and Holohan then went to the guardroom, where they dispatched some prisoners to rescue their wounded comrade.

Next, Holohan joined his brother, Pat, and Eamon Martin, and they began laying the long fuses from the canister bombs. Five minutes passed, and all was ready.

Lieutenant Daly watched attentively as the wounded soldier was carried into the guardroom, before he turned to the group of prisoners, which included the horrified Playfair family, saying: 'The Fort is to be blown. You have five minutes to clear out.' He added that if any of them were seen heading towards the city they would be shot, before shouting, 'Now leave!' The frightened group did not need to be told twice.

He called to the Volunteers to withdraw from the Fort and ordered the captured weapons to be loaded onto the cab. As the rebels rushed out, the demolition squad, which included the Holohan brothers and Eamon Martin, accompanied by a covering team of two, patiently waited for the last of their comrades to leave. Everything was going according to plan.

Tim Roche drew his pistol and shouted at the cabbie 'Don't try anything now', as numerous Volunteers ran towards them, weighed down with extra Lee Enfield rifles slung across their shoulders. Roche grabbed the horse's bridle to hold it steady, while the driver felt a sudden feeling of dread overcome him. He recalled the fate of another cabbie several decades earlier, known as 'Skin the Goat', who was press-ganged into helping with the Phoenix Park Murders and subsequently sentenced to many long years in prison.

'Are we ready?' Martin asked his two comrades as they began lighting the fuses. A loud hiss prompted the three to make their hasty escape from the Fort, followed by the pair of men who had covered them. Once outside they saw their squad dispersing, and in a minute or so, the area around the Fort was empty. As the five men ran towards the cab, they found Mellows, Roche and Lieutenant Daly sitting around it, waiting for them. Garry Holohan jumped onto his bicycle while the others joined the three men with the terrified cabby. 'To Blackhall Place, please,' said Roche, his polite manners providing little relief to the petrified driver, who said nothing. He whipped the horse and they moved off, following Holohan who was now a short distance in front, acting as a lookout.

Suddenly, Lieutenant Daly spotted the Playfairs' eldest son, 23-year-old George, sprinting through the Park's Islandbridge Gate, having bolted to raise the alarm. He shouted, 'Stop him!' to Holohan. Cycling in hot pursuit, Holohan saw Playfair make a dash towards a policeman before running on again. Holohan pedalled hard, out through the Park's gate where it met the Chapelizod Road, and it was here that he saw his target make the right turn onto Islandbridge Road. He turned the same corner and leapt off the bike, drawing his handgun as he did.

Playfair ran up the driveway of the house at No. 1 Park Place, the first of three houses diagonally facing the road junction, as Holohan coldly levelled his pistol. The terrified revenue clerk banged desperately on the Georgian door as the Volunteer took aim. The door opened, presenting Playfair with the brief hope of safety before three shots rang out. The housemaid who had answered his knocking screamed as the mortally wounded man slumped in the open doorway, shot in the abdomen. Holohan turned away but kept his handgun out, thinking he might yet have to deal with the constable, but there was now no sign of him.

He cycled back towards the Park's gate, where the cab was now exiting. A dull boom sounded out from behind them, and the seven men in the carriage gave a loud cheer. Their exuberance was premature, however, as the High Explosives Room had not succumbed to their improvisations, and the noise they had heard was merely their failed effort to penetrate its wall. Holohan rode forward again and they moved towards Parkgate Street and the city, keeping their eyes averted from the unfolding tragedy in the doorway to their right where the horrified housemaid was doing her best to comfort the slowly dying man.

Lieutenant Daly suddenly sensed that something was wrong when he saw Holohan stop in the middle of the road and look back at them. The jarvey was told to slow down and come to a halt a short distance behind him. Fingers slipped onto the triggers of handguns. Ahead of them, a gun carriage bearing a coffin followed by a military guard approached. As it passed, the rebels waited with bated breath for any sudden move. They did their best to avoid drawing attention, which was not an easy task considering their driver's increasing nervousness. They waited, and sweated, as the column passed them, before moving off again. Daly ordered the man facing him to watch their rear for any sign of military movement from Islandbridge Barracks.

Holohan soon drew level with the Royal Barracks. The River Liffey was to his right and the Barracks' entrance archway was 100 yards to his left. The road in front was teeming with soldiers in British uniform being issued with instructions and extra ammunition. The rebellion appeared to have begun. The small convoy came once again to a stop. Their battalion area was only minutes away, but they were now deep within enemy territory.

Holohan cycled forward and saw groups of soldiers crouching and kneeling behind the 4-foot-high quay wall just ahead of him. He turned and pedalled the short distance back to the cab. They then made the decision to split up. Daly, Mellows and Murphy left the cab to proceed on foot, armed with revolvers, while the rebel column, with Holohan still cycling in front, pressed on, turning away from the quays as they moved towards the main gate of the Barracks, at which point Holohan turned right onto Benburb Street, and was followed by the cab. The street was thronged with troops, some carrying wounded comrades and others preparing to go into battle. The palpitating jarvey was warned not to try anything or he would get the first bullet. They would run the gauntlet. As they moved along the road, many soldiers stopped and stared at them, but no challenge came.

When they made the left turn onto Blackhall Place, they felt a huge sense of relief, as the road was completely deserted. The horse strained as the driver whipped it to increase their speed in spite of the slight uphill climb, having been assured it was not much further. They turned right onto North Brunswick Street and were met by the sight of Volunteers hastily building a barricade across the road. As they approached, Holohan cycled forward, causing the rebels there to reach for their guns. County Cork native Captain Dinny O'Callaghan, of the 1st Battalion Irish Volunteers, recognised him immediately, however, and settled his men with the words: 'They are ours, lads, lower the guns.'

The captured weapons were quickly unloaded and passed across the barricade. The jarvey looked apprehensively at Tim Roche who gave him the nod to clear off. As the clatter of horse hooves faded into the distance, Holohan picked up the bicycle and threw it onto the barricade. He laughed loudly as he suddenly realised that he had been cycling a ladies' bike, before he clambered over the barricade.

George Playfair died of his wounds later that night.

2

The Battle of City Hall

'Good luck, Seán, for we won't meet again.'

In Liberty Hall on Dublin's Beresford Place on the afternoon of Easter Sunday, 23 April 1916, Commandant James Connolly was in a foul mood. He had earlier been shown the countermand order placed in that day's *Sunday Independent* newspaper by the man in charge of the Irish Volunteers, Eoin MacNeill. This order cancelled all Irish Volunteer manoeuvres for that day, and effectively put an end to the Irish Republican Brotherhood's plans for a nationwide insurrection.

At 3.30 p.m., approximately 200 men and women of Connolly's Irish Citizen Army lined up outside Liberty Hall regardless and awaited orders from their outspoken and burly commandant, who soon appeared on the building's steps. After briefly inspecting their ranks he ordered: 'Right turn, prepare to march!' whereupon he joined the head of their two columns. They then set off across the River Liffey via the nearby Butt Bridge, which led them onto Tara Street, before they turned right on to Great Brunswick Street. Their route then skirted Trinity College and eventually brought them to the top of Grafton Street, from where they wheeled right and made their way back to Dame Street. As the marching men and women approached Dublin Castle, the seat of British colonial power in Ireland, tensely muttered rumours circulated among them they were 'going it alone', but they eventually passed its gates and continued on their march up Lord Edward Street, turning right after Christchurch to make for the south quays. It was almost evening by the time they returned to Liberty Hall. The Castle was safe for now.

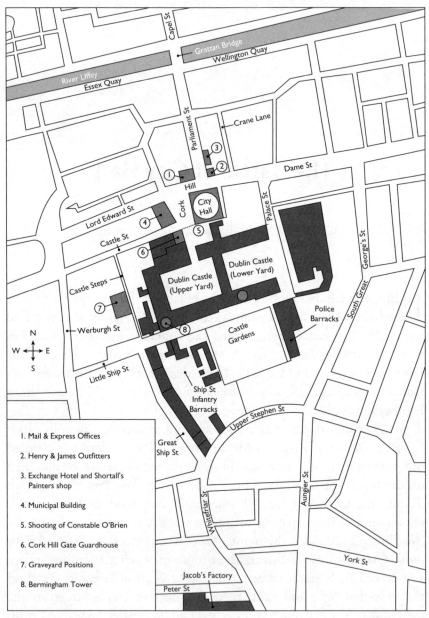

City Hall, Dublin Castle and surrounding area.

As the well-drilled Citizen Army members lined up once again outside the Hall, dressed in their distinctive bottle-green uniforms and slouched hats, Connolly was sent word from Pádraig Pearse, who was still inside with the other IRB leaders. After heated discussions the planned Rising had been set to begin at noon the following day, Easter Monday, 24 April. It was on.

Connolly immediately sprang into action. He ordered all members of the Citizen Army to remain at Liberty Hall overnight, with the exception of those who had to report for work. They were instead given instructions to return by noon the following day.

At 11 a.m. the next morning, as the Irish Volunteers and Citizen Army were gathering amid the feverish activity at Liberty Hall, 33-year-old Captain Seán Connolly and his detachment of 40 men plus a handful of women prepared themselves and their weapons for their attack on City Hall. The captain would lead the assault. This large and imposing building, dating from 1779, lay just outside the gates of Dublin Castle at the junction of Parliament Street and Dame Street. Their armaments included revolver pistols, single-shot rifles and the more rapid firing Lee Enfields. As they were setting off, James Connolly approached the captain and vigorously shook his hand, saying, 'Good luck, Seán, for we won't meet again,'[1] before he himself hurried towards the much larger force that was preparing to march from the same building to the GPO.

Captain Connolly's group then turned as a unit, to the tune of young Private William Oman's bugle call, and marched across Butt Bridge. Many among them shared their commandant's sense of foreboding of the trip being a one-way affair. As Captain Connolly and his men crossed the Liffey on what had become a sunny spring morning, one of the men asked if they were going to take Dublin Castle as well as City Hall. He replied: 'It would be too great an area to defend, and with a Red Cross Hospital on site, too many mouths to feed.' As their march continued along Tara Street, in almost identical order to the previous day, they were spotted by their captain's brother Joseph, who had just finished his shift at the fire station. He waved enthusiastically to the unit and wished them luck, before rushing off towards Liberty Hall to join his own Citizen Army outfit, which had been detailed to St Stephen's Green.

Soon afterwards, Captain Seán Connolly and his unit, which included another of his brothers, 15-year-old Matty, reached the end of Dame Street, where they broke into smaller sections. Sergeant Martin Kelly then set off with a detachment to capture the offices of the *Daily Express* and *Dublin Evening Mail*,[2] which were in a four-storey red-

Sergeant Martin Kelly, who was in charge of the Citizen Army unit that wreaked havoc on the Dublin Fusiliers from his men's position close to City Hall. BARRY LYONS

brick building on the western corner of Parliament Street, where it met with Cork Hill. Sergeant Elliot Elmes and his group went about seizing Henry & James Outfitters, a similar building on the opposite corner of Parliament Street. William Oman and four others had been ordered to occupy the viaduct overlooking Ship Street Barracks at the rear of Dublin Castle. The remainder under Captain Connolly would storm City Hall itself, leaving a small squad under Sergeant Tom Kane to take its guardhouse and provide cover while the other positions were being occupied.

As they approached the main entrance of the Castle at Cork Hill, 45-year-old Dublin Metropolitan Police Constable James O'Brien rushed to close its gate. A loud crack of a rifle rang out, and the veteran policeman from Limerick fell to the ground, shot in the head. Connolly's men had drawn the first blood of the Easter Rising.

This sudden plunge into action prompted Sergeant Kane to rush forward while firing into the Castle's guardroom, quickly forcing the surrender of the small, startled group of troops inside. They were swiftly taken prisoner. The insurgents set about constructing a small barricade around the guardroom entrance. The other sections simultaneously assaulted their assigned positions upon hearing the same gunshot, while a small group opened fire on a cluster of British troops who had run up Parliament Street to investigate. The soldiers immediately retreated, and were then pursued by a single rebel who sprinted towards them pointing his gun, before he turned and dashed back towards City Hall.

Sixteen-year-old William Oman's detailed objective at the viaduct posed the greatest challenge due to its significant distance from the launching point for the rebel attack. He and his men began their assault by sprinting up Castle Street, with City Hall at their backs. They broke through a nearby tenement house to their left and, rushing through its rear, they came upon an old graveyard. They crossed the uneven half-acre of ground, before Oman, displaying a tactical awareness that belied his youth, opted to man a separate position to the viaduct, which afforded the same field of fire but offered additional cover for him and his men. As soon as they were securely emplaced in their improvised positions, they noticed movement inside Ship Street Barracks. They swiftly undid their rifles' safety catches and began firing through its windows, forcing the surprised troops inside to rush for cover as shards of broken glass flew and bullets smashed into the walls around them.

At this time Sir Matthew Nathan, the 54-year-old British Under-Secretary for Ireland, was holding a meeting in his first-floor offices inside the Castle. Also present was Ivor Price of British Intelligence and Arthur Norway, a prosperous gentleman from Cornwall who was in charge of the GPO. They had been discussing the possibility of severing the telephone lines of the city's civilian population while the army rounded up the leaders of the Irish Volunteers. Rumours had been circulating for some time in the Castle about an imminent rebellion. They realised they had left it too late when the sharp, piercing cracks of rifle fire reached them. Price ran to the window overlooking the Castle's main gate before turning to Nathan, saying that the rebellion appeared to be already under way. He hurriedly pulled his service revolver from its holster and began firing at the rebels now guarding the gate.

Price telephoned the nearby Ship Street Barracks and informed the officer in charge that a full-scale attack on the Castle had begun, while Nathan armed the constables on duty and then with their help locked its upper and lower gates. He was joined by a handful of British troops who had managed to scramble from the barracks, narrowly avoiding the fire from Oman and his men just above them.

In the meantime, about three quarters of a mile away, Irish Citizen Army Sergeant George King and an Irish Volunteer from their 3rd Battalion succeeded in opening a manhole cover on the corner of

Lombard Street East and Great Brunswick Street, their movements covered by comrades keeping watch from the nearby street corners. They set about cutting the Castle's vital communication cable with London.

Having locked the Castle gates, Sir Nathan returned to his office and telephoned Military Headquarters in the Phoenix Park to inform them of the attack. Next, he picked up the receiver of his direct line to London, but as he waited for an answer the line went dead. He exclaimed to Price: 'They have cut the lines!' He ran to the nearby Telegraph Office just off Dame Street, which would have been taken by the insurgents had they not been misinformed by a lady nearby that it was full of military. From here he wired London about the rebellion.

Captain Seán Connolly and his force entered City Hall via its basement on the eastern side at Exchange Street. A section was dispatched to its huge domed roof while the remainder set about barricading its ground-floor windows. To gain entry, the Citizen Army women had to climb over the tall black wrought-iron gates at the steps on the building's Castle Street side, hoisting their long skirts as they did, much to the amusement of several small clusters of onlookers who peered out from the nearby laneways, keen to see what was going on. Once inside, the Chief Medical Officer of the Citizen Army, 42-year-old Dr Kathleen Lynn, ordered a field hospital to be set up on the ground floor, and a kitchen on the first. She could now hear gunfire from the roof.

Meanwhile, about 2 miles from City Hall, Colonel H. V. Cowan at Military Headquarters in the Phoenix Park telephoned Richmond, Portobello and Royal Barracks and ordered troops to rush to the immediate relief of Dublin Castle. He then placed an urgent call to the Curragh Army Camp in Kildare and requested Brigadier General Lowe to mobilise the 1,600 men of the 3rd Reserve Cavalry Brigade under Colonel Portal and advance to Dublin, before this line, too, went dead. A dispatch was then sent to the nearby Marlborough Barracks on Blackhorse Avenue ordering the 6th Reserve Cavalry Regiment to advance to the city centre.

A short time later, a large force of the 10th Royal Dublin Fusiliers marched out of the Royal Barracks on Benburb Street towards Dublin Castle. They immediately came under rifle fire from rebels positioned in the Mendicity Institute across the river and other positions which were springing up throughout that part of the city. However, they managed to cross the Liffey and, by using various backstreets, made their way through Christchurch and eventually to the cluster of narrow intersections around Longford Street. Here they connected with a company of the Royal Irish Rifles which had been advancing from Portobello Barracks having detoured along Mercer Street to avoid the recently taken rebel stronghold in Jacob's biscuit factory.

At 1.30 p.m. William Oman's small group of rebels were securely emplaced in their elevated position overlooking Dublin Castle and its surrounding area. Harassing fire was a growing problem and bullets regularly whined through the air close by, but their position gave them safe cover. Oman was the first to notice an ominous-looking force of about 200 khaki uniforms making its way towards Ship Street Barracks. His men immediately opened fire on the troops but they made it into the Barracks relatively unscathed, rushing through the arched entrance which sat halfway down the hill of the street to its right. The troops covered each other in sections and avoided the many rebel shots that ricocheted wildly off the cobblestones and walls around them. The tables turned once they gained the Barracks and soon Oman and his men came under fire. Within half an hour the Castle's Bermingham Tower was swarming with British Army snipers. In spite of being a dangerous nuisance, they nevertheless posed little real threat to Oman and his men as their position provided them with adequate cover. The teenager's last-minute improvisation regarding the tactical placement of his men was proving to be an inspired one.

The men on the City Hall roof were not so fortunate. Just after 2 p.m. an intense firefight developed between themselves and the Castle's newly arrived garrison. Captain Seán Connolly made a circuit of the roof's massive copper dome to check on his men, all the while doing his best to stay under the cover of its various-sized chimneys. He fired numerous rounds into the Castle grounds as bullets ricocheted around the roof nearby. British troops in the Castle hugged its many concrete parapets as the rebel bullets screamed back at them. In the Castle's yards, small groups of soldiers dashed here and there, trying to avoid being hit. Connolly peered around the massive green dome to take another aim. A multitude of shots whizzed by, and one smashed into his chest. As he collapsed, Nurse Jinny Shanahan rushed to his aid while Dr Lynn was summoned from her improvised operating table below them inside the Hall. She came promptly, but the wound was mortal and Connolly died, while his brother Matty watched helplessly, sobbing. The captain, who was also an actor based in the Abbey Theatre, was the first rebel officer to die during Easter Week. He would not be the last.

In the meantime, the ferocious firing continued around them as Lieutenant John O'Reilly took command of the City Hall garrison.

At roughly this time, the British also lost their first officer when 21-year-old 2nd Lieutenant Guy Vickery Pinfield of the 8th Royal Hussars was ordered to lead an attack on the main Castle gate.[3] Without a moment's hesitation, he assembled several of his men and together they charged towards their objective. When Pinfield fell to the ground, shot in the chest, his men rushed to his aid but the shot, fired from a nearby window, was lethal. The attack stalled while the lieutenant was dragged to cover. The writer and pacifist Francis Sheehy-Skeffington[4] witnessed the officer's fall and rushed to his aid, despite the obvious danger to himself, but to no avail.

At 4 p.m., in the nearby Kingsbridge Railway Station, over 1,000 well-armed troopers of the 3rd Cavalry Brigade arrived from the Curragh Camp. As they had had to leave their horses and mules in Kildare, they set about commandeering baggage carts from the station to carry their machine guns and numerous ammunition boxes. Civilians and railway workers did their best to stay out of the way. Rumours about what was happening in their city were circulating wildly and the warm spring air was electrified with anxiety and apprehension. Orders were barked and whistles blown as the troopers' boots and equipment clattered on the immaculately polished floors of the station; eventually, the soldiers fell into line. Their sense of excitement was soon justified. As soon as the cavalrymen left the safety of the bustling terminus they came under fire.

Captain Seán Heuston and his group of Volunteers in the Mendicity Institute on Usher's Island fired on the troopers as they marched eastwards from the station where he himself had previously been an employee. His men were aided by other small groups of rebels in the nearby Guinness Brewery. The cavalrymen took to the more sheltered back streets and advanced on Dublin Castle.

They arrived in its vicinity after a half hour's march. The first to see them coming was William Oman from his elevated vantage point. His men engaged the troopers whose return fire was immediate, relentless and extremely effective in pinning down the Citizen Army men, who were forced to abandon their position. Oman gave as much covering fire as he could under the intense hail of bullets and when his men were clear he succeeded in escaping himself. The men of the Cavalry Brigade, meanwhile, were welcomed as heroes by Sir Nathan. The threat to the Castle had been averted.

Captain Carl Elliotson, a young English cavalry officer, wasted no time once he received his orders and rushed between the Castle's many buildings, pointing out tactical positions to machine-gun crews and doing his best to remain undetected by the rebels.

Within minutes, City Hall came under fire from these crews. The Castle's huge and immensely thick stone walls suddenly echoed to the loud hammering of the Lewis and Vickers guns. The Lewis guns spewed drum after revolving drum of red-hot bullets into the ground floor of City Hall from the Castle's upper rooms and apartments, while the belt-fed Vickers guns covered the roof. Razor-sharp shards of glass from the windows of City Hall and wooden splinters flew everywhere. Shots ricocheted around inside like pinballs, bouncing off the internal stone pillars, and lumps of plaster and concrete clattered onto the marble floor where the Citizen Army men and women crouched helplessly under the barrage. To raise one's head meant almost certain death. Some were wounded where they lay, as arbitrary luck determined the casualties. Their piercing cries began to mount, prompting the nurses to slide on their bellies along the floor to render whatever aid they could.

The Lewis gunners turned their attention to the rooftop and, combined with the tremendous destructive power of the water-cooled Vickers guns, they turned the dome into something resembling a huge inverted green sieve. Concrete, metal splinters and clay shattered all around the Citizen Army men, covering them in dirt and dust as they lay prone behind the roof's ornamental parapet. But the traffic was not all one way: eager rebels fired back at their assailants through the roof balustrades when they could. The well-oiled bolts on their rifle barrels slid back and forth with every shot. The British soon realised they could not expect a quick victory in spite of their increasing numbers and superior weaponry.

As their machine guns clattered away above their heads, the British ground troops inside the Castle formed up for an assault. They assembled two platoons for an attack on its main Cork Hill Gate where their earlier attack had failed. Tom Kane and his men positioned at the guardhouse doorway fired manically into the first platoon now rushing at them, but the sheer weight of attacking troops forced them to retreat inside, where they locked the heavily reinforced door behind them. The British now held the main Castle gate. They opened it, allowing the enthusiastic second platoon of troops to rush out headlong towards Cork Hill and the front entrance of City Hall, and straight into the gunsights of the rebels in their two outposts at the junction of Parliament Street. The rebels there wasted no time. The bunched-up troops were now exposed in a wide, open area which sloped downwards to the east and was surrounded on all sides by three- and four-storey buildings. A deafening roar echoed as the Citizen Army rifles blasted their enemies relentlessly and without pity, forcing the British to make a hasty retreat for the relative sanctuary of the Castle. They left 20 of their comrades dead or wounded on the street, groaning in agony in the warm spring evening.

The British quickly changed tactic. They armed themselves with the plans of the Castle and descended into its cellars. They then assembled squads of cavalrymen who stumbled through the subterranean dank corridors by torchlight until they finally emerged from the labyrinth at an opening just under the rear windows of City Hall. From here they pulled the pins of their hand grenades and lobbed them inside, before rushing like madmen at the openings created by the terrific blasts.

The rebels on the rooftop threw caution to the wind. They stood up to get better shots at the attackers below. Captain Elliotson was ready for such an opportunity. He tapped the machine gunner next to him on the head and indicated the direction in which to aim his fire. The rebels suddenly lost another leader. Lieutenant Jack O'Reilly, standing at over 6 feet 6 inches tall, was mown down in a hail of bullets. His men crouched for cover once again under the incessant fire, while some jumped through the roof's skylight to reach the men and women on the floors below and reinforce them.

The hard-pressed rebels on the ground floor rushed to the rear of the Hall, firing wildly at the troopers now climbing through its windows. Men fell in agony as their blood splattered the ornate floors and walls, their bloodied faces contorted in pain as shell casings clattered noisily all around. But weight of numbers soon began to prevail as more soldiers emerged from the cellars and the attack was pressed home. The British were in.

The half-deafened rebels retreated in panic to the first-floor landing to regroup. The evening sunlight struggled to penetrate the thick fog of dust and gun smoke as it swirled in the turbulent air of City Hall, the ground floor of which was now teeming with the military. They now crept nervously towards the foot of its staircase while the rebels upstairs waited, hearts pounding and wide eyes staring out from filthy faces. Their dry throats gulped for moisture in the thick heat and dust. Below them the troops began their climb, swiftly reaching the halfway point.

Suddenly, a succession of blinding flashes and a hellish roar signalled the unleashing of complete pandemonium on the khaki-clad soldiers. They were met with close-range volleys of bullets which tore into them from the many rebel rifles and pistols. Men fell backwards, some doubled over, while others danced like rag dolls under the rain of bullets. Those behind were knocked down in turn as their broken bodies tumbled. Loudly bellowed orders from their non-commissioned officers (NCOs) combined with sheer bloody-minded rage and dogged determination compelled the remainder to press forward, but they could not. They slipped on the blood of their comrades before they fell under the relentless fire from above.

As the panicked survivors from this dreadful ordeal were eventually forced back down the marble steps, they ran headlong into another wave of their own men rushing into City Hall. In the confusion and dusty half-darkness, both groups mistook each other for rebels. Their bayonets parried momentarily, slashing and stabbing wildly as they fought for their lives while their enemies fired again from the first floor.[5]

Quickly realising the terrible mistake, a British captain ordered an immediate withdrawal. He left a group in place to cover the bottom of the stairs and prevent a rebel counter-attack. He then reorganised his men for another assault, this time in much greater force. The insurgents upstairs took a brief respite while they reloaded their magazines and quenched their parched throats.

The British troopers charged again. The rebels mercilessly cut down the first among them, but their sheer numbers carried the attack forward. A brief and vicious firefight ensued on the landing before the surviving Citizen Army men were finally forced to capitulate.

Back in the surrounded guardhouse at the Castle gate, Sergeant Kane and his men feared the worst as the British infantrymen smashed at its door with sledgehammers, while outside a section of troops with fixed bayonets stood at the ready. The door creaked and buckled before finally collapsing. The troops stormed in but, to their surprise, found the guardhouse empty except for the tied-up guards. A cupboard knocked over on its side revealed the insurgents' escape route. A grating had been removed and the Citizen Army men had climbed down through the piping below. None of the soldiers was eager to follow.

The British troopers inside City Hall now began a mopping-up operation, leaving some rather apprehensive sentries on the first-floor landing in case of a counter-attack from the roof. They moved cautiously throughout the ground floor. In the gloom their torches picked out many dead and wounded men along with the women of the garrison who had gathered in small clusters around the white pillars.

Dr Kathleen Lynn stood up in the darkness. She raised her hands above her head as she approached the British troopers, but turned her face away from the sudden glare of their torches. She shouted, 'We surrender! There are only wounded and Red Cross personnel here!' She was removed from City Hall with the others and taken to Dublin Castle.

From the secured ground floor, the British cavalrymen moved in more significant numbers to the first floor, much to the relief of their nervous sentries. From its landing they slowly fanned out and began searching for hidden enemies, with bayonets at the ready, and came across some Citizen Army women, one of whom – Jinny Shanahan – was not in uniform and was mistaken for a prisoner. When questioned about the strength of the rebels on the roof she turned this misunderstanding to the insurgents' advantage, replying, 'There are hundreds upstairs – big guns and everything'.[6] The exhausted British soldiers were in no mood for a night battle on the roof against such a 'numerous' force, so the inevitable clash was postponed until first light.

Only a dozen or so exhausted rebels now remained on the roof. They prepared themselves as best they could for the final onslaught, cleaning and checking their weapons. They ate and drank what they had but as the perceived imminent threat slowly dissipated and the drizzly night wore on they began to relax a little. Guards were posted to watch the skylight as machine guns rattled away at the nearby Henry & James outpost. Some of them dozed restlessly on the roof's cold stone surface using whatever shelter was to hand, while others waited tensely to see what the following morning would bring. The only real disturbance came from the ever-eager snipers on the Bermingham Tower who fired at the slightest hint of movement and from the intermittent sounds of fighting on the street below.

The British Command by now had also turned their attention to the rebels occupying the Henry & James position and the adjacent *Evening Mail* offices. A brief firefight had taken place around Cork Hill and Dame Street in the darkness and the British had managed to cross the street without casualties. They then forced the barricaded door of Henry & James and stormed inside. Sergeant Elmes realised that the continued defence of his position was hopeless and he accordingly ordered an immediate withdrawal. He and his men escaped through the rear of the building into Crane Lane, and made for the Volunteer headquarters at the GPO. They left behind them the body of a 15-year-old private from Gloucester Street (now Séan McDermott Street) named Charles D'Arcy who had been shot by a sniper.

Back in the Castle at around midnight, Captain Elliotson received fresh orders. He was to take 100 men and his machine guns and crews and proceed to occupy the Shelbourne Hotel and from there to 'have a go'[7] at the rebels in St Stephen's Green. His men prepared to move their guns as quietly as they could in the darkness as their replacements waited close by.

Opposite the Henry & James building, Sergeant Kelly and his men prepared for the inevitable attack on their own position. Kelly checked each of his men and ensured they had a plentiful supply of ammunition. As the night wore on, however, the anticipated attack never came, so he ordered his men to take turns at snatching some sleep. The only disturbance was numerous shouts of 'Surrender in the name of the King!' aimed at them, to which the reply 'Go to Hell!' was repeatedly bellowed back across the road.

Sergeant Elmes and his squad eventually crossed the river and reached to the GPO, where he reported to Commandant-General James Connolly on the situation at City Hall. The commandant was silent for several moments, as if pondering his prophetic parting words with Captain Séan Connolly the previous day. Elmes made it clear that Sergeant Kelly was still holding out with his men in the *Evening Mail* building.

Just before dawn on Tuesday 25 April, British troops inside City Hall finally began moving quietly up the stairs towards the roof's skylight. The numbing fear felt by many reminded the veterans among them of waiting to go over the top. Their hearts raced. Many smoked and drank from their canteens and checked their weapons, anything to take their minds off the hell they felt they were about to face. The previous day's butchery left few of those who bore the heavy responsibility of being the first through the skylight with any optimistic illusions about the outcome for them, particularly so as they assumed a much larger force awaited. Machine gun fire clattered away in the distance.

The rebels also prepared themselves for the inevitable, with the added anguish of knowing there could be no retreat from the City Hall roof. They knew they stood little chance of seeing their loved ones again. The only constructive thing to do as they waited was to check their weapons' safety catches and magazines constantly and control their breathing as best they could, trying not to allow their imaginations to focus on the large and vengeful force that must be massing below. When daylight broke the Castle's machine guns erupted into life, suggesting the attack was imminent.

In the meantime, back in the GPO, Commandant-General Connolly instructed John Scollan of the Hibernian Rifles to take his 18 men and 9 Volunteers from Maynooth and to occupy the Exchange Hotel on Parliament Street. This building was situated on the left-hand side of the street as one faced City Hall. Any British troop movement down Parliament Street from the Castle was to be dealt with from this new position. With latecomers arriving throughout the various Volunteer Battalion areas of operations, the rebel strength in the city was steadily growing, and the longer Dublin Castle could be contained, the better.

Back inside City Hall, the British soldiers' torturous wait continued, until suddenly the machine guns at Dublin Castle ceased firing. For a couple of nerve-shredding moments the only sound was the distant rhythmic staccato of heavy machine guns being used elsewhere in the city, before an officer's loudly barked order prompted the men to launch themselves up through the skylight. They fired wildly as they went. The waiting rebels opened fire and cut down the first few assailants, who twisted in agony as the bullets ripped at their insides. More and more troopers poured out onto the roof, stepping over their fallen comrades, and began to overwhelm the hard-pressed and worn-out rebels. Soon it was all over. City Hall had fallen.

To the men in the *Evening Mail* offices the sudden silence from the roof of City Hall meant only one thing: they were next in the firing line. With increasing regularity, the same shouts of 'Surrender in the name

The facade of City Hall. NATIONAL LIBRARY OF IRELAND

of the King!' sounded out in the cold early morning air. They knew it would not be long. Sergeant Kelly ordered one of his men to fire a single shot in answer to every call to surrender and told the others to hold their fire until it was time.

Meanwhile, Commandant Scollan and his men began creeping cautiously up the lower end of Parliament Street. As they approached the Exchange Hotel they heard the single rifle shots from the top of the street being fired in reply to the repeated surrender demands. Once their objective was secured they took up firing positions on the roof. Scollan, from St Joseph's Avenue in Drumcondra, ordered Tom Byrne and Ned Walsh, both from Dominick Street in Dublin, to take some men and occupy the roof of Shortalls next door to the hotel in the City Hall direction. Walsh's teenage son made to leave with them, but Commandant Scollan turned to the boy, saying, 'Not you,' ordering him home to much protest. It was the last time the boy would see his father alive.

As the morning wore on, the 5th Battalion of the Royal Dublin Fusiliers under Major Robert Robinson, having arrived in the vicinity shortly after dawn, had positioned themselves appropriately throughout the Castle and were busily making their final preparations for the attack against the *Evening Mail* building. Confidence was now growing among the young troops as they were aware that there remained only a handful of rebels holding the position. Many of the Fusiliers were from Dublin city itself and the irony of lining up to fight to the bitter end against an enemy from the same city, albeit in a different uniform, was something they tried to put to the back of their minds. The sooner their job was done the better.

After a while, Sergeant Kelly's Citizen Army men saw what they had been waiting for. Two large lines of enemy riflemen had formed up in firing positions in the upper yard of the Castle, preparing to attack. To their astonishment, the troops had ventured into plain view before their rifle sights. Kelly said: 'Get ready! Fire only on my order!' The men took deep breaths as they steadied themselves and waited.

At noon the Fusiliers opened fire on them. Kelly's men crouched with their heads held low as scores of bullets peppered the red-brick facade of the *Evening Mail* building. Shots flew through the shattered windows and the outside walls protested under the drumbeat of rounds crashing against concrete. The infantrymen confidently formed up to attack. In the deafening chaos Kelly screamed the order to fire. The subsequent unrelenting volleys from their elevated firing positions cut swathes out of the ranks of their would-be assailants. The entire front of the *Evening Mail* building was soon hidden behind plumes of red dust and thick grey rifle smoke.

Many of the additional Fusiliers waiting to form the first assault wave paled when they witnessed the seemingly incomprehensible carnage the rebel fire visited on the ranks of their comrades. Their NCOs encouraged them with shouts of 'Stick with me, lads, and you'll make it. It's only thirty yards!' The bullets whining backwards and forwards across the street, however, were far less comforting than the well-practised reassurances from their corporals and sergeants.

For two hours a rifle battle was fought in the street with no sign of the rebel fire diminishing. Major Robinson eventually ordered his machine guns to the fray. The dreadful ear-piercing cacophony was amplified accordingly. After several 9-yard belts of Vickers ammunition had been spewed across the street at Kelly's stubborn stronghold, Major Robinson ordered Second Lieutenant O'Neill to advance and capture the rebel post. O'Neill shouted to his platoon to fix bayonets. The young men whose grim task it was to answer that call did their best to deal with their paralysing apprehension. Some shook so much that their bayonets slipped from their hands and clattered to the ground. 'Keep it together, lads,' was the repeated command from their NCOs between the dry cracks and deafening peal of the incessant rifle and machine-gun fire.

O'Neill then blew his whistle to sound the charge and his men rushed out of Cork Hill Gate, where they were greeted by a lethally concentrated barrage from the rebel position to their front which decimated them. The Fusiliers scrambled back inside the gate. Major Robinson now ordered all troops in City Hall to its roof to increase the rate of fire on the building.

O'Neill rallied his men inside the gate, while ordering the troops of the following wave to join his ranks. A deafening echo of supporting fire filled the streets as he then ordered the second charge.

As they dashed once again down Cork Hill, men fell all around, rebel bullets making loud and obscene thuds as they struck from point-blank range, but the survivors pushed on and made its outer wall where they then managed to smash its door open. O'Neill ordered his men to rush inside, but as they struggled to enter they were again cut down by the tenacious defenders, whose fire was now added to by several of Scollan's men in Parliament Street firing from across the road and whose presence had been unknown to the assailing Fusiliers. A half-hour later, the heavily barricaded entrance was still being fought for with no quarter given by either side.

A third wave of troops rushed out in support from the Castle. More young men fell as they were hit trying to make the 30-yard killing ground of the wide, open street. Commandant Scollan's riflemen strained to get a better view of the troops from their positions around the Exchange Hotel and when they could they added to the stream of lead that tore into them. Minutes later, another wave emerged from the Castle, followed by another shortly thereafter. Slowly but surely, the Fusiliers forced their way inside the *Evening Mail* building where they began clearing its ground floor of rebels. Over a hundred of their number waited nervously on the street just outside, hugging the walls of the buildings for cover, ready to rush inside once the signal was given.

It soon was and the Fusiliers began storming the staircase where they were met by a small but viciously determined group of defenders under Sergeant Kelly who fought like trapped animals. The battle turned into an appalling close-quarter affair, with the numeric superiority of the Fusiliers counting for little in the confined space. The walls shook with the cacophony of rifle and pistol fire, added to by the abusive shouts and curses of men frantically trying to kill each other, until just after 3 p.m. when a sudden quiet descended signalling that the *Evening Mail* offices had fallen.

Small clusters of bewildered-looking civilians now began gathering in the area towards Christchurch a hundred or so yards to their west. The captured garrison was expected to be led out at gunpoint, but with no sign of any rebels some of the crowd began to disperse. A short time later, some locals received the shock of their lives at the sight of four men in Citizen Army uniforms sprinting towards Grattan Bridge: having escaped from the Exchange Street side of their former fortress, they had launched themselves at full speed down the cobblestoned street towards the River Liffey.

Guards were then positioned at the fallen position. The Dublin Fusiliers quickly re-formed and began advancing down Parliament Street with their backs to City Hall, keen to secure the area. The intensity of the firefight they had just endured had, however, hidden the presence of the 25 or so rebels under Commandant Scollan, who now knew they were next in the firing line.

Suddenly, and seemingly out of nowhere, the infantrymen on the street fell victim to another merciless barrage, unleashed upon them from the Exchange Hotel, which was just in front of them and to their right. The hapless young soldiers stood little chance. Under a withering hail of fire from several floors of the hotel and nearby buildings, they were cut to pieces. After some time they re-formed again to charge the position, this time at full speed down the short and narrow stretch of road and now supported by a squad who had made for the rooftop of the Henry & James building. They began lobbing grenades at their nearby enemies. Once again, the men on the street were stopped dead in their tracks by the cannon-like booms and shattering cracks of rifle and pistol fire from John Scollan's men, which resonated thunderously between the enclosing four-storey facades of the street's buildings. The troops were utterly exposed here and their only option was to fall back again in disarray towards City Hall. No further attacks were launched.

Twenty-three Royal Dublin and Inniskilling Fusiliers lay dead and wounded on the pavements and cobblestones of Parliament Street. On the roof of Shorthall's shop, next door to the Exchange Hotel, Ned Walsh had been critically wounded by a grenade blast, his stomach torn wide open by the explosion. Tom Byrne did his best to help his stricken comrade, while Walsh fell into shock. He died in agony later that night.

The British then posted spotters on the rooftops of both recently overwhelmed corner-facing positions that had proved such a thorn in their sides. Their next move was to ascertain enemy strength on Parliament Street itself. They feared having to clear the street one building at a time and their recent experiences left them with few illusions about what that grim task would entail.

At 4.30 p.m., however, Scollan received an order that put an end to the killing in the area. He was to withdraw immediately to the GPO. He and his men made their escape out of the back of the Exchange Hotel into Crane Lane and aimed for East Essex Street and eventually the River Liffey, carrying Ned Walsh with them on a makeshift stretcher over the Ha'penny Bridge, having patched the dying man up as best they could.

The British Army spotters eventually noticed that the rebels had pulled back. Their troops then slowly and nervously proceeded down Parliament Street and, much to their relief, found it free of the enemy. In spite of the recent carnage the threat to Dublin Castle had been repulsed. Sir Matthew Nathan wired London with the news.

3

Northumberland Road, Mount Street Bridge, Boland's Bakery and Mills: Part 1

'Ten in the mag, none in the breech.'

The two children – a boy and a girl – could barely contain their excitement at the sudden surprise of seeing their father, Captain Frederick Dietrichsen. Their mother was similarly delighted at the unexpected sight of her dashing 33-year-old husband who marched with his battalion of infantrymen from the East Midlands in England. It was Wednesday 26 April 1916. The calm blue waters of Dublin Bay, filled with small craft of just about every variety, presented a beautiful backdrop to the touching sight of the captain from Nottingham, a lawyer by profession, hugging and kissing his wife and children as the crowds that had gathered to cheer the arrival of their liberators waved Union Jacks. Many locals ran from their homes presenting sweet cakes, tea and sandwiches to the surprised young British Tommies who smiled broadly as they marched behind their officers. In just over an hour, however, Captain Dietrichsen would be dead.

At 11 a.m. on Easter Monday, 36 men of C Company, 3rd Battalion, Irish Volunteers, held a short conference at a street corner in Upper Mount Street, situated between peaceful and picturesque Merrion Square and

42

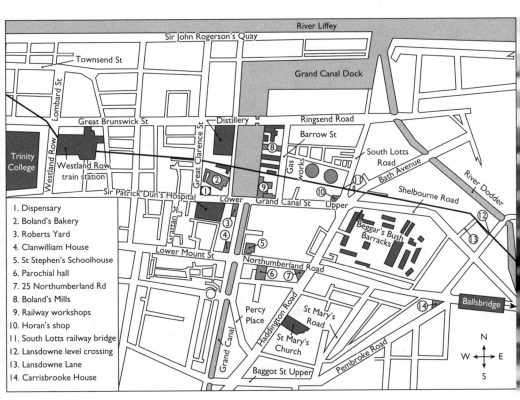

River Liffey

Sir John Rogerson's Quay

Townsend St

Lombard St

Grand Canal Dock

Great Brunswick St

Distillery

Ringsend Road

Barrow St

Great Clarence St

Trinity College

Westland Row

Westland Row train station

Gas works

South Lotts Road

Bath Avenue

River Dodder

Shelbourne Road

Sir Patrick Dun's Hospital

Lower   Grand Canal St   Upper

Grattan St

1. Dispensary
2. Boland's Bakery
3. Roberts Yard
4. Clanwilliam House
5. St Stephen's Schoolhouse
6. Parochial hall
7. 25 Northumberland Rd
8. Boland's Mills
9. Railway workshops
10. Horan's shop
11. South Lotts railway bridge
12. Lansdowne level crossing
13. Lansdowne Lane
14. Carrisbrooke House

Lower Mount St

Northumberland Road

Beggar's Bush Barracks

Ballsbridge

Percy Place

Haddington Road

St Mary's Road

St Mary's Church

Grand Canal

Pembroke Road

Baggot St Upper

N
W ← → E
S

Irish Volunteers 3rd Battalion area of operations.

Dublin's Grand Canal. Lieutenant Simon Donnelly, the 25-year-old officer in charge issued his final orders before departing for Boland's Bakery on Lower Grand Canal Street, accompanied by 18 of his men. From there his plan was that they, along with the remaining companies of the battalion, would block access to the city from the bakery's adjacent bridges and contain any enemy forces that might attack them from nearby Beggar's Bush Barracks. The remaining men, under the command of a 27-year-old lieutenant from the South Circular Road in Dublin named Michael Malone, simultaneously moved out in the direction of nearby Mount Street Bridge with a similar mission in mind.

This was a quiet and well-to-do suburb of the south city. The still waters of the canal were lined with leafy rows of trees, with a towpath on either side. Barges drifted slowly and lazily along through its many sets of lock gates to and from the Grand Canal Dock, which flowed into the River Liffey less than a mile away. Picturesque three- and four-storey-over-basement Georgian houses occupied both sides of the idyllic waterway. Nearby Northumberland Road boasted some fine red-brick dwellings that ranked among the most exclusive that the city had to offer.[1]

Lieutenant Malone's plan was to occupy four separate positions in this location. By holding these positions, his sections, along with the rest of their battalion, would be able to hamper, harass and hopefully, in the minds of the Rising's planners, prevent any newly landed British reinforcements from entering the city from the direction of Kingstown Harbour (now Dun Laoghaire) situated about 6 miles to their south. In this sense the entire surrounding area was strategically vital to the Irish Volunteer army's ultimate goal.

When they reached Mount Street Bridge Malone's men split up and made for their designated positions. Section Commander Séamus Grace and two young Volunteers occupied 25 Northumberland Road, situated on its crossroads junction with Haddington Road. Commander Patrick Doyle, and three Volunteers – Joseph Clarke, James McGrath and William Christian – occupied the Parochial Hall, located on the same side of the road at about half distance between No. 25 and the canal. Commander Denis O'Donoghue accompanied by three Volunteers occupied St Stephen's Schoolhouse on Northumberland Road but on its opposite side, and closer to the canal.

These three positions commanded the southern approaches to Mount Street Bridge, while Clanwilliam House, occupied by Commander George Reynolds from nearby Ringsend, and four Volunteers (Patrick Byrne, Daniel Maher, Willie Ronan and James Doyle), overlooked the bridge itself from the canal's opposite side, as well as all of their positions along Northumberland Road. This rendered the final position of paramount importance to the entire operation.

As soon as the houses were occupied, the rebels set about barricading them. Clanwilliam House was to be turned into a fortress. The basement's huge coal stock was wrapped in blankets and pillow cases to make sandbags, which were stacked up at the house's many sash windows, and most of the furniture was used to block the building's entry points. The rebels were careful to issue the house's furious occupants with a receipt for the commandeered goods in order that they be properly compensated following the implementation of the Republic that Reynolds and his men were about to fight to the death for. They were then moved to a nearby house for their own safety while their most precious valuables were locked in one of the huge building's rear rooms for safekeeping.

Lieutenant Malone eventually joined the three-man garrison at No. 25 when he was satisfied that the other three positions were being properly

No. 25 Northumberland Road, the position from which two highly trained Volunteers, with almost suicidal determination, held off two British battalions for six hours. NATIONAL LIBRARY OF IRELAND

prepared, and he oversaw the fortification of the corner house. Malone, a carpenter by trade, was adept at using whatever wooden furniture was available to create the most effective of obstructions. His handiwork would soon prove lethal. This particular house had been 'donated' to the rebel cause by a sympathiser and overlooked the wide road junction, giving those inside a major advantage over any attacking force. There would be very little cover available to any unit assaulting the building from a distance of 50 yards or so, and they would then have to contend with a railing, a wall and the concrete steps leading to the front door, before dealing with the fortified structure itself.

While these positions were being consolidated, Lieutenant Donnelly, under the supervision of 33-year-old Commandant Éamon de Valera, was busy ordering the men who had just forced entry at the main gate of Boland's Bakery to their various defensive positions. The bakery building sat on the junction of Lower Grand Canal Street and Clarence Street. Seventeen-year-old Andrew McDonnell from Rathgar, whose choice of weapon that day was a pike, was handed a shotgun by the lieutenant and

ordered to the roof overlooking Grand Canal Street with instructions
to shoot at any British soldier he saw. He quickly hid his trusty pike and
took position.

Other Volunteers throughout the bakery took up similar firing
positions while a handful of men from B Company went to the building's
stables, situated to its rear, where they smashed through a wall. The
rubble was used as a base for a ramp up to the railway line just behind
the bakery. Other B Company members then took up positions on the
line. This would link them with their fellow Company men 500 yards to
their rear, who had just occupied Westland Row train station. While this
was under way, Commandant de Valera set up his headquarters, along
with a first-aid post, in the building's dispensary.

Shortly after Boland's Bakery had been consolidated, Dublin-born
Captain Joe O'Connor, the 35-year-old commander of A Company,
moved out from the position to which he had initially been detailed in
the adjacent railway workshops and ventured south along the railway
line towards Lansdowne Road with a dozen or so men whom he divided
into sections. The first of these was detailed to dig a trench that straddled
both sides of the line while the second was to occupy a small cluster of
two-storey houses that led to Horan's shop at the corner of South Lotts
Road and Grand Canal Street. This position would effectively cover the
front entrance to Beggar's Bush Barracks. Volunteers Tom and Christy
Byrne were led to Lansdowne Road level crossing where they smashed
the points and dug a trench under the supervision of Captain O'Connor,
who then returned the half mile or so to the railway workshop where he
oversaw the final defensive preparations of its various sheds. He placed
several men in the windows overlooking the yard before assigning half a
dozen or so to various positions among the nearby water towers, which
overlooked his own positions as well as Grand Canal Street and its
bridge. Soon afterwards, Lieutenant Donnelly ordered the remaining C
Company members in Boland's Bakery to drive the bread vans onto the
bridge where they were to be overturned and used as barricades.

With C Company covering his right flank, O'Connor was now feeling
increasingly confident, particularly as stalwart men such as Malone
and Grace formed its vanguard. This made up somewhat for his earlier
apprehension regarding the dangerous lack of numbers forming their
ranks as they had set out before noon to get to grips with an empire. As
if to add to the sentiment, Volunteer Lieutenant Joseph O'Byrne, from

Dartmouth Square in Ranelagh, who with 17 men had occupied various positions in and around Boland's Mills, soon signalled the approach of half a dozen or so men whom he had seen crossing Ringsend drawbridge, heading in their direction. The welcome reinforcements were detailed throughout the area of the grey fortress-like building which sat at the junction of Barrow Street and Ringsend Road, where they promptly set themselves to increasing the surrounding fortifications.

Back in Boland's Bakery, Volunteers Seán O'Keefe and Andrew McDonnell were ordered by Lieutenant Donnelly to reinforce the few men occupying the position in Robert's Yard, a builders' suppliers on Grand Canal Street's junction with Clanwilliam Place. They took up position there on a corrugated roof and waited in the afternoon sun, chatting nervously to relieve the frightening realisation that several months' training was finally being put into practice against an enemy whose response would, no doubt, be swift and brutal.

That enemy did not take long to engage them. The sudden shattering of the relative peace and quiet in the area at about 2 p.m. signalled 3rd Battalion's first hostile contact with the British Army in the form of a patrol from Beggar's Bush Barracks. Robert's Yard came under fire from a turf bank on the far side of the canal. The cracks of several rifles rang out across the still waters and were answered by a multitude of weapons that varied in both pitch and calibre. The patrol was rapidly driven back through the gates of the barracks.

Two hours later, Commander Reynolds in Clanwilliam House heard several shots being fired some distance to the south and hastily grabbed his spyglass. He saw a number of uniformed figures lying prone on the road close to Malone and Grace's position in No. 25 Northumberland Road. Lieutenant Malone had seen them coming from a distance of about 200 yards, roughly 40 troops of the Home Defence Force named the Georgius Rex. Due to their advancing years they were more often referred to by witty Dubliners as 'the Gorgeous Wrecks'. They had spent the morning on field manoeuvres in the Dublin Mountains and were returning on foot to Beggar's Bush Barracks. As they approached, Malone and Grace took up their firing positions and waited until the troops had almost reached the street corner before both of them opened up. The exposed men scattered but never returned fire. They made a desperate dash for the relative safety of their barracks, leaving four men dying on the street corner.

Shortly beforehand, Major George Harris, their battalion commander, had led a much larger contingent of his middle-aged infantrymen towards the same barracks from the Shelbourne Road direction, having split his ranks of men in Ballsbridge following a warning of rebel activity in the Haddington Road area.

Captain O'Connor's section of men on the railway line had seen the larger body of Major Harris's troops coming, preceded by a motorcycle outrider[2] who passed their vantage point oblivious to the numerous gunsights converging on his decelerating figure on board the noisy Triumph which he manoeuvred around the street corner with impressive agility. They waited tensely until the head of the main body of troops had reached the corner of Shelbourne Road and Haddington Road before they let loose with their weapons. Several fell under their fire before their panicked major screamed an order to scatter and make for the gates of the barracks. Many rushed to climb its walls and were helped over by others waiting on the far side. Major Harris and the men at the front of the column sprinted towards a protruding section of wall which partially shielded their scramble inside the gate. O'Connor's men fired manically at the clusters of troops as they sped away.

Back up the road, Lieutenant Malone quickly realised that the hapless middle-aged infantrymen had no ammunition for their rifles and ordered Grace to cease fire. O'Connor's men, on the other hand, fired until the last troop had rushed inside the gate, leaving a dead man and several wounded behind them.

Medics soon arrived to collect the dead and dying troops from both ends of the road, while the men in No. 25 reflected on what had just happened. Killing was not a business that pleased any Volunteer, but their vantage point over the road junction was a particularly lethal one, especially when manned by two experienced marksmen whose highly tuned skills complemented each other. A short time later this point was proved when they came under sniper fire from the house diagonally across the junction from them, No. 28. The sniper, recently dispatched from the barracks just 100 yards to its rear, became a dangerous nuisance to the four insurgents for a time, until Malone managed to shoot him dead through a window with his Mauser, while Grace drew his fire.

Just after Major Harris's veterans had been routed, Volunteer Lieutenant Seán Guilfoyle and the four other men who had been ordered to occupy the houses next to Horan's finally succeeded in mouse-holing[3] as far as the red-brick corner store, much to the bemusement of the terrace's many residents. Once inside, they piled sacks of sugar and foodstuffs against the doors and windows before taking up firing positions which gave them an excellent view of the main barracks gate, 100 yards to their front and left.

Unfortunately for Colonel Frederick Shaw, commander of the barracks, this new rebel position was consolidated only minutes before he ordered a platoon of troops to make a sortie to the railway line to dislodge the insurgents. As they exited through the wrought-iron gates they turned right and moved cautiously down the sloping street where they were suddenly met with a hail of shots from Guilfoyle's small squad. They promptly retreated to the protection of the 10-foot-high granite walls of the barracks whereupon Colonel Shaw ordered its gates to be locked. The incandescent officer beckoned several men to take up positions on the nearby rooftops inside the barracks, before a sniper duel began between the men there and the two rebel sections close to the road junction below.

As the Volunteers and British shot their volleys, another patrol was hastily assembled inside the Barracks, which it left by climbing over the rear wall. The troops moved stealthily through the nearby houses and made the dash across Shelbourne Road undetected. They reached the railway line, but came under increasingly accurate fire as soon as they began advancing north-westwards towards Boland's Bakery. The dozen or so exposed infantrymen were forced back under fire to the point from where they had left the barracks earlier before they scaled its wall to rejoin their platoon. The sniping continued.

As the hot spring day turned slowly to evening things gradually settled in the area of C Company's four positions on Northumberland Road and Clanwilliam Place. The weary Volunteers began to settle down for the night. Malone and Grace and their accompanying pair of teenagers swapped shifts getting some sleep and the same pattern was repeated in the other rebel-controlled buildings: some dozed while others watched. The civilians in the surrounding houses stayed put, fearing any movement in the fading light would draw fire. They grabbed what rest they could get in their homes, nervously praying and hoping that the horror visited on the Georgius Rex would not be repeated. Upcoming events, however, suggested that God was not listening.

St Stephen's Schoolhouse on Northumberland Road, the focal point of numerous assaults by the Sherwood Foresters. MILITARY ARCHIVES

The only real movement in the entire area that night was from the bakery, where Simon Donnelly, having been promoted to captain, had asked for some volunteers for a mission. At this point the two young rebels McDonnell and O'Keefe had been recalled from Robert's Yard. McDonnell was feeling somewhat invincible, as all 17-year-olds do, particularly at having seen off the troops who had opened up on them from the turf yard earlier. He did not hesitate when he heard the request, and stepped forward enthusiastically along with nine others.

Captain Donnelly, from Wexford Street in Dublin, began to rub large amounts of the bakery's plentiful supply of flour on to the Volunteers' backs to enable them to identify each other in the darkness. They then set off in pairs spread 10 feet apart along the tracks with Commandant de Valera leading them. Every so often the word '*tirim*' (Irish for 'dry') was quietly announced by the tall and awkward rebel leader as a password for the group to get by their own trenches unhindered. When they reached the gasworks they ordered its small workforce to leave. Their pistols and rifles, combined with the assurance that several hundred more rebels were en route, persuaded the night-shift workers to comply. The subsequent dismantling of several large machines with half a dozen crowbars plunged the entire south-eastern section of the city into darkness. De Valera then led the patrol back to the bakery where they, too, rested.

At dawn on Tuesday 25 April, Lieutenant Malone rose early from a restless sleep and left No. 25 through its back door, and made his way to the schoolhouse. There he found Commander O'Donoghue in a state of alertness having just finished checking on his position. The two men spoke for a while before coming to the conclusion that tactically the schoolhouse did not have much to boast about, as it was set too far back from the road and offered its occupants limited visibility. Accordingly, O'Donoghue and his three men were detailed back to Boland's, much to the premature delight of the building's caretaker. Malone then crossed the canal bridge and had a meeting in Clanwilliam House with Commander Reynolds.

As they assessed their situation Malone and Reynolds agreed that they would need reinforcements if they were to hold their positions. Malone spoke of the irony of having just dispatched O'Donoghue before Patrick Byrne was sent to Boland's Bakery with a request for additional men. Byrne made the journey but returned a short time later without the expected handful of riflemen, but instead with some food supplies in the form of bread and cake. A somewhat perplexed Reynolds then sent him back with orders to seek out Lieutenant Simon Donnelly to inform him of their precarious manpower situation.

Byrne did as he was ordered and found that the man he sought had just been promoted to captain. His newly promoted officer in charge ordered four men to reinforce Clanwilliam House,[4] ensuring that they were given extra ammunition for their Mausers. Richard Murphy from South William Street, Patrick Doyle from Milltown in south Dublin, and two brothers, Thomas and James Walsh, whose mule named Kaiser had earlier transported most of that same ammunition, gathered their equipment and prepared to move out. As they were leaving, Donnelly told Byrne to return afterwards to Boland's, to be used as a dispatch runner. All the departing men were told to watch for snipers in the Lower Mount Street area as they left Boland's Bakery through its Clarence Street gate.

Three hundred yards away in Clanwilliam House the fortifications continued for most of the day, and by early evening were approaching completion. After almost two days of rebel renovations the house seemed ready to withstand a siege. Reynolds decided that the best vantage point overlooking their proposed combat zone was to be found in the first-floor drawing room with its three heavily fortified windows overlooking the bridge allowing an unobstructed view along the entire length of Northumberland Road. The side and rear rooms on the same level overlooked Lieutenant Malone's proposed escape route in Percy Lane should he need it, and provided a commanding view all along the canal bank on its Percy Place side.

Half a mile away, at around 6 p.m. Lieutenant Joseph O'Byrne and several men manning the loft in Boland's Mills heard an unfamiliar whistling sound from the direction of the River Liffey. This was swiftly followed by the deafening crash of a shell as it smashed through the thick concrete wall next to them, before it too was followed by another, a few seconds later. Red-hot metal and brick flew throughout the confined space and several sacks of flour were burst open by the flying debris. Soon, the upper rooms were completely engulfed in thick, choking dust. For about ten minutes, visibility was all but impossible. Luckily for the rebels their only casualty was Volunteer Seán McGrath, who suffered a gash across his face. The shots had come from the gunboat *Helga* from Dublin's quays before she steamed south to Kingstown while O'Byrne's men dusted themselves off and settled back down as the sound of small arms fire grew throughout the city centre.

As the light began to fade, several civilians had begun to venture out in the area in search of food and other necessities. The local inhabitants, however, were not the only ones beginning to suffer hunger pangs. There was little food to be had in the barracks, a situation aggravated by the presence of the many 'Gorgeous Wrecks,' whose somewhat dishevelled appearance following their recent tribulations now lent some justification to the nickname. Colonel Shaw decided on a simple solution: the officers would be fed, and the ranks would go hungry.

One sympathetic civilian who had ventured out towards dusk approached the wide pavement at the front of Clanwilliam House where he whistled, assuming he did not already have Commander Reynolds' attention. He most certainly did, as did any passer-by, as all movements were monitored closely. This particular individual had just heard some sketchy information regarding heavy fighting in the St Stephen's Green area, information he felt compelled to pass on to the uniformed stranger in his upstairs battlement. The plucky civilian was not the only bearer of news that day. Just down the road Captain O'Connor had received word of the latest English edition of the *Daily Mail* being on sale in the shops that were still open in the city. That could only mean one thing: the port was still open to ships.

Back in Northumberland Road, the two teenagers who had accompanied Malone and Grace were ordered to leave the position. Volunteers Byrne and Rowe protested vigorously before their lieutenant insisted they obey his instructions. This left only himself and Séamus Grace to man the house. What they lacked in numbers, however, they made up for in weaponry, expertise and determination. Malone had claimed many victories during the various Volunteer sharpshooting tournaments and Grace had spent significant time training with the Canadian Infantry before being recalled to Ireland for the upcoming Rising. They had Lee Enfield rifles and various pistols; Malone himself was armed with a 'Peter the Painter' Mauser semi-automatic pistol. This came with a large wooden stock which, when attached, gave the weapon a truly vicious edge. It could then be held like a rifle, but had a much quicker rate of accurate fire. Their motivation was unquestionable. Malone's younger brother had been killed the previous year serving with the Royal Dublin Fusiliers in France, ironically one of the same British Army regiments now fighting against the rebels in Dublin. Grace had spent time serving with one of the world's best infantry units before being recalled by a telegram which read, 'We are waiting for you,'[5] prompting him to make a clandestine escape from Canada with his beloved Enfield. Their lack of numbers, it seemed, would be adequately compensated for.

Commander George Reynolds back in Clanwilliam House had similarly sent a teenage Volunteer home the previous day, when Daniel Maher had become very ill. There were many teenagers among the Irish Volunteers and Citizen Army that week, but the commanders preparing to hold this small cluster of positions had some idea of their strategic importance, and what their enemy would be prepared to do to capture them. Accordingly, it seems they wanted to spare the youngsters.

At this point, Reynolds had been more or less confined to his fortress overlooking the canal bridge for almost 36 hours and he longed to stretch his legs. To leave the house would, however, have been almost impossible, not to mention highly risky, without having to squeeze oneself through the same basement window through which his earlier reinforcements had struggled. He contented himself with his breezy upstairs vantage point for a time. In the distance, machine guns and rifles reported intermittently. As darkness descended he ordered his men to cease what they were doing, and in the slowly creeping silence of the house the menacing sound of gunfire, the frequency of which had increased dramatically, could be heard in the surrounding streets. The men knew their time was coming. They returned to their work on the front door's barricade which helped keep their minds from the dread all soldiers feel of impending combat, and when they were fully satisfied with their labours, and welcome exhaustion had overcome their jumpiness, they settled down for some sleep, leaving lookouts as they had done the previous night. The continuing sound of distant gunfire provided the weary rebels with a sinister lullaby in the cold April darkness.

Shortly after 4 a.m. on Wednesday 26 April, the SS *Tynwald* and SS *Patriotic* pulled into Kingstown Harbour while the *Helga* was slowly making its way northwards again along Dublin Bay. The arrival of the two troop ships was watched from the shadows by a cyclist, who immediately began pedalling towards the city.

The *Tynwald* and *Patriotic* carried elements of the 59th Midland Infantry Division of the British Army who had crossed the Irish Sea overnight from Liverpool. It took several hours for them to disembark and attracted the attention of scores of the small port town's curious inhabitants. Many of the raw recruits among them believed they had landed in France and were pleasantly surprised to find how well the locals spoke English, particularly the blushing local ladies responding to 'Bonjour, Mademoiselle'. They were disabused of this notion and told that they had landed in Ireland for the task of quelling the rebellion that had broken out in Dublin city. The early morning sunshine and sense of welcoming fanfare that surrounded their arrival belied this reality, and their officers seemed unconcerned that they had arrived without their machine guns due to the fact that their embarkation officer's orders were that men were needed and not guns. He had ordered all of their heavy weapons to be left at the dockside in Liverpool,[6] a command that was to have tragic consequences for the young infantrymen eating a hastily provided breakfast before preparing to march.

Part of 59th Division was made up of the Sherwood Foresters Regiment, commanded by Brigadier Colonel Maconchy. After Captain

Dietrichsen, the 2/7th Battalion[7] adjutant, and his fellow regiment officers had enjoyed breakfast at the local Royal St George Yacht Club, they received orders to advance on foot to Dublin city centre. The Foresters did not have any maps, so local shops and hotels were hastily relieved of theirs. It was then decided that the 2/5th and the 2/6th Battalions would proceed inland along the Stillorgan–Donnybrook route, and the 2/7th and the 2/8th Battalions would follow the Coast Road, advancing through picturesque Monkstown and Blackrock and eventually through Ballsbridge. The 2/7th would lead with C Company to its front, A Company in support, B Company at the rear, and D Company as a reserve. Once this route had been cleared of rebels, the 2/8th Battalion would press on to Trinity College with the Royal Hospital in Kilmainham being the ultimate objective for both.

Shortly after 8 a.m., a tremendous ringing echoed in the Dublin docklands, bringing any half-dozing Volunteers to a state of abrupt readiness. The *Helga* had returned and was shelling Liberty Hall. Her first salvo smashed into and ricocheted off the metal superstructure of the Loop Line Bridge which partially shielded Liberty Hall from her sights. For several hours the dull thuds of artillery became more and more frequent as the ship's cannon, supported by two nearby 18-pounder field guns, zeroed in on the building which had spawned the insurrection she had been summoned to help crush.

In Boland's Bakery, meanwhile, Captain Donnelly picked four men and dashed across Lower Grand Canal Street to relieve the Volunteers in Robert's Yard. They took up the same firing positions as their comrades had previously held on the corrugated steel roof of its tallest building.

Helga's call to battle brought a great sense of urgency to 3rd Battalion's area of operations. Captain O'Connor moved through his positions on the railway line, checking on his men, and was soon approached by the clandestine cyclist who informed him of the arrival of the troopships several miles to the south. He knew their time was approaching. He sent word back to Boland's Bakery to order reinforcements to the line and instructed Volunteers Séamus Murphy and Seán O'Keefe to take position in the railway workshop yard.

The order 'Ten in the mag – none in the breech!' was loudly bellowed by various sergeants throughout the ranks of the 2/7th and 2/8th at 10.30 a.m., as they exited the port area of Kingstown to begin their march toward the city. Five miles of friendly territory stood between them and the enemy and accidental discharges would not have befitted their proud march.

Most of the young men who had been shipped in to regain for the British Empire her second city were tired from their relatively sleepless night and were heavily laden with supplies and equipment. Their high morale compensated, boosted by the welcome given to their arrival from the countless civilians who lined the streets to greet them with warm enthusiasm.

As they entered Blackrock, Captain Dietrichsen stepped out of the line to embrace his young family. His wife was a native of Dublin and, fearing for their children's safety because of the ever-increasing Zeppelin raids over England, she had moved with the children to live with her parents who were local wine merchants. The company sergeant barked at the ranks of men to keep in line as Dietrichsen reassured her. As he rejoined his battalion, he reflected on how lucky this turn of events was for them. He had expected to be in France, up to his neck in muddy trenches, not knowing when or if he would see his family again. Now it would be a relatively simple matter of sweeping aside a 'minor rebellion' before enjoying some unexpected leave with his loved ones.

Back towards Mount Street Bridge, Lieutenant Malone, having been informed by a runner from Captain O'Connor of the troop landings, was hastily checking the various positions. He found them all to be well fortified and the men fully ready. He then ventured the further 400 yards south to Carrisbrooke House, the three-storey building situated on the corner of Northumberland Road and Pembroke Road, and found it deserted. This concerned him greatly due to its tactical position, covering as it did any left-handed manoeuvre the British might make should they decide to proceed towards Baggot Street Bridge, which was unguarded at the time.

The garrison of Volunteers detailed to hold Carrisbrooke House had opted to take up various sniping positions throughout the surrounding area rather than concentrate their number within a single and easily outflanked position, and as they were not under Malone's command, he was powerless to do anything about it. He returned to No. 25 Northumberland Road where he and Grace now waited anxiously and made their final preparations. They filled whatever containers they had to hand with water and placed them in the various rooms of the house.

They were under few illusions about what they would face, and knew their impending struggle would be a thirsty one.

By noon, both British battalions had marched as far as Ballsbridge. The parched ranks of troops were ordered to rest so they fell out on both sides of the wide road and drank from their canteens. Several hundred impeccably dressed onlookers cheered and encouraged them, having alighted from the Spring Fair taking place in the showground of the nearby Royal Dublin Society, in spite of the rebellion now gaining momentum in the city. The officers, meanwhile, set up their headquarters in Pembroke Town Hall, situated at the junction of Merrion Road and Anglesea Road, where they assessed the situation. Intelligence was received of a rebel presence in the schoolhouse on Northumberland Road. Accordingly, this building became their number one target.

Inside the town hall, Lieutenants Colonel Fane of the 2/7th and Oates of the 2/8th received their orders: the 2/7th would take the schoolhouse south of Mount Street Bridge, and then the 2/8th would pass through and advance as far as Trinity College and wait for the rest of the regiment. It all seemed relatively simple.

In Clanwilliam House, word had come from the industrious cyclist that thousands of British troops were marching in their direction from Kingstown. Reynolds ordered his men to take position. Their training and commitment were about to be tested.

In the first-floor drawing room, five men placed themselves at the three barricaded front windows, Reynolds in the centre with two men on either side. Tom and James Walsh moved to the windows at the side and rear of the house, and began checking their fields of fire. Word also reached the Parochial Hall where they too made ready. The Volunteers there had a narrow line of vision as the building was set back slightly from the road. They could not deal with any troop movement until it was almost level with their position so they watched the buildings opposite and waited.

In the meantime, the disconcerting situation at Carrisbrooke House was still playing heavily on Malone's mind. If the British marched up Pembroke Road instead of Northumberland Road they would have virtually unopposed access into the city. He considered ordering Grace to accompany him to the position, sensing that the surrounding rebel snipers would have a much greater chance with their assistance. He took one last look through his spyglass, scanning Northumberland Road and Ballsbridge.

Suddenly he shouted to Grace, 'They're here!' The khaki-coloured mass of the British Army was advancing from the Dodder Bridge about half a mile to their south. Both men rushed to their firing positions, Grace at the front windows and Malone at the side overlooking Haddington Road and Northumberland Road. Malone attached the stock to his Mauser which clicked neatly into place while Grace pulled back the bolt on his rifle and released its safety catch. The wait was over.

As the head of the Sherwood Foresters neared the Shelbourne Road junction a loud volley of shots rang out from the direction of Carrisbrooke House. The cracks reverberated throughout the quiet suburb. A rebel sniper had found his mark and one of the troops slumped to the ground clutching his stomach. The rest immediately returned fire while medics rushed to the man's aid. Rifles were aimed and shot wildly by the inexperienced recruits, but they eventually reached and stormed the house, only to find it empty.

The sharp echoes of the same shots filled those in No. 25 Northumberland Road with a nerve-shattering sense of urgency. Malone and Grace crouched at their posts, nervously smoking to relieve the tension. They had eaten very little over the previous few days but the gnawing hunger that had plagued them was now gone. Their hearts raced, their mouths went dry and their stomachs began to churn. They surveyed the road and all its potential hidden dangers.

The 2/7th advanced. When they reached St Mary's Road, a left-handed junction with Northumberland Road, they halted. They had been warned of Volunteer snipers on the railway embankment close to Grand Canal Street on their right flank, so a small section of troops was sent back through Lansdowne Park to patrol the Shelbourne Road area and deal with any such threat.

C Company then advanced towards the schoolhouse. The young conscripts' hearts pounded as their boots clattered in step towards the unknown. The sound of gunfire in the background did little to steady their nerves, or their protesting bladders. Somewhere ahead of them lay an unseen enemy.

They pressed on in their perfect formation almost as if they were on the parade ground.[8] They gripped their rifles with sweaty palms and shaking hands. The atmosphere was now completely the opposite of the exuberant fanfare that had greeted them earlier in the day. On Northumberland Road they were no longer surrounded by pretty girls and cake-bearing well-wishers; instead, they imagined hawklike eyes sizing them up through rifle sights. They were right.

As the Sherwood Foresters reached the junction with Haddington Road, Malone and Grace let loose. The crossroads became a scene of carnage as Malone's semi-automatic smashed into the British ranks while Grace fired his bolt-action rifle with well-trained speed and lethal precision. Once in action their natural fear subsided and their training took over. The raw recruits beneath them on the street stood no chance. Their comparative lack of training left them both stunned and stupefied. Those standing or kneeling while trying to shoot back fell as they were hit, prompting those around them to lie helplessly still on the ground in the hope their turn would not come, but they too were shot where they lay. Some tried to find cover but it was impossible in the chaos. What little training they had was designed for field warfare in continental Europe. Here they found themselves in the leafy suburbs of south Dublin, on cobbled streets, under intense, close-range, high-velocity fire coming from several directions at once. One young infantryman dislocated his shoulder when his rifle recoiled as he tried to fire back. Needless to say, his shot went astray, but he was one of the lucky ones. Within seconds ten of his comrades lay strewn on the road, including Captain Dietrichsen. He was eventually carried into No. 26 Northumberland Road, directly across the street from No. 25, where he passed away while being tended to.

The dumbfounded Sherwood Foresters soon received the shouted order to charge forward. Their few weeks of training now somehow overcame their desperate fear and those close to the front of the Company automatically jumped to their feet and rushed at the corner house. Several assaulted its side railings while others rushed for the steps up to the front door. They pressed forward under the dreadful fire of the two Volunteers. Gun flashes emanated at terrific speed from the upstairs windows, noticed briefly by rushing troops who feared the worst momentarily until their pals fell screaming next to them, providing them with a microsecond of relief at their own survival. But those who made the steps ran headlong into a new nightmare. The same steps were clearly visible from Clanwilliam House roughly 200 yards away and Reynolds and his men there wasted no time. Their

Lieutenant Michael Malone, C Company 3rd Battalion Irish Volunteers who held his position against impossible odds and inflicted appalling casualties on his enemies. NATIONAL LIBRARY OF IRELAND

rifles boomed at the bunched-up cluster of khaki uniforms scrambling for Malone and Grace's front door. The Foresters were cut to pieces. Those who turned and ran from the hell had no idea where the fire was coming from and in their disorientation they panicked, increasing their vulnerability to the two men upstairs still firing furiously down upon them. Those back on the road sought cover where they could, provided with a brief breathing space as Malone and Grace dealt mercilessly with their retreating comrades.

Colonel Fane reacted quickly and decided to try to outflank No. 25. He summoned Major Hanson, and ordered him to advance with three platoons from B Company up Haddington Road to its left, with additional orders to secure Baggot Street Bridge and then to move back down via the canal bank towards Mount Street Bridge, in order to attack the schoolhouse from behind Malone and Grace's position. A single platoon from the same Company was ordered to remain on Northumberland Road.

The disorientated young men from C Company soon collected themselves and laid a covering fire against the rebel position to cover Major Hanson's manoeuvre, but their fire was wild and inaccurate. The troops had barely shot their rifles during their six weeks of basic training in the English midlands. B Company rushed forward, losing several men to Malone's rapid fire before making their left turn onto Haddington Road where the rebel lieutenant opened up again. His Mauser held a magazine of ten rounds and could be emptied in less than as many seconds. It was designed for precisely this type of warfare. Its nickname 'Peter the Painter' came from the Siege of Sydney Street in London that had taken place five years earlier during which a handful of anarchists from the Baltic States held off several hundred policemen and soldiers, killing and wounding many. The same weapon in the hands of a skilled marksman such as Malone amplified its killing power greatly. Every squeeze of his trigger was met with the horrific sight of a pair of hands clutching at a wound or flying wildly in the air, or with the obscene collapse of a lifeless body shot through the head in mid-sprint. The 6-foot-high granite wall opposite Malone's position was soon stained red while the narrow gaps between the road's cobblestones became wet with blood oozing from the wounds and urine from the involuntarily releasing bladders of those perishing beneath his vantage point.

Soon, about 20 men from B Company lay dead and wounded in the street on Haddington Road. The expressions on the faces of the unfortunate infantrymen who had fallen to Malone's rapid fire varied. Some lay motionless with their vacant eyes revealing a still warm but lifeless and bloody corpse. Others screamed and twisted in agony, while several looked dazed, as if detached suddenly from reality, having entered another unfamiliar and terrifying realm of half-existence as their life ebbed away.

Hanson nonetheless successfully reached his objective at Baggot Street Bridge. He left a single platoon to guard both the bridge and the surrounding area, and with the remainder he moved back along the canal bank towards Percy Place and Mount Street Bridge. They pushed forward cautiously, convinced that their enemy was directly in front of them in the schoolhouse. They attempted to gain access to the houses just across from the perceived rebel strongpoint whose perpendicularly positioned front doors would be shielded from the enemy's view, but were suddenly plunged into confusion as scores of bullets began smashing into the walls and pavements all around them. Several fell as the disorientated troops, believing the fire was coming from the very buildings they were trying to enter, attempted to storm through the front doors, but it was impossible. More of the panicked young Englishmen fell as they were forced to flee under the guns of Reynolds and his six Volunteers across the canal, and from the men further down in Robert's Yard. Unable to find any way out, they rushed for cover along its coping stones on the opposite pavement which stood at between 12 and 18 inches high, and afforded just enough shelter for the terrified Sherwood Foresters to lie down next to. The fire then escalated to such a level that the civilians in the nearby houses found their sitting rooms and kitchens assailed by the intense volleys. They huddled together as their windows were smashed in on them and shots ricocheted into their ornate parlours. Several became victim to stray bullets.

A half-mile to the east of the developing carnage, Lieutenant O'Byrne's men in Boland's Mills were beginning to come increasingly under sniper attack. It was not long before any rebel movement towards the adjacent drawbridge drew vicious enemy fire, and communications between the Mills and the bakery became all but impossible. The sudden increase in the intensity of the battle had the Volunteers on the railway line on edge and any hint of movement below them drew the sights of their weapons. Lieutenant Guilfoyle in Horan's corner shop ordered his men to increase their fire at the barracks to their front. It was imperative not to allow the troops inside to force an exit and turn the flank of the Volunteers around Mount Street Bridge.

Back at No. 25, the firing died down somewhat. Most of the young military had found some cover behind the many rows of steps leading up to the surrounding houses on the southern side of the crossroads, and were firing at the rebel position as best they could. Malone and Grace drew breath and waited. Corpses littered the road junction and the many wounded groaned in agony in the warm afternoon.

Soon it was C Company's turn to enter the fray once again. A whistle shrilled, heralding the charge across no man's land, and 60 or so terrified young troops began another charge towards the schoolhouse. They began to fall as soon as they reached the crossroads. Grace fired again and again without any hint of emotion at the ranks of troops below as they rushed past his position. Malone joined him at the front of the house while a large section of troops broke away and charged for

The Parochial Hall on Northumberland Road, another of the rebel positions that decimated the 2/7th Battalion Sherwood Foresters on Wednesday 26 April 1916. MILITARY ARCHIVES

a second time at their front door, leaving their main body of men to press on up the street towards the schoolhouse ahead and to their right. Again, this section of young troops were shot to pieces on the steps of No. 25, completely unable to make any progress against its barricaded door and falling victim to the gunmen both above them and on the far side of the canal.

As the main force rushed at the schoolhouse they came abreast of the Parochial Hall on their left. They were unaware that it was occupied by rebels until a deafening volley of Mauser bullets smashed into them from point-blank range. Men tumbled obscenely sideways into their comrades as the life left their collapsing bodies. The Company had ventured into a carefully laid trap. Additional rifles and pistols now opened up on them from Clanwilliam House. The four Volunteers in the Parochial Hall soon struggled to see past the tear-inducing smoke that filled the rooms from which they fired wildly.

Spent brass cartridges clattered to the floor as they shot volley after volley from rapidly overheating guns. Grace added to their misery from behind with his lethally fast and accurate marksmanship while Malone kept the rest of the Regiment's heads down behind the crossroads. The slaughter was appalling. Only 12 from the original 60 reached the schoolhouse, but, unable to enter its barricaded doors or windows and powerless to advance or retreat, they were picked off by the Clanwilliam House sharpshooters. A lucky few found cover and waited, shaking and panting.

Colonel Fane looked on in horror through his field glasses as his men were mown down. From his sheltered position at the St Mary's Road junction he assessed the situation. In the confusion he still believed that the schoolhouse was the main rebel stronghold.

In Clanwilliam House, Reynolds prepared his men for what now lay ahead. He told the Walsh brothers covering the side and rear windows that they were to keep Percy Place and Percy Lane clear of British troops, fearing that its use as an escape route from No. 25 and the Parochial Hall was becoming increasingly inevitable. He then instructed both pairs of Volunteers manning the windows to his immediate left and right to train their rifles on the opposite sides of Northumberland Road: those on his right would aim to the left and vice versa, while he would cover the centre, creating a lethal crossfire in the leafy street.

Meanwhile, the two brothers at the house's side windows were firing on the troops of B Company with gusto, pinning them down against the canal's coping stones. They fired at the tops of their backpacks protruding from above the low wall. Every so often a canvas haversack was seen lumbering along and a shot was fired into it, causing the soldier beneath it to expose himself momentarily under the force of the impact. If the infantryman reacted quickly he could successfully crawl back to cover, but on several occasions the rifle fire was quicker. When the brothers scored a hit, the hapless victim's comrades had no choice but to crawl either around the body or over it, rendering themselves vulnerable to the same guns. Major Hanson was shot in the arm as he and his troops tried to creep along the pavement away from the bridge. Several of his men continued, but the Walsh brothers were ready. There was a gap of about 4 feet between two sections of stones at a point roughly halfway along the length of Percy Place. As soon as they saw khaki crawling through the gap they shot. They could hardly miss.

Major Hanson lost a significant amount of blood and was soon unable to command any longer, so a sergeant took control. Feeling there was no way out, he ordered a full-on charge at the schoolhouse. It seemed better to 'have a go' than to crawl on the ground to annihilation. The young troops bravely jumped to their feet as ordered and ran headlong into another wall of bullets. As they charged they were cut to pieces by Reynolds and his pair of snipers on either side, their lethal fire now added to by the four riflemen on the roof in Robert's Yard and O'Byrne's men in the loft at Boland's Mills, who were also bringing pressure to bear on the platoon of troops holding Baggot Street Bridge. Progress was impossible.

Tom Walsh's rifle eventually overheated and jammed. He ran out to the landing of Clanwilliam House and shouted to his brother James to come and clean their guns. He then rushed back to his position to find three bullet holes in the window frame right where his head had been only moments earlier. He briefly studied the angle of the bullet holes and concluded that the British had now placed snipers in the bell tower of St Mary's Church on Haddington Road. This presented them with an unexpected problem: as strict Catholics they struggled with the idea of shooting at the house of God,[9] particularly, no doubt, as they might be imminently making His acquaintance, but necessity soon overcame their inhibitions and once their rifles were cleaned and had cooled down they did their best to reply to the source of the British fire. They warned Commander Reynolds of the new danger.

At this stage, in spite of all the evidence to the contrary, Colonel Fane still believed that the abandoned schoolhouse represented the main enemy threat. He decided on a new plan to outflank it. He instructed Captain Wright to proceed with A Company towards South Lotts Road, and from there to turn onto Grand Canal Street, with the aim being to manoeuvre into a position that would allow them to take the building from its rear.

Captain Wright's Company initially retreated towards Ballsbridge before making for Shelbourne Road, where they drew alongside the huge side walls of the barracks, and were unexpectedly met by Colonel Shaw, whose head suddenly popped up above its parapet. He ordered Captain Wright to hand over a platoon of his troops. The captain reluctantly agreed to the demand of his higher-ranking officer and ordered Sergeant Hardy to take a platoon to bolster the barracks while he himself pressed on with his diminished remainder, until they approached the wide junction at Horan's where a wall of fire greeted them from both the shop and the railway line. Captain Wright and his men retreated.

By mid-afternoon Fane's situation was becoming desperate. He had suffered serious losses to two companies of troops, and not a single insurgent had been wounded, killed or captured. He held Baggot Street Bridge, but could not advance past Northumberland Road and his casualty rate was growing by the minute. He sent a runner back to headquarters in Pembroke Town Hall with the message that he needed bombs and machine guns in order to press on. The returning message contained instructions to contact Captain Jeffares, the officer in charge of the Elm Park Bombing School situated 2 miles to the south of Ballsbridge.

Soon, however, the Volunteers suffered their first fatality, when Patrick Whelan, positioned in the loft of Boland's Mills, was shot just below the eye by a sniper. He died within a minute.

Fane promptly contacted the Bombing School, before deciding to change his plan of attack. He now called his reserve into play. D Company of the 2/7th, under Captain Cooper, would move forward and occupy the houses opposite No. 25, and from there they would start laying covering fire from three directions into the house. The ragged remainder of C Company under Captain Pragnell would then advance up Haddington Road and cut through Percy Lane to the canal bank to reinforce Major Hanson's B Company, the remainder of which was still pinned down in Percy Place. From here they would capture Mount Street Bridge.

D Company soon trained its sights on No. 25. Numerous rifle barrels protruded from the gardens of the red-brick houses along the road, and from behind whatever cover they could find. A whistle sounded and they commenced firing. Clouds of dust and masonry were sent flying from the walls of the house as the ear-shattering volleys crashed into its brickwork and remaining glass. Captain Pragnell and his men raced to pass the position, but not before Malone opened up once again with his Mauser. The earlier scene of carnage and mayhem was then repeated as troops crumpled under the bullets, but, just as they had done earlier, the remainder pressed on. They made the right-hand turn into Percy Lane where they spread themselves along its entire length. When their forward troops emerged onto Percy Place with the canal directly in front of them, the rebels in Clanwilliam House, Robert's Yard and Boland's

Mills opened up on them with several fearful bursts. Streams of red-hot lead flew at the laneway's intersection, shattering the concrete wall on its western side. Malone's escape route had to be kept open at all costs. The rebels fired like madmen at C Company who then followed their orders to the letter. They left the comparative shelter of the laneway in spite of the ferocious fire, leaving only a handful of men there, and emerged onto Percy Place to reinforce Major Hanson, but were cut to pieces under the rebel guns once they revealed themselves. By now C Company was decimated. Captain Pragnell himself soon became a casualty, leaving the hapless troops huddling behind the coping stones on the canal bank virtually leaderless.

Both the rebels and the British were by now beginning to feel the strain and soon an uneasy calm descended on Northumberland Road. After a while, only the sickening groans and cries of the dying and wounded broke the disturbing silence. The Volunteers in Clanwilliam House took turns cleaning their weapons while Malone and Grace kept watch several feet back from their windows where they drank huge gulps from dusty water vessels. During the relative calmness, the military began quietly making their way through the houses and gardens along the entire length of the road south of the crossroads.

After an hour of this strange stillness, Reynolds peered out from behind his position in Clanwilliam House and was met with a terrifying sight. He beckoned his men to come and have a look. As far as the eye could see there were khaki-clad troops – behind hedges, trees and garden steps – but their eyes were drawn to what looked like four huge snakes crawling towards them from about 300 yards. The Volunteers rushed back to their positions and took aim at the khaki mass – loading, aiming, firing, reloading – firing non-stop into what seemed to be a pulsating beast. The Parochial Hall rebels stood by, ready to join the fray, before a whistle repeatedly shrilled and the Sherwood Foresters leapt to their feet to charge at the schoolhouse, only to be cut down in their tracks again. The whistle blew yet again, and yet again they charged. Their inexperience was their undoing, but their courage was undeniable. Each time the whistle blew, they rose as one and charged with their pals, and fell at each other's side under the murderous hail. The Sherwood Foresters were being slaughtered.

Several nurses and doctors from the nearby Sir Patrick Dun's Hospital on Grand Canal Street approached Clanwilliam House with complete disregard for their own safety and requested permission to tend to the many British wounded. A ceasefire was hastily arranged and the medics soon set about their work, the nurses' capes and doctors' white over-jackets soon resembling the aprons of slaughterhouse workers. They comforted the young Englishmen as best they could under the conditions, and saved the lives of many who otherwise would have slowly bled to death. The wounds they treated were appalling. The rebel Mauser bullets were large in comparison to the smaller .303 calibre rounds used by the British, and were inadvertently mistaken for 'dum-dum'[10] rounds by the troops who yearned for revenge.

During the ensuing ceasefire, small crowds of onlookers gathered on Lower Mount Street, despite the obvious danger and the fact that several civilians had already fallen victim to stray bullets. A crescent of onlookers two to three people deep formed across the road next to Love Lane, 100 yards to the rear of Clanwilliam House, where they remained for some time.

The British troops used the temporary ceasefire to move their men forward stealthily, to gain a better advantage for their next attack. The rebels, however, were quickly alerted to the somewhat devious tactic and began shooting once again, taking great care to avoid hitting the medical staff who continued about their work with great resilience.

The battle's centre of gravity was now shifting slowly towards Clanwilliam House and the bridge it dominated. Malone and Grace's position was still under constant fire and they found it increasingly difficult to find targets without attracting a hail of British lead. Scores of dead and wounded lay in the street and in the well-tended lawns. Numerous and significantly better-armed reinforcements were, however, on the way. In the meantime, the British who had bypassed the position still had their eyes fixed on the schoolhouse as their primary target.

They crouched in gardens and behind trees and steps, until they heard the piercing shriek of a whistle. The loud cry of 'Good Old Notts'[11] accompanied the high-pitched blast and signalled the charge of another 30 or so young Englishmen, who ran headlong to their destruction. Those at the front of the attack were the first to fall, forcing those behind to leap over their crumpling bodies whilst sidestepping the brave doctors and nurses, before meeting the same fate. Another large group followed, tripping on debris and slipping on blood and human tissue before they, too, halted, seemingly unable to come to terms with the utter futility of their endeavour.

A machine gun began to bark loudly in the afternoon air. Puffs of smoke flew from the bell tower of St Mary's Church on Haddington Road as the belt-fed Vickers gun was aimed at Clanwilliam House. Those inside bellowed curses as they scrambled for cover while doors inside the house were violently torn from their hinges. Chunks of plaster and shards of broken and splintered chandeliers rained down on them. The carpet soon began to smoulder with the intense heat of the rounds that ripped into it while a piano in the corner of a room played a macabre sonata as bullets smashed its keys to smithereens. On the road outside, the doctors and nurses continued to work.

In Pembroke Town Hall, Brigadier Colonel Maconchy sent orders to Colonel Oates of the 2/8th Battalion that he was to send a company of men along Grand Canal Street to outflank the rebel positions. Before the men could move out, however, he received an order by telephone from General Lowe, the British commander-in-chief stationed at headquarters in the Royal Hospital at Kilmainham, which read: 'No deviation from plan. Maintain frontal attacks against Mount Street Bridge.' The general was not going to be forced from his plan by a handful of 'undisciplined rebels'. Colonel Maconchy mounted his horse and rode to Northumberland Road to assess the increasingly grim situation for himself.

Once there, he met with Colonel Fane, whose arm had been bandaged following a wound from a stray bullet. Fane informed his superior officer that taking the bridge would require the remainder of his 2/7th, with the full support of the 2/8th Battalion, and that casualties would continue to be very high. The Brigadier Colonel returned to Pembroke Hall where he telephoned General Lowe. He informed him of the true gravity of the situation and the measures that would be required to take the bridge. He then asked the General if crossing the canal at this particular point was such a necessity, and hung his head when he heard the reply: 'At all costs.'

Maconchy then informed Colonel Oates of the disastrous situation affecting the 2/7th and ordered him to 'take the 2/8th Battalion, and overrun the schoolhouse at all costs ... at all costs mind,'[12] and from there advance as far as possible into the city.

Every 20 minutes or so another whistle sounded on Northumberland Road and the ragged remainder of the 2/7th charged at No. 25, the schoolhouse and the bridge, only to be cut down time and time again by the concentrated fire of the Volunteers. It was hopeless. Their own weight of numbers seemed to work against them. In a situation reminiscent of the Battle of Thermopylae, the huge force found itself hemmed into a confined space with little cover and driven again and again at a well-concealed and barricaded foe who were few in number but well-armed, well-trained, highly motivated and presented repeatedly with targets at such close range they could hardly miss.

At 5 p.m., however, the future for Malone and Grace's position suddenly began to look bleak. Captain Jeffares arrived with the main body of his men. They brought hand grenades and an ample supply of explosives. Jeffares immediately set about planning his attack. No. 25 would be dealt with first.

For the next half hour, attack after attack was laid against the battered position. Malone and Grace, both of whom were now utterly exhausted, half-deafened and with their throats parched from stifling heat and acrid gun smoke, moved frantically from room to room, and window to window, firing relentlessly down into the ranks of attacking troops. There was no respite. Two of the Sherwood Foresters, under instruction from Captain Jeffares, managed eventually to fix an explosive device made from guncotton to the door, and rushed back as it blew from its hinges. The entire building shook and surrounding windows shattered with the blast.

The remaining platoon from B Company rushed at the house once more, while those in front stormed through its doorway, screaming and shouting like madmen hell-bent on revenge, only to find the hallway inside heavily barricaded. Malone and Grace raced out to the landing and furiously emptied their magazines into the bunched-up and horrified troops on the porch, several of whom fell clutching at their wounds while their panicked comrades stepped over them, trying to escape the claustrophobic deathtrap. The two rebels upstairs ran back to the windows and fired again. Across the canal Reynolds was heard shouting, 'Good old Mick!'

The writing was now on the wall for No. 25, and fully aware of this inevitability, Malone ordered the position's abandonment. During a brief lull he told Grace to go downstairs and wait for him to follow. Both men at this stage were completely spent. They had faced odds far beyond their expectation and had fought those odds to a standstill for over six hours with little respite. Their soot-covered faces bore the strain of what they had endured. Grace felt a tremendous fear grip him at this point, as if the adrenalin built up during the day sought to render him with a form of paralysis he could ill afford as they prepared to make their escape.

The next British attack relieved him of his torment. Once his animal instincts kicked in, he felt completely fearless as he shot his overheating weapon manically through the ground floor's front window. He heard the disconcerting sound of the back door being smashed in and turned to fire a couple of shots before his gun jammed, leaving him with no option other than to rush for the basement. Once there, he ran his pistol under a cold tap before aiming a couple of shots through the rear window. A hand grenade was lobbed through the same smashed pane of glass which sent him running for cover in a tiny alcove. He was just in time to avoid the full force of the blast. As he waited there for death his half-shattered eardrums barely registered his lieutenant shouting, 'I'm coming Séamus!' The young troops storming into the ground floor had other ideas, however, and fired mercilessly into the rebel officer as he descended the stairs, shooting his Mauser before he collapsed in front of them. His smoking Mauser still pointed at the uniforms of the very army for which his younger brother had died fighting.

An urgent shout then filled the hallway, 'There's another one in the basement!' Grace was out of options. He fired his unjammed pistol at the silhouettes the troops made in the basement doorway before hearing another two grenades ominously tumbling down its wooden staircase. Pure instinct launched him behind a cooker, which had been knocked over by the first blast, just milliseconds before the deafening explosions plunged the smashed basement into complete darkness. He lay there deafened and stunned. He vaguely heard the English accents of troops as their hobnailed boots crunched on broken glass just on the other side of the cooker that had saved him from oblivion seconds before. He then heard the shout, 'Clear the street!' from just outside as the troops left the basement. Without thinking, he launched himself up the steps and fired several shots into the various rooms of the house that led to the back door. He sprinted out into Percy Lane where several half-stunned troops fell to his pistol before their comrades gave chase. Grace hid in a coal shed.

The British military had finally taken the first position in the Battle of Mount Street Bridge. The Parochial Hall became their next objective.

4

Northumberland Road, Mount Street Bridge, Boland's Bakery and Mills: Part 2

'Boys, isn't it a great day for Ireland?'

Captain Joe O'Connor briskly checked on his men's positions up and down the railway line as the battle 300 yards west of them escalated. He ventured into Horan's shop from its rear and saw several riflemen taking a breather while their comrades fired away at the barracks. A sense of urgency gripped them as a breathless Volunteer arrived, saying, 'The British are advancing along the tracks!'

Captain E. Gerrard, an artillery officer who had been on home leave from Athlone[1] but who had reported for duty to Beggar's Bush Barracks on Monday evening by scaling its rear wall, had led another patrol from the same section of wall, and, using ladders, had climbed on to the tracks close to Lansdowne Lane. Colonel Shaw had ordered him to take the patrol and remove the rebels from the railway line and if possible to deal with the problem in Horan's. Captain O'Connor, however, had placed pickets all along the line earlier, 100 yards apart, and it was not long before one of them brought news of the enemy's arrival.

O'Connor rushed to the railway line, grabbing six of the Volunteers closest to him. They formed a line abreast and advanced to meet the threat.

By the time Captain Gerrard realised that their presence had been discovered it was too late for the NCO at his side. Sergeant Gamble collapsed dead just as the loud crack of rifles from O'Connor's men reached them, shot through the head. Gerrard ordered a return volley, but the startled troops surrounding him barely took time to aim their guns before the next rebel fusillade spun him around, knocking him over as he was hit in the arm. O'Connor's men increased their speed of advance. Gerrard swiftly came around and ordered a fighting retreat. His men needed no encouragement. They hastily turned and made for the barracks' entry point, harassed now by the rebels at the level crossing on Lansdowne Road. Once over the wall, the captain's condition rapidly worsened. His loss of blood had been compensated for by the adrenalin that fuelled his retreat, but he now began to go into mild shock. He was taken to the first-aid station, his brief part in the rebellion's suppression now at an end.

The single volley his troops had fired, despite barely taking the time to aim effectively, had, however, borne fruit for them in avenging the death of their sergeant. As O'Connor turned back he came across Volunteer Christie Murphy who was lying on the railway tracks clutching his chest. He knelt down next to him and did his best to provide comfort as his comrades prepared carefully to move him rearwards to the dispensary.

In Northumberland Road, the attacks against the Parochial Hall rapidly grew in momentum. Untroubled by fire from their rear at No. 25, overwhelming numbers of troops were now free to join in the onslaught. The rebels inside the building were unable to view their assailants until they were almost level with them, and were reliant on Reynolds' men in Clanwilliam House to hinder their approach. They held out for as long as they could against constant grenade attacks, firing wildly at the troops who temporarily exposed themselves to hurl them, but their supplies of ammunition were getting low. When the inevitable order was finally given to pull out, they rushed from the Parochial Hall through its rear onto Percy Lane, where they ran straight into the British troops gathering there in force.

When the half-stupefied rebels appeared in front of them, the Foresters in the laneway reacted with uncontrolled anger. They punched and kicked them until a British officer grabbed Volunteer Joe Clarke by his collar and placed his revolver at his head. He pulled the trigger but missed, having turned his head away and moved his hand suddenly while firing the shot which happened to fly into a neighbouring garden being used as a field-dressing station. The army doctor in charge there rushed to the laneway and furiously ordered the officer to cease fire, much to the relief of half-deafened Clarke and his small battle-weary group.

Following this development, Colonel Oates informed the men of the 2/8th Battalion of a new plan of attack. The school and houses around Mount Street Bridge held by the rebels were now the main objective. B Company would lead the attack, with A Company in close support to press home the attack and C Company in reserve (D Company of the 2/8th were on a ship crossing the Irish Sea from Liverpool and did not reach this particular battle).[2]

At about 6.30 p.m., B Company, under 22-year-old Lieutenant Harold Daffen from Worksop in Nottingham, went into action. They spread themselves along the road and in the nearby gardens opposite the schoolhouse, keeping their heads down in order to avoid the fire from across the canal. Reynolds' Volunteers did their best to disrupt them but were now finding themselves increasingly hard pressed to control the escalating mayhem caused by the Vickers gun in the St Mary's Church. B Company soon opened fire on the schoolhouse with a broadside volley from the entire length of the road. The school's red brickwork was pulverised by hundreds of Enfield .303 rounds. What was left of its windows disintegrated while inside the walls and wooden roof beams struggled with the weight of lead that tore into them. The ensuing attack was badly co-ordinated, however, and the infantry rushed at the building while the machine gun was being reloaded, allowing the rebels in Clanwilliam House time to raise their heads to aim and fire, once again with fatal efficiency. The attack stalled and the troops became pinned down on the left-hand side of the road.

Trying desperately to drive the attack forward, Captain Quibell of A Company moved his men to the road's right-hand side and laid down covering fire against Clanwilliam House. Lieutenant Foster of the 2/7th now seized his chance and with an assault squad with fixed bayonets he rushed the schoolhouse. His men hurled themselves over the railings and through the main gate and quickly succeeded in forcing the door, only to enter and find the building completely deserted except for the bullet-riddled bodies of the caretaker and his wife which were grotesquely sprawled out on the floor. They soon found themselves joined by the remaining men of D Company 2/7th, under the command of Captain Cooper, who had come through the rear of the houses at the back of the schoolhouse.

Clanwilliam House in ruins. Nothing had prepared the young British infantrymen for the storm of lead that greeted them as they launched attack after attack against this position. NATIONAL LIBRARY OF IRELAND

Captain Cooper then ordered them all to move out and take up firing positions behind the 2-foot-thick and 4-foot-high granite canal wall next to the small road adjacent to the schoolhouse, which directly faced Clanwilliam Place. A large advertising billboard there shielded many of them from the eyes of the rebel gunners but also made it difficult for them to aim at a target. To add to their predicament, they soon began taking fire from Robert's Yard, diagonally across the canal, and also from the rebels in their elevated position in Boland's Mills, 500 yards away to their right.

The closely bunched men soon attracted most, if not all, of the fire from Clanwilliam House and the advertising hoarding was rapidly shot to pieces. The Vickers gun then began to spit streams of lead at Reynolds and his hard-pressed rebels once again while, simultaneously, A company directed their rifles at the upper floors of the house. The rebels retreated from their windows and took up firing positions further back into their rooms where they were not as visible to the British riflemen and machine-gunners.

Lieutenant Daffen blew his whistle, summoning the troops of B Company to jump to their feet once again and rush at Mount Street Bridge. He was the first to die. Meanwhile, Captain O'Connor, now back in the railway workshops, barked repeated orders to his men to fire from the railway line and the water towers next to him. Their efforts were augmented by their colleagues in Boland's Mills to their rear where the Volunteers had an almost unobstructed view of the Bridge. The accompanying avalanche of bullets ripped into the sides of the charging Sherwood Foresters from their right, and was matched by a frontal broadside from Clanwilliam House. The result was devastating. Each of B Company's officers was wounded in the same charge. Without effective leadership, the attack stalled and the Foresters fell back yet again in disarray.

The same Company launched attack after attack at the bridge, with a seemingly never-ending supply of men, only to be beaten back time and again. The dead and wounded were heaped in obscene piles and once more the doctors and nurses felt compelled to place themselves in the firing line. Some of the medics themselves became casualties. It is fair to say that if they had not done what they did under such dangerous circumstances the number of deaths from wounds among the young Englishmen would have been staggering. To their surprise, as the doctors and nurses moved from victim to victim they discovered several young troops and NCOs who were uninjured, but who were lying there as if dead in the middle of the bridge, awaiting the next attack and using this 'head start' to their advantage. When the whistle blew again, these 'dead and wounded' infantrymen sprang to their feet and made it to the front railings of Clanwilliam House where they lobbed several grenades at its barricaded windows. The explosions rocked the front of the building but did little damage, while below the rebel guns the troops were again forced back to the cover of the bridge wall.

Reynolds ordered Willie Ronan and Jimmy Doyle to take up firing positions in the top-floor windows of Clanwilliam House, hoping to draw some of the increasingly accurate British fire away from its drawing room. It was next to impossible for them to mount the staircase as most of it had by now been shot away but they somehow managed to scramble up. Meanwhile, the Vickers bullets blasted the front and side of the building and continued the bizarre sonata with the piano slowly being smashed to pieces in the side room.

Ronan found himself overlooking Mount Street Bridge once again while Doyle chose the side room that dominated Percy Place. His choice almost proved fatal. He stood on a table to get a shot at a British sniper in a house opposite the canal and was knocked out by the impact of the shattered stock of his own rifle smashing into his face, having been hit by a bullet from the same sniper. He came to as Commander Reynolds handed him a new rifle. Reynolds positioned himself at the centre window. The fighting then escalated as small fires began to break out throughout the house. At this stage, the rebels were beyond the limits of endurance. Seven of them faced the remnants of two well-armed battalions bent on revenge, whose unrelenting fire rendered it almost suicidal to raise one's head. They were exhausted and parched. Their hands and faces resembled those of unwashed coalminers. Their eardrums rang with the unending firing and their shoulders ached from the bruising effect of almost continuous recoils. Their eyes were completely bloodshot, while their dry throats called for reinforcements which never came.

'Boys, isn't this a great day for Ireland?' shouted Patrick Doyle.[3] 'Isn't it that!' replied Tom Walsh just before Doyle was hit in the head by a bullet. He slumped unceremoniously to the floor, dead. As if they smelt the blood, the machine-gunners intensified their fire and mortally wounded Dick Murphy in the same room. Sensing that something had gone horribly wrong, both Walsh brothers rushed into the room as Murphy passed away next to the sprawled body of Doyle. Tom Walsh drew breath as he scanned the room for ideas. He spotted a mannequin lying in a corner. He grabbed the dummy and placed it in position at one of the windows to draw the British fire. His brother knelt over the two bodies momentarily, but there was little time for prayer.

At this point the British troops were unaware of the actual rebel strength in Clanwilliam House or in nearby Robert's Yard. They more or less controlled the bridge, but were still unable to make the 30 yards or so from there to the railings of their main objective without suffering heavy casualties. Once exposed, they faced defilade fire from the Volunteers shooting from the windows above, and enfilading them from their right at Robert's Yard as well as other positions further back. B Company of the 2/8th had by now been severely mauled. All of its officers and many of its ranks were either dead or wounded. Their reserve of C Company under Captain Cursham was now called into action. Its men emerged

British infantrymen taking stock on Northumberland Road. Two battalions were completely shattered along this stretch of affluent Dublin suburb. De Valera Collection UCD, courtesy UCD-OFM Partnership

from the shelter of St Mary's Road and advanced with trepidation along Northumberland Road, passing the scores of dead and wounded now being attended to by their own army medics.

Deafening exchanges of shots continued across the still canal while the remaining British officers of A Company pulled back from the bridge to make room for their reserves to pass through, while they themselves regrouped at the schoolhouse before taking position behind the canal wall to provide covering fire for their advancing comrades.

As the evening shadows grew, fires began to break out in Clanwilliam House. The repeated grenade blasts outside made the building shudder with the impacts while its walls were constantly peppered with bullets. The Volunteers did their best to deal with the fires, all the while under immense pressure from the machine gun up in the church bell tower. James Doyle peered out briefly from behind his window and noticed C Company forming up in increasing numbers behind the canal wall to attack.

In time, it became impossible for the rebels to man their upstairs windows, such was the weight of fire now being aimed at them, so they moved back several feet. Two of them ventured back as far as the landing, where they struggled to maintain their balance on tables while getting an effective shot. They were running low on ammunition, but still hoped for imminent reinforcements.

The British prepared themselves for the showdown. Captain Quibell, having taken charge of C Company, blew his whistle and charged forward, joined by Captain Cursham and Lieutenant Foster with his remaining men of the 2/7th. As they reached the brow of the bridge, the five remaining Volunteers once again opened fire. The troops threw themselves to the ground, but when the firing from Clanwilliam House died down they leapt to their feet and rushed on, lobbing grenades as they went. One NCO hurled himself over the 4-foot high railing, such was his eagerness to throw his grenade, which he did with great energy, only for it to bounce off the second floor wall where it flew back towards him and exploded next to his head. His shattered body was blown sideways and crumpled like a sack. Captain Quibell was among those wounded by rebel bullets as he crossed to the railing, as was Captain Cursham. The Company command passed to Lieutenant Foster, who pressed on.

Volunteer Captain O'Connor was now alongside his men at the water towers, where he too fired like a madman at Mount Street Bridge. He could sense that the end was near for the battered rebel position. Percy Place was teeming with military, and small units were making their way along the northern side of the canal on Warrington Place. His men fired and fired again, almost without pausing for breath. Their minds were focused on one thing alone: shooting at the mass of khaki swarming around the bridge. The noise was deafening, the smells of combat nauseating. The men next to him were filthy and parched, but their growing fatigue was an unlikely ally: it helped dull the emotion of what they were doing to their fellow men 300 yards away.

In spite of the deluge of lead both from in front of them and to their right, British troops eventually began to swarm into the front garden of Clanwilliam House. From here they were partially sheltered, at least from the rebel fire from above. Foster wasted no time. The house's door was too heavily fortified to allow entry but he managed to get to a side window and lobbed in a grenade, before rushing in just after the ensuing explosion had displaced the window's obstructions.

The military now began to pour across Mount Street Bridge. Seeing this, the Volunteers close to the water towers fought with an animal intensity and viciousness. They desperately wanted to save their comrades. The deafening din built to a crescendo before the man next to Captain O'Connor screamed in pain. O'Connor shouted at him, 'Are you hit?' His face twisted in pain as he replied, 'No, but my bloody hand is stuck to my gun,' prompting the captain to help peel the man's hand from the burning gun breech, leaving a clump of skin sizzling on the red-hot metal. The captain began shooting again, rejoining the rebels all around who were firing like automatons. Plumes of smoke could now be seen from the windows of Clanwilliam House.

Reynolds knew the time had come to withdraw from the rebel keep so the order was shouted around the building to pull out. The section commander stood up to make his move but was shot as he turned. Tom Walsh heard him cry out as he was hit and scrambled up what was left of the staircase to try to help him, but it was too late. Reynolds muttered, 'Mick ... Mick,'[4] and died.

The four remaining Volunteers manning the beleaguered position – James Doyle, Willie Ronan, and Thomas and James Walsh – rushed to the basement, firing frantically as they went. Meanwhile, the British were gaining access to the ground floor in significant numbers. They moved from room to room in the smoky half-darkness, lobbing grenades and following in their wake, shooting like madmen at those they assumed were crouching in corners aiming pistols back at them.

The staircase was next. As the ground floor filled with dense, acrid smoke, Lieutenant Foster led the charge to the first floor where he was met by the silhouette of what he thought was a rebel in the front window. He pulled the pin on a grenade, counted for a couple of seconds as he drew a deep breath and lobbed it into the room, before exhaling vigorously while wrenching the heavy and bullet-riddled door closed to shield him from the blast. Rising from a protective crouching position he then rushed into the drawing room to finish off his enemy, but turned away when he realised it was the mannequin set up by Tom Walsh.

The dummy had been blown to pieces but had bought the Volunteers precious seconds. The lieutenant and his men fanned out to search for those who were now below them escaping through a 2-foot-wide basement window into the back garden, before scrambling over the wall to safety.

Soon the entire house was ablaze, and the British moved back out onto Lower Mount Street. The rebels in Robert's Yard carried on firing as best they could, but with the fall of Clanwilliam House their position was hopeless. When Captain O'Connor sent word back down the line that the position had fallen to the enemy, Captain Donnelly ordered the abandonment of Robert's Yard. As Section Commander O'Donoghue led the men out over its wall they felt the heat of Clanwilliam House burning behind their backs, and they prayed quietly for those who had held it for so long, fearing the worst had befallen them.

In the still spring evening Clanwilliam House rapidly became an inferno, a funeral pyre for Volunteers Doyle, Murphy and Reynolds, whose bodies were consumed by the flames. All that remained of them when the fire abated was half a human leg.

The Battle of Mount Street Bridge was over. De Valera now feared an assault on Boland's Bakery would immediately follow and ordered his men to prepare. Donnelly, on the other hand, was convinced that having received such a bloody nose the last thing their enemy was planning was a night assault. He favoured resting his men.

Order was slowly restored to the shattered area around Mount Street Bridge and Northumberland Road while the Sherwood Foresters consolidated their positions. They licked their wounds while many civilians ventured outside, shocked by what had happened along the three-quarter mile length of their hitherto peaceful and tree-lined street and at the scores of young men who lay here and there, groaning in agony as their wounds were treated. The casualties numbered 234, of which 18 were officers.

The regiment eventually regrouped and were hailed as heroes by the much relieved locals. Colonel Machonchy arrived astride his horse and congratulated his victorious but utterly exhausted men to the enthusiastic applause of the residents, whose torment, however, was far from over.

As night drew in, Lieutenant O'Byrne's problems dealing with the increasing sniping around Boland's Mills were escalating greatly. He

A British Army checkpoint on Mount Street Bridge after the fighting. The dead and wounded had formed into 'obscene piles' on this bridge as the fighting here reached its climax. National Library of Ireland

found it impossible to pinpoint a source for the buzzing rounds that now ricocheted regularly from the walls of his position. The rifle cracks seemed to come from everywhere, echoing around the surrounding red-brick townhouses and the imposing granite walls of his own position. He sent two Volunteers on a patrol under cover of darkness to see if they could throw any light on their growing predicament. They returned within the hour, reporting that they had observed a uniformed man moving at the window of a house in nearby Barrow Street. O'Byrne decided to investigate.

At 11 p.m., both he and the pair of rebels stormed through the front door and discovered two terrified men from the Georgius Rex. They handed their rifles over to the menacing intruders but assured O'Byrne and his men that they lived in the house and had nothing to do with any sniping, emphasising that they had no ammunition for their guns. A search of the house confirmed this, which inclined the lieutenant to give the men the benefit of the doubt. They returned to their position in the loft of Boland's Mills, untroubled for a time by snipers.

At 2 a.m. on Thursday, the exhausted Sherwood Foresters were relieved by Lieutenant-Colonel Taylor, accompanied by his 2/6th South Staffordshire Battalion, who immediately took to the rooftops along Lower Mount Street and began sniping at Boland's Bakery and the rebel positions along the railway line. The battered infantrymen from Nottingham and Derbyshire returned to Ballsbridge where they were rested for the remainder of the night in the showgrounds.

With the following dawn came greatly increased sniper fire. Captain O'Connor ordered the two Volunteers manning the level crossing at Lansdowne Road to retreat towards the various other rebel posts on the line, expecting an imminent attack. He sent orders to the men to hold their fire until they had a clear shot. His instincts were correct. A patrol soon began advancing towards his positions. It was immediately driven back, but another swiftly returned with greater numbers. A tense firefight then ensued for a time before the troops pulled back again, satisfied with their probing attack. O'Connor knew they were only testing the strength of his positions.

One ingenious Volunteer devised a plan to place two of their ample supply of shotguns into a metal pipe with a string attached to both triggers. The resulting boom, amplified by the pipe, was considered very impressive. Several of these devices were then hastily put together and placed further south on the line. When the anticipated attack came it was in platoon strength, but when its officer heard the terrifying blasts from the pipes, even though no casualties were sustained, he considered it prudent to avoid contact until more information was available as to the killing power of such a menacing-sounding weapon.

Captain O'Connor had little time to savour this small victory, however: an aggressive British patrol had penetrated into a small section of the southern end of the railway workshops and its men were rapidly digging in. As they did, they fired their weapons to cover several others who manoeuvred themselves between the huge engines and sheds placed throughout the yard. There was no time to waste. If O'Connor did not act quickly, enemy reinforcements would soon swarm in and his Company headquarters would be lost.

Section Commander Joseph Guilfoyle and several of his men began shooting from the upstairs of the headquarters in the direction of the incursion. Their rapid fire forced the intruders to keep their heads down. Their repeated volleys ricocheted from the huge metal hulls of the railway engines several troops were hiding behind, making loud ringing noises as sparks flew wildly all around. The troops darted about as they replied with their rifles, seriously wounding Volunteer Leo Casey.

O'Connor hastily summoned a dozen or so men from both inside and around his building and shouted at them to fix bayonets. Guilfoyle's relentless rifle fire continued as the captain prepared to blow his whistle, signalling to Guilfoyle and his men to cease firing immediately when they heard the high-pitched shrill that would herald their charge. Suddenly a man next to him fell to the ground.

He looked down and saw that Tom Traynor had been shot in the face. A 6-inch gash had been torn across his cheek. O'Connor blew the whistle. Guilfoyle's section stopped shooting and the Volunteers charged. As they closed in, enemy shots zipped by their heads and clattered off the surrounding concrete and metal. The onrushers began shouting and screaming as their adrenalin focused on the enemy to their front they knew they must kill or dislodge at all costs.

As their yells amplified with every advancing step the terrifying sight of such fanatics unnerved the young Englishmen in the yard. They panicked and ran. Several of their rifles fell to the ground as they sprinted from the rabid-sounding roars that were now accompanied by the booms of Mausers.

Soon it was all over. O'Connor's hugely relieved men swept around the yard and saw that it was once again secured. The two wounded Volunteers were treated. Leo Casey was now deathly pale. Things then quietened down – but not for long.

During the previous evening, the British had moved an artillery piece mounted to the back of a truck into Percy Place. Its opening volleys zeroed in now on Boland's Bakery and several explosions tore through the rebel position. Captain Donnelly reacted swiftly, and organised the remaining sacks of flour to be placed in such a way as to create a series of 'bomb proof' locations. The one remaining bread van was blown to pieces by one of the shots. Twisted metal and shattered glass, oil and burning fuel were everywhere.

The sudden deluge of explosions prompted de Valera to order Captain Donnelly to hoist a flag on a pike and place it in a location that would draw the artillery fire away from their hard-pressed comrades. When Andrew McDonnell, who had been standing next to the captain, heard the instruction he exclaimed enthusiastically that he had a pike. When the reply, 'get it, man,' came, he did not need to be asked twice. He retrieved it from its hiding place, and watched proudly as Captain Mick Cullen left with it to hang a golden harp flag from the disused distillery tower close to their position. A few moments later it was fluttering above them in the light breeze.

It was immediately effective. The amount of ordinance aimed its way suggested an extreme hatred of everything the emblem stood for. The first shell missed altogether and landed in the Liffey, close to the *Helga* who replied in kind, elevating her gun towards the clearly audible source of her 'attacker'. Cullen and the Volunteer who had accompanied him to the tower smiled wryly from the basement they had rushed to. On the far side of the Grand Canal Dock, Lieutenant O'Byrne watched with keen interest from the loft of Boland's Mills as several more shells missed their mark. Soon, however, the gunners' aims improved and the concrete tower was hit with several loud explosions. O'Byrne realised that his elevated position could be next so he began to reposition his men, including their dead comrade from the previous day, Patrick Whelan. There had been no time to inter him.

Soon Volunteer McDonnell saw his pike take a direct hit from a passing shell. As it fell, it caught on a railing close to a water tower, its flag now askew but flying nonetheless and still drawing the wrath of the gunners. The next shell struck a huge water tank, which collapsed, spewing several thousand gallons of frigidly cold liquid into the building beneath the flag. McDonnell was horrified as he knew several Volunteers were positioned inside that particular building. Several hundred rats now rushed out of the building, followed by three half-drowned men spilling out in confusion, one of whom shouted, 'I can't take it any more!'

Peadar O'Mara, Seán Guilfoyle and Tom Cassidy, meanwhile, were still manning the windows in Horan's shop. They were trying desperately to knock out a machine-gun post that had been set up by the British in the nearby Beggar's Bush Barracks. They were under such heavy fire at times that the woodwork in the building was beginning to smoulder. Another Volunteer was zeroing in on the bell tower in St Mary's Church, the source of such recent tribulation to Clanwilliam House. The tower was now a nest of snipers. The small cluster of men in Horan's knew that their beleaguered position had to hold. Their lieutenant had made it clear to them that if it was lost it could mean the end of 3rd Battalion.

For the rest of that long day, the rebels withstood the numerous probing attacks which came their way. The sniping, however, was a different matter. Certain areas along the railway line had been marked out as safe but these were few in number. The constant threat was beginning to play on the nerves of men whose expressions bore the unmistakable strain of battle. Volunteer Peadar Macken became victim to the inevitable carelessness that accompanies the dilemma of being ordered to carry on when there seems very little with which to carry on. When a comrade slipped near him and accidentally discharged his gun, Macken was hit and died at the gate of the bakery facing the street which today bears his name. His body was brought initially to the dispensary and eventually buried in the building's yard.

When the long and torturous day drew to a close, Séamus Kavanagh was posted to the railway line from the bakery. Simon Donnelly was patrolling its tracks when Kavanagh called him over to bring his attention to Captain Cullen who appeared to be in a bad way and had been ranting for some time. Their conclusion was that he was suffering from shell shock.[5] Kavanagh was ordered to take Cullen to a nearby stable and try to settle him. Cullen was not the only officer suffering from such disconcerting symptoms. Their own commandant's intermittently irrational behaviour became a source of great concern that night to the men on the receiving end of his seemingly conflicting orders. He had not slept in days, and at one point was nearly shot by his own men, having forgotten their password.

An air of desperate tension hung over the entire area that night, never more evident than when Lieutenant O'Keefe tripped on a length of barbed wire while checking on his men's positions on the railway line overlooking Lower Erne Street. One of his increasingly jumpy men reacted by shooting the officer in the arm, ending his rebellion with a wound that was treated the following day in Sir Patrick Dun's Hospital. Further south along the line, the positions were being called in to the Bakery. The rebels then consolidated their positions from Westland Row Station to South Lotts Road. Horan's was still in the fight.

Back in the upper floors of Boland's Mills, Lieutenant O'Byrne watched the lurid glare from the city centre as Sackville Street burned, a mile to their north-west. O'Byrne was as sensitive as the rest of his men to human vulnerability in the small hours of the morning, particularly on one such as this, and the flickering shadows repeatedly presented to his exhausted eyes the illusion that his dead comrade, 23-year-old Patrick Whelan, was moving every now and then. He would make sure to bury the Ringsend man in the morning.

O'Byrne did not renege on his commitment. As Friday morning broke, Volunteer Peter Byrne assembled several large pieces of wood into the rough shape of a coffin, and a few members of the garrison buried their comrade in a shallow grave in the yard of Boland's Mills. Their movements were not wasted on the British riflemen who, in spite of being denied a clear line of shot, improvised in their enthusiastic efforts to kill their enemies, by aiming carefully at the smooth concrete walls close to where the rebels were carrying out the burial, hoping to score with a lucky ricochet.

As the morning progressed, the sound of battle in the background continued. O'Connor had been summoned by de Valera during the long night to receive an unexpected promotion. He was now Vice Commandant of 3rd Battalion. One of his first duties was to patrol the various garrison areas to check on the well-being of the men. His impression was not an optimistic one. They were utterly exhausted and expressed concern about the dramatic increase in the reports from the artillery and the machine guns in the distance. Many feared the worst.

He instructed the various captains and lieutenants to ensure that their men were properly rested. Meanwhile, the situation in Boland's Mills was a cause of concern, as the line of communication was highly unreliable due to the intense activity of the snipers. The elevated position in its reoccupied loft was tremendously advantageous to their cause, as O'Byrne's men could see for miles all around and would be the first to know of any attack in force that was sent their way. He directed several men who, having been rested for a couple of hours, were sent through the rear gardens and yards of the terraces of small houses along the western length of Barrow Street to set up a line of communication. When this was in place, O'Connor set off to check on O'Byrne, who came down from the loft to meet him. Both men were tired but in good spirits.

In the meantime, Colonel Taylor, of the 2/6th South Staffordshires, received fresh orders. He was to proceed with his battalion to Trinity College and from there he would aid with the isolation of Dublin's Four Courts from the rebel headquarters in the GPO. His present position would now be occupied by one of the North Staffordshire battalions, whose number would be bolstered by elements of a battalion from the Lincolnshire Regiment, which was moving towards the city from Ballsbridge.

As the day wore on, the distant thunder of the artillery pounding Sackville Street was ever present. O'Connor feared the same treatment might soon be coming their way. He consulted with his commandant regarding contingency plans for an escape. The reply was concise: there was none. The two men discussed the options. One of those was a potential escape along the Grand Canal, which would allow them eventually to break away to the Dublin Mountains, while the other was a breakout through the Canal Docks, which would set them in a southbound coastal direction, with the same ultimate destination in mind. The Vice Commandant then relayed this to his officers and emphasised that he wanted the men rested, even if it meant standing down some of their guards for a time. They would need to be in good shape and the results of their enforced rest periods since the morning were already visible.

Friday night was a long and harrowing one. The city centre was in flames and the glow could be seen for miles around. Civilians gathered in their droves in places like Howth Head and Killiney Hill to watch. Lieutenant O'Byrne had an almost bird's-eye view in Boland's Mills. Throughout their various positions men had crouched and rested all the while keeping their eyes peeled for any hint of movement from the enemy. Both military and rebel positions were lit up intermittently by the flames engulfing Sackville Street, and eager snipers waited to pounce at any opportunity.

When Saturday morning arrived the city had quietened somewhat. A smoky haze hung in the calm air as an exhausted O'Byrne scanned his men's positions. As his gaze veered towards the drawbridge just below, a sudden sense of dread overcame him. Margaret Naylor, a young local woman, had ventured onto the bridge with her three children, but before the Lieutenant could cry out to warn her of the snipers, a shot rang out. Mrs Naylor collapsed to the ground. Her children pulled at her while they cried and pleaded with her to get up, unable to comprehend what had happened to their mortally wounded mother and why. O'Byrne turned his head away, knowing there was nothing he or his men could do to help. The children were spared by the snipers, but their particular tragedy was only beginning. Within hours of the shooting of Mrs Naylor, her husband – the children's father – 36-year-old John, would be gassed to death in France where he was serving with a unit of the Dublin Fusiliers.

The air around Grand Canal Dock was no less heavy as the afternoon came and went with a general tapering off in the hostilities. The din of the last few days was strangely absent as rumours of the surrender of their headquarters began to filter through to the ranks of the weary men of 3rd Battalion Irish Volunteers. Most of the men under de Valera and O'Connor laughed off such apparent idiocy, while they cleaned their weapons and partook of stale rations and cigarettes.

5

St Stephen's Green and the Royal College of Surgeons

'Five minutes' notice.'

When they reached Davy's pub, Joyce stepped forward. The wooden door nearly flew from its hinges with the force of the kick he then administered to it before stomping inside. When the pub's startled landlord saw him standing there in his Citizen Army uniform with his rifle lowered towards the floor his initial surprise quickly turned to anger. He slammed his fist down on the counter and shouted: 'That's it – I'm giving you a week's notice, Joyce.' The young rebel's abrupt reply – 'And I'm giving you five minutes' notice, Mr Davy!' – left the landlord speechless. Joyce raised his rifle and fired two shots at the bottles on the shelves just above the landlord's head, showering his now terrified employer with glass and liquor. Davy ran from the pub followed closely by several of his shocked patrons. The Citizen Army men immediately began throwing anything that was to hand – tables, chairs, stools and crates – up against its windows, which they smashed with their rifle butts. They then prepared for the inevitable arrival of the British soldiers.

The area of St Stephen's Green had been selected as the target to be occupied on Easter Monday by the main body of the Irish Citizen Army for the Rising, and was to be under the command of Dublin-born 42-year-old Commandant Michael Mallin, himself a British Army veteran. His second in command was the flamboyant 48-year-old

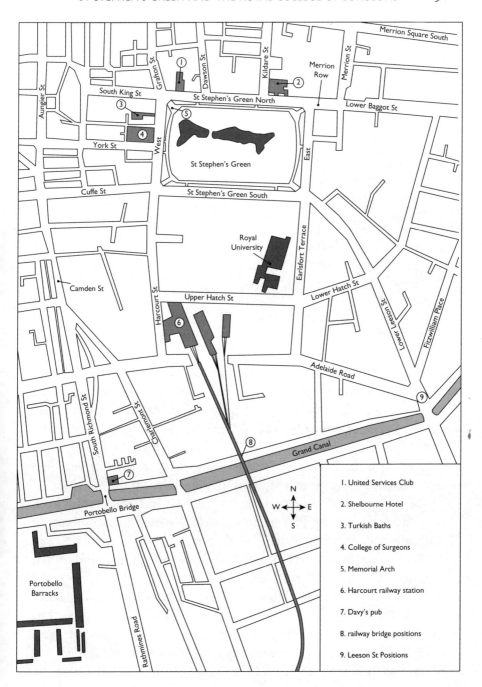

Irish Citizen Army operational area, St Stephen's Green and various outposts.

Vice-Commandant Markievicz of the Irish Citizen Army. Also a founder of Na Fianna, she played a pivotal role during the fighting in and around St Stephen's Green. MILITARY ARCHIVES

Countess Constance Markievicz, the London-born aristocratic daughter of a knighted Arctic explorer.[1] Four major routes to the city converged on St Stephen's Green, those being Baggot Street/Merrion Row, Lower Leeson Street, Harcourt Street and Cuffe Street. Several smaller routes also led to St Stephen's Green. Its central position among these routes, coupled with the fact that it had its own freshwater supply, made its capture and subsequent defence a priority objective for the insurgents.

The main perceived threat to their positions in St Stephen's Green came from the nearby Portobello Barracks, situated in the suburb of Rathmines, about a mile to their south. Four outposts were therefore to be taken in order to prevent the British from rushing troops from that direction. Captain Richard McCormack was detailed to oversee the securing of these positions. His own mission was to seize Harcourt Street Railway Station, and a sergeant named Joseph Doyle, accompanied by nine men, would occupy Davy's pub, which overlooked the Royal Canal at La Touche Bridge (more commonly known as Portobello Bridge) and stood directly in the path of any likely British advance into the city.

James Joyce worked in Davy's pub as a bottle washer, and knew the area well. His task was to provide details of the quickest escape route from the outpost should they need it. He could not have been happier with this, as there was no love lost between himself and Mr Davy, whom he regarded as a cruel and heartless boss.

Support was to be offered to the Davy's section from its left flank at the nearby railway bridge overlooking the canal. The officer in charge there was Lieutenant Michael Kelly. Another supporting position in the area was to be taken by Captain John O'Neill with a squad of his men.

Sergeant Frank Robbins, from North William Street in Dublin's North Strand, was given the task of securing any eventual escape route for the four outposts back to St Stephen's Green, a plan which would involve a retreat through the nearby Iveagh Gardens on Upper Hatch Street, and eventually to St Stephen's Green.

About 15 minutes after Captain McCormack's section had begun their southbound march from Liberty Hall where they had initially mustered, they came across the junction of St Stephen's Green and Grafton Street. Here they had their first encounter with the British Army. Their general orders were to hold fire that day until the various positions were occupied, unless, of course, it became necessary. These orders were about to be tested as the men were confronted with the unnerving sight of a British calvary officer and his orderly approaching them on horseback at a distance of about 200 yards. They continued undeterred, crossing Grafton Street's junction with South King Street before moving onto St Stephen's Green West, with the park itself to their left. As the distance between the rebels and the horsemen decreased, the tension began to mount. The Citizen Army men kept their eyes on their captain, who then, to their complete surprise, offered the smartest of salutes to the horsemen as they drew level. The marching unit followed suit. The rather puzzled-looking British officer then smartly raised his cane to his cap in return and rode on, while McCormack's men muttered to themselves in disbelief. A few moments after they had passed each other, however, the cavalrymen turned to follow them.

They began to shadow the suspicious-looking group. When his unit finally reached the top of Harcourt Street just outside the station's main entrance, McCormack stopped suddenly and turned to check on the pair who had also halted. He turned to Sergeant Doyle and ordered: 'Keep your eye on them; if they give you any trouble you know what to do'. He then entered the station with his main body of men.

Doyle remained outside with a group of nine men and monitored the mounted soldiers. Then, just as he was about to set off towards Davy's, they trotted up Harcourt Street towards him. His slipped the cover off his holster and he let his hand rest on his revolver, but to his relief the horsemen rode on by, before stopping at the next corner at the junction of Harcourt Road.

The sergeant and his men moved off, keeping their eyes fixed firmly on the cavalrymen. If they turned left from Harcourt Road onto South Richmond Street, heading towards Rathmines, it could mean only one thing: they were trying to raise the alarm. Doyle, however, knew a shortcut that would cut them off. Just before the junction of Harcourt Road and South Richmond Street there was a small side street. He ordered his men there. They dashed through the shortcut and arrived abreast of South Richmond Street forming a firing line directly in the path of the oncoming horsemen who had made the expected left turn. A single shot was fired causing the two to turn and gallop as best they could on the street's cobblestones back towards Harcourt Street. Some civilians crouched in shock at the sudden rifle crack. Meanwhile, Doyle's men re-formed into a column and marched on Davy's, where Joyce subsequently took delight in booting its door in.

When Commandant Mallin and his group of 39 men reached St Stephen's Green, they split into several groups and entered through its many different gates. Mallin himself entered from the west, through the small gate next to the Lord Ardilaun statue. Almost as soon as he had set foot inside he was set upon by James Kearney, the park keeper,[2] who demanded to know precisely what he and his men were doing. When Mallin explained, Kearney insisted on helping to evacuate the women and children. Mallin quickly detailed some men to evict the scores of startled bank-holiday revellers. Several shots were fired into the air to expedite matters. The measure was effective. Several British soldiers who had been enjoying a lazy walk in the park suddenly found themselves taken prisoner by various clusters of men in dark green military attire whose unambiguously fierce expressions and pointing bayonets suggested that co-operation would be the order of the day.

As soon as St Stephen's Green was secured, its heavy wrought-iron gates were closed and barricaded with park benches, nearby carts and anything else that could be used. The north-west gate facing Grafton Street was kept temporarily open to allow Countess Markievicz and her troops to enter a short time later, before it too was locked and barricaded.

Soon afterwards, a 29-year-old police constable named Michael Lahiff approached this gate and tried to climb over, but was pushed back by the pair of men guarding it and told he would be shot if he did not clear off. The Citizen Army had very little time for the Dublin Metropolitan Police. Less than three years earlier, many of its members had been involved in violent street battles with them during the strikes of the 1913 Lockout. The constable's colleagues had brutally supressed the actions of the workers during the latter part of this lengthy struggle, resulting in many injuries and several civilian deaths. The Countess soon heard the commotion and rushed back to the gate to issue the policeman with a second warning, which he ignored with equal disdain. She raised her pistol as the sentries simultaneously raised their rifles. The policeman was not impressed and kept trying to force the gate. Two shots rang out and the constable was blown backwards off his feet before collapsing to the ground. His body lay on the wide pavement in front of the park's ornate limestone arch in a growing pool of blood and grey matter. Several civilians screamed while others ran away.

Once their sentries had been posted, the men inside the railings grabbed pickaxes and shovels and began digging trenches. Various assortments of additional tools were 'liberated' from the park keeper's shed for those who had arrived empty handed. Several slit trenches were dug in the park's bushy areas facing Dawson Street and Kildare Street, and several more were placed where the other main roads converged with the park. The trenches were dug to a depth roughly waist deep, with a step built in to allow weapons and supplies to be kept close to hand. The earth and soil dug up was placed to the front and rear of the trenches as added protection.

The situation in Harcourt Street Station, which reached a state of near-pandemonium when Captain McCormack and his men had stormed inside, was now beginning to calm down. When they had initially rushed in, he had ordered all the waiting passengers onto the platforms, whereupon several women and children had panicked. To add to the confusion, some men had locked themselves inside the station's Ticket Office. The sound of gunshots in the confined space provided sufficient shock to persuade them to comply with the captain's instructions, and eventually some semblance of order was restored to the scene. As if to add to the somewhat farcical episode, a Crown soldier unexpectedly

Lieutenant Michael Kelly, who held a Citizen Army outpost in the Portobello area, before leading an attack in St Stephen's Green. James Connolly, his commandant-general, is pictured behind him, above right. BARRY LYONS

discarded his uniform jacket and asked if he could throw in his lot with the rebels, much to the disgust of an elderly gentleman standing nearby, who loudly proclaimed his revulsion at being in the presence of a turncoat. McCormack's growing frustration reached its high point when he ordered five of his men to commandeer a locomotive engine, and use it to block the railway tracks, but discovered that the station's signal man had locked himself into his signal box and blocked all the points, allowing no trains to be moved.

Lieutenant Kelly was keen to get his section of men into position, and moved out from the station heading south along its tracks to give support to the men to his right in Davy's. Captain O'Neill's squad moved out simultaneously.

McCormack, meanwhile, ordered some of his own men to take up sniping positions along the tracks and also to guard the area to the rear of Kelly and his men. Slowly they pulled out of the station.

Back in St Stephen's Green, Commandant Mallin had reached the conclusion that with so few of his men available, the beautifully landscaped park was completely undefendable. It contained open and predominantly flat ground and was surrounded by tall Georgian buildings, a fact that would present an enemy with an obvious advantage.

Had Mallin had the luxury of a full complement of fighting men, he would have been in a position to occupy the more strategically important buildings, in particular the Shelbourne Hotel. The five upper floors of this particular building, built in 1824, provided a commanding view of the entire surrounding area, as well as dominating the uphill approach towards St Stephen's Green via Kildare Street. With less than half of his garrison present, however, he decided against storming the hotel. He had received intelligence regarding the presence of several high-ranking British officers in the Shelbourne, which would have made its capture an even more attractive prize, but he realised that assaulting it would have resulted in casualties he could ill-afford. It would also have spread the remainder of his troops too thinly on the ground outside.

His immediate priority now was to blockade the streets that met with St Stephen's Green. Accordingly, he issued orders to stop any vehicles, including trams, motor cars, cabs and dray carts. After numerous passing drivers and their passengers were relieved of their horse-drawn wagons and cars, the same vehicles were used to form the frameworks for barricades which quickly began to take shape. Mallin then selected several houses, and inserted two or three men into each. Some of these positions were left deliberately unbarricaded to create the illusion of their being vacant in an attempt to lure in any unwary British troops.

Guests in the Shelbourne Hotel noticed two trams which stopped abruptly outside the entrance. The passengers and drivers were ordered to alight. This disturbance drew several curious guests to the large front windows for a better view. Some British Army officers who were in the hotel at the time rushed out through the revolving door, drawing their pistols as they went. When shots rang out from the Green from positions they found impossible to pinpoint, they dashed back inside, ordering the guests away from the windows while they did their best to return fire. They fired several shots but with no effect. Fearing an imminent assault on the hotel, the British decided that their limited pistol ammunition would be better saved for such a close-quarter struggle.

At roughly the same time, Sergeant Doyle's men at Davy's had their first taste of action. A British patrol from Portobello Barracks, home of the Royal Irish Rifles, had stumbled upon their position and after a brief exchange of fire had been forced to retreat. They soon returned, however, in platoon strength and accompanied by a machine-gun crew. They had been ordered to overwhelm the position and then to advance on Dublin Castle

The infantry's forward section opened fire on the building to keep the insurgents' heads down, supported by fire from the gardens along Lower Rathmines Road, while a two-wheeled Maxim machine gun was set up close to the bridge where it was partially shielded by the foot-high canal wall. They did this under fire from the upper floors of the pub, before they formed themselves into two lines on the southern bank, the first lying prone behind the canal wall, while the second took up a kneeling position just behind them. This was done under the cover of the machine gun, which had shattered the tranquillity of the Georgian Dublin suburb with its deafening drumming. Cement on the pub's outside wall began to disintegrate under the hail of bullets. The remaining glass in its windows was shattered, and the shards fell on the men inside while bullets ricocheted around them. Pictures were knocked from walls and glasses and bottles were smashed on its shelves and countertops. The rebels mounted a spirited defence which very nearly killed the British officer in charge at the bridge. His uniform was perforated by several bullets but he somehow escaped without a serious wound.

The still air in the surrounding area soon stank of gunpowder and echoed to the high-pitched cracks of 50 or so rapidly firing Lee Enfield rifles, and the deeper-sounding gun that pumped its lethal load into the rebel position at the rate of 500 rounds per minute. Unfortunately for the rebels, it became impossible to sustain a defensive action under such unrelenting machine-gun and rifle fire. Belt after belt of ammunition was fed into the insatiable British gun, while the infantrymen around reloaded and fired steadily. The rebels slipped away, guided to the rear of the pub through its cellars by Joyce. Their comrades to their left on the railway line provided as much covering fire as they could before they too pulled back.

The men from Davy's now fell back along Camden Street, pursued relentlessly by the troops. Unable to make their planned escape into Hatch Street due to enemy fire, they instead sprinted towards Jacob's biscuit factory. Captains McCormack and O'Neill and Lieutenant Kelly's men, meanwhile, retreated along their originally planned route into Hatch Street where they rushed into the nearby Iveagh Gardens, whose paths were hastily traversed by a line of bottle-green uniforms rushing to reach St Stephen's Green.

Soon afterwards, a 28-year-old Irish Volunteer from Seville Place named Liam Ó Briain was making his way towards the city centre from Rathgar where he had spent the night. On the way, he was met by Volunteer Harry Nicholls who informed him that the rebellion was back on, a fact underlined by the sudden rifle cracks and the din from the Maxim gun that echoed along Lower Rathmines Road.

Nicholls suggested that they make for the nearest garrison. Their route to the city was blocked by the numerous and highly agitated British troops around Portobello Bridge, however, so they used laneways and side streets, and eventually came to St Stephen's Green. They explained their predicament to a sentry, who invited them to climb its 6-foot-high railings. This they did – with care – and when Ó Briain's feet touched the ground, he felt a great pride swell up in him, announcing to all that 'He was in the fresh-born Irish Republic'.[3] Both men immediately sought out an officer, and relayed what they had come across at Portobello, before they joined the ranks to help prepare their positions.

In St Stephen's Green itself the rebel barricades were growing both in size and number, and the entire position was slowly being disconnected from the surrounding streets. A tense excitement was in the air and morale was high. The Citizen Army found itself putting months and years of training to its intended use, and as the afternoon wore on found its number increasing. Every once in a while the many sentries were approached by an eager young face at the railings, identifying him- or herself as a fellow volunteer ready to join the fight.

Having assessed the developing situation, Mallin decided that he needed a position not only with a commanding view of St Stephen's Green, but one which could also act as a line of retreat if necessary, and which would be suitable for defensive purposes.

The Royal College of Surgeons, dating from 1784 and located on the western side of St Stephen's Green, fitted the bill. It was an incredibly strong two-storey-over-basement building, 60 feet wide and with a relatively flat sloping roof, which itself was surrounded by a 2-foot-high parapet that would provide excellent visibility and reasonable cover to a rifleman firing through its balustrades. Its seven upper windows added to its attractiveness as a tactically defensive position, providing an excellent view over the park and the surrounding streets. From the St Stephen's

Green side it could only be assaulted through the thick wooden front door, as the lower windows sat behind an 8-foot gap between the pavement and the basement windows. It had a single side entrance on York Street, which, when barricaded, would copper-fasten the building's impenetrability. Mallin had also received some intelligence regarding a large store of weapons and ammunition in its basement rooms, making it an even more tempting prize.

A section of men under Sergeant Frank Robbins was sent by Mallin to gain initial access to the College.[4] They did this by forcing its front door at gunpoint. As they entered they found themselves somewhat unsettled by the many specimen jars that seemed to fill its walls and countertops. Its rooms were draughty and cold, but large enough to hold their entire garrison. Satisfied with this, most of Robbins' section made for the roof, where they surveyed the area and took up firing positions. The remainder then set about barricading the doors and windows.

As the day wore on, the park's fortifications grew considerably. Newcomers continued to arrive and were immediately put to digging trenches. Many curious civilians had gathered around the park and were mocking the rebels. Their insults generally were ignored, however, due to the intensely absorbing and frantic activity on the 'Republic' side of the railings. Eventually, a silence fell on the area, occasionally broken by shouts of 'Help us over, lads!', as increasing numbers of new arrivals descended on the position.

At one point a middle-aged man was spotted by the sentries approaching a barricade close to Dawson Street. He attempted to wrestle his dray cart from the fortification and paid no heed to their demands for him to stop. The sentries fired several warning shots above his head, which only seemed to anger him. He turned and ran at the railing that shielded the sentries. Another shot rang out. The man tumbled forward. Some civilians who heard the shot turned as he fell and ran to his aid, and found him dying on the ground at their feet. Several rushed off to seek help, while others ran shouting for the police, one of the civilians turned to say: 'We'll be coming back for you, damn you!'[5]

Gunshots could now be heard almost continuously in the distance, as Lieutenant Bob de Coeur left St Stephen's Green in the evening's fading light with a section of 20 men which included Liam Ó Briain. They made their way along Lower Leeson Street, with orders to occupy a number of the Georgian houses overlooking the nearby canal bridge.

They split into two groups of ten as they advanced up the gently sloping hill, weighed down by numerous canister bombs. When they reached their intended positions, those being the two houses on either side of the broad junction of Leeson Street and Fitzwilliam Place/ Adelaide Road, they knocked on the doors. Both sections then stormed inside, informing the houses' affluent and surprised owners that their dwellings had been commandeered in the name of the Irish Republic. They barricaded the ground floors and basements, and climbed several flights of stairs before reaching the rooftops, where they found excellent footing. Each roof was surrounded by a parapet which offered additional cover. Any attempt by the British to cross this bridge to attack St Stephen's Green via Lower Leeson Street would now be met with a rain of bullets and canister bombs from a well-covered, elevated position.

About a mile to the north-west at around 10 p.m., Lieutenant Grant of the 10th Royal Dublin Fusiliers left the embattled Dublin Castle with a handpicked section of 12 men and made for the Shelbourne Hotel. Once there, they barricaded its entrances and emptied its front bedrooms. Grant then ordered the section to remain in the hotel while he returned to the Castle to report that his orders had been carried out.

Back in Leeson Street at around midnight, some of the Citizen Army men were dozing in the attics of the recently occupied houses when they were roused by their sentries, who had heard the tramp of a column of men marching in the darkness towards the bridge from its southern side. The insurgents quietly slipped through the skylights onto the rooftops of both buildings. Glancing across the road at each other they saw the men opposite moving into firing positions. Deep breaths were drawn as their weapons' safety catches clicked off. The column reached the brow of the bridge and de Coeur shouted, 'Fire!'

The men on the bridge scattered under a sudden storm of bullets which sent sparks flying from the cobblestones. They replied to the sudden and unexpected onslaught of muzzle flashes with shouts of 'Volunteers! Volunteers!' Fortunately for them, no canister bombs were thrown and the shooting came to a sudden stop. After sending several angry shouts skywards, the shaken men of the 4th Battalion Irish Volunteers under Lieutenant Larry Murtagh continued their march towards the city, while the men on the rooftops retreated under their parapets, cursing.

In Dublin Castle, meanwhile, British Cavalry Captain Carl Elliotson, having spent the evening engaging the Citizen Army there, had just received orders which stated: 'Take one hundred men and machine gun crews, occupy the Shelbourne Hotel and have a pop at the rebels entrenched in St Stephen's Green.'

By 2 a.m., Elliotson and his men were set to make their move. Weighed down with machine guns and boxes of extra ammunition, and with loaded rifles at the ready, they began a cautious advance towards the Shelbourne. They were led by Lieutenant Grant who acted as a guide. Their march in the dark was a short but nerve-racking affair but they soon arrived on Kildare Street and made the final dash to the hotel's rear in small groups, having avoided any hostile contact. Elliotson now ordered a section of men and a Lewis machine gun into the United Services Club, which faced St Stephen's Green, but on the far side of Dawson Street. This presented a better scope of fire against the park, and would cover any surprise attack against the hotel itself from its right flank.

The men and women in St Stephen's Green huddled together in the shallow trenches for warmth against the cold and drizzly night air. They grabbed what little sleep they could. The only apparent movement was from the Citizen Army men providing some finishing touches to their barricade just outside the Shelbourne, where Johnnie McDonnell and Phillip Clarke were placing heavy-duty chains through the wheels of carts under the supervision of their lieutenant, Thomas O'Donoghue.

By 3.30 a.m. on Tuesday, Elliotson's machine gun had been hauled up to the fourth floor of the Shelbourne. Its crew peered cautiously out of the window, and in the half-light saw the rebels still at work on the barricade. Each window facing the park and Kildare Street, of which there were approximately 60, was manned by one or two riflemen. By 3.50 a.m., the entire front of the Shelbourne Hotel bristled with weapons and a Vickers machine gun stood at the ready.

Moments before 4 a.m., Lieutenant O'Donoghue and his two men were applying the finishing touches to their barricade. The lieutenant looked up, alerted by the sound of a window being raised at the hotel's top left corner. A terrible realisation gripped him. He screamed: 'Get back into the Green! Get back into the Green!' but it was too late. Captain Elliotson gave a shrill blast with his whistle.

The machine gun erupted into life. Strobes of blinding flashes emanated from the facade of the hotel as the trenches in the park were hosed with bullets from both the Vickers and the rapidly firing rifles.

St. Stephen's Green (from Shelbourne Hotel) Dublin.

A rare photograph, taken shortly after the Rising, from the vantage point of a British machine-gunner in the Shelbourne Hotel. The rebel positions in St Stephen's Green were hosed with fire from here in the early hours of Tuesday 25 April 1916. The Royal College of Surgeons is situated just above the centre of the picture, its rooftop visible above the treeline. It was from there that most of the effective resistance was mounted against the British forces in and around St Stephen's Green. NATIONAL LIBRARY OF IRELAND

The cacophony echoed around the buildings surrounding the park, amplified by the cold early morning darkness. The rebels in the trenches froze with terror as the earth churned around them. Just outside the park railings, Phillip Clarke was mown down as he and his comrades sprinted for the Green.

In the trenches just beyond the 6-foot railings, some attempted to return fire but were unable to aim properly. Any effort was met with a fury of bullets. They pressed themselves as hard as they could into the earth.

Phillip Clarke moaned in agony as he attempted to crawl to some kind of cover. He was bleeding heavily from several bullet wounds. Mallin, who had rushed to his position close to the Shelbourne gate, suddenly leapt to his feet and dashed to his aid. Bullets smashed the railings and the ground around him as he ran towards the wounded man, but he somehow managed to drag him to the relative sanctuary of St Stephen's

Green. His luck held, unlike that of his wounded Citizen Army comrade who died moments later.

For three nerve-shredding hours the machine-gun and rifle bullets ripped into the rebel positions, pinning them in their trenches. The section in the United Services Club added to their misery with their drum-fed Lewis gun. Some of the younger insurgents lost their nerve and tried to make a dash from the nightmare, but luckily for them their older comrades dragged them to cover and did their best to settle them.

They were not all so lucky, however. One 16-year-old insurgent named James Fox, from Slane in County Meath, sprinted from his trench in panic towards the railings on the Green's northern side. Those close by screamed for him to get down but he kept going. Shouts of 'Duck!' turned into silent appeals of 'Please God, let him make it.' He scrambled through the bushes and almost made the railings when the machine gun caught him. He twisted and jerked as his body was mercilessly riddled and was driven back through the bushes before he fell onto the lawn where the machine gun gave another blast to make sure he was finished. As the torrent of lead ripped into it, the teenager's broken and shattered body danced, leading the gunners to believe he still lived, which attracted even more fire.

The men around the roof of the College of Surgeons returned fire savagely in an attempt to suppress the stream of bullets from the Shelbourne's many windows. They also poured fire on the United Services Club to their left. Countess Markievicz, from her vantage point inside St Stephen's Green, temporarily silenced the Lewis gun, shooting furiously from her Mauser pistol, but it was firing again within minutes.

The British began to take casualties. They were, however, immediately tended to in conditions far better suited to war than the makeshift dressing station in the bandstand in St Stephen's Green.

Just after 7 a.m., Commandant Mallin concluded that his positions on the northern side of the park were completely untenable, and he issued the order to pull back to the south-west side towards the junction with Cuffe Street and Harcourt Street. The many trees and undulating ground in the park provided better cover from the machine guns, and his escape route to the College of Surgeons on his left would be easily accessible from here, and well covered by the riflemen on its roof.

The rebels began slithering along the ground towards the south-west, using the park's many bushes to cover their retreat. They took up firing positions behind the hillocks there. They now relished their chance to repay their tormentors and opened up enthusiastically on the Shelbourne and the United Services Club, providing covering fire to their comrades still inching their way towards their position.

Mallin was concerned, however, that the proximity of so many of his Citizen Army personnel in the one location would leave them vulnerable to an infantry attack from a variety of directions should the British decide to launch one in force, so he gave the order to evacuate to the College of Surgeons. A handful of men were to remain close to the gate, while orders were sent to the men on the south-eastern corner of the park, near the Leeson Street/Earlsfort Terrace junction, to spread out and take up sniping positions. This would provide some cover for their withdrawal to the College of Surgeons, and enable them to harass any attempted incursions into St Stephen's Green by the military.

Their dash to the College of Surgeons would be carried out in small groups in much the same way as the men and women had entered St Stephen's Green. They would run across the exposed street and hope to make it before the machine-gunners found their mark. They would be particularly vulnerable here to the Lewis gunner in the United Services Club, and planned to time their runs for when the light machine gun was being reloaded. This would allow them precious seconds to cross under the somewhat less lethal attention of the riflemen, who would be hindered by their own men firing from the College roof.

Margaret Skinnider, a 23-year-old schoolteacher from Glasgow who had taken a week's leave to travel to Dublin for the insurrection, was sent by Mallin to make contact with Lieutenant de Coeur in Leeson Street and to relay the order for him and his men to pull back. Mallin feared that if the British took the park the section would be cut off.

Word was soon sent to Mallin that the men detailed to provide covering fire were ready, and that those set to make their escape were in position. The perilous crossing was soon under way. Captain Joseph Connolly was the first to sprint across, quickly followed by several small clusters of rushing men.

A horrific scene then put a stop to the evacuation. A rebel on the roof of the College of Surgeons was caught by a machine-gun burst. He slumped forward over the parapet and his blood splattered over the facade of the College. Those by the gate froze as more rounds pulverised him and peppered the wall around, sending shards of red-tainted masonry flying. The paralysing tension was broken moments later when David O'Leary appeared suddenly on the roof with several others, who under a hail of bullets, tried to drag the seriously wounded man to cover while their neighbouring riflemen hit back with everything they had. Joseph Connolly, meanwhile, now rushed to the roof where he sprang into action, using his firefighting skills to their utmost. To the astonished gasps of those watching from the park, he stood up, completely exposing himself to enemy fire as he lifted the broken body of his comrade clean from the parapet. When he and the others were clear a huge cheer went up inside the park.

Groups began to sprint once again across the road to the College of Surgeons, where they passed Sergeant Robbins who, with some other men, was providing covering fire from the street close to the York Street entrance. This side of the College was fully shielded from the British gunners. The relieved insurgents who had just crossed then added to the covering force, aiming at the machine-gunners. Some exclaimed their delight at the opportunity to shoot at men who had so energetically just tried to kill them.

The machine-gunners' apparent bloodlust seemed to intensify when the women, somewhat hindered by their long skirts and white aprons, attempted the crossing. The Red Cross markings worn by many went either unnoticed or ignored by the cavalrymen.

As the rebels' covering fire intensified, their gun barrels overheated proportionately. Sergeant Robbins shot his rifle like a man possessed. He entered a trance-like state, ignoring any thought for safety as he fired relentlessly at the military, using every expletive that came to mind to punctuate his shots. All the rebel men and women made the crossing.

Once everyone was safely inside the College, its doors were locked and fortified. Robbins had calmed down considerably as he entered into the main lecture hall, where he saw a crowd of his comrades gathered around the wounded man who had been so dramatically rescued from the roof. Pushing his way through, he realised that the deathly pale victim was his friend Private Michael Doherty, and he had received at least 15 bullet wounds. His clothes were soaked in blood and he was barely conscious, a merciful fact considering the appalling injuries he had sustained. As bandages were frantically applied and prayers whispered, Robbins knelt down by him and muttered emphatically, 'You're a gonner, and the Lord have mercy on you.'[6]

The debris-strewn main lecture hall in the Royal College of Surgeons. It was used primarily as a rest area by its Citizen Army garrison. The only source of natural light was from its skylights above and so was therefore impervious to small-arms fire. A mattress can be seen to the fore in the picture. ROYAL COLLEGE OF SURGEONS IN IRELAND

Another photo of the wreckage of war in the main lecture hall, Royal College of Surgeons. ROYAL COLLEGE OF SURGEONS IN IRELAND

A selection of the canister bombs which were so popular with the insurgents, in spite of their volatility and unreliability. They consisted of gelignite, plus whatever 'shrapnel' was available, such as nails and bolts. They were used throughout the rebel-held areas during the insurrection, with varying levels of success. Royal College of Surgeons in Ireland

The evacuation of St Stephen's Green was, however, a complete success. It had taken less than an hour for approximately 120 men and a dozen or so women to transfer themselves under fire from St Stephen's Green to the College of Surgeons. Michael Doherty was eventually removed to the nearby Mercer's Hospital. He survived the wounds he received that day, only to succumb to the Spanish flu epidemic in 1918.

The College was now to be turned into a fortress. Its unwelcome occupants were split into three groups, the first of which was to man its loft and roof, the second to rest, and the third to work on augmenting the defences. The tasks were detailed to be performed in shifts.

The day passed swiftly and the garrison rested and recovered from the previous night's ordeal. The men alternated their tasks between strengthening the fortifications and roof duty, where a vicious sniper battle had developed steadily with each passing hour. The rapacious British machine-gunners also strafed them at every opportunity. The balustrades around the College's parapet were regularly chipped with shots that whined as they ricocheted wildly throughout the small open section of the rooftop. On the more sheltered side of its slates, holes were cut into the angled garret of the roof, allowing riflemen to sit on the rafters beneath and fire in relative safety through them.

During the mid-afternoon, Mallin called an officers' meeting in the lecture hall, having devised a plan to deal with the United Services Club and the Shelbourne, an endeavour that would require a significant measure of luck. Sergeant Robbins would take a large section of men and begin tunnelling towards Grafton Street from the Turkish Baths which were next to the College on its northern side. Only a narrow laneway separated both buildings. Each subsequent 'mouse-holed' building would then be garrisoned by two or three men. The aim was to get as close to the corner of South King Street as possible. From there, Lieutenant Michael Kelly would sprint with another squad under the cover of darkness across the top of Grafton Street, and from there set fire to the houses on its junction with the north side of St Stephen's Green. It was hoped that from here the fires would spread to the United Services Club, and that if their luck held they could then manoeuvre themselves to threaten the Shelbourne Hotel.

The rebels soon set off. Nothing about this mission would be easy. To begin with, they had to cross from the College roof to the Baths balancing on a plank of wood, weighed down with rifles, pistols, and canister bombs. Then they had to contend with the bullets constantly whizzing by, threatening their every step across the 30-foot drop to the street below.

The mission met with success initially, and by 5 p.m. they had tunnelled as far as South King Street. Lieutenant Kelly and his handful of men waited patiently for darkness to descend before making their next move. A runner was sent back to the College to inform Mallin of their readiness. He returned with a message stating that at 10 p.m., both the College and the rebel snipers in the park would open fire simultaneously to keep the military's heads down, allowing them to make their perilous dash across the wide road junction.

Accordingly, at 10 p.m. the rebel garrison and its outposts opened up. The British rifles and machine guns quickly answered the call to battle, and St Stephen's Green once again became an amphitheatre of noise, smoke and muzzle flashes. Then, at 10.15 p.m., Kelly ordered his assault squad to cross to the top of Grafton Street. They dashed across and knelt to prepare their incendiary bombs.

Unexpectedly, the rebel fire began to taper off, and soon the only thing audible was the barking of the enemy machine guns. Countess Markievicz appeared in the darkness on the corner of South King Street where she did her best to conceal herself while beckoning the confused squad to her. Their plan had been abandoned. Mallin feared the British had got wind of the attack and were readying themselves with their own ambush. Another group who had recently been dispatched from Jacob's biscuit factory in support had opened fire on the United Services Club from close to where the attack was due to be launched. This, he feared, had alerted them that something was up and he felt it best to play it safe. They returned to the College of Surgeons through their mouse-holes and settled down for the night.

As Wednesday dawned, the firing between both sides intensified for a time before dying off somewhat. In the chilly morning air a sense of unreality abounded. The streets were completely deserted. The city itself seemed to be in a state of shock.

As the hours passed and the temperature rose, sniper fire began to escalate. Sporadic cracks bounced from the faces of the Georgian buildings surrounding the park, contrasting with the intermittent echoes of both the Vickers gun in the hotel and the Lewis gun in the United Services Club. With the reports of the insurgents' weapons, the atmosphere in the normally pleasant St Stephen's Green was strangely disturbing.

What followed the morning chorus of exploding gunpowder was most peculiar: the park keeper was suddenly seen walking through St Stephen's Green, having ventured out from his lodge close to Earlsfort Terrace where he had spent the previous 24 hours as far back from his windows as possible.

Fighting men from both sides were fixated by him as he proceeded to feed the Green's ducks with breadcrumbs. Many of the weary rubbed their eyes to ensure they were not seeing things. When he finished, he calmly made his way back to his quaint dwelling, keeping his eyes squarely ahead, as if the surrounding battle was a thing he had neither issue with nor interest in. As soon as he was clear, the firing began again.

The park keeper ventured into the battle zone again that evening to repeat his task. The ducks did not go hungry during the fighting in St Stephen's Green.

Inside the Shelbourne, Captain Elliotson, having rested during the night, had been treated to an exceptionally worthy breakfast and was now reviewing the overall situation. The insurgents in the Green were preventing him from effectively engaging the College of Surgeons. His men positioned at the windows found themselves under constant and highly accurate harassing fire. The machine-gunners were often singled out with deadly precision. Several gunners had fallen to Mauser bullets, the horrific power of which was evident from the dreadful wounds they inflicted. Large chunks of red brick had been displaced from the hotel's frontage by the huge rebel rounds, while the ornate wallpaper and plush carpets began to bear the unmistakable marks of battle. The floors were littered with spent .303 rounds, the sulphur-like smoke from which filled the air, while bloodstains splattered the walls, doors and floors.

Elliotson had no desire to continue in what was descending into a battle of attrition, so he devised a plan to infiltrate the park and flush out the rebels by bullet or by bayonet. His men were then to begin sniping at the College, and once they were securely entrenched he would summon additional machine guns from the nearby Trinity College, situated only 300 yards to their rear, and place them in the Green.

The hotel's crystal chandeliers danced from the vibrations of the machine gun on the fourth floor as Elliotson assembled 30 or so men for the mission. Haughty laughter was heard coming from the rooms immediately behind them, where the guests and the high-ranking military had been placed for their protection. Some of the staff officers dipped the tips of their cigars into complimentary brandy, as they recited tales of military glory to each other. One particularly brash redcap boasted loudly of his days in the Boer War, stressing the point that had he been in charge here, the rebels would have been cleared from St Stephen's Green in a much more expeditious fashion. Elliotson bit his tongue and carried on instructing his men.

The British patrol reached St Stephen's Green without incident, but were unable to root out the rebels. They had a good idea where to find them, as spotters on the hotel's roof had identified their positions from the telltale smoke that followed their shots. The many hedges and bushes inside the unfamiliar park, however, made it difficult to navigate, and rendered the troops particularly vulnerable to ambush. They took to the deserted rebel trenches just in front of the hotel, where they discovered weapons, food and medical supplies abandoned in haste during Tuesday morning's onslaught. Then the sniping began again, until the park keeper returned.

Since Easter Monday, Margaret Skinnider had proved to be a very useful dispatch rider, and seemed completely fearless when presented with orders to run the increasingly lethal gauntlet of British sharpshooters on her bicycle. There were few such messages on Wednesday, however. Instead the Glaswegian woman passed the day watching with increasing envy the men firing through the holes cut into the roof. Countess Markievicz noticed her and suggested to Mallin that he put her shooting skills to good use. Skinnider changed out of her civilian clothes into her uniform[7] and Mallin assigned her to a loophole. The decision was a productive one: several times she strained her eyes to pick out a target 300 yards or so away in the hotel or the park and her aim was true. Roughly half a dozen enemy soldiers fell to her rifle.

For the remainder of Wednesday, the comparative quiet in St Stephen's Green was at odds with the rest of the city, where the dramatic escalation in violence resounded throughout the streets. Mallin did his best to keep his men busy in spite of the relative lack of activity. Hunger was becoming a problem, aggravated by the unexpected lack of distraction.

By Thursday food was in critically short supply. A search of the College's basement turned up nothing of any nutritional value, but revealed 89 Enfield rifles complete with bayonets and 24,000 rounds of ammunition. These were immediately put to use. Meanwhile an urgent dispatch was sent to the nearby Jacob's garrison requesting food, and for any Citizen Army members there to report. A large patrol returned later with sacks of cakes and flour, but it was not nearly enough to feed the men and women holding the College.

Most of the rebel men remained in the loft and on the roof that day, where some rested, while others maintained the duel with the British snipers and gunners. Those who slept were too exhausted to find themselves disturbed by the ear-shattering gunshots around them, and the enemy bullets that ricocheted from their surrounding parapet.

The women, in the meantime, set themselves to an increasingly urgent task. They left the College as enemy rounds whizzed through the air around them, making for Mercer Street, whose narrow profile provided them with some cover. Several British patrols had ventured through the area prior to this but had been beaten back from South King Street. The area around Mercer Street and Bow Lane fell between two very closely positioned rebel garrisons, those being the College itself and the nearby Jacob's biscuit factory. This gave the women some freedom of movement. They descended on the back streets in the Grafton Street area to commandeer what food they could get their hands on, all the while scanning the surrounding streets for khaki uniforms. They then hitched up their skirts and filled them with whatever they could muster, even buying supplies from local shopkeepers. In the midst of the destruction of Dublin traders still needed to trade. Many business proprietors felt that in the increasing chaos of Britain's second city, it was more prudent to protect one's property and business despite the obvious risks, by being there one's self, rather than trusting a prized asset such as a shop to mere lock and key. As the reports of the artillery now flattening Sackville Street became more and more frequent they soldiered on, hoping and praying that they'd be spared a similar fate.

Once the supplies had been brought back safely to the College they were distributed fairly, no one was left out. The women became a very welcome sight to the hungry rebels manning the upper rooms and the roof. The eagle-eyed British snipers did not view them with such affection, and singled them out once they realised what they were doing. The women continued undeterred.

The stand-off continued meanwhile between the trench fighters from both sides in St Stephen's Green, and between the College, the United Services Club, and the Shelbourne. The British later placed a Lewis gun in the small red-brick University Church on the southern side of the Green. After it became an increasingly dangerous nuisance a rebel patrol under the command of Margaret Skinnider was sent out from the College to set fire to the buildings to the west of the Church, in the hope that the fires would eventually spread and force the position's abandonment. The mission failed and resulted in several rebel casualties including one fatality, 17-year-old Fred Ryan. Skinnider was seriously wounded, and when she was eventually hauled back to the College a stretcher team was assembled with orders to take her to the nearby hospital. She refused, opting instead to take her chances in the College and stay where she felt she could still be of some help.

The firing escalated for a time and then ceased once more when the plucky park keeper returned to his ducks. All the while, Mallin moved among the men and women under his command, checking on them and encouraging them.

A sentry manning one of the College's barricaded windows was approached by Mallin, who suddenly waved him to one side. With his Mauser, he fired a shot at an unseen target inside the park. A round screamed past his head in reply and smashed into the wall behind him. Mallin instantly began firing his semi-automatic repeatedly at where he had seen the telltale wisp of gun smoke, before exclaiming, 'Got him!' He then smiled at the sentry, saying, 'A sniper was at the railings, but that'll keep them back.' He then moved off to another position, leaving the young man feeling confident and keen to live up to the example just set by the Citizen Army commandant.

One young Na Fianna member, a teenage boy who was rapidly losing his sight due to an eye disease, had arrived with Countess Markievicz on Easter Monday. The youngster had constantly pleaded with the riflemen on the roof's rafters to be allowed to fire at the enemy. On Thursday evening, they gave in. He was helped up into one of the loophole positions and handed a rifle. A comrade then helped him to aim in the direction of the Shelbourne. He did his best to impress his peers, and fired shot after shot in that direction while quietly murmuring prayers under his breath.

The irony of a half-blind sniper firing across a park, where its caretaker was feeding ducks in the middle of a battle, provided amusement to the ranks of insurgents. It did not provide sufficient relief, however, to assuage the effects of having had very little food or sleep for over four days. Men fainted at their positions. The growing problem seemed to affect the younger rebels more than the older ranks, who reassured them as best they could, and did not let them miss out on rations when sleep inevitably overcame them. The torment continued for the rest of that long evening and night. Hungry men kept watch in the darkness. The slightest noise jolted the exhausted sentries. In the Shelbourne, on the other hand, the finest of food was provided to its defenders, and the weary were provided with comfortable quarters.

By Friday 28 April, all communications with the rebel headquarters in the GPO had been severed. The starving and exhausted rebels on the roof of the College of Surgeons could see the many fires burning in their city, with the thunderclaps of enemy artillery now almost constant.

As midday approached, Mallin ordered all wounded to be transferred to the nearby Mercer's Hospital, and the uninjured men to return to their posts. He was keen to maintain strict order, knowing that having to fight a battle of attrition against boredom and hunger would test the discipline of his garrison to an even greater extent than any enemy action.

Almost mercifully, in the early afternoon, British fire from St Stephen's Green and the Shelbourne Hotel increased suddenly. Something was afoot. The rebels readied themselves, soon replying to the increased firing in kind. It seemed that they were being softened up for an attack, so they prepared. The sudden danger was like a tonic to them. They darted about, making sure their defensive plans and measures were still ready for whatever would be thrown at them. Rifles appeared in increasing numbers through the holes in the roof, and the windows below. Bolts were pulled back, loading the barrels of scores of guns whose sights probed for khaki in the bushes in front of them. Their fortress bristled. They knew it would hold.

They waited, but the attack never came.

After a while, as their friends and comrades began to faint around them, the strain that had accumulated in many insurgents began to vent itself with loud cries of 'Will they not just attack and get this over with!'

Captain Elliotson's attitude had changed significantly since Wednesday's patrol was sent into St Stephen's Green. He was now quite happy to play the waiting game. Word had reached him that the insurgents' various positions in the city had been individually isolated, so he wisely decided against risking heavy casualties in a potentially catastrophic full-on attack. He had been reinforcing his men in the park since late on Wednesday night with elements from the Staffordshire Regiments, who had brought word of the costly capture of Mount Street Bridge. The harsh lessons from there were not wasted on the young cavalry officer.

The stand-off continued throughout Friday. As the sniping persisted all day, the terrible hunger and exhaustion worsened among the rebels. Meanwhile the well-fed and well-supplied British waited. The ever-reliable park keeper returned in the evening.

As dawn broke on Saturday some of the women made another sortie to find food. Yet again, the machine gun in Shelbourne blazed away, and was answered by the rebel riflemen who revived themselves for the fight. Inside the park, both rebel and British snipers continued taking potshots at one another. For the rebels in their slit trenches conditions were extremely challenging. Any movement was highly dangerous and, just like their comrades in the College, they were suffering terribly from lack of food and sleep. Unlike the College garrison, however, they did not have the luxury of being able to relieve themselves, other than to perform nature's functions where they crouched while trying not to get their heads blown off. They were under constant pressure now from the Lincolnshire and Leicestershire Regiments, whose riflemen added to the regular stream of fire being poured at them from positions around the Green's Merrion Row junction. They held on nonetheless, succumbing to sleep when the circumstances permitted, their brief slumbers juxtaposed against equally brief and vicious firefights.

Early Saturday afternoon saw the firing die down once again, before both sides stopped firing completely. A strange calm then descended on the area. Apart from the flocks of birds which darted and glided about, not a single movement could be detected from either inside the park or from the surrounding streets which normally bustled with trams, cars, carts and thousands of civilians.

In the half-distance, a horse's hooves could be heard. The accompanying high-pitched neighing suggested that the beast had broken loose, having probably been driven mad over the previous nights and days. It appeared to be dragging a metal chain as it darted about. Hundreds of animals in the city had been driven insane by the fighting.

The men and women in the garrison looked around at each other curiously, relieved at the chance to draw breath, yet disturbed with the unexpected silence and uncertainty. Shots could still be heard in the distance, but only sporadically.

The famished garrison waited.

6

The South Dublin Union and Marrowbone Lane

'Have you come to read the gas meters?'

The South Dublin Union was a 50-acre hospital complex located 2 miles south-west of Dublin city centre, sandwiched between Kilmainham and the middle section of the South Circular Road. It served as a refuge for the poor, the sick, the old and infirm. Its numerous buildings and surrounding grounds were to be taken and held by the 4th Battalion Irish Volunteers, led by 35-year-old Commandant Éamonn Ceannt, early on Easter Monday. The Union and its outposts were to be used as the rebel forces' main point of resistance in the south-west of the city. From here, the battalion's Volunteers would be in a position to prevent British Army troops rushing to the city centre from the nearby Richmond Barracks and Royal Hospital,[1] and later from the Curragh Army Camp in Kildare. Its dominating position overlooking Kingsbridge Railway Station, through which these troops would have to pass, presented a huge tactical advantage to the insurgents.

The battalion's main section initially mustered in Emerald Square, a small enclosure of two-up two-down terraced houses close to the Coombe/Dolphin's Barn area. The countermand order had left it seriously under-strength and less than a fifth of its men were present. This led to a feeling of subdued anxiety throughout its depleted ranks, which their commandant did his best to assuage with his echoing words of encouragement, followed by his loudly barked orders.

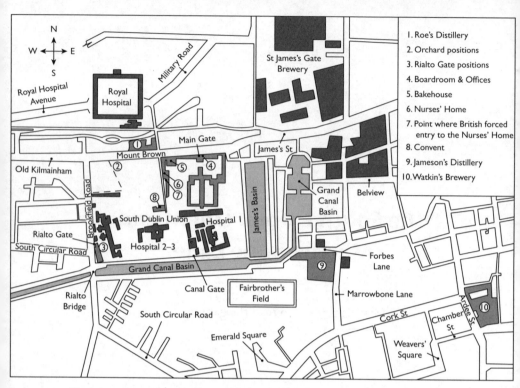

1. Roe's Distillery
2. Orchard positions
3. Rialto Gate positions
4. Boardroom & Offices
5. Bakehouse
6. Nurses' Home
7. Point where British forced entry to the Nurses' Home
8. Convent
9. Jameson's Distillery
10. Watkin's Brewery

Irish Volunteers 4th Battalion area of operations.

Various outposts had been selected to provide support to the Union garrison. These consisted of Jameson's Distillery[2] on nearby Marrowbone Lane, which would come under the command of Captain Séamus Murphy of A Company. Next was Watkin's Brewery on Ardee Street, about three quarters of a mile to its east, under Captain Con Colbert of F Company. Finally, Roe's Distillery on Mount Brown, just to the northwest of the Union, was to be occupied by a section of C Company men under Captain Tommy McCarthy.

The most strategically important of these supporting positions would be Jameson's. Its main distillery building was several storeys high, and had both all-round visibility and excellent defensive cover. The entire complex was surrounded by a 12-foot-high granite wall. Its imposing fortress-like structure dominated the south-eastern side area to the rear of the Union and was ideally positioned to guard it from attack.

As Commandant Ceannt's stirring words roused the spirits of his apprehensive men, the dozen or so of their remaining comrades who had been selected to capture Watkin's Brewery departed with Captain Colbert, the 27-year-old from County Limerick. They had just been relieved of six

Commandant Éamonn Ceannt, 4th Battalion Irish Volunteers. His battalion's tenacious defence of the South Dublin Union drew tremendous respect from his enemies. NATIONAL LIBRARY OF IRELAND

men who had been detailed to reinforce the planned attack against the Magazine Fort, but were nevertheless feeling enthusiastic and confident. They had sent several scouts ahead to the area around Wellington Barracks on the South Circular Road to ensure that their path was clear, and also to determine whether or not its garrison was on to them. Their rendezvous was arranged for the area surrounding Weaver's Square. When they met up, Captain Colbert summarily outlined to the remaining Volunteers their upcoming tasks. They then loaded their rifles and quick-stepped the 200-yard journey eastwards along Chamber Street before storming into Watkin's Brewery. Its bemused shift workers offered no attempt to hinder the menacing-looking men whose zeal suggested the unambiguous benefit of their immediate co-operation.

Back in Emerald Square, meanwhile, Commandant Ceannt's command to march signalled to the assembled men that there was now to be no going back. They drew breath, and set themselves to what lay ahead.

Captain Murphy's section of about 40 Volunteers wasted no time. They rushed into Marrowbone Lane and forced the gates of Jameson's Distillery. Preceded by scouts, 41-year-old Vice Commandant Cathal Brugha marched onwards with two columns of men consisting primarily of members of D Company, through the narrow, twisting streets at the rear of the huge Guinness complex. As they approached Echlin Street, the strong aroma of hops and malt filled the air, and they came under the curious gazes of bank-holiday onlookers. A horse-drawn cart followed, filled to capacity with implements of war such as rations, ammunition boxes, canister bombs and rolls of barbed wire, and was flanked by several guards who scanned the area for the military and the police.

When they arrived at the T-junction with James's Street they turned left and increased their pace. The main Union entrance was just 500 yards ahead and to the left. Captain McCarthy ordered his dozen men to break off to the right towards Roe's Distillery. Within minutes the main Battalion section had reached the imposing granite wall surrounding the Union's huge wooden entrance gate, behind which sat their objective.

Vice Commandant Brugha and Lieutenant W. T. Cosgrave saw to it that there was little resistance at the gate. Commandant Ceannt and around 35 men from both B and C Companies made for the Union's Rialto entrance, on its west side, where the guard was persuaded at the point of Ceannt's pistol to hand over his keys. Once inside, Ceannt detailed Captain George Irvine to the entrance's defence along with a section of eight men. Next, he ordered Lieutenant William O'Brien to take two 6-man sections. The first of these was to occupy an area known as McCaffrey's Orchard, a wide, open, grassy piece of uneven ground to the Union's north-west. The area here was surrounded by a thick brick wall overlooking Kilmainham. The second section, under Captain Seán McGlynn, was to place itself further east along the Union's north-facing wall opposite Roe's Distillery.

Ceannt then ordered the remaining men to barricade the other Union entry points to the south with items appropriated from its various hospitals and outbuildings. The many inmates and staff were ordered to stay out of the way as the Volunteers set about commandeering whatever they could find. Carts, bedsteads and mattresses, as well as office furniture and gardening equipment were hastily piled up by rebels, who worked with tremendous energy considering their small number. When their tasks were completed they fell back from their defences and began ensuring that they were adequately covered by effective fields of fire. Here there would be no margin for error.

The 4th Battalion Quartermaster, Volunteer Peadar Doyle, was sent to a position in the convent in the centre of the Union grounds. He knocked loudly on the door and was answered by an elderly nun. 'Have you come to read the gas meters?' she asked, to which Doyle smilingly replied: 'No, Sister, but we are in a hurry.'[3] The nun stood aside.

Soon Ceannt was as satisfied as he could be, given the circumstances, and made his way to join Brugha and Cosgrave, who had set up their headquarters in the three-storey nurses' home, not far from the main Union entrance. They finalised their defensive plans and prepared for the struggle ahead. They would not have long to wait.

They had anticipated an initial British advance from nearby Richmond Barracks along the straight stretch of road in Old Kilmainham overlooked by McCaffrey's Orchard, and were not disappointed. A half-mile to their west, a company of the 3rd Battalion Royal Irish Regiment, many of whom had recently returned from action in France, was being hastily assembled inside the barracks which sat next to the Grand Canal in Inchicore. General word of the insurrection had been received at this stage throughout Dublin's various garrisons. They had been given orders to move out, and to proceed with haste towards Dublin Castle.

A short time later, their commander, Major Holmes,[4] assembled an initial 100 men. Ammunition was distributed and orders issued. When the men had checked their weapons and equipment they formed into four lines, and marched at speed to the South Circular Road/Kilmainham junction, where they came to a sudden stop. From there the major could see several heads in the distance to his right just above the parapet of the Union's boundary wall. He ordered a party of five troops led by a sergeant to move forward as a probe. He then watched as the cautious group was allowed to pass the rebel position unhindered. The sergeant's squad continued up the hill until they came abreast of the Union's main entrance, where they fired several shots at the boardroom windows just above. The Volunteers inside were ordered not to return fire.

Holmes then mustered 20 men under Lieutenant James Malone to follow the five. They began their advance in a column five deep and four across, moving forward apprehensively, their eyes firmly fixed on the silhouettes of their enemies' heads against the blue afternoon sky, until they reached the junction of Brookfield Road.

Suddenly, the Volunteers fired. Three of the troops twisted and fell to the ground, while the others found themselves exposed in the open under another deafening volley. The troops had ventured into a trap. The surrounding garden-less terraces of red-brick houses and the open street into which the Volunteers fired from the wall above left the infantrymen helplessly exposed, until a British NCO managed to kick in the door of a nearby tannery. As Lieutenant Malone scrambled inside he saw the man next to him fall, having been shot in the jaw. He grabbed for the shoulder straps of the young infantryman but was then hit himself. He passed out, and came to a short time later to find his men firing back in frenzy at the rebels.

Major Holmes was quick to react. He ordered the rest of his men to take up covered firing positions at the crossroads, while Lieutenant Colonel Owens ordered the remainder of the battalion forward in support. An additional company was rushed into the nearby Royal Hospital, through its huge medieval gates facing Kilmainham Gaol. They sprinted all the way down its quarter-mile-long avenue, before reaching the three-storey building where they rushed to its upper floors. From there, 80 or so rifles quickly engaged the insurgents in McCaffrey's Orchard. The overpowering din was added to by a Lewis machine gun which opened up on the rebel position from the Royal Hospital roof.

At roughly the same time, two additional companies were sent forward from the barracks to storm the Union's barricaded Rialto entrance. The infantrymen rushed eastwards along the South Circular Road, watched intently from nearby windows by the terrified inhabitants whose curiosity had been roused by the unfamiliar sound of scores of clattering footsteps. Their initial assault on the gate was fruitless, as it was heavily reinforced and covered by Captain Irvine's men positioned just inside, who were using a frail-looking corrugated steel and wood panelled building as their outpost. The two officers leading this attack then tried to enter the Union from further up the road towards the canal, having spotted an alternative entry point.

Back inside the Union, Lieutenant O'Brien's section in McCaffrey's Orchard were being overwhelmed by firing from the Royal Hospital. They were eventually forced back, leaving behind a dead Volunteer – John Owens – along with two badly wounded men who could not be moved. O'Brien's remaining men were forced to run in retreat across exposed ground towards the nurses' home under a withering hail of fire. Captain McCarthy's men in Roe's Distillery provided some covering fire, but when they did the British gunners poured everything they had at them. The diversion did, however, provide several precious seconds of respite for O'Brien and the others, who continued their run eastward. The odds were stacked against them. A wide, open field larger than a football pitch separated them from their headquarters, and the routed men's frantic movements were pursued by the rifle sights of the many veterans firing from the Royal Hospital, most of whom had honed their skills of marksmanship firing on German troops carrying out similar retreats across no man's land. O'Brien and his men sprinted from position to position, before the frighteningly depleted group eventually reached the relative safety of their headquarters.

The Lewis gunners in the Royal Hospital were then free to turn their attention to Captain Irvine's position at the Rialto gate, which was soon riddled with bullets. Its nine occupants, led by the 38-year-old Enniskillen native, dived for cover with the patients still trapped inside, as hot lead, wooden splinters and shards of corrugated metal flew wildly at them. One 17-year-old Volunteer named John Traynor, whose home was less than 200 yards away in Shannon Terrace, was killed after being shot through the eye. Under the relentless pressure a rebel runner was dispatched to the nurses' home for reinforcements, but was hit in the leg as soon as he left cover. His loud cry as the bullet knocked him flying signalled to Irvine and his men that they were now on their own. A two-man rescue party ran out and pulled him back to cover, where the blood gushing from his wound was bandaged efficiently as he groaned in pain.

Just outside the Union, the pair of officers who had attempted entry at the Rialto gate began pushing up the South Circular Road with their men towards the Grand Canal. As they did, they filled the upper floors of the nearby red-brick houses to their right with riflemen. From the bay windows they now enjoyed the combined advantages of good visibility and excellent cover. A captain in the Royal Irish, Alfred Warmington from Naas in Kildare, then ordered a platoon to advance to the Union's canal entrance on its southern side, while he, Lieutenant Ramsay and a squad of men made an attempt at a 4-foot-wide gate facing Mount Shannon Road.

This small gateway, however, funnelled the attacking force into such a confined area that the few Volunteers now occupying the first floor of the hospital in that section of the Union could hardly miss them. Their rifle sights fell upon 26-year-old Lieutenant Ramsay from Ballsbridge as he led the first assault. His men smashed in the gate before he charged inside, running straight into a volley of shots that killed him instantly. His shocked troops dashed for cover behind the small chapel while their fellow infantrymen fired manically into the Union from the surrounding houses. The area soon reverberated with repeated rifle reports.

The British Enfield rifles shot rapidly. Their high-pitched cracks sounded out oddly against the dull cannon-like booms of the rebel Mausers, which fired at a much slower pace but with far greater velocity and range. Captain Warmington then led a second charge, again rushing the gate before he too shared the same fate as Lieutenant Ramsay. His head and body were shattered by a volley. His men looked on in horror as his half-collapsing, half-sprinting body fell horrifically under the impact of lead.

The attack was called off and for a time a stunned silence prevailed. Across the open ground between the chapel and the hospital building, the similarly accented voices of Irish troops in British Army uniforms and those wearing Volunteer garments arranged a temporary ceasefire to allow the soldiers to gather the bodies of their two fallen officers. Outside on the road, a teeming and angry mass of khaki waited at the ready.

A short time later the same infantrymen prepared for another assault, laying down an unrelenting barrage of covering fire on the western section of the Union. They were then joined once again by the Lewis gunner on the Royal Hospital roof. Every window and doorway became a target, while movement and return fire from the Volunteers became next to impossible. Under the ferocious assault the military stormed in. They launched themselves at the corrugated building housing Captain Irvine's small section to their left. There, rebels held them off as best they could but were quickly overwhelmed. Soon, the parched few who were still standing emerged from their ruined position with their hands in the air. The rebels manning the nearby hospital building retreated eastward. The British had secured their first foothold in the South Dublin Union.

But it was not over for Captain Irvine and his men. They were surrounded by a menacing ring of fixed bayonets. The British junior officer in charge demanded to know from Irvine where the rest of the men were, refusing to accept his repeated assertions that they were all directly in front of him. The officer approached him and stared directly into his eyes, saying, 'You all know the rules of war where rebels are concerned – they are to be shot without trial.'[5] A firing party was hastily assembled, until, luckily for Irvine and his terrified men, a more senior officer appeared shouting at the officer to stop and to 'Take these men to Kilmainham!'

When the 50 or so troops dispatched to the Union's southern side arrived at its entrance, situated halfway along the length of its 10-foot-high boundary wall, they too employed the tactic of rushing forward, hoping to overwhelm the enemy inside. They ran straight into an avalanche of fire, this time from their right, where the insurgents from their elevated positions in Jameson's Distillery unleashed a torrent of shots at the troops who rapidly became clustered at the narrow entry point. Volunteer Robert Holland had just arrived in the position and was a particularly lethal sharpshooter. He was armed with several rifles and was accompanied by a member of Cumann na mBan[6] who reloaded his weapons as he fired. He almost single-handedly stopped the attack. He shot rapidly at the huddle of khaki uniforms and saw several of them fall. He emptied his Enfield magazine with the speed of the most seasoned of marksmen, his hand furiously sliding the gun's greasy bolt backwards and forwards between shots, before being handed a Mauser rifle, while his female comrade then reloaded the Enfield with a fresh clip.

When Holland fired the German-made gun, a huge ball of flame shot from its long barrel like a miniature flamethrower as its massive bullet spun through the air towards its victim. The gun's recoil smashed repeatedly into Holland's increasingly bruised right shoulder, often knocking him back about 3 feet from his perch, before he was handed the next weapon with which to take aim. Second Lieutenant James Calvert, from County Armagh, was shot in the head by one of Holland's high-calibre bullets.

At the back of Hospitals 2 and 3 meanwhile, which sat to the British soldiers' right as they entered, six Volunteers under the command of

Captain Douglas fFrench Mullen were preparing to deal with the onslaught through the canal gate. They were crouching in a narrow trench. The captain sternly instructed the terrified men not to fire without his orders. However, all six Volunteers opened fire almost simultaneously upon a soldier who had climbed a telegraph pole at the canal wall. Mullen looked around at the men, saying, 'Although I did not give the order to fire, it was damn good shooting.' The British private was shot to pieces. He fell from the pole and his body fell into the canal.

The Royal Irish persevered and eventually forced their way in, driving the few Volunteers back from their trench. They beat a hasty retreat towards the upper floors of Hospitals 2 and 3, under sporadic covering fire from several other rebels who had taken position there earlier. They left one wounded man behind. He lay in agony in a growing pool of blood as enemy boots clattered all around. The attacking troops, meanwhile, rushed forward to link up with their units who had successfully overcome the Rialto gate. They pushed on relentlessly.

The British forces had by now gained three points of access to the Union, one from its south and two from its west. To their frustration, however, they lost their bearings amid the maze of avenues that intersected the many hospitals and outbuildings. Rifle, pistol and shotgun fire rained down on them from the surrounding floors. Volunteers appeared suddenly at windows, firing, then quickly redeployed to another vantage point, firing again. This terrifying scenario was repeated over and over, while rebel reinforcements arrived from the complex's northern section. Shots cracked and echoed around the buildings, the bouncing reverberations from which made it impossible to pinpoint the enemy. Acrid gun smoke began to waft through the hospital corridors and wards, adding to the terror of the patients.

When the same troops reached the interior of the hospitals, however, the fighting rapidly degenerated into unprecedented ferocity. Vicious running battles ensued along corridors whose adjoining wards were filled with staff and patients. Hand-to-hand fighting involving rifle butts, knives and bayonets took place in the confined spaces and narrow passageways, where silently concealed rebels lunged at their onrushing foe. The pandemonium was amplified by the hysterical screams of many patients, and the repeated shouts and appeals from the Union staff for the madness to stop. Neither set of protagonists was initially able to gain any advantage in the confusion.

At one point during this episode, Volunteer Lieutenant James Kenny, accompanied by Dan McCarthy, who had been holding the ground floor of one of the hospitals, became involved in a fierce firefight with four British soldiers along one of its corridors. Both men repeatedly concealed themselves in doorways to load their guns before stepping out to fire again and again as they sought to hold their position from the advancing troops. When McCarthy suddenly fell, hit by a bullet, his lieutenant threw himself down next to his groaning comrade, and adopted a prone position to aim his rifle. Several well-aimed shots persuaded the attackers to take off, prompting Kenny, whose blood was up, to charge with his bayonet after the soldiers while roaring like a madman. They fled.

Kenny then ran into Volunteer Jack Doherty, just as more British reinforcements arrived. They attempted to hold them but retreated under a murderous hail of fire which separated the two men. Kenny fell back towards his headquarters, where he ran into Commandant Ceannt. In the ensuing chaos both men became trapped in a narrow cul-de-sac. They waited for the worst.

After some time, things fell eerily quiet. It seemed that both sides needed time to draw breath. The sudden and unexpected change in circumstances allowed Kenny and Ceannt to make their escape to the nurses' home.

A young nurse, Margaret Keogh from Leighlinbridge in County Carlow, assumed that a ceasefire was in play. She rushed down a staircase seeking to tend to the wounded, only to be shot in the stomach by a terrified British private. She died in agony some time later, in a bed next to Dan McCarthy, who was being treated for his wound, having at this point been taken prisoner.

Further spells of shocking violence alternated with brief periods of equally terrifying silence which stretched endurance to breaking point. As clusters of men from both sides became separated and lost, many removed their boots to silence their movements. Then when shooting started again, beds, cupboards and tables were overturned as cover was desperately sought.

Superior weight of numbers ultimately allowed the British to prevail, and the Volunteers eventually either surrendered, which roughly half a dozen did, or fled from the hospital. As those who had avoided becoming trapped in the maze of wards ran, the surrounding air hissed with the .303 rounds that whipped around them. Most of the retreating men made for the relative security of the nurses' home, covering each other in turns. They quickly regrouped there, expecting more of the same, but the men of the Royal Irish were done for now.

After a relatively quiet hour or so had passed, a mission was set in place to re-enter McCaffrey's Orchard in an attempt to rescue the wounded in the open field. Commandant Ceannt was deeply troubled at the thought of his men lying unattended. Volunteers James Coughlan and William McDowell, along with two of the Union's inmates, were then sent out. They entered the Orchard through a door at the rear of the nurses' home. As they advanced apprehensively, they spotted the six Volunteers 30 or so yards to their right under Captain McGlynn who were lying prone in firing positions. McDowell and Coughlan took up position on the left, while the two inmates were told to take cover by a nearby wall.

Intense rifle fire erupted from the bushes to their front, immediately added to by the machine gun in the Royal Hospital. McDowell was a relative newcomer to the Irish Volunteers, having been detailed to the 4th Battalion only the previous Friday. Coughlan shouted at him to keep his head down and his heels flat. As bullets whizzed around their heads, an order came back down the line from Captain McGlynn: 'Retreat!' The last man on the left was to return and reopen the door at the rear of the nurses' home and from there to cover their withdrawal. Coughlan looked to his left and found no one there: it was down to him.

He scrambled rearward and succeeded in opening the door. He then threw himself down and began firing wildly at the many sources of enemy fire. Over a period of several minutes, which must have resembled an eternity, his fellow Volunteers filed past, the last of whom was Captain McGlynn. He was then ordered to close and barricade the door. His immediate thoughts were of McDowell and the pair of inmates, but McGlynn assured him that there was no one left out there alive. He glanced around the area, before a shower of bullets smashed into the door frame around him. He needed no further persuasion. McDowell and the inmates had been killed in a burst of fire from Rialto.

The wounded insurgents who had remained in McCaffrey's since the early afternoon were now at the mercy of their injuries. They would remain unattended and exposed in the open. Towards dusk, a messenger was sent out to the British officer in charge to negotiate a temporary ceasefire to collect the wounded. The reply was concise: no negotiations were possible, as all their officers were dead.

As Monday evening descended a disturbing atmosphere fell on the Union. The uneasy calm that had crept in with the darkness was punctuated only by the odd crack of gunshot. The traumatised inmates and patients did their best to cope with the horror they had witnessed, while the rebels sought much needed food and rest. Supplies of rations and ammunition were distributed and the religious among them prayed. Any movement outside was met with the clicks of safety catches being undone. There was little rest that evening for the 4th Battalion, several of whom, in their weaker moments, questioned their sanity for having volunteered for this apparent lunacy.

Their enemy also regrouped, and some among them reflected on the vicious and wholly unexpected battle in a city that for many was their home, having woken the previous morning expecting nothing more traumatic than a boring bank holiday in a barracks. In the background the barking of machine guns could be heard from the city.

Tuesday morning broke to the dull rhythm of drum after drum of Lewis gun ammunition being poured into the Union grounds. Sporadic bursts of rifle fire were aimed with increased precision at the Volunteer strongholds in the northern section of the Union. The British firing positions in the Royal Hospital dominated any exposed ground, and made communication between the remaining rebel positions extremely hazardous. Runners frequently found themselves cut off, while bullets zipped around them and pummels of earth and masonry flew as the bullets struck close by.

Ceannt and his men in the nurses' home found themselves harassed with increasing frequency by bursts of intense fire as the morning wore on. Both sides prepared for what they believed would be the final British assault to clear the Union. The insurgents repeatedly checked their weapons. They turned the buildings they held into a labyrinth of tunnels and barricades. Fields of fire were checked each time a position was adapted.

The British also checked their weapons and stocks of ammunition. The ferocity of the previous day's fighting did not bode well for any force attacking the clusters of buildings and open areas approaching the insurgents' headquarters. They waited with agonising apprehension, drinking from their canteens to relieve the growing warmth as midday approached. Then, to their astonishment, an order came to the British troops. 'Retire from the Union.'

The infantrymen began to pull out in small groups. Abandoning positions for which at least three highly respected officers and numerous private soldiers had died left many with a bad taste in their mouth, yet there was unspoken relief at being spared the prospect of another round of close-quarter combat with opponents who fought like demons. Rebel sharpshooters soon realised what was going on, and their eyes hunted for any momentary lack of discipline on the part of the retreating men. As the troops dashed from position to position the air all around resounded to clusters of low-pitched booms as their Mausers sought out moving targets. To counter this, the British Lewis gun was again brought into play, with its abrasive 'thud-thud-thud'.

There was to be little respite for the weary troops once they had left the Union grounds. From the cover of its western wall they were re-formed into their platoons and companies and ordered to provide covering fire for an attack on Jameson's Distillery. Since the previous afternoon that particular position had fallen into the crosshairs of the British military planners. Several hundred reinforcements were now brought in from the surrounding areas, including 50 or so Cavalry Lancers.

Their objective was four storeys high in places, with numerous windows, as well as its formidable outside wall. It also contained a small 'crow's nest' type of structure, which was built on stilts and could hold four or five men who, once inside, had a commanding view over the entire city of Dublin. It was almost perfect as a defensive position, a fact that significantly disturbed the British soldiers whose job it now was to capture it. Cavalry traditionally presented a great advantage to an attacker in open country. Their speed of movement combined with the troopers' renowned commitment and expertise had turned many a battle. Attacking a building that looked more like a fortress, in what was predominantly a built-up area, on the other hand, left several infantrymen's jaws gaping at the apparent naivety of the plan.

Several platoons of the 3rd Battalion Royal Irish Regiment took positions on both sides of the canal at the rear of the Union, and in Fairbrother's Field, south-west of Jameson's Distillery, close to Rialto Bridge. Various other units were moved into Cork Street, where they formed up in preparation for the attack. The movements of the latter mass of men were noticed by Volunteer Thomas Young, who, with a small section of others, was manning a footbridge across Marrowbone Lane.

Young and his section opened fire on the troops at their earliest opportunity, which was at around 2 p.m. Their fusillades sent the troops scurrying for cover, but seemed to act as a cue for the enemy attack to begin. Soon Jameson's Distillery was under fierce fire from the scores of troops to its west, while the horsemen, supported by infantry, having mustered in James's Street and Thomas Street, attacked from its north.

The scene surrounding the distillery then descended into horror. Myriad puffs of thick smoke flew from its many windows, and thunderous cracks of gunfire resounded throughout the surrounding streets. Rebels rushed from window to window, firing relentlessly as they changed position. The huge rounds from their Mausers inflicted terrible wounds on the advancing horsemen as they negotiated the cluster of side streets that led them straight into the rebels' rifle sights. Bones of humans and animals alike were heard shattering under the bloody and grotesque impacts. The accompanying infantrymen, who sought shelter where there was little to be found, witnessed comrades being torn apart by rounds that hurled blood and tissue into their own faces. The carnage continued for two hours as the assault ebbed and flowed from several directions. The attackers found the streetscape between Jameson's and Echlin Street claustrophobic and disorientating. The echoes of shot bounced from the huge walls throughout the area, suggesting fire was coming from several directions.

Astonishingly, the troops in Cork Street were completely contained by Young and his small section, aided as they were by Volunteer riflemen taking numerous potshots at them from the distillery's southern side. Meanwhile, the bodies of infantrymen attacking from the west side began to litter the nearby canal bank, and civilians in their tiny homes nearby pressed back from their windows.

Repeated orders to fire rang out from the distillery's many vantage points, while the infantrymen and cavalrymen pressed on. Their tactics were hopeless against such a fortress, but their bravery in maintaining the attack was undeniable, and was admired greatly by the insurgents. In the cobbled streets a cavalryman, trapped under the weight of his fallen horse, clawed with increasingly bloody hands at the concrete beneath him to escape the ricochets that crept ever closer, before he too was shot. His supporting infantrymen looked on helplessly. A single soldier eventually reached the distillery's outer wall at Forbes Lane, only to be cut down in a hail of bullets.

The foot soldiers in the open ground along the canal soon began retiring in sections with each trying to cover the other, all the while under devastating fire. Their dead and wounded were strewn on the ground. Some of the infantrymen attacking from Rialto had fallen into the canal, having been wounded, and subsequently drowned. Stricken men cried out for medics. As the attack to the distillery's north faltered and the soldiers withdrew, the piercing screams of dying horses filled the air.

The sheer folly of using cavalry to attack a fortified building was grotesquely illustrated some time later when a lancer's horse wandered aimlessly around the front of the distillery just beneath Young's vantage point, dragging its limp rider behind over the hard and bumpy ground. The dead man's foot was wedged into its stirrup. The Volunteers turned their heads away from the sickening sight.

Inside the Union, when the partially rested rebel garrison realised the Royal Hospital machine-gunners' ammunition supplies were not inexhaustible, they grew increasingly confident about sending communiqués between their positions. Messengers ran between the buildings in short rushes, knowing that instant death could come at any second from the crack of an enemy rifle that they would not even hear. Ceannt and his men continued fortifying the many offices and rooms of the nurses' home, and the well-practised tactic of tunnelling was exercised throughout their positions. Morale among the 4th Battalion, Irish Volunteers was now very high.

Later on, Thomas Young, who was still positioned on the Marrowbone Lane footbridge, implemented a hand-signalling system that would allow him and his small section to communicate with the distillery's numerous sentries. Messages were then sent back and forth to Volunteer Ned Neill who was manning the main gate. At one point Young noticed a messenger boy with a bicycle looking through a gap between the gate and the huge wall that supported it, so he immediately signalled his comrade, who promptly opened a small wicket gate and stepped outside to confront the youngster. When he asked him what he was doing the boy pointed to some trussed-up chickens in the bike's wicker basket before answering nervously: 'Delivering them to the Viceregal Lodge.' Neill promptly commandeered the chickens and told the boy to give the Lord Lieutenant his compliments. The messenger boy replied: 'For

Marrowbone Lane Distillery. Its 'crow's nest' is clearly visible to the top right of the picture. This rebel position came under repeated and sustained attacks from the British military during the fighting around South Dublin Union, whose rear it was used to protect. MILITARY ARCHIVES

fuck's sake, Mister!' He threw the bicycle against the distillery's wall and shouted angrily: 'Take the fucking bike as well!'[7] and walked off into the side streets.

Over in Watkin's Brewery on Ardee Street, meanwhile, Captain Colbert was getting restless. He sent a runner with an urgent dispatch to Major John MacBride, the nearest available senior commander who was less than half a mile away in Jacob's biscuit factory. He stated that their position had as yet made no contact with the enemy, but stressed that if they were attacked in force, they would be very vulnerable owing to their continuing deficiency in numbers. This was in spite of extra men having filtered in to the brewery overnight. The runner dashed through the back streets near St Patrick's Cathedral and returned later in the evening with orders from MacBride to leave Watkin's Brewery and to relocate to Jameson's Distillery. Once there he was to assume joint command with Captain Murphy of the distillery and of its smaller outposts throughout Marrowbone Lane.

At roughly the same time in Roe's Distillery in Mount Brown, Captain Tommy McCarthy had come to the same conclusion as Colbert, feeling that his men would be put to better use in the Union itself. Unfortunately, its main gate was too heavily barricaded to allow him to make any communication with Ceannt. He subsequently made the decision to evacuate the building, instructing his few Volunteers that it was now 'every man for himself'. Some simply returned through the streets to their homes, doing their best to avoid the increasingly vigilant British patrols, while others eventually made the journey to join Colbert's men in reinforcing Jameson's. There was little further significant action in the area on Tuesday, save for both sides tending their wounded and preparing once again to kill each other.

Captain Colbert rested his men for the night, until just before dawn on Wednesday, when he ordered them to begin making their way to Jameson's Distillery. They planned to filter as silently as possible through the tightly packed terraces of the Pimlico area, before reaching Marrowbone Lane.

Just before they left they removed their boots. The final quarter mile of their journey was through an area that would be closely surveyed by enemy snipers, eager to exact revenge for the previous day's bloody nose at the hands of Captain Murphy's garrison. Stealth would be essential.

Thomas Young was still positioned with his small unit manning the footbridge as dawn began to break. His men did their best to fight sleep as they scanned the area all around. Cork Street was still infested with enemy troops but the area was ominously quiet. Young's mother, who lived nearby, had recently been summoned to Watkin's Brewery with a request to bring as many overcoats as she could muster to help conceal their weapons as they moved out. She obliged with enthusiasm, and then volunteered to act as a forward scout.

She signalled to Christopher Byrne that the way was clear all the way from the eastern end of Cork Street before he led the men, including Young's two brothers, in two lines, one on either side of the road. Colbert brought up the rear. Soon they were stealing through Pimlico. Any moment a shot might ring out, followed by a deluge of lead from a British patrol or ambush. They scrutinised every nook and cranny of the narrow side streets, while straining their ears for any sound that might betray an enemy keen to take advantage of their temporary exposure. The loud barking of dogs alerted by the unfamiliar sounds and smells did little to calm their nerves.

As his mother approached the distillery, Young signalled to Ned Neill to open the wicket gate. His heart pounded as he watched her in turn signalling behind her that the way ahead was clear. His men stood up and held their rifles at the ready. They took aim at any potential source of a target and turned their bodies to allow each of their fields of fire to make 90-degree arcs. Their guns rotated sideways as if mounted in turrets, as their wide unblinking eyes strained to cover Young's mother, her two sons and her comrades. Soon they were in. The wicket gate was swiftly closed behind them. Colbert was the last inside, after Young's mother, who ensured her sons were safe before telling them to lace up their boots. Thomas Young breathed a sigh of relief.

Captain Murphy greeted Colbert, knowing the extra fighting men would come in very handy. He briefed him on the previous day's attack and on the situation in general. He laughed when Colbert mentioned the great number of riflemen he appeared to have positioned in the upper floors of the huge building, before pointing out numerous small poles and broom handles with Volunteer coats and hats on. The inanimate rebels were quickly replaced with real ones. The ruse, however, had proved quite effective during the recent attack, as evidenced by the bullet marks surrounding Colbert's men's new firing positions.

Back in the Union, Wednesday morning unfolded as Tuesday evening had ended, with relative quiet throughout its outposts. The daily routine of looking after their hundreds of charges was followed to the best of their ability by the nurses, doctors and ward matrons. Gunfire could be heard throughout the day from the other parts of the city.

Back on the footbridge as the morning progressed, Young saw to it that his section took turns resting. It was apparent that the streets to Marrowbone Lane's north presented less of a threat than they had perceived during the long night.

Meanwhile, another young boy had ventured into the area, seemingly oblivious to any threat. To Young and his men's utter amazement the youngster approached them from the north, driving three cattle towards Cork Street while he himself strolled nonchalantly 30 or so yards behind. As he looked around at the evidence of the previous day's fighting he became distracted and unaware of Ned Neill quietly opening the distillery gate, having been signalled by his wide-eyed comrade on the footbridge. Two Volunteers dashed out and drove the cattle inside. When the boy turned and realised they were gone he looked perplexed. He walked towards the footbridge looking upwards and asking: 'Have you seen my three heifers?' Young shrugged his shoulders and replied: 'No cattle came this way' while he and his men did their best to conceal their amusement. The boy stood there for a time while the insurgents struggled not to laugh aloud at his confusion.

The joviality was short-lived. Jameson's soon came under constant sniper fire from several directions. A Volunteer named Mick Liston had positioned himself in the crow's nest, and for some time had managed to avoid the growing numbers of bullets that hissed around his flimsy perch. His head was grazed by two bullets simultaneously, with neither penetrating his skull. He was knocked to the floor and came around feeling disorientated and dizzy, with his hands covered in blood from having instinctively clasped his head when falling. He eventually clambered down with considerable difficulty from his position and made for the dressing station. Once there, the astonished medics treated him for two similarly shaped lacerations and an agonising headache whose vice-like hold increased by the minute. He rested while word of his miraculous escape filtered through the garrison, prompting his good friend Robert Holland to join him while taking a break. The previous day had been Holland's 19th birthday and Liston was quick to offer his best wishes in a strong, if now somewhat slurred, Dublin accent.

Their amicable conversation soon veered towards the increasingly hazardous enemy sniper fire. Holland then left Liston to rest, and took up a position in one of the upper rooms facing the scene of the previous day's failed British assault from the distillery's west, accompanied by Cumann na mBan volunteer Josie O'Keefe. Once there he began scanning the huge green area to his front with his field glasses. A short while later the heavily bandaged but impossibly keen Liston returned to the crow's nest.

Holland continued to seek out enemy activity, until his eye was drawn to the area between the canal and the Union wall where he spotted the tip of a rifle sticking out from behind a tree. He then noticed movement behind some nearby tree trunks and bushes. O'Keefe was hurriedly dispatched to Liston's position above to explain what they had seen. They then coldly prepared themselves. Spare rifles were made ready and several young Volunteer women stood by, ready to reload. They waited patiently for the opportunity to pounce, until after about 15 minutes one of the troops carelessly revealed himself. Two shots echoed out in rapid succession from Jameson's. The soldier buckled and slumped to the ground in full view. His dozen or so comrades, realising their location had been exposed, did their best to return fire as they retreated along the Union wall towards Rialto Bridge. Many of them were shot.

The arrival of pitch darkness on Wednesday night presented an opportunity for the British to move more men into positions from which to launch another attack on the distillery. They spent the early hours of Thursday morning digging in on both sides of the nearby canal and in Fairbrother's Field. As dawn broke, the insurgents woke to the sight of the enemy's vastly increased numbers.

A tense stand-off ensued for several hours, during which British sniper fire began to increase in concentration. The insurgents manning the distillery's windows were regularly forced back as they heard the brief high-pitched screams of incoming rounds. The heavily bandaged Liston soon abandoned the crow's nest and returned to the floor below, considering his previous day's uncanny escape to have fully utilised his quota of good luck. The fire then escalated again, until it erupted into a torrent at approximately 10 a.m., when it seemed that the entire canal bank erupted.

Several platoons of infantry leapt from their recently dug slit trenches and made a dash for the distillery's outer wall. They were met with a hail of bullets, matched in ferocity by the covering fire from their own side as they continued their advance. The noise rose to a cacophony of thunderclaps, coming and going in terrifying firecracker-like clusters. It was accompanied by scores of muzzle flashes followed by plumes of smoke which formed into low clouds and drifted abreast of the advancing infantrymen. British bullets smashed into and shattered the walls of the distillery while the troops pressed on. They ducked and sprinted between the raised mounds of earth that covered their alternating rushes toward the insurgents' position. Many crouched and knelt as they aimed their Enfields at the telltale wisps of smoke betraying the Volunteers' firing positions. The rebels moved further back from the windows and fired repeatedly, filling the rooms with dense, stinking cartridge fumes. Several troops fell under their fire, but many more succeeded in making the distillery wall. Their comrades rushed forward with growing confidence that a victory was finally close. Soon the military were swarming around the distillery, and preparing to attack with grenades.

Captain Colbert clearly saw what was about to happen from his vantage point in the distillery's top floor. He grabbed a squad of his men, and rushed down several staircases from the top floor carrying canister bombs, which they then lit and lobbed over the outer wall. The detonations were followed by several terrible screams as shrapnel ripped into those who had thus far successfully braved the rebel fire. Colbert's counter-attack managed to halt the momentum the assaulting troops had built up. Several of their NCOs were hit by flying shards and fell to the ground. When another shower of bombs followed, the few remaining uninjured British retreated hastily. They did so under continuing covering fire from their own lines, but harassed all the way by the Volunteer marksmen, who once again exacted a very heavy price. In the grassy area facing Jameson's west side, the wounded and dying groaned in pain. Shocked residents from the nearby terraces to the south of the carnage looked on in disbelief, unable to draw their gaze away from the terrible spectacle. More than a few were sent scurrying by stray bullets.

Later in the afternoon, Colonel Oates of the 2/8th Battalion Sherwood Foresters was leading a large group of his battle-weary men, who had been billeted in Ballsbridge the previous night, to new positions inside the Royal Hospital. Several much needed horse-drawn ammunition and supply wagons accompanied their marching column. They were accompanied by the Brigade Headquarters Transport and some Royal Engineers. The men from the 2/8th Battalion formed the vanguard of the column, while their Regimental colleagues of the 2/7th formed the rearguard, which was deemed to be the safest position for the bruised battalion following its decimation the previous afternoon.

Volunteer Thomas Gay, an intelligence officer under Colbert's command, stealthily monitored the officers from the Sherwood Foresters as they stood on the South Circular Road and consulted their maps. Once the column had passed Wellington Barracks, which was on their left as they marched, Gay rushed to the distillery to report to Colbert that a large force was heading their way. Colbert detailed his men to their positions and ordered them to stand ready.

As the troops approached Rialto, moving ever westward, they came under sporadic rifle fire from the Union and the distillery, which intensified as their forward sections tried to cross the bridge.

Brigadier Colonel Maconchy ordered a single supply wagon forward to test the accuracy of the insurgents' aim. It was driven at great speed across the steep arching bridge in full view of the rebels by its courageous driver. Both he and his cargo made it across, but the volume of shot sent his way suggested that anyone who followed would not be so fortunate. The British officers considered their options for a time before formulating a plan.

Captain Martyn, second in command of the 2/8th, moved out with a small section from D Company to clear Rialto Street of a sniper, which they promptly did. Simultaneously, Captain Dimock with A Company began filtering throughout the many side streets along the South Circular Road to secure both of its flanks against enemy sharpshooters. C Company, meanwhile, secured the line of advance, observed all the while by the bewildered local inhabitants and shop owners.

The column stalled for a time while reinforcements from the Royal Irish Regiment, under Major Sir Francis Fletcher Vane, were brought up from Portobello Barracks.

D Company, under Captain John Oates, Colonel Oates' son, was then ordered, along with the reinforcements, to advance as far as possible into the Union with a view to distracting the enemy's attention, allowing the transport to cross the bridge. Overall command for the attack fell to Captain Martyn, who was himself awaiting a promotion to Major.

The troops re-entered the Union virtually unopposed initially as the insurgents had remained in its north-eastern section surrounding their headquarters. The doctors and nursing staff inside the complex, who could see the troop movement from the many windows, did their best to carry on, in spite of the imminent threat of Monday's mayhem being revisited upon their charges. As the infantrymen advanced eastwards with fixed bayonets they formed waves to cross the open ground, spreading themselves into skirmish lines. This allowed them some freedom of movement to fire and manoeuvre in alternating groups as they pressed on. They advanced over open ground towards Ceannt's headquarters, watched now by eagle-eyed rebels on its first and second floors.

They troops hurled themselves at the ground initially when their machine gun from the Royal Hospital to their left opened fire in support. Each 47-round drum that fed the gas-operated Lewis gun spewed its rounds at the roof, walls and windows of the nurses' home. The men inside scrambled for cover as shots ricocheted from window sills and embedded themselves in the ceilings and inner walls, filling the air inside with thick clouds of plaster and dust.

The crouching troops then jumped to their feet and charged. The rebels now let fly. Ceannt, Brugha and Cosgrave darted from position to position, pointing out running targets to riflemen who shouted back 'Yes sir!' before their perspiring hands forced the butts of their 4kg rifles into their shoulders to shoot. The scenario was repeated over and over. The insurgents' ears rang with every shot. Several advancing troops fell as bullets tore into their bodies, but the majority pressed forward. Their machine gun continued firing just feet over their heads.

The mayhem intensified as the British weight of numbers soon had them swarming into the yard to the front of the nurses' home, while its rear was pulverised with lead. The ferocious rebel fire cut down several more of their fast-moving enemies. Cracks and loud booms echoed within the confines of the yards and buildings, intermingled with barked orders, curses and the screams of the wounded. The troops were eventually driven to ground throughout the maze of buildings surrounding the nurses' home, where they frantically scanned the walls and windows all around for both targets and cover.

The three-storey building that contained the rebel headquarters was adjoined by a long thick-walled hospital building which was about half its height, and approximately 150 feet in length. The troops led by Captain Martyn reached its outer walls several times, only to be driven back repeatedly until finally several of his men succeeded in smashing in a door to gain access. Once inside, they launched themselves along its corridor until they reached the thick dividing wall that separated the rebel headquarters now next door to them. They began digging through the wall, using their bayonets and anything else within their grasp. The ward patients trapped inside did their best to remain calm in the face of the terrifying brutality all around. Next door the rebels were still firing ferociously at the troops who were once again swarming outside.

When they finally bored a hole, one soldier put his head through. There came a loud bang accompanied by a flash, and the infantryman's body slumped forward, shot through the head by Volunteer Jack Doherty. James Coughlan and Captain fFrench Mullen, who were next to Doherty, prepared for the worst.

The dead soldier's furious comrades yelled insults and obscenities before retreating momentarily. Captain Martyn then ordered Oates to fetch some hand grenades. He departed but soon returned. Several bombs were lobbed through the improvised abrasion. Their deafening bangs were immediately succeeded with small-arms fire as Martyn and three others entered the dusty chaos of the adjoining building through the hole in the wall, where they were soon joined by Captain Oates. Several Volunteers on the ground floor rushed out of the building's side windows facing the bakehouse, training their weapons on any soldier who might follow.

The British troops found themselves in a hallway, where they were confronted with what appeared to be an impregnable barricade blocking off a staircase. Officers and soldiers began pouring in to reinforce them, and soon a satchel's worth of hand grenades was hurled over a small gap between the obstruction and the ceiling just inches above. One of the grenades bounced back and nearly killed several of the troops. The building shook to its foundations under the repeated explosions. At one point it seemed that the entire roof would cave in.

From a broken window upstairs Ceannt's attention was drawn to a small cluster of British soldiers who had been ordered by Captain Martyn to make their way to the bakehouse. This greatly alarmed the commandant. He realised that if they took control of that building it would cut his positions in two, presumably the reason Captain Martyn had ordered its capture. He scrambled from the nurses' home to alert the men at the Union's front gate. The remaining insurgents who were holding on to the upper floors of their headquarters mistook his abrupt exit for a retreat. They quickly followed.

They scurried through a labyrinth of tunnels and eventually made the front gate, while in the bakehouse just to their rear the disorientated English soldiers sought out their enemies. Unable to make contact in the claustrophobic cauldron of chaos they ventured back outside, leaving two men to guard the position.

The rebels gathered themselves and prepared for the inevitable. One Volunteer asked Ceannt if he planned on surrendering or fighting to the end. His reply was short and simple: 'A fight to the finish.' As soon as the words had left their commandant's mouth his fighters made their way back through the mouse-holes to their headquarters.

Never the type to back away from a fight, Vice Commandant Brugha had been running down the main staircase of the nurses' home towards the barricade when he charged directly into a grenade blast. His shattered body suffered no fewer than 25 wounds from the bombing and more than one enemy bullet. His torn uniform was covered in blood and dust and he was unable to stand. He sat on a small landing with his legs parted for balance and, mustering all his strength, reloaded his Mauser, trying his best to manoeuvre the metal parts between fingers that were slippery with his own blood. He continued firing at the frustrated British below him still savagely trying to force the barricade.

The infantrymen began to make ground. But the first man to penetrate was confronted with the vision of a nihilistic and apparently suicidal madman, covered in coagulating blood and dust as it oozed from his mouth, ears and nose, singing through blood-red teeth: 'God Save Ireland!' while firing his semi-automatic. The apparently deranged Vice-Commandant then began directing an imaginary force who appeared to be rallying to his aid from above. He shouted: 'You ten men cover this barricade – you ten men come with me.'

The barricade held. His enemies were baffled and his comrades were inspired. As they entered the nurses' home in increasing numbers, they regrouped and succeeded in driving the attackers back. At this point the insurgents seemed to have lost all regard for their own survival.

The Sherwood Foresters were now utterly exhausted. They had faced annihilation the previous day and were by now out of ideas. They retreated from the building and eventually from the surrounding area, having been sent word that the brigade had succeeded in crossing Rialto Bridge. The riflemen and machine-gunners in the Royal Hospital covered their retreat.

The insurgents grasped at the opportunity to draw breath. The attack had left them shattered. Many collapsed onto the rubble-strewn carpets, their legs no longer able to support them. Their officers moved about checking on them, issuing cigarettes and making sure every man had water to drink, fearing they might momentarily have to face the same hell again. Cathal Brugha, the former travelling salesman from Dublin, soon lost consciousness, and was not expected to live.

The decision was eventually made for a full retirement by British forces from the South Dublin Union. No further attacks would be planned or made. General Lowe, in overall command, was happy to contain the rebels inside while he set about tightening the British grip on the main Volunteer headquarters in Sackville Street. Arrangements were made regarding the wounded and the dead throughout the vast complex.

As evening approached, coffins were transported into the Union from Rialto on a horse-drawn carriage to deal with the many victims of the fighting, some of whose remains had lain outside for over three days. Meanwhile, one of the British privates who had been left to guard the bakehouse had found himself cut off. His comrade had fallen to a volley of rebel fire that rendered him temporarily unconscious. He managed to remain undetected, having come to shortly after his comrades had retreated. He had quietly tended his dying companion, terrified of what would become of him should he be captured. When the carriage arrived unexpectedly in his vicinity the young soldier seized the opportunity to play dead. His 'corpse' was collected along with that of his friend and several others, and taken to Rialto, where the many locals who had gathered received the fright of their lives when the lid from his coffin shifted, revealing his 'resurrected' body. Such a vision at Easter left the devout Catholics among them gaping as they hurriedly blessed themselves. The young private then reported for duty once again.

By Friday the South Dublin Union had been left in its entirety to the Volunteers. The insurgents' morale reached its zenith as they took the opportunity to rest, eat and treat their wounded. No communication was now possible with the other rebel garrisons still fighting in the city, but Ceannt was fully aware that, in war, contact between forces was frequently lost, albeit temporarily, and he had no reason to fear the worst.

The sound of fighting from the city centre had intensified greatly that day, which was an obvious cause for concern, and reports from the distillery of a bright red glow over the entire city centre from the many fires the previous night suggested that, overall, things from the Republican point of view were not going according to plan, but the Volunteer Commandant knew that his responsibility lay with his 4th Battalion, which had acquitted itself with great distinction, a sentiment shared by the British officers regarding the incredible bravery shown by their own men.

The staff and inmates of the South Dublin Union, in the meantime, carried on, hungry for news from outside as to when the conflict would end. Many wounded soldiers and rebels alike had been treated by the Union's medics, who spoke very highly of the demeanour of the young men in both sets of uniforms. Great gratitude and respect was reciprocated by the combatants to those who chose to stay and take care of the weak and infirm in spite of the danger to themselves.

The men and women in Jameson's also rested that day. Rifles were cleaned and ammunition replenished. Those manning the watch positions scanned the surrounds while numerous sniper battles took place in the morning. During the early afternoon, however, the firing died down.

The seemingly spontaneous ceasefire prompted numerous Red Cross personnel to enter Fairbrother's Field. They began digging pits. Volunteers and British soldiers alike looked on as the pits were filled with the corpses of young soldiers. An area of field roughly 300 yards long was littered with bodies which awaited interment. A desolate quiet hung over the battlefield, punctuated by distant sounds of artillery. The silence in the area lasted for several hours until a single shot rang out. Soon the sniper battles were once again under way.

Dublin city centre blazed that Friday night. The conflagrations could be seen by young Robert Holland as he took a break from his position and wiped away the gunpowder soot that had become caked into every pore in his face. He and his comrades were covered in black dust and dirt from the firing they had maintained – for hours on end at times during the British infantry assaults. They were utterly exhausted, and yet elated. Young men and women, teenagers as many of them were, had held and held again, and they had no reason to assume that the situation was not similarly positive throughout their newly founded Republic. The number of Volunteers in the distillery had increased now to over 140. Morale was as high as it could be, so high in fact that a ceilí dance was planned for Sunday night to celebrate their continuing success.

Sunday, however, turned out to be very different.

7

Jacob's Biscuit Factory

'I think, my boy, you better send for the Fire Brigade.'

Easter Monday 24 April saw 36-year-old Volunteer John MacDonagh rubbing his eyes. It had been a long morning already, and it was not even 7 a.m. His brother Thomas, the Tipperary-born commandant of the 2nd Battalion, had been sending dispatches to mobilise its men since the crack of dawn. John looked out from the first floor of his temporary headquarters in 130 St Stephen's Green, listening to the chorus of chirping birds, oblivious to the tribulations of humankind. In a few hours it would all begin: they were about to cross the Rubicon.[1] Soon they would leave their temporary headquarters and set up their field headquarters in the imposing, fortress-like Jacob's biscuit factory, where they, like their comrades elsewhere, would strike a blow for the Republic.

About 2½ miles to his north, in Father Matthew Park, situated just off Windsor Avenue in Fairview, former Olympic cyclist Michael Walker and his brother and fellow Olympian John had just been handed a list of men from G Company by their Vice Commandant, 31-year-old Tom Hunter. They were tasked with finding each of the listed men and instructing them to be at St Stephen's Green by 11 a.m. Hunter, from County Cork, then checked on the small squad who had remained in the park overnight, guarding the vast stock of supplies and ammunition that had been stored in its pavilion since the failed mobilisation resulting from the countermand order the previous day. Satisfied that everything was in order, he dispatched a runner to find

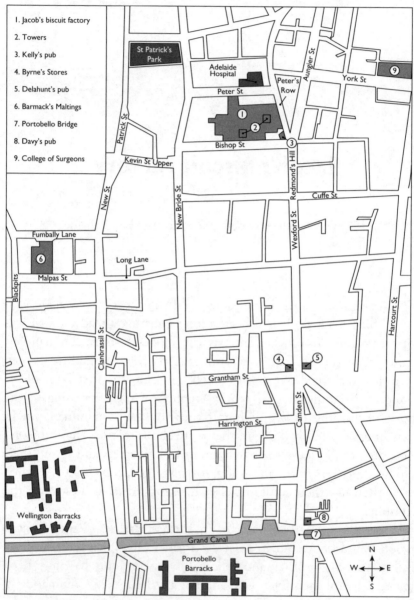

1. Jacob's biscuit factory
2. Towers
3. Kelly's pub
4. Byrne's Stores
5. Delahunt's pub
6. Barmack's Maltings
7. Portobello Bridge
8. Davy's pub
9. College of Surgeons

Jacob's biscuit factory and various 2nd Battalion outposts.

Lieutenant Thomas Slater of C Company, and to issue the Dubliner with instructions to mobilise his men.

Lieutenant Slater soon arrived at the park with word that he had dispatched orders to his Volunteers to assemble as instructed. He and

Hunter waited, as men gradually arrived in small groups. They issued the men with ammunition and dispatched them in twos and threes to St Stephen's Green. The two men waited as long as they could to allow for stragglers and latecomers, before Hunter eventually passed over joint command of the men and the stores in the park to Enniscorthy native Captain Tom Weafer and Dubliner Captain Frank Henderson, with orders to get to St Stephen's Green as soon as the remainder of the battalion turned up. Hunter and Slater hailed a passing hackney cab from nearby Fairview Strand, and instructed its curious driver to take them to 130 St Stephen's Green.

Séamus Pounch – another young Dubliner and a captain in Na Fianna – and two of his comrades in full uniform had been heading for their headquarters in Dawson Street when they met Garry Holohan on his bicycle. He explained that he had a job on, but that as they were in uniform they would be of no use. He ordered them instead to gather up their equipment and report to the nearest battalion. The three youngsters hurried to their homes and grabbed what they could, before they met up again to seek out the nearest sign of action, which turned out to be the mustering of 2nd Battalion at St Stephen's Green West.

Over breakfast that morning, Volunteer Seosamh de Brún had decided to spend the day at the seaside. Leaving his house on Amiens Street, he walked towards North Strand until he noticed a group of uniformed Volunteers at its junction with Seville Place, near the landmark 'Five lamps'. Thinking that it looked like a Company mobilisation, he walked over and asked if that was the case. When told that it was, he decided to walk the mile or so to Father Matthew Park to find out what exactly was happening. On his way he chanced upon Captain Weafer. He asked the officer if the parade was general. The reply was clear and concise: he was to get to St Stephen's Green by 11 a.m. His trip to the beach would have to wait. He hotfooted it home to change his casual outfit into something more formal and warlike, before he grabbed his gun and headed for the Green.

Back in Father Matthew Park, the confusion sown over the previous two days still lingered. Word had somehow reached the remaining officers that the mobilisation was again cancelled. Curses of varying degrees were muttered by the increasingly frustrated men who looked to their officers for some sort of certainty. Captain Weafer decided to go and see Commandant Pearse, while Henderson and Lieutenant Oscar

Traynor, a 30-year-old Dubliner, disbanded the Volunteers temporarily and billeted them in the nearby terraces of houses.

Seventeen-year-old William Stapleton received some very curious glances from his fellow passengers on the tram as it trundled towards the city centre. He stood in its centre aisle with a bandolier and a small rucksack slung across his chest. This, however, was not the reason for his fellow travellers' whispers regarding the appearance of the uniformed teenager; rather, it was the shotgun he held that drew their attention. It was nearly as tall as the young Volunteer.

Fifteen year-old Dubliner Vincent Byrne, meanwhile, was striding enthusiastically up Grafton Street with his .22 rifle when he bumped into Lieutenant Shiels of his Company. Shiels asked the youngster where he was going. When he explained that he had been mobilised to St Stephen's Green the lieutenant sternly told him to go home. Devastated, the teenager slowly turned to walk back down the normally busy shopping street. He bucked up, however, when his section commander, Mick Colgan, told him 'not to mind' the lieutenant. Young Byrne then marched proudly at Colgan's side towards the Green.

Just inside the Green, Michael Walker was sitting amongst the men of G Company, when 23-year-old Lieutenant Dick McKee ordered him back to Father Matthew Park to find out why the other battalion companies had not yet arrived. Walker set off on his bicycle, pedalling almost as swiftly as he had done in Stockholm four years previously,[2] as he sped down Dawson Street on his northbound journey, which he made in excellent time. When he arrived he found about 100 men waiting in the park, seemingly unsure of their next move. Walker put them out of their misery, bearing as he did word that the insurrection was imminent; but now, according to Captain Frank Henderson, there was a problem with transport for their supplies. Henderson told Walker to inform McKee that as soon as he could commandeer the required number of vehicles he would follow him to the Green.

Towards the junction of St Stephen's Green West's with South King Street and Grafton Street, Lieutenant Slater and Vice Commandant Hunter had arrived at No. 130, where they found most of the Volunteer captains present. Commandant MacDonagh laid out the battalion's general plans, which had been heavily revised following the countermand order. The main body was tasked with taking over Jacob's

Lieutenant Dick McKee, who, with several others, bore the brunt of the civilian backlash against the insurgents in the Fumbally Lane/Clanbrassil Street area, while they covered their battalion to their rear in Jacob's biscuit factory.
MILITARY ARCHIVES

biscuit factory, which sat between Bishop Street and Bride Street, roughly a quarter of a mile to their west.

The biscuit factory was a large structure dating from the 1850s whose frontage partially faced Aungier Street. Strategically, it was tremendously important as it was very close to the rear of Dublin Castle, and sat between St Stephen's Green, soon to be commandeered by Commandant Mallin, and the South Dublin Union. It denied the enemy an uninterrupted route from Portobello Barracks in Rathmines to the city centre, while its outposts, which would soon be in place on Malpas Street and Fumbally Lane to its south-west, and Camden Street to its south, would hinder any city-bound movement from Wellington Barracks on the South Circular Road.

As MacDonagh and his officers meticulously went over their plans, Seosamh de Brún had arrived just outside the Green. He checked his watch: 11.30 a.m. Looking around, he became aware of the usual sightseers that an assembly of Volunteers inevitably drew. He also noticed Detective Johnny Barton of Dublin Castle's G Division, who was watching their movements with keen interest.

At 11.40 a.m., MacDonagh and the 2nd Battalion's officers left their temporary headquarters and joined the assembled Volunteers outside.

The officers proceeded to check the numbers of men that they had present from each Company, while MacDonagh's attention was drawn to a formidable-looking man dressed in a distinctive and impeccably tailored blue suit, who was approaching them on foot from Grafton Street. MacDonagh went over and shook the man's hand and, following a brief conversation, both he and the man he would shortly introduce as Major John MacBride joined their ranks.

At 11.50 a.m., MacDonagh shouted the order to fall in. His brother John then joined him at the head of the column, while 47-year-old Major MacBride, who hailed from Westport in County Mayo, flanked the commandant on his other side. The major gave the order to march, whereupon the men of the 2nd Battalion moved out. Behind them encouraging shouts of, 'Now or never boys!'[3] came from behind the railings of St Stephen's Green from the Citizen Army members who had just arrived and begun occupying their own positions.

Within a few minutes the column had arrived at its destination, where they halted along the entire 200-yard length of Bishop Street. Some of the men then forced entry to the biscuit factory. The door at its Bride Street end was heavily barred, but a window at the Peter's Row side was quickly and easily forced, allowing Volunteers to begin hoisting each other up. Major MacBride, acting with his characteristic dash, was one of the first in. Soon a sledgehammer was procured and the main door was smashed open. Hackney carriages began to arrive, disgorging their cargoes of weapons and ammunition, before being ferried into Jacob's through the gates which were now ajar. The battalion quartermaster, 39-year-old Michael O'Hanrahan, oversaw that all the supplies were brought inside and accounted for correctly.

Michael Walker, meanwhile, had cycled back to St Stephen's Green from Fairview, but was flummoxed to find none of his battalion there. A comrade appeared and said, 'Walker, get to Jacob's.' He promptly set off again.

As Walker pedalled towards the biscuit factory, Vice Commandant Hunter and a large group of Volunteers stood on Bishop Street while the main body of rebels entered the huge building. As soon as they were in, Hunter barked the order to move out. He and Lieutenant Dick McKee led their force on another quarter-mile march towards Fumbally Lane, a narrow 100-yard-long street to the right of Clanbrassil Street. They passed New Street, where Volunteers Séamus Pounch and Vincent

Byrne were detailed to a 12-man section under Lieutenant Billy Byrne with orders to occupy the tenement houses on Malpas Street, which lies parallel to Fumbally Lane 100 yards further south. When Hunter arrived in Fumbally Lane, he ordered his men into three groups, the first of which was to occupy Barmack's Maltings, and the second to occupy several tenements overlooking the approaches from New Street and Clanbrassil Street. The third, under Lieutenant McKee, was to barricade both ends of Fumbally Lane and to throw another across the width of New Street.

Once inside Barmack's, the men took to its upper floors where the windows overlooked Blackpitts. All potential approaches to the city from either Portobello or Wellington Barracks were now covered. De Brún listened closely as Hunter informed the men that the Irish Republic had been declared in Dublin, concluding his address with the enthusiastic claim, 'We are in action!'[4] A loud cheer rang out, followed by Hunter's order to smash the windows. Within seconds the narrow streets rang to the sound of breaking glass and, ominously, rifles began to poke out from the empty window frames.

The inhabitants of Malpas Street were not the type to take their eviction lying down, and furious shouts of, 'You should be fighting the Germans!' were levelled at the Volunteers, who carried on emptying the houses, using their gun barrels to emphasise their intent. Then, as soon as their tenants had been rendered homeless, the houses were loopholed and fortified. These positions would be the first defensive line against an enemy attack from the South Circular Road.

Several police constables soon arrived in the area, keen to exercise their authority. Their determination to remove the rebels waned when they were confronted with the business end of numerous gun barrels. They were taken prisoner as the first shots of the Rising rang out in the distance.

Similar cracks could be heard in the air as Captain Weafer returned to Father Matthew Park and recalled the men. The scrap was on and they were now to get supplies to the GPO. He set off with the main body of 50 men, accompanied by the supplies, which had been loaded on to a truck and a horse and cart. Captain Leo Henderson had just left ahead of him with an advance guard of 30 men, while Henderson's brother and fellow captain, Frank, was with the rearguard of another 30.

All was well until they reached the brow of Clarke's Bridge, which straddled the Royal Canal on the Ballybough Road, where the air suddenly crackled around them with a brief succession of bullets and the rapid mechanical thud of machine-gun fire, which came from behind and to their left. Weafer ordered the advance guard to locate the enemy, and the rearguard to retrace their steps and take up defensive positions commanding the Tolka Bridge half a mile to their north, next to Richmond Road. Weafer then rushed on ahead with the rest of the men to the GPO.

One of Leo Henderson's scouts discovered the source of the shooting, and informed his captain that the British were advancing towards Annesley Bridge from Fairview. Henderson quickly got his men down Spring Garden Street and into firing positions on both sides of North Strand's wide roadway, in Annesley Place and Leinster Avenue, where the terrified residents pleaded with them to leave.

An unexpected and withering hail of fire greeted the British advance guard as they crossed Annesley Bridge. Extra machine guns were brought into play by the military, but determined resistance by Henderson's men knocked out two of them, and eventually forced them back from the bridge. The Volunteers in Leinster Avenue also managed to trap some troops in East Wall and take them prisoner. After an hour with no sign of another attack, Captain Henderson ordered his men to fall back to the GPO.

In Jacob's, meanwhile, the Volunteers were busy barricading and fortifying the position. The empty window frames were sandbagged with huge flour sacks. They had no qualms about breaking the windows on the upper floors, but some of the lower floors had highly decorative stained glass. The order was given to put them out nonetheless. MacDonagh set up his headquarters on the ground floor, as the sound of intense machine-gun fire resounded to the south.

Just after 1 p.m. a squad of Citizen Army men under Sergeant Doyle came racing down Camden Street, having been forced to evacuate the position in Davy's pub, the source of the machine-gun fire that had alerted MacDonagh. A large formation of soldiers from Portobello Barracks was hot on their heels. They had originally planned on escaping to the Stephen's Green garrison, but their planned route through Hatch Street had been denied to them. They made their way instead to the nearest garrison. Jacob's immense walls were a welcome refuge and, once inside, several Volunteers rushed to the corner of Bishop Street and Redmond Hill, where they waited in ambush for Doyle's pursuers.

About 30 men of the Royal Irish Rifles formed the advance guard of a larger force following the Citizen Army men down Camden Street. When they reached the corner of Redmond's Hill and Bishop Street they found themselves in a trap. The tall surrounding buildings echoed to the volley of shots that confronted them. Six men fell to the cobblestones as soon as the Volunteers opened fire. Their screams and shouts could be heard among hastily barked orders to retreat. After several seconds a couple of them had stopped moving, while others clawed and kicked at the ground in agony. The remainder returned to the main force, after doing their best to move their wounded men out of harm's way. When they linked up close to the junction of Camden Street and Harrington Street, they found themselves under sniper fire from one of the immense towers in the biscuit factory. Safe positions were swiftly taken up, out of the line of fire.

When Volunteer Joseph Furlong and three other men arrived at the biscuit factory they found a hive of activity. They hoisted each other up and, as they were helped in through the windows, they were told that the rifle reports they had just heard were their garrison's first encounter with the British military, and that an attack was imminent. Once safely inside, they reported to their company commander, 28-year-old Captain Patrick Moran, who was in conference with Commandant MacDonagh. When their turn came to speak, they told Moran that they had only one handgun between the four of them. MacDonagh handed Furlong his Mauser C96 pistol, and Moran ordered them to report to Section Leader Gerry Boland who, at that time, was tunnelling through from Jacob's into the adjoining pub, Kelly's, which had a commanding view over the junction with Redmond Hill, Wexford Street and beyond.

On Clanbrassil Street at roughly the same time, Volunteer Seán Murphy of the 3rd Battalion was en route to his home, having been out for a stroll in the Harold's Cross area, until the cracks of gunfire from various parts of the city suggested that, in spite of the countermand order, something was afoot. At his house he found three other members of his unit waiting for him, who told him of their Company's planned assembly on Earlsfort Terrace. He dispatched a man to see if their comrades were still there while he changed into his uniform and waited with the others. The tone of their conversation alternated between great excitement and subdued dread. Eventually their comrade returned and told Murphy that they had dispersed from Earlsfort Terrace, adding that the Citizen Army held nearby Harcourt Street Station, but had not been able to help him regarding the whereabouts of the 3rd. His wife then told him that Volunteers had occupied Barmack's Maltings.

Meanwhile from the windows in Barmack's, Seosamh de Brún was watching the hostile crowd that had been steadily gathering near their barricades. To his curiosity, two women pushed their way through the crowds, and handed two buckets over to the rebels beyond the fortification. One of the buckets was sent up to Barmack's and was found to contain hot tea.

More ominously, at the New Street end of Fumbally Lane, a man had been observed taking notes and watching the positions. Believing he was a plain-clothes policeman from G division, he was ordered to move on or face a bullet. He refused to move and was shot where he stood.

A quarter of a mile away in Kelly's pub, Joseph Furlong had just sealed the doors of the premises' bar area, while the Volunteers inside took up positions at its windows. Section Leader Boland distributed canister bombs to each firing position. It was decided to test one. After the area outside was checked for civilians and found to be clear, a fuse was lit and the bomb thrown out onto the road. An impressive explosion followed, albeit with little destructive effect, but the men were not disheartened. Smashing concrete with improvised explosives was one thing: human flesh was quite another. The rebels waited confidently.

At 3.30 p.m., continuous gunfire could be heard from the South Dublin Union, about a mile to his west, as Seán Murphy brought his three men down from Clanbrassil Street and reported to Vice Commandant Hunter, who detailed him and his men to the wide junction of Patrick Street, New Street and Kevin Street, about 200 yards to their north. Hunter was happy to employ whomever he could to help deal with the increasingly hostile locals. All around Barmack's, civilians were emerging in force, singing and dancing to English songs and pelting the men on the barricades with stones. At one point a man made a grab for a Volunteer's rifle, before he was unambiguously warned to let go. He held on, until a shot from the same rifle tore through his body. The man's eyes held a brief and terrible look of disbelief, before his dying frame slumped against a wall which had just been splattered with his blood. The shocked locals dispersed, although they soon returned to remove the dead man, and the stone throwing and insults began again, with increased wrath.

Later in the evening, Hunter received word from Seán Murphy via a runner that huge numbers of British reinforcements were crossing from Back Lane into Ship Street Barracks, adding that he would need extra men to engage them. By the time the runner returned with a handful of additional Volunteers, however, the soldiers had already made the gates of the barracks. Their arrival brought a huge increase in gunfire, which left Murphy and his men fearing for the Citizen Army garrison, who by the sounds of things were being given a rough time in City Hall and around Dublin Castle.

On the north side of the River Liffey in the meantime, Captain Leo Henderson had reported to Commandant Connolly in the GPO and been ordered to return to reinforce his brother Frank and his men now holding the Tolka Bridge and the Fairview area.

Volunteer Padraig O'Ceallaigh had been at the Fairyhouse Races in County Meath earlier in the day, when he heard rumours of disturbances in the city. He returned to the capital at the earliest opportunity to pick up his two rifles from his home in Clontarf. He went on foot to the GPO via narrow back streets and alleys, while keeping his eyes peeled for military patrols. Sporadic rifle fire echoed all around. Once inside the GPO, he took in the feverish activity in the building before approaching Commandant Pearse, who informed him that his 2nd Battalion held Jacob's. O'Ceallaigh set off, but not before Pearse requested that he leave behind his Savage automatic rifle along with its ammunition. Very reluctantly and doing nothing to hide his displeasure at being asked to hand over his prized possession, he unslung the Savage and handed it to Pearse. He then left through the building's Prince's Street exit, and made his way to Ha'penny Bridge and eventually the biscuit factory. On the way he noticed excited groups of people gathering on the south quays. The repetitive thuds of machine guns coming from Dublin Castle in the early evening promised a show not to be missed – but from a safe distance.

At 8 p.m., Vice Commandant Hunter received a dispatch from Commandant MacDonagh, ordering him to pull back to Jacob's. The outposts had successfully accomplished their job and the Volunteers were now embedded in the factory. With the two huge towers that provided visibility for miles around now fully manned, any movement from the Portobello direction would be clearly visible.

Hunter spread the word and the men slowly started to pull back from the barricades and buildings, closely followed by the 'separation women' and 'shawlies'⁵ whose hostility had grown as the day wore on. In spite of two horrific fatalities in their midst earlier they seemed fearless, indeed some were even trying to drag the Dublin Metropolitan Police prisoners free as they were marched towards Jacob's at rifle point.

When they reached Bishop Street, the ire reached new levels of volatility. As the Volunteers waited for the factory gates to be opened, the growing crowd pelted them with stones, bottles and whatever else they could grasp. Every curse known to man or woman was flung at the rebels, who rushed inside as soon as the gates were opened, and felt great relief at being detailed to their new positions.

William Stapleton was ordered to form part of a guard over the main gate while its barricade was built up again. While this was being done, the crowd outside, whose number had now swelled to over a hundred, suddenly surged forward in an attempt to force the gate, smashing at it with a variety of implements. The Volunteers did their best to control both themselves and the enraged mob. Commandant MacDonagh and Major MacBride came to the scene, looking concerned. They then noticed several paraffin-soaked pieces of sacking being pushed under the gate before being ignited. Stapleton and two others quickly pushed the rags back out before they could cause any damage. MacDonagh then ordered him to remove the shot from his shotgun cartridges, and to fire one or two blanks through the iron grid at the top of the gates in the direction of the people to frighten them off. His plan worked. After two loud bangs, the mob went quiet and then slowly dispersed.

Those who had just entered found the factory in a state of defensive readiness. All the windows and doorways had been sandbagged with huge sacks of flour, while tactical defensive positions had been set up throughout. The garrison hurried around performing their various tasks covered from head to toe in flour, as their captains encouraged them, their own uniforms now showing up as pale green beneath the fine, white powder.

Vincent Byrne was brought to a window position overlooking Peter's Row by Volunteer Mick McDonnell. Once there he was handed a sack of tin cans and told to throw them out the window, so that if any enemy attempted an assault by stealth in the dead of night, they would stumble over the cans and signal their presence. Byrne was then handed another sack, which was filled with biscuits and cocoa chocolates. The 15-year-old sat down and gorged himself.

Seosamh de Brún and a number of men were soon shown to their billets for the night, which turned out to be the engine room and the boiler house at the base of one of Jacob's gigantic chimneys. The men threw themselves down on the tiled floor and began to relax. They tucked into rations and smoked, while they nervously joked together and tried to get some sleep. Their next picket was in four hours. The hard floor beneath them did nothing for their prospects of a good night's rest, however, and in de Brún's case matters were not helped when Pat Callan said to him, 'Suppose a shell struck it and the damn thing crashed?', pointing at the chimney above them. De Brún was no more immune than the rest of humanity to the power of suggestion, particularly during the hours of darkness. He assured Callan that such a thing would not happen, but the idea had now been firmly planted in his own head. De Brún had a restless four hours.

At approximately 2 a.m., 21 Volunteers under Lieutenant Shiels proceeded to occupy outposts at the junction of Lower and Upper Camden Street. Fifteen of them took over Byrne's Store on the corner of Grantham Street, and six were detailed to Delahunt's pub opposite.[6] Here they waited, taking turns trying to rest. Opportunities to slumber were few, however: the machine-gunners in St Stephen's Green and Dublin Castle saw to that.

Early on Tuesday morning, an advance in force was made from Portobello Barracks to try and reach Dublin Castle. As its spearhead of 20 infantrymen approached Grantham Street, they came under fire from Delahunt's and Byrne's. Both positions were overrun, however, after reinforcements were called forward to bolster the attack. When the troops eventually forced entry into both positions, they found them abandoned.

Back inside Jacob's, the buccaneering Major MacBride was making his presence felt. He had taken over command of the fighting men in the factory and surrounding areas, his years of experience and his proven cool head under fire making such a move inevitable. Soon after the British assault up the road, a Volunteer rushed into his headquarters room to present him with a somewhat exaggerated report that thousands of British troops were advancing down Camden Street and that the Grantham Street positions had fallen back on Jacob's. 'That's all right,' was MacBride's confident reply. The messenger became concerned that the major did not understand the importance of his words, so he repeated them. MacBride emphasised again, 'That's all right,' and turned to John MacDonagh beside him as if they had been having a relaxed conversation, and said, 'So I played my King and won the game.' The Volunteer went away satisfied that there was nothing to be alarmed about, particularly with such an accomplished card player in command.[7]

MacBride calmly went to the position's south-eastern corner of Redmond Hill and Bishop Street and prepared the men. They watched the spearhead of the British troops come into view and waited. Astonishingly, the troops had followed the same route as their comrades the previous afternoon when they had been routed. Then, just as the enemy soldiers reached the street junction, a massive volley of rifle fire tore into them. Several fell while others tried to return fire, but found themselves helplessly caught out in the open. The order of retreat rang out, and several infantrymen instinctively hauled at the leather shoulder braces of their wounded comrades to pull them out of the line of fire. Their officer in charge subsequently decided that a different route would be the order of the day and word was sent back to Portobello that the Bishop Street area was heavily garrisoned.

Sixteen-year-old William Oman of the Citizen Army, who had been forced out of his position overlooking Ship Street Barracks during the fighting for Dublin Castle, had spent the night hiding from the hostile crowds at his grandmother's house in Blackpitts. With the arrival of morning the youngster decided it was time to rejoin the fight, and he made for the nearest rebel garrison, which happened to be Jacob's. His comrades who had retreated from Davy's vouched for him when he attempted to gain entry, and he was brought before MacDonagh and MacBride. MacBride questioned him about the action at the Castle. Both men were impressed with Oman, who was then assigned as MacDonagh's orderly. His first task was to acquaint himself with the various positions and officers throughout their stronghold.

Another teenager, Vincent Byrne, was taken from his post and put in charge of a pair of prisoners who had been detailed to peel potatoes, and was soon marching them to their tasks under guard. When Seosamh de Brún noticed them passing, he could not help but laugh loudly at the sight of the small-framed Byrne escorting the pair of 6-foot policemen across the building. 'Fancy,' said one Volunteer, 'the ignominy to which two pillars of the most detested force in the British administration in

Ireland had been reduced. Have not the tables turned? The baton no longer holds sway, oh the memories of 1913.'[8]

Up in the towers the rebels were coming under increasingly heavy fire. Machine guns from both Portobello and Dublin Castle were now sending streams of bullets at them. The threat was negligible, however, as long as they held themselves low.

Of far greater concern were the escalating sniper duels being fought against the eagle-eyed riflemen in Portobello. Volunteer Michael Molloy, a compositor by trade who had proudly overseen the printing of the Proclamation, was sent up to one of the towers to add his keen eye to the fray. The first thing he noticed when he scaled the huge ladder to the vantage point was that his fellow snipers were firing down on the Barracks without the use of the powerful field glasses they had. Both the barracks and the canal bridge were a considerable distance from the tower, which left him confused as to how they could possibly hope to hit a target. One enthusiastic rebel was only too happy to impress Molloy with their genius. He explained that the soldiers' shining belt buckles, together with their glinting bayonets, showed them up very distinctly as targets. Fascinated by this, he grabbed the field glasses and watched.

Dubliner Thomas Pugh, meanwhile, was in the rest room and library on the top floor of Jacob's, relaxing with several others in the heat under its glass roof and windows. Suddenly one of the panes shattered, sending men scattering for cover. A sharpshooter had them in his sights. Word was rapidly sent to the towers that there was a sniper in the St Patrick's Park direction.

Ned Lyons, who was on the same tower as Molloy, then changed his direction of fire from Dublin Castle towards the park. He adjusted the sight on his rifle to 300 yards and waited. With his unblinking right eye he scanned the area thoroughly from the length of his gun barrel, while his breathing slowed and his finger rested on the trigger. A nearby Volunteer with field glasses did his best to help but to no avail. The sniper was well hidden. This was a patient man's game. Suddenly, Lyons noticed a slight movement at a distance. He held his breath, paused, and his finger squeezed slightly tighter. A flash of reflected sunlight came from the target area, followed by the loud crack of shot as his weapon recoiled into his shoulder. He had his man.

As the day progressed, the rifle and machine-gun fire became continuous, while extra barricades were set up throughout the ground floor. Barbed wire was spread across the main inner yard. If the enemy managed to break in, he would be made to fight for every inch of ground.

Back on the north side of the city as the sun began to set, word was brought to Captain Frank Henderson and his brother Leo by a scout that they were about to be caught between two large enemy forces, one coming from Drumcondra, and the other from the Malahide Road. The 66 men in total prepared for the fight that would soon be to hand. A short time afterwards, however, word came from James Connolly to retire to the GPO, immediately if possible. Accordingly, they set about pulling out, taking their prisoners with them, and slowly made their way to the city centre.

Things in Jacob's settled down considerably on Tuesday night, where Seosamh de Brún found himself on guard duty. The machine guns and rifle fire had died away almost to nothing in their immediate area, to be replaced with the sounds of armoured cars driving around the dark side streets to reconnoitre the factory positions.

Early the following morning Séamus Pounch was detailed by Michael O'Hanrahan to lead a patrol to obtain supplies of food from the nearby area. He was handed a warrant signed by Commandant MacDonagh, stating that he was an officer of the Irish Republican Army and as such was duly authorised to requisition foodstuffs.

He apprehensively left the factory, knowing that small clusters of enemy troops were scattered around on South Great George's Street and Mercer Street, and also to his south in the Portobello direction. He therefore posted men at each potential contact point, with orders to fire a shot if the enemy appeared. Then he and the remainder of his detail went to Carvey's Shop on Wexford Street, and commandeered a sizeable measure of lard, before they temporarily retraced their steps back towards the biscuit factory. They then turned right into Cuffe Street, where they entered Quinlisk's Store, and liberated sacks of potatoes and several trays of bread. Pounch was delighted with the haul, but realised that he and his men would be unable to carry such a large amount of supplies and defend themselves if attacked. Looking around while his mind searched for solutions, he noticed that a small crowd of civilians had gathered to see what was happening. Pounch and a few men approached; he informed them that they had just been conscripted into service. Luckily, these civilians were a lot more co-operative than those who had recently laid siege to the biscuit factory.

William Oman, the Citizen Army teenager who served in three garrison areas during Easter Week, those being City Hall/Dublin Castle, Jacob's biscuit factory and the Royal College of Surgeons. NIALL OMAN

Pounch and his large convoy returned to Jacob's, where the ever-inquisitive MacBride questioned him regarding the conscripts and seemed to enjoy the story thoroughly. Pounch then asked if he could reward the press-ganged civilians with some bread. 'Two loaves apiece,' was the reply.

After a while, the rifle and machine-gun fire intensified throughout the city, and soon the regular booms of artillery shells were added to the growing din. Those manning Jacob's Peter Street windows began to receive the full attention of the British Lewis gunner in the Bermingham Tower of Dublin Castle. Meanwhile, the snipers in their own huge towers had made Portobello Bridge a no man's land for the British soldiers. To set foot anywhere in the 20 yards between its side rails meant certain death.

By evening, the intensity of fire increased even further, suggesting an attack was imminent. The men were told be on their guard and extra sentries were posted. As they then waited at their positions, many wondered if their time had come. One excitable sentry later rushed into the headquarters room to notify his commanders of a great fire raging somewhere on the north side of the city, from behind the Four Courts. MacBride looked back at the young Volunteer and said 'I think, my boy, you better send for the Fire Brigade.'9

MacBride checked the men's positions. His presence had a soothing effect on those under his command, the trademark of the greatest of tactical military commanders: the ability to calm his men's nerves just by being there.

As night fell, Seosamh de Brún found himself on guard duty in the short corridor that led from the factory's front gate to its machine room. The surrounding echoes of gunfire had died down, with the exception of the snipers from both sides. He was now exhausted and longed for his relief. The creeping silence did little to alleviate his yawns and he resisted the urge to sit, instead pacing up and down. He began thinking, not the best activity for a tired soldier, particularly on night watch. In the event of an enemy attack, his position would bear the brunt, and he alone would be called to fend for the Irish Republic until the arrival of his comrades, no doubt alerted by the gunshots that would have signalled his own demise. He looked at his Lee Enfield rifle and his razor-sharp bayonet and thought, 'What the hell are we fighting for in any case? Can't this damn thing called freedom be achieved in any other ways?' A burst of machine gun fire from Dublin Castle rudely jolted him from his thoughts and he noticed that dawn had arrived. It was now Thursday morning.

Reports came in from Commandant de Valera that the Volunteers manning Westland Row train station were hard pressed and running low on ammunition. MacDonagh decided to send a sortie to relieve the situation. Lieutenant Donal O'Reardon was put in charge of a party of 20 cyclists selected for the task. MacDonagh gave them a short but detailed briefing. Among their number was de Brún, who was not banking on their chances.

De Brún breathed deeply as they left the biscuit factory by an exit on Peter Street. It was the first time he had been outside the building since Monday and the dust-free air felt invigorating. They moved off and by the time they reached St Stephen's Green South they had picked up considerable speed. Their pedals resisted their efforts as they began to climb Lower Leeson Street, but the Irish Volunteers were a fit bunch of men and carried on as if it was nothing, even teasing a comrade named O'Rourke who had two long feathers sticking out from his cap, calling him an Indian Brave. To their disbelief, by the time they reached Fitzwilliam Square not a single shot had been fired in their direction. As they turned down Merrion Street their speed increased to match the downhill gradient, but also led them directly into the sights of the Staffordshire Regiment, who opened fire from the northern end of Merrion Square. The 20 rebels jumped off their bikes to reply in kind. Soon increasing numbers of infantrymen arrived from Lower Mount Street to add to the rate of fire against them. O'Reardon realised it would be suicidal to proceed and ordered a withdrawal.

Using their handguns, they began a fighting retreat, shooting while pedalling for all their worth along Merrion Square South, where the park was to their left. They heard enemy bullets whizzing just inches from their faces as they sped along the length of Fitzwilliam Street, before turning right onto Leeson Street, making once again for St Stephen's Green. As the corner of Harcourt Street came into view, a machine-gunner opened up on them. They pedalled furiously towards York Street, where the College of Surgeons garrison took up the fight on their behalf. O'Reardon shouted out to zigzag, as rounds richocheted off their wheel spokes. Suddenly the man on de Brún's left was hit. They all jumped off their bikes to help while several took up firing positions to cover him. The man initially appeared to have a leg wound, so two comrades carried him back to Jacob's, covered by the others.

When de Brún arrived back at the factory he found Volunteer John O'Grady to be in a more serious condition, having been shot in the groin and the shin. He had lost a tremendous amount of blood and his face had the chalk-white pallor of death. Commandant MacDonagh sent a runner across the road to the Adelaide Hospital to fetch a doctor, who refused to come until forced at gunpoint. When the ill-tempered doctor finally examined O'Grady he announced that there was little hope for the wounded man, but assured them that he would get the best of attention in the Adelaide. A pair of O'Grady's comrades then stretchered him the short distance there, only to return shortly afterwards with the grim news that he had died on admittance.

An hour or so later, William Oman was in the headquarters room with Major MacBride and Commandant MacDonagh when a Volunteer knocked on the door and informed the men that there was a woman at the gate dressed in widow's weeds with an emblem of the Royal Dublin Fusiliers pinned to her coat. She claimed to have a dispatch for the Commandant. MacDonagh ordered the woman to be brought to him. She was blindfolded and escorted in. Oman watched as she was brought forward, before the blindfold, which had covered most of her tiny face, was removed. To his surprise the woman slapped him on the shoulder, saying, 'Hello, Bill'. She was Chris Caffrey, a good friend of his family's, and had just come from the College of Surgeons. She gave MacDonagh the dispatch, which she had carried the short distance inside her mouth, and after having had a quick catch-up with Oman she returned to the College, with a message to Commandant Mallin to expect food and reinforcements.

MacDonagh ordered Oman to assemble the Citizen Army men in Jacob's. As soon as darkness had fallen, half a dozen had gathered on the ground floor, where their number was added to by several Volunteers. All were loaded down with sacks of flour and cakes. Lieutenant O'Reardon would lead the men again. Then, to Oman's surprise, MacDonagh turned to him and told him that he wished to keep him there. Oman replied, 'You are in command, sir.' Just as the men were leaving, however, MacDonagh changed his mind and instructed Oman to proceed with the others. They got to their destination without a hitch, having listened to the city being pounded as they darted between the tightly packed clusters of workshops, pubs and tenement houses lining the narrow streets that led them back to the ranks of their army.

On Friday the roars of the city's impending destruction were almost constant, while the factory's day began as had the previous three, with the sniper and machine-gun fire commencing as soon as the sun had risen. Throughout the day the men carried on with their duties, increasingly apprehensive about the growing uncertainty all around. The men on the towers had a bird's-eye view of the destruction caused by the British artillery. A huge haze of dust and smoke hung in the spring air over the capital, while in the background the constant clatter of battle was audible. The sharpshooters did their best to bring the fight to the enemy, sensing that the showdown was about to happen, and feeling frustrated at their isolation and comparative impotence. Their eyes strained for enemy targets, and periodically a crack rang out, followed by the frustrated curse of a miss, or the cheer for a kill.

As night approached a general alarm sounded, prompting the garrison to jump to readiness. It seemed the time was at hand. The inevitable full-scale assault on their position was viewed with equal measures of eagerness and terror by those who rushed to the barricade overlooking the main gate where the coming attack was expected. Scores of rifles poked out across the sacks of flour, as everyone waited tensely for the explosion that would blow the gates from its hinges. They waited, and waited. No attack came. The men's demeanour fluctuated between relief and frustration as they stood to.

John MacDonagh turned to an elderly bespectacled man at the barricade, having not noticed him in the factory prior to when they had stood shoulder to shoulder together while preparing to face death. MacDonagh asked him when he had arrived. 'I was here from the start,' was the reply. He then asked if he had a family. The man replied that he did, adding, 'I was never able to do much for them, but isn't this the grandest thing I ever could do?' Both men turned their faces and watched the gates again.

A sense of foreboding returned to the garrison on Saturday morning when word came down from the towers that rising numbers of British soldiers were moving into positions around St Patrick's Park. They could also see civilians being removed from the area, and word had come that the Adelaide Hospital was preparing for evacuation. The noticeable lull in the artillery and gunfire from the rest of the city suggested that men and artillery were being moved in their direction. Once again, the men stood to arms. Seosamh de Brún counted his rifle ammunition: 60 rounds. Would it be enough if the building was shelled and they had to fight their way out?

He would have to wait and see.

8

The Four Courts

'You are all going to hell for this.'

Second Lieutenant Godfrey Hunter was at the head of a troop of about 50 mounted cavalrymen of the 5th and 12th Lancers. It was early afternoon on Easter Monday. Their orders were to escort a wagon train of ammunition from North Wall Quay to the Magazine Fort in the Phoenix Park, a journey of about 3 miles. There were four carriages in all. They were completely oblivious to any threat to them until they arrived abreast of the Four Courts, which was to their right as they travelled. They noticed shards of glass from the many broken windows littering the wide pavement outside the building. They then noticed armed men darting about on its roof 40 feet above. As their horses' hooves clattered on the cobbled street, their 26-year-old lieutenant ordered his men to be on their guard.

Volunteer Lieutenant Peadar Clancy quietly told his small squad to make ready. They were manning the half-built barricade where Church Street meets with the quays. Bolts were pulled back on their rifles, there was a soft metallic click as each chamber was filled with a round while the rebels took aim. Their shoulders hugged the metal plates at the end of the long wooden stocks of their guns as tightly as possible, as they squinted along the barrels to line up the sights. Their fingers squeezed slowly on their triggers. In the Four Courts the rebels did the same. They found excellent cover along the roof parapet, and their elevated position

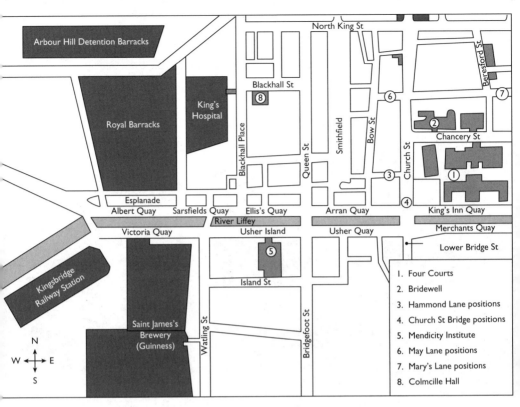

Irish Volunteers 1st Battalion operational zone (Four Courts and surrounding area).

gave them a tremendous advantage over the nervous horsemen passing with increased haste below them.

Clancy's men were first to fire at the head of the troop, followed swiftly by the snipers on the roof. The deafening volleys cut into the cavalrymen from their front, side and from above. Plumes of gun smoke shot from the building's smashed windows as the rounds flew at the soldiers, knocking them from their saddles as both they and their horses fell to the ground screaming under the onslaught. The Volunteers fired again, while Hunter's horsemen tried to rush westward along the quay, only to be driven back while more of their number fell before the rebel guns. Their broken bodies tumbled from their mounts, hitting the ground with tremendous force. Men writhed on the cobblestones, clutching at gashes in limbs and torsos while sparks from bullets peppered the paving close by. The spooked horses scattered about, neighing in terror. There seemed to be no way out: the river was to their left, and to their right the forbidding wrought-iron railings surrounding the Four Courts barred the entrance to the pair of small rectangular enclosures that could have

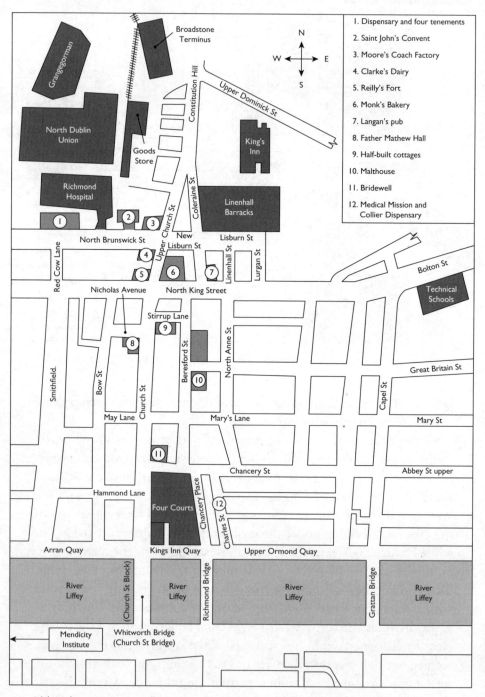

Irish Volunteers 1st Battalion operational zone (North King Street and surrounding area).

provided some temporary cover from Clancy's men and the rooftop snipers.

The rebels fired unrelentingly and without a shred of mercy. Hunter struggled to regain control. He had to turn his four ammunition wagons in a confined space that was becoming increasingly littered with wounded men and horses. He shouted for the drivers to turn and for the cavalrymen to provide return fire, but it was hopeless in the chaos. Hardly a shot was aimed back at the rebels. Some of the Lancers kicked wildly at their horses, galloping forward to where they presented easy targets for Clancy's men. They were cut down and fell before his barricade. Horses were shot as they thrashed in agony on the ground.

The cavalrymen eventually succeeded in turning away from the view of the riflemen at the barricade, but their relief was short-lived. Thomas Smart and five other Volunteers had anticipated their retreat and rushed from the Four Courts' Chancery Place exit to take up position along Ormond Quay. Their shots began to tear into the horsemen as they sought escape. The Lancers made a sudden dash into Charles Street, from where several made a break for the side roads at the back and the left flank of the Four Courts, while Lieutenant Hunter spotted an opportunity.

A three-storey red-bricked building, the Medical Mission, faced the Four Courts' side entrance on Chancery Place and had Charles Street at its rear. Hunter screamed at his men to enter its gates. Once inside he quickly uncoupled the wagons from the horses, which were then let loose. His men unloaded the wagons and barricaded the entrance with them. Defensive positions were then taken up throughout both the Mission and its adjoining buildings.

A number of the men who had not heard his command galloped past the gates of the Mission. Two of them made for the Bridewell police station, where they rushed inside and locked its gates. Their remaining comrades were less fortunate. The sudden chaos had left them lost and leaderless. They cursed loudly as they attempted to navigate the maze of narrow streets and laneways. Shots whined through the warm air from unseen positions. A pair of them reached Church Street, but found themselves hemmed in on all sides by buildings and barricades. They shouted loudly, urging their mounts on, and galloped towards the barricade at the junction of North King Street. This in itself proved difficult, as the ground had been strewn with broken bottles in order to hinder precisely such a charge. One of them pointed his lance towards his increasingly visible enemies while his comrade fired his rifle from the saddle, aiming wildly. One shot hit a two-year-old boy, John Francis Foster, behind the ear as his mother wheeled his pram towards Father Mathew Hall to escape from the sudden danger.

Commandant Edward Daly ordered a volley of shots from the rebel-held barricade. Rifles cracked and boomed and the horseman fell. He was dead before his body hit the ground. His lance-wielding comrade halted before urging his horse forward again. Daly steadied his pistol arm across the shoulder of a Volunteer named Kelly[1] and another shot rang out. The cavalryman slumped forward and fell unceremoniously from the saddle as his now riderless horse charged on, before being brought under control by the rebels. They turned the sweating animal and slapped it hard to make it run back down towards Lower Church Street in order to confuse any more cavalrymen who might follow.

Just yards away, a priest ran out from Father Mathew Hall and grabbed the child from the arms of his screaming mother. He ran with the boy to the nearby Richmond Hospital, desperate to save him, but it was too late. The boy was dead.

Daly's men took the badly wounded Lancer's weapons and ammunition and one of them attached a tricolour flag to his lance. He wedged it into a manhole just outside a nearby pub. Shots rang out into the air in salute while the Lancer was carried by some nearby volunteers to the same hospital as the boy.

Meanwhile, Lieutenant Hunter's cavalrymen prepared their positions in the Medical Mission, and waited.

Shortly before they had received their bloody nose at the hands of the insurgents, Commandant Daly, a 25-year-old native of County Limerick, and the youngest of the Irish Volunteers bearing that rank, had mustered his men of 1st Battalion in the grounds of Colmcille Hall on Blackhall Place. This sat just to the north of the River Liffey about half a mile to the west of the Four Courts. It was shortly after midday on Easter Monday.

Daly's second in command, 35-year-old Vice Commandant Piaras Béaslaí stood next to him as he addressed approximately 120 men. Their numbers were severely depleted, but Daly expected that many more from their 400-strong battalion would eventually show up once the fighting had started. He outlined the mighty endeavour that lay ahead of them, before suggesting that anyone who felt the task was too great should step

The Medical Mission on Chancery Place, where Lieutenant Hunter's Lancers sought refuge. Its facade came under heavy fire during the fighting around the Four Courts. MILITARY ARCHIVES

out. At this, two men walked slowly forward from the line. They were relieved of their weapons. Before they set off, they wished their former comrades the best of luck, but insisted nevertheless that they were all mad.

The battalion's objectives that afternoon consisted of taking and holding a number of positions in the area surrounding Dublin's Four Courts, a hugely imposing building that dated back to the late 18th century, and dominated the north quays to the west of the rebel headquarters in Sackville Street. To consolidate the battalion's hold on the area, various outposts would be occupied while barricades were constructed in the surrounding streets. The area to the north, consisting of North Brunswick Street, North King Street, and the approaches to Dublin's northern suburbs via Broadstone and Phibsboro, were to be taken and held. This would facilitate an escape from the city should the Volunteers need to withdraw in that direction and link up with their 5th Battalion, under Commandant Thomas Ashe, which would be fighting in the surrounding countryside.

Their overall strategy was to prevent the military from sending reinforcements to the city centre from its north-west. This would not be an easy task due to the large numbers of British Army barracks located in their proximity, not to mention the large numbers of troops that would inevitably arrive by train in the nearby Kingsbridge Railway Station once word of the insurrection had spread.

Daly had proved himself to be an excellent tactician during the many Volunteer preparations and manoeuvres that preceded the Rising, and despite the obvious apprehension he felt when faced with such a heavy responsibility that day with so few men, he set them to their tasks with methodical efficiency. Their objectives were quickly taken.

First to fall to them was the Four Courts, when 20 or so Volunteers under Captain Frank Fahy and Lieutenant Joseph McGuinness stormed its Chancery Place entrance. Thomas Smart initially held the guard there at pistol-point while the rebels rushed inside to consolidate the huge building.[2] Windows and doors were barricaded with anything that was within reach: tables, chairs and benches were piled up against its entrances. The windows were smashed in with rifle butts and then reinforced with benches, doors, and with hundreds of leather-bound books that were discovered in the archives and administrative rooms. The many inner staircases were blocked off, leaving just enough room for Volunteers to pass, but allowing them to be quickly sealed in the event of the building being stormed by the enemy. A first-aid post was set up. The building's inner chambers and long corridors, normally thronged with those wearing horsehair wigs and sombre gowns, echoed to the sounds of breaking glass and the clatter of footsteps rushing to and fro with the heavy equipment to construct the defences of their newly found fortress.

As soon as the raising of a tricolour flag on its roof signalled that the Four Courts had been secured, Vice Commandant Béaslaí deployed the other sections to their positions, while Daly set up his headquarters in Saint John's Convent on North Brunswick Street. Many weapons had been deposited in safe houses throughout the area in the preceding weeks, and a section of men were handed the addresses and instructed to gather up the small arsenal.

Father Mathew Hall, a large red-brick building situated at the junction of Church Street and Nicholas Avenue, was next to be taken by the insurgents, and was immediately converted into a supply post and field hospital, while outside, the first of a formidable series of barricades began to take shape across Church Street: paving slabs were dug up with crowbars, while local buildings were pillaged of their contents and a nearby builders' yard also proved very useful.

Captain Fionán Lynch, the 27-year-old in charge of F Company, ordered a barricade to be built on Upper Church Street with mattresses, bedsteads and furniture taken from surrounding houses, along with pallets and sacks of grain from the nearby Monk's Bakery. Five hundred yards to the south, Lieutenant Peadar Clancy oversaw the construction of another barricade at Church Street's junction with the quays. This was reinforced with carts and other vehicles, as well as furniture and the contents of several nearby pubs.

The men of G Company under Captain Nicholas Laffan built several more across North Brunswick Street, and occupied many of the surrounding buildings, which they fortified in the usual manner, barricading doors and windows and knocking tunnels into walls with picks and axes. Soon afterwards, Volunteer Liam O'Carroll and several men from A Company took position in the Richmond Hospital Dispensary, across the road from Red Cow Lane. They built a pair of barricades on either end of the lane, and another across its width. Laffan, meanwhile, set up his company headquarters in Moore's Coachworks on the junction of North Brunswick Street and Church Street. His men simultaneously occupied Clarke's Dairy, just across the narrow street to his south.

Numerous other barricades were erected hastily around the small clusters of surrounding road junctions that would soon bear witness to some of the most vicious street fighting yet seen by a modern army.

On the eastern side of North King Street, one was built outside Langan's pub on the corner of Coleraine Street. Beer barrels, tables and chairs as well as nearby vehicles were used. Section Commander Tom Sheeran then ordered his unit to take up positions inside the pub and to fortify it. Next, he ordered them to help with the construction of another two barricades, one across Coleraine Street and another on Lisburn Street. Local residents watched this activity and many of them shouted curses and insults at the insurgents.

At the junction of Church Street and the western stretch of North King Street was a pub named Reilly's, which would soon become known as 'Reilly's Fort'. Lieutenant Jack Shouldice of F Company, from Ballaghaderreen in County Roscommon, and his group of half a dozen men took up position there. Using the building as a base they then placed another barricade, employing much of the pub's contents, across North King Street, completely sealing off the junction. From the four floors of Reilly's they had a commanding view of the lower end of Church Street and in particular the eastern side of North King Street; this latter fact would have lethal consequences for their enemies in the days and nights ahead. Diagonally across the road junction from Reilly's, Frank McCabe and a small section took position to cover Shouldice's rear. From their building's upper floors they aimed to hinder and prevent any attack from the Smithfield direction to their west.

In the midst of these rebel positions stood the Bridewell police station. The Lancers' frantic dash into the building had not gone unnoticed by Lieutenant McGuinness in the Four Courts. He ordered Michael Flanagan to assemble a squad to root them out. Shortly afterwards, the lock of the main gate was shot out, and the rebels stormed inside. The two Lancers and 23 policemen were swiftly locked in the building's cells in its basement.[3]

On the opposite side of the river, on Usher's Island, members of D Company, which had been seconded to the GPO garrison, set up a small blocking post in the Mendicity Institute, a refuge for the homeless. The Volunteers there, under the command of 25-year-old Dubliner Captain Seán Heuston, had been ordered by Commandant Connolly to hinder any troop movements into the city while the other Volunteer battalions and Citizen Army units embedded themselves in their chosen positions. The building was expected to hold out for three to four hours once the enemy counter-attack began in earnest.

When the outposts were secure, the rebels began to occupy strategic buildings such as Monk's Bakery, which overlooked the Church Street/ North King Street junction. Many other houses and buildings were occupied, much to the disdain of their residents who suddenly found themselves homeless and forced to rely on help from their neighbours in their own overcrowded dwellings. Abuse was heaped upon many of the Volunteers by the wives and families of soldiers from the very regiments Daly's men were preparing to fight. At one point, the local residents had to be held back at bayonet point while they vented their fury at the men who were holding Monk's.

Any occupied building was rapidly and efficiently adapted for defence. Small holes were bored into walls allowing snipers the benefit of unseen vantage points, while tunnels were dug between buildings to allow covered movement between them for both men and supplies. The entire area soon became a warren of carefully crafted defensive positions. Set in a streetscape such as this it presented a potential nightmare to an attacker.

Shortly after the Lancers had been driven from the quays, Volunteer Joseph MacDonagh was helping to build a barricade in Hammond Lane, a narrow roadway sitting between the west wing of the Four Courts and Smithfield. Father O'Callaghan, a local priest from Saint Paul's Church on Arran Quay, could see nothing but evil in the actions of the men who had unleashed such destruction upon the cavalrymen, and who appeared to be preparing to repeat the carnage on a much grander scale. He approached MacDonagh's position on foot, pointing towards the scene of the ambush, shouting, 'You are all going to Hell for this!'

Captain Seán Heuston and his 12 Volunteers across the river had clearly heard the repeated volleys of shots from the Four Courts which had so recently dispersed the Lancers. He did not have to wait long for his own turn to fire his weapon. Shortly after 12.30 p.m. he shouted to his men to prepare themselves. To his west, approximately 400 men of the 10th Battalion Royal Dublin Fusiliers, under Lieutenant Colonel Esmonde, had just been given urgent orders to advance from the Royal Barracks on Benburb Street to the relief of Dublin Castle, and having accomplished this, to recapture City Hall from the clutches of the Irish Citizen Army.

Their advance column, consisting of just over 100 troops, left the huge barracks via its main gate and marched eastwards along Ellis Quay, directly across the Liffey from Heuston's position in the Mendicity Institute. As they entered Heuston's rifle sights, 34-year-old Lieutenant Gerald Neilan drew his sword to order a charge. Two shots rang out from across the river, one of which hit him in the face. Heuston blew his whistle. A broadside volley then thundered from the Mendicity Institute, as 13 or so bullets smashed into the ranks of soldiers who had not been able to pinpoint the source of the shots that had taken down their officer. Several fell wounded close to the dying figure of Lieutenant Neilan, whose younger brother Arthur, ironically, was a Volunteer serving in the Four Courts.[4]

The 10th Dublin Fusiliers were a well-trained battalion, and their initial shock was quashed by the discipline of their training. They

Captain Sean Heuston of D Company 1st Battalion Irish Volunteers, and also a prominent Na Fianna member. The 26 men under his command fought a ferocious battle against overwhelming odds in the Mendicity Institute on Dublin's south quays, even hurling live hand grenades back at their attackers. NATIONAL LIBRARY OF IRELAND

crouched en masse behind the 4-foot-high river wall and returned fire as best they could. They were, however, unable to advance any further. The Mendicity Institute was quite a large building with many well-concealed firing positions on its upper floors.

Esmonde was quick to react. He called for his remaining men and for his machine-gun sections to provide immediate support. Three hundred troops poured from the rear entrance of the barracks on to Arbour Hill. From here they advanced downhill along the narrow road towards Blackhall Place and Benburb Street, under the gaze of local residents who looked out from their red-brick terraced houses and quaint cottages. The machine-gunners took position in the buildings close to Queen Street Bridge. Heuston, along with his small group, prepared for their attack. Heuston himself took position in a window that overlooked the bridge, accompanied by Volunteer Patrick Stephenson. They primed their canister bombs.

The Fusiliers soon opened up with a salvo of machine-gun and rifle fire. Heuston's men ducked as stray bullets whined through the air and shards of granite were sent flying. The loud, echoing staccato of the machine guns terrified the local civilians, many of whom clasped rosary beads. Lieutenant Charles Grant, leading the advance, then used the cover of the guns to rush across the bridge with his infantrymen.

Heuston and Stephenson saw them coming. They held the fuses of the canister bombs over burning candles as they prepared to light and hurl them. Stephenson cursed to himself, however, when he saw that the flame would not take: the fuses would not light. Stephenson muttered angrily that the best they could hope for was to injure an enemy soldier with the sheer weight of the impotent projectile.

Then, to their surprise, the soldiers made an unexpected left turn eastwards onto the south quays. The remaining troops followed suit. The rebels managed a few token shots, but their aim was inaccurate due their enemy's incessant covering fire. A sharp-eyed spotter quickly and capably directed the British gunners' aim at any hint of movement from the institute's barricaded windows and made it almost impossible for the men inside to raise their heads.

Captain Heuston realised that the British Army at present had a more pressing target in sight than his small outpost. He also knew that a thorn in their side such as the Mendicity Institute would not be left unchecked by the military for long. He set his men to reinforcing the position, following which they checked their ammunition supplies. The disconcerting realisation that their canister bombs were all but useless made it clear that every round would count.

For the remainder of the afternoon and evening, the area of the Four Courts was deathly quiet, apart from the odd rifle crack. The Irish Volunteers continued to dig in, their strength added to by increasing numbers of their comrades who were steadily and stealthily filtering into the area. Vice Commandant Béaslaí ensured that all newcomers were properly directed to effective defensive positions, where they sighted their zones of fire, checked their equipment and did their best to deal with the excitement and the terrifying magnitude of what had been unleashed against the world's mightiest empire. Civilians huddled apprehensively in cold and crowded tenement houses, while the Lancers in the Medical Mission waited for relief under the menacing gaze of the rebels in the east wing of the Four Courts.

Shortly after midnight, a small British outfit used the cover of darkness to transport a much-needed ammunition wagon from the

Royal Hospital in Kilmainham to Dublin Castle. The first mile or so of their journey was uneventful. They whispered quietly to one another as they continued their manoeuvre along the southern quays heading eastwards, having successfully avoided detection by the Volunteer sentries in the nearby Mendicity Institute.

As a soft drizzle fell on their faces their hopes of the trip continuing peacefully were shattered by a fusillade from the far side of the river. Peadar Clancy's men had seen them coming despite the darkness. The 27-year-old Lieutenant from County Clare shouted at his men to open fire from their positions around their barricade. They let loose on the soldiers with everything they had. The cement and brick of the relatively low river wall on the southern quay that covered the crouching troops was sent flying under the impacts of the high-calibre bullets. The wagon was hopelessly exposed. The men who had been trying to manoeuvre it through the melee of flying metal were forced to abandon both it and its cargo.

For Clancy's men the increasing daylight at roughly 4 a.m brought with it a chance to examine the contents of the wagon. To their delight they found several dozen Enfield Rifles and thousands of rounds of ammunition.

Tuesday morning heralded a day unlike any other in living memory for the citizens of Dublin. Twenty-four hours earlier the city had been preparing for a warm and relaxed Easter holiday. Now they woke to the unknown. As thousands of local civilians roused themselves from their restless night, rumours abounded about similar rebellions breaking out all over the country. Divisions of German infantry were expected to be landing on remote beaches throughout the island to support the uprising. No possibility or conspiracy seemed too far-fetched or improbable.

In the Mendicity Institute, Captain Heuston's men were beginning to run low on food. Heuston had, after all, been ordered to hold the position for a few hours at best, but seizing the initiative, he had decided to hold it indefinitely. He sent word of his decision for the approval of Commandant Connolly in the GPO, and requested reinforcements and supplies should that approval be forthcoming.

Volunteer Seán McLoughlin was used as a runner and, with characteristic enthusiasm, returned several hours later with an additional 12 men, having carefully led them westward through the back streets.[5]

Heuston's lookouts observed them cautiously making their way along the north quays towards the bridge below and prepared to give covering fire as they approached. Luckily, their crossing turned out to be uneventful. They filtered across the river in small groups and succeeded in avoiding the attention of the British machine-gunners. Soon McLoughlin introduced Volunteer Lieutenant Dick Coleman to Heuston, who warmly welcomed the officer and his men. Coleman's unit had brought plenty of ammunition with them, but food was still in short supply.

Later that afternoon, at the northern end of the 1st Battalion's operational area, the British managed to install a battery of two 18-pounder field-guns inside the grounds of Grangegorman Hospital close to its Medical Officer's Residency. The sights on these guns, which formed the very backbone of the Royal Field Artillery, were then trained on the barricade that had been built to traverse the North Circular Road, close to its Charleville Road junction, between Cabra and Phibsboro. This position was manned by 30 Volunteers from B Company, under the command of Captain James Sullivan. It overlooked the railway line from Broadstone, and several rebels, one of whom was an engineer, had been dispatched by Sullivan to blow up its tracks. If this measure was successful it would prevent troop reinforcements using the Kingsbridge–Amiens Street line, which also ran partially beneath Phoenix Park.

This barricade held the utmost importance in terms of the necessity for the battalion to hold open a northbound route through the Phibsboro area. It would allow the entire Volunteer army in Dublin an escape route from the city should they become overwhelmed by enemy forces in the capital. Fifteen to twenty men manned the barricade itself, while others, including the unit's best sharpshooters, were positioned in vantage points throughout the gardens of the nearby houses, where they took up positions around their concrete steps overlooking the approaches to the barricade.

The first salvo of 84-millimetre shells from the British artillery unleashed a terrific burst of shrapnel directly above the heads of Sullivan's men who fell to the ground, shocked by the assault of red-hot flying metal. Nearby windows shattered and local residents ran screaming for their basements. The quiet suburb was hurled into panic and chaos as another salvo exploded into the air. Hundreds of razor-sharp, bullet-sized chunks of shrapnel flew at terrific speed, slicing into the trees behind which several rebels had sought shelter. Sullivan's terrified men made their bodies as small as possible and held their arms over their heads, instinctively shielding their half-shattered eardrums from the deafening bangs that accompanied the lethal torrent. The windows of the houses that did not initially succumb to the explosions now shattered under a hellish hailstorm of shrapnel that ripped into the bedrooms and parlours of the suburban homes. The Volunteers were pinned to the ground beneath the repeated blasts.

The stretch of road between Prussia Street and St Peter's Church was witnessing a scene more familiar to those living in towns throughout north-eastern France and Belgium than a peaceful and well-to-do suburb of Dublin inhabited primarily by professionals and prosperous families. However, it suited the experiences of the Royal Dublin Fusiliers, whose mission it now was to remove the rebels from their fortification. As shrapnel tore into the barricade they crept forward from their positions near Prussia Street and moved from garden to garden, dashing from one position of cover to another, until they closed on the barricade. The artillery ceased abruptly. The Fusiliers charged at the barricade.

A hundred or so troops rushed the fortification, screaming like possessed demons as they ran with their bayonets pointed at Sullivan's men who had now begun to recover from their initial shock. The rebels fired again and again at the advancing khaki-uniformed men who zigzagged as they rushed ever closer, until the ferocity of the Volunteers' fire forced them into nearby gardens for cover. The rebels struggled to contain the furious assault of the Fusiliers until their sharpshooters began to take their toll and swung the balance. The barricade held.

Sullivan briefly checked his position. His wounded were moved from around the barricade into nearby gardens and placed with their backs to the sets of steps that shielded them from the violence. There they were given first aid and cigarettes, while those who had not been wounded prepared to face the same hell once again.

The Fusiliers charged a second time, following another brief salvo of deafening shrapnel bursts, but the replying rebel fire once again stalled their advance. Nevertheless, the barricade was beginning to show the strain. A prolonged silence developed, broken only by the odd shot that accompanied the taunts and insults that now flew in both directions. The vulnerability of his position to artillery fire was emphasised to Sullivan by another salvo of shells which finally convinced him that the position was no longer tenable.

He arranged for a small rearguard to remain in place while he prepared his men's escape towards Glasnevin. They moved out towards Phibsboro, passing St Peter's Church, before taking a sharp left and turning through the many lanes and back streets at the rear of the northern section of Phibsboro Road. They came under fire as they emerged on to Connaught Street, however, and Sullivan became separated from his men. He was forced to go to ground in a laneway.

The remainder eventually resurfaced from the red-brick terraces at Cross Guns Bridge, which straddles the Royal Canal, before they pressed on along Prospect Road. Once there, they found themselves pursued and harried by several small but determined squads of military whose shots zipped past their ears as they ran.

They soon reached Glasnevin Cemetery. Once inside, they crouched behind tombstones to shoot back. After a time their pursuers gave up, allowing B Company's breathless men to escape. Their rearguard surrendered after a brief firefight and were taken prisoner. Sullivan reached the GPO the following morning, having successfully avoided many military patrols.

As the afternoon wore on, Commandant Daly decided that his headquarters would be better situated in Father Mathew Hall, as it was more central to his operational zone. As soon as the new location was suitably adapted he consulted with Piaras Béaslaí. The pair assessed what had happened so far, 24 hours into the rebellion, and felt that things overall were progressing quite satisfactorily. The battalion was now well entrenched, more and more Volunteers were turning up, and there were adequate supplies of food, medical supplies and ammunition.

Daly's main concern was with the proximity of the Broadstone railway terminus, a quarter of a mile to his north. When Seán Howard had arrived earlier with a dispatch from Captain Sullivan, indicating that he would have to abandon the North Circular Road positions, Daly realised it was imperative that they take the terminus before the British did. Denying the enemy the use of a railway station had obvious military advantages, but Broadstone's elevation would also afford its occupiers a panoramic view of his positions. He had originally planned to capture it the previous day, but was prevented from doing so by his battalion's unexpectedly low turnout. As soon as their meeting was finished, Daly ordered a section of a dozen men under Captain Denis O'Callaghan to perform an initial reconnaissance there.

Captain O'Callaghan soon set off with his men, including Volunteers Garry Holohan and Eamon Martin, both of whom had been involved in the storming of the Magazine Fort the previous day. They cautiously made their way up the gently ascending hill towards the terminus via Nugent's Lane. Distant pops of gunshot could be heard throughout the city. The men eventually reached the concrete gates of the railway terminus. Holohan suddenly saw a khaki-clad figure flit across the entrance to its large administrative building. He signalled to the men behind to take firing positions. Eamon Martin moved up beside Holohan just as a shot rang out from the terminus. His weapon fell from his hands and Holohan saw his friend stagger back several steps before collapsing, having been hit in the side. Martin groaned as he fell and lost consciousness, while Holohan and the others scrambled for cover on the ground and prepared to fire back. The building appeared to be occupied in strength by the military, who had filtered in the previous night. A heavy shoot-out developed during which Volunteer Seán Moore, with apparently suicidal courage, ran under fire across 50 yards of open ground to the doorway of the building and glanced inside, where he saw large numbers of Dublin Fusiliers in well-placed firing positions. He then sprinted back to inform his captain, who quickly ordered a fighting retreat. The station would be left to the military.

The rebels on the roof of Moore's Coachworks just beneath the terminus on North Brunswick Street aimed their rifles carefully at the puffs of smoke that betrayed the location of the British in the terminus providing covering fire for their retreating comrades. Garry Holohan's brother Patrick was among those furiously emptying their rifle magazines over the heads of the Volunteers who retreated in good order, carrying their heavily bleeding comrade. They ran in short bursts, while several turned briefly to add to the covering fire. They made it back to North Brunswick Street, with the exception of one man, Seán Cody, who became separated from the main body, having apparently been singled out by British riflemen firing from the King's Inns building.

As the bullets thumped into the ground around Cody's feet and whizzed by his head he was forced to seek cover in a side street. A local woman beckoned him to her flat on the top floor of a house. He took up a position in a window and began firing at the soldiers he could see crouching behind piles of railway sleepers and in the engine sheds of the terminus. He swiftly used up his ammunition, firing furiously at the troops who could not pinpoint the source of the fire. As he made his escape onto the street below the Fusiliers realised that the house was being used by an enemy rifleman and they peppered it with dozens of Enfield rounds, while Cody made his escape to rejoin the Volunteers on North Brunswick Street. From here several dozen of them trained their rifles back to the scene of the recent firefight hoping to catch any would-be pursuers in the open. The troops, however, had been ordered to hold a cordon at the terminus. There would be no pursuit. For now at least, it appeared that any threat to Daly's north could be contained. Eamon Martin was rushed to Richmond Hospital for treatment.

The Volunteers had thus far displayed a tenacity that was soon to become the curse of the young British soldiers who were hastily being assembled on the far side of the Irish Sea and whose unfortunate job it would be to dislodge them. The Volunteers' line of retreat, however, was now gone. Before the bulk of British reinforcements had set sail from Liverpool, their military cordon on the city's north side was successfully in place.

Commandant Daly's immediate priority was to contain the situation. He spent Tuesday evening and night securing his positions, and concentrated his defences to his north along the east-to-west axis of North Brunswick Street. His battalion looked forward to the third day of the Irish Republic with some optimism. Their numbers were steadily increasing and the men and women had proven up to the job so far. The setback of losing their hold on the Phibsboro area was compensated for by the growing belief that without artillery support, the Crown forces would struggle to cope with the well-drilled street-fighting tactics of the Volunteer army as a whole.

Just before dawn on Wednesday, Seán McLoughlin was preparing to venture out once again from the Mendicity Institute on a mission to find some much needed food supplies with Patrick Stephenson. They made their way to the GPO. The 26 men they left behind alternated their duties in shifts. Those who were not on watch duty did their best to sleep, their hunger growing by the hour.

Later that morning, several rebels approached the Linenhall Barracks gate, on Coleraine Street, and began smashing its massive door with sledgehammers. Captain O'Callaghan, who had led the reconnaissance on Broadstone terminus, and his men took up firing positions at the building's main gate. Inside the building were 29 British Army Pay Corps clerks and a solitary policeman. They initially refused O'Callaghan's demand to surrender, until several canister bombs were lobbed at them. These men were not combat troops and were, in any case, hopelessly cut off. They were escorted to Father Mathew Hall as prisoners. O'Callaghan then searched the building, and decided to set it ablaze, as he did not have nearly enough men to occupy it. Cans of oil and flammable paint were poured throughout the building before it was set alight. The inferno spread to nearby buildings and could be seen for miles.

Captain Laffan, meanwhile, had become greatly concerned that his positions in North Brunswick Street were at risk of being cut in two due to the recent southbound advances made by the Dublin Fusiliers from the North Circular Road and Broadstone. The prospect of their artillery pounding his positions also greatly disturbed him. He ordered a barricade to be placed at the southern end of the tunnel connecting Upper and Lower Grangegorman, assuming that this route would be used by the enemy in the event of an assault. Soon afterwards, a skirmish erupted between his men around the tunnel and Fusiliers who had been sent to harass them, until the unexpected arrival of the Master of the nearby North Dublin Union put a stop to the shooting. Captain Laffan, having listened to the master's pleas for a ceasefire, ordered his men not to fire their weapons towards the heavily populated Union unless they came under a direct assault.

Commandant Daly at this point had adopted a fully defensive posture. He began to strengthen and reinforce his positions in the North King Street and Church Street areas. He appeared to sense what was coming.

Back across the river things had begun to heat up. Since shortly after dawn, approximately 300 Dublin Fusiliers had established themselves in the many buildings and narrow side streets between Watling Street, Thomas Street and the Mendicity Institute. Small squads of men had been ordered to tunnel through the walls of the buildings that adjoined the rebel-held position. Infantry privates and NCOs waited tensely for their officers to order them forward.

On the stroke of midday the machine-gunners on Queen Street once again unleashed a torrent of lead. The rebels' hunger was instantly forgotten as their survival instinct took over. They threw themselves on the floors of the Mendicity Institute to avoid the stream of bullets that drummed against its thick brickwork and smashed into the inner walls and ceilings, knocking plaster and dust everywhere.

The gunners ceased firing to allow their assault troops to close in. The rebels were quick to react. They sprang to their barricaded vantage points as if practising a well-drilled ambush tactic. Wild shooting was then let loose from the Institute's windows as they struggled to contain the military's multi-directional assault. The surrounded rebels fired like madmen. Those with Lee-Enfield Rifles slid their bolts forward and backward at speed and reloaded a magazine after every ten shots, mimicking the 'mad minute' method of firing practised by the best infantrymen, who could fire 15 to 20 rounds per minute, given the proper motivation, and motivation was not found wanting in the building where 26 now faced 300.

The intense fighting dragged on with the military gaining ground as their weight of numbers inevitably allowed them to press forward. Soon they were close enough to pull the pins on their Mills bombs (hand grenades) which they then hurled at the Institute's windows. The assailants were horrified when several of the hissing, fist-sized fragmentation grenades came hurtling back at them – picked up and thrown back by the desperate rebels – before exploding among the clusters of troops who had been preparing to follow the echoing detonations with rushing bayonets. One of the British bombs landed on the Mendicity' Institute's floor next to Liam Staines, who picked it up and threw it back, but just after it left his hand a terrific blast sent both him and Richard Balfe flying. Balfe appeared to be dead. Back outside, the advancing troops found themselves temporarily stunned. They soon regrouped and launched another attack which met similar fierce resistance and after a time it too finally stalled.

A lull then developed, allowing both sides to regroup. Weapons were reloaded and checked while parched men gulped water from their canteens. Soon the machine guns barked angrily again. The building was peppered as before while the rebels waited, their tired minds tortured with the prospect of imminent death. The waiting was unbearable, and the tension was aggravated by the sound of hammering coming from the walls all around. They expected holes to appear at any moment, followed by enraged enemy troops.

They did not have to wait long till the next assault. The Fusiliers rushed from several directions at once and the insurgents darted from position to position doing their best to force them back. All the while the attackers drew ever closer in spite of their mounting casualties.

The rebels, on the other hand, were spared heavy losses, such was the effectiveness of their fortification.

Fearing that the position would be overrun, the Volunteer captain shouted the order to prepare to evacuate. He gathered some men to check the Island Street exit. This had been planned to facilitate their escape to the area around the Guinness Brewery and from there to the South Dublin Union. As soon as they reached the exit they came under heavy fire. Heuston did not hesitate. He ordered his men to lay down their arms: the time had come to spare them from a massacre. A ceasefire was then arranged while the Volunteers took time to destroy their weapons before marching out of the Island Street gate under a white flag.

Volunteers McLoughlin and Stephenson, who had left the Mendicity Institute earlier to find food, arrived back on Arran Quay while the British were launching their first attack. The two Volunteers were unable to cross the bridge to join their comrades. Laden down with sacks of food, they concealed themselves in an alley and watched the assault unfold. Realising that the sheer weight of the attack made the Mendicity Institute's position untenable, they slipped back to the Four Courts to warn Commandant Daly of what would be coming his way. They left the sacks of food in the alley, and eventually returned to the GPO the following day.

This, however, was not the end of the drama at the Mendicity Institute. After the last men had left the building carrying their wounded, a rifle discharge from a British private killed 40-year-old Volunteer Peter Wilson. What had been a relatively calm capitulation erupted suddenly into fury. The surrendering rebels hurled venomous accusations at their captors who, in turn, harassed and threatened their prisoners. They demanded to know how many more of them were hiding inside the Institute, refusing to believe that such a small force had held the position for the best part of three days. Their officers entered the fray and quickly regained control. They ordered the building to be searched, and when satisfied that everything was as it seemed, instructed their men to escort the small garrison to the Royal Hospital with their hands above their heads.

With Heuston now out of the way, the military were able to seize control of the buildings on the southern side of the river. They began inching their way eastwards along the quays until they were in position almost directly opposite the Four Courts. The inhabitants of the buildings did their best to stay out of the way of the well-armed and highly agitated Dublin Fusiliers. The fact that they were named after Ireland's capital did not mean that all its rank and file were from either the city or county. A sizeable number came from the surrounding counties while more came from Ulster. Others came from Britain, and had little time for their adversaries or the Dublin citizens, many of whom they believed to be rebel sympathisers. The irony of this was that thousands of relatives of the same civilians were fighting alongside their own comrades in a no less bloody field of conflict, for a cause they felt to be no less patriotic, and a great deal worthier.

At roughly the same time, Volunteer Lieutenant Liam O'Carroll from A Company was carrying out inspections in the east wing of the Four Courts, having rested for a couple of hours following another check on the North King Street positions.

He and his men were alerted by the sight of an ambulance parked on the opposite side of the river to their east at the junction of Essex Quay and Wood Quay. A faint, curious but disconcerting digging noise could be heard from behind it. O'Carroll decided not to take any chances. He unslung his rifle from his shoulder and opened fire on the vehicle. Several shots rang out in quick succession before he saw the ambulance speeding away, revealing a field gun pointing directly at the Four Courts.

A huge puff of smoke belched from the muzzle of the gun less than a second before the three-storey wall outside O'Carroll's position was struck by its shell. The blast shook the entire room while those inside fell to the floor, scrambling for cover. O'Carroll looked around, completely stunned. Seconds later, another deafening explosion rocked the building.

Con O'Donovan and another Volunteer were in the room directly beneath O'Carroll when the second shell flew through its unmanned window. It hit the wall inside and exploded. O'Donovan and his comrade fell to the floor under the impact. As both men lay helplessly under the collapsing ceiling they wondered if they were still alive. Nothing could be seen but fine white clouds of cement dust. Shouting could be heard from above, but the ringing in both men's ears made it sound distant and faint. O'Carroll shouted through a hole in the ceiling: 'Are you alive down there?'

The lieutenant then bellowed to his fellow marksmen in the nearby rooms to open fire. Several volleys were shot across the river, causing sparks to fly from the metal plate armour of the drab-green field gun. The artillerymen quickly abandoned it to seek shelter in Exchange

Lieutenant Peadar Clancy, 1st Battalion Irish Volunteers, was heavily involved in the constant rifle fire around the Four Courts/Church Street area. He was instrumental in seeing off a troop of British Lancers on Easter Monday. He succeeded in capturing a huge haul of much-needed arms and ammunition that same night. His behaviour on Wednesday 26 April at Church Street Bridge, when he led an almost suicidal assault, completely bewildered his enemies. NATIONAL LIBRARY OF IRELAND

Street. O'Carroll and the other rebels looked on with relief. Marksmen were ordered to keep their sights trained on the gun.

As Wednesday evening drew on, the sniper fire aimed at the Four Courts began to intensify steadily. Fusiliers in houses they had recently occupied provided a source of considerable harassment to the Volunteers. The British also placed snipers in the bell tower of Christchurch Cathedral, and in the Sacred Heart Church on Merchant's Quay, directly across the river from the pillars of the Four Courts. Soon Peadar Clancy's men at the Church Street barricade came under fire from the concealed riflemen in the bell tower. The troops who now filled the upper floors in the terraces of houses on Usher's Quay added to the pressure.

By early evening, Clancy's frustration was beginning to show. Any movement was met with the crack of an enemy rifle. His men regularly peered through small gaps in their barricade to identify enemy positions, but any attempt to engage them was met with a spray of metal and wooden splinters sent up from the structure as rounds smashed into it. The rate of fire continued to grow, suggesting their post was being softened up for an attack. Soon he had had enough.

To the utter astonishment of their enemies, Clancy and Thomas Smart climbed over their own barricade carrying cans filled with petrol. They sprinted across Church Street Bridge as the soldiers on its far side began firing at them. Several bullets smashed into the ground around the pair but failed to hit either them or the containers of fuel, which would have instantaneously turned them into human fireballs. When they reached the southern end of the bridge, they sheltered temporarily by its side walls before making a mad dash across the open stretch of road, again under intense fire. They managed to pour the petrol from the cans through the ground-floor windows of the nearest house facing them, and set the fuel alight.

The fire blazed up as Clancy and Smart ran for their lives back across the bridge, again attracting volleys of bullets. They managed to climb back across their barricade to safety. Astonishingly, neither of them had received so much as a scratch during the suicidal action. No. 1 Usher's Quay was rapidly consumed by roaring flames, as noxious plumes of thick smoke gushed from its roof and windows.

The flames swiftly spread to the next two houses in the terrace and soon the British riflemen were fleeing from the entire block. The intense heat and choking black smoke rendered all of their vantage points from Usher's Quay to St Augustine Street unusable. Any plan to cross the bridge was abandoned. The first three houses were completely destroyed in the flames and eventually collapsed, leaving the road strewn with rubble.

Meanwhile, at the opposite end of the Four Courts, on Chancery Place, the Medical Mission was being sized up by the rebels with a view to removing the Lancers who had occupied the position since Monday and were proving to be a nuisance. The cavalrymen had left the North Wall to escort the wagons on the Easter bank holiday with very little by way of rations and had not been able to grab any sleep. Most of their horses had bolted after being let loose by their riders who had rushed for cover in the Medical Mission, and the animals who remained were suffering from lack of food and water and the maddening strain of constant gunfire. Some had been wounded and had to be shot, a grim task for those ordered to carry it out. Any opportunity to repay their tormentors was seized with great determination and energy, and the horsemen proved a significant threat to any man who carelessly presented himself through the few exposed sections of the Four Courts' barricaded windows.

The rebels spent a great deal of time improvising a large bomb, and planned to place it as close to the Mission as possible. They initially manoeuvred it to the inside of the Four Courts' Chancery Place gates, before loosing a ferocious broadside of covering fire from the entire east-facing wing of the building, which enabled several men to cross the road unhindered. The red-brick facade of the Medical Mission began to disintegrate as the bullets riddled it. The noise was deafening. Second Lieutenant Hunter, who had shown such composure under fire while his men were ambushed on Monday, was shot inside the Mission and killed instantly. His men dived for whatever cover they could find as their gallant officer lay prostrate on the floor before them.

The Volunteers placed their bomb at the Mission's door and retreated in haste, expecting a huge explosion at any second. However, the only burst of noise came from the rifles of the Lancers who fired at the retreating rebels as they rushed through the small yard back inside the gates of the Four Courts. Lieutenant Paddy Daly[6] who had led Monday's assault in the Phoenix Park, was shot in the right arm as he ran.[7] The bomb failed to detonate and the stalemate with the Medical Mission continued.

The overall British strategy in Dublin was to isolate the GPO from the other rebel positions, which would then allow them to contain and attack each one in turn. As the daylight faded over the city their sights fell upon Capel Street, the narrow half-mile-long road that stretched from Bolton Street at its northern end to Grattan Bridge at the quays. It was flanked by three- and four-storey buildings and situated directly between the Volunteer headquarters and the Four Courts area. Accordingly, it presented a valuable strategic target to General Lowe, who surveyed his street maps from a mile away in the Royal Hospital.

From that same hospital the 2/6th Sherwood Forester Battalion were soon dispatched under orders to march to Dublin Castle and, once there, to ready themselves for their attack across Grattan Bridge with the objective of capturing Capel Street and securing a line as far as Great Britain Street. The machine-gunners positioned around Queen Street Bridge were relocated towards Smithfield to support this move. This was done with great caution as the entire area was a warren of civilian houses and small industrial buildings, any of which could conceal an enemy sniper. A heavy Vickers machine gun was ordered to the roof of Jervis Street Hospital. Once there its crew determined its best position, and then ensured that the mounting tripod and gun itself were placed correctly, with plenty of ammunition close to hand. Adequate 'crest-clearance' was established, i.e. an unobstructed line of fire to its enemy target, whose engagement range was then ascertained before the weapon's sights were adjusted accordingly, in this case the 500-yard distance to the Four Courts. The gunners then scouted out secondary positions for their weapon, in the event of things becoming 'too hot' where they were. The crew's NCO took on the role of spotter. He sought out targets and directed the gunner's aim, while the third man loaded in each 250-round belt, before assisting its feed into the gun.

The air throughout the entire area stank with the noxious smoke from Linenhall Barracks. As darkness descended, the glow from the burning building could be seen for miles around. Several nearby buildings also contained potentially disastrous amounts of their own flammable materials.

The civilians in the area were beginning to suffer terribly. As the third day of the rebellion drew to a close, pantries had been emptied of food and many basic necessities were scarce. The smoke from the burning barracks permeated the floors of the draughty tenement buildings, which were filled with young and old alike, heaping misery upon misery. They did their best to cope with the uncertainty and contagious apprehension that worsened in the night. To those living in the North King Street area that apprehension would soon prove to be justified.

A comparatively peaceful Thursday morning and early afternoon saw sporadic sniping and combat between both sides, but nothing to the degree of the developing carnage in nearby Sackville Street. Then the Sherwood Foresters under Lieutenant-Colonel Hodgkin received the order to march to Grattan Bridge. They launched their attack at 4.30 p.m. Thunderous bursts from the British artillery, now blowing Sackville Street to pieces, echoed between the buildings on either side of the river.

The machine-gunners to the west of the Four Courts opened up initially to support the assault, followed by the heavy belt-fed Vickers gun in Jervis Street. The infantrymen waited apprehensively on Parliament Street while behind them two armoured Daimler lorries approached the bridge from the City Hall direction. The trucks had been loaned to the British forces by the Guinness Brewery in order to help suppress the rebellion. Large curved sheet-metal boiler housings had been riveted onto their flatbeds in such a way as to provide an armoured 'shell' into which would fit 18 soldiers and one officer, while the driver's cab was surrounded by sections of armour plating with narrow visibility slits cut into each. Five of these armoured trucks had been constructed in the Inchicore railway works, 3 miles to the west of the city centre.

The first appearance of one of these monstrous improvisations on Grattan Bridge was met with a hailstorm of fire from the rebels in the Four Courts, but it crossed to the northern side where it disgorged its cargo of men, who stormed into the buildings on the corners of Lower and Upper Ormond Quay, before the truck retreated across the bridge to replenish its cargo. The second truck waited for the signal that the buildings facing the quay had been secured before it too crossed under equally ferocious fire. Its 19-man squad was deposited at the junction of Great Strand Street to commandeer the corner buildings on both sides. The terrified civilians watched helplessly as their worldly possessions were used to barricade the junctions that fed onto both sides of Capel Street. This leapfrogging was repeated over and over with both vehicles revving their engines fiercely as they hurried to and fro. After several hours, all of the eight side streets that fed into Capel Street were barricaded and their respective overlooking corner buildings were occupied. In spite of the armour plating, the endeavour suffered several casualties, as the sheer volume of lead launched at both trucks resulted in several rounds penetrating the small firing holes bored into the structures.

When this process was eventually completed, all of the buildings that sat between the new British outposts and barricades were searched in turn for rebels. The bewildered and hungry inhabitants of Capel Street could do nothing but pray that their ordeal would soon end. The repeated blasts of artillery that resounded through the narrow passageways of Mary Street and Strand Street, however, did little to allay their fears.

When darkness had begun to descend and their commanding officers were satisfied that the entire length of the street was secure, the remaining British infantrymen began crossing Grattan Bridge in small groups. Once on the bridge, however, there was very little cover available to them. Its walls consisted of cast-iron balustrades which overlapped each other diagonally but left significant gaps. The rebels in the front rooms on the upper floors of the eastern side of the Four Courts pounced at the chance to alleviate the frustration caused by their helplessness in the face of the Daimlers, and fired manically but effectively, in spite of the increasing harassment from the Jervis Street machine-gunners. Dozens of rounds struck the bridge while beneath its five under-arches, spouts of water flew up as ricocheted shots splashed into the Liffey. The rate of fire increased as the Volunteers zeroed in. Soon, Foresters' rifle barrels

The bullet- and shell-damaged Four Courts building. NATIONAL LIBRARY OF IRELAND

could be seen poking through the rectangular gaps in the bridge's western side as the men knelt to return fire. They aimed at the flashes betraying the positions of the rebel riflemen but, under pressure, their shots were wild and inaccurate. Their remaining Companies then made the dash from behind them on Parliament Street, sprinting to gain the bridge's northern end.

Lieutenant Frank Shouldice, meanwhile, scanned the surrounding rooftops from his perch in the Jameson Malt Tower, near the corner of Beresford Street and North King Street. His spyglass finally revealed what he had been searching for: muzzle flashes in the darkness. The crack marksman fired three shots and the Vickers gun in Jervis Street fell silent, its position having quickly become 'too hot' for its crew, who now lay bleeding in agony among the smoking brass shells of several hundred spent rounds.

Untroubled now by that gun, the rebels in the upper rooms beneath the dome of the Four Courts added to the rapid fire being aimed at the bridge. British snipers in Christchurch and on Merchant's Quay answered but were kept busy by the Volunteers in the front rooms of the Four Courts which directly faced them. Casualties began to mount among the young troops on the bridge, but they eventually succeeded in crossing. Medics rushed from Parliament Street to tend to their wounded and remove the dead.

All four companies of the 2/6th had crossed the River Liffey and were now dispatched to the surrounding areas. A Company, under the command of Acting Major Heathcote, was deployed to secure the area to the north, between Capel Street and Cole's Lane. C Company, under Captain Jackson, was sent eastwards along Upper Abbey Street towards Liffey Street, while D Company, under Captain Tomkins, occupied the area between Cole's Lane and the northern end of Sackville Street. The British had succeeded in driving a wedge between the command areas of Commandants Daly in the Four Courts and Connolly in the GPO.

B Company, meanwhile, under Captain Johnson, set about organising a rescue bid for the trapped Lancers to their west in the Medical Mission. They sent a Daimler from Capel Street. It manoeuvred awkwardly through the narrow side streets and lumbered into Charles Street, backed up by a platoon of riflemen who sprinted from various positions of cover to provide supporting fire, all the while scanning the surrounding buildings for snipers. Eventually, the vehicle was backed up to the gates of the Mission, aided by suppressing fire from both inside the building, and from the troops supporting their rescue.

The driver grimaced with the strain of waiting once he was parked, feeling helpless. The terrifying ringing of the huge rebel rounds on the truck's hull throughout the afternoon had sent shockwaves reverberating through his skull, leaving his nerves all but shredded. The driver's slit allowed little or no view and the surrounding darkness, intermittently lit up with muzzle flashes, was menacing. All it would take was one grenade or bomb to finish them all. Soon enough, though, the vehicle was filled with cavalrymen and their walking wounded, and the relieved driver sped away. His relief was short-lived, however: he had to make more than one trip.

The second rescue mission was even more daunting. Infuriated by the success of the first evacuation, the rebels now threw caution to the wind. Cascades of sparks flew from the steel exterior of the huge truck as it backed up once again. The Sherwood Foresters strained to reply to the fire but it seemed to come from everywhere. To their relief, the lorry was quickly filled with the remaining Lancers, including the body of Lieutenant Hunter, and it drove off. The riflemen retreated in its wake, to the dismay of the surrounding Volunteers. The vehicle delivered its second cargo of exhausted and hungry cavalrymen to the safety of their own lines where they were to be debriefed, rested and fed, and their wounded tended to.

While this dramatic series of events was unfolding, British sniper fire in the North King Street/Brunswick Street area was beginning to cause serious problems to the nearby rebels. The stinking smoke from the burning barracks permeated every nook and cranny occupied by Volunteers and civilians alike and some began to suffer the effects of inhalation. To move in search of clean air, however, meant risking a bullet from a faraway gunman who was not hindered by eyes that constantly watered with the irritation of filthy fumes. Snipers from various British units had been moved to the high ground north of Constitution Hill and they, like their comrades in the Christchurch bell tower, methodically surveyed the landscape for targets.

That night the entire area was lit up by the inferno at Linenhall Barracks. The fires had spread and flammable containers from the surrounding buildings had exploded, adding to the chaos. The rebels were ending their fourth day of insurrection in an atmosphere of destruction, uncertainty and hunger, set against a backdrop of constant artillery fire to their east. The civilian inhabitants close to the barracks prayed together, huddled in their homes, and sheltering in the houses of their neighbours, without food, and struggling to breathe when the wind blew the caustic fumes their way. Shadows from the dancing flames flickered in the surrounding streets and laneways, attracting shots from jumpy snipers. Little rest was available that April night, although permanent sleep came to several, as stray bullets and shells indiscriminately raked the area.

The British now prepared to implement the second part of their plan to clear Daly and his men.

9

North King Street and North Brunswick Street

'Just one more push.'

At 11 a.m. on Friday morning, the 2/6th South Staffordshire Battalion under the command of Lieutenant-Colonel Henry Taylor crossed the River Liffey over Butt Bridge, next to Dublin's Custom House. Once across, its men passed the shattered Liberty Hall on their left, before marching under the dominating Loop Line railway bridge onto Lower Gardiner Street. Looking up, the infantrymen saw a cordon of riflemen on the rooftops of the four-storey-over-basement Georgian houses lining both sides of the road covering their march. They stopped when they reached the junction of Talbot Street, and moved swiftly across in small groups. Many glanced to their left as they did, and witnessed the start of the climax of the fighting around the GPO 300 yards to their west, before rushing forward across the 20-yard crossroads in order to prevent themselves from falling victim to one of its riflemen. A barricade on their left provided some cover, while their own troops manning it fired towards North Earl Street and the GPO. The noise in the area was deafening.

The South Staffordshire Regiment consisted primarily of young men from 'The Black Country', the area to the north and west of England's second largest and most industrial city, Birmingham. They were tough soldiers and hard men, having spent most of their civilian lives living and working in harsh conditions: prior to enlistment, most had worked for long hours in the region's coalmines or in factories, performing back-breaking work for poor wages, which rendered them chronically susceptible to ill health and living in poor housing. They did not expect life to be easy in any way or forgiving, and accordingly were themselves unforgiving, particularly towards those trying to kill them.

They advanced along Upper Gardiner Street, then turned left, towards the Parnell Monument. They avoided the fighting around Sackville Street and eventually made their way to Bolton Street where their command post was set up in its massive technical college. Capel Street, just behind them, had been made safe by the Sherwood Foresters, but the road in front was unsecured. Troops from A Company were dispatched to the many flats and tenements there, where its men brutally ordered the terror-stricken inhabitants out of their homes. Many of these refugees flocked to the college, where a growing number sought shelter from the escalating violence. Firing positions were then set up to cover North King Street to their west. This was to be the jump-off point for their attack.

North King Street's three-quarter-mile length sat directly along the axis of the final piece of the British cordon in Dublin city. It was imperative that it be taken and held. The 2/5th South Staffordshire Battalion was assembling in the Queen Street area, and the plan was to link the two battalions along North King Street.

The Volunteers they were about to face were men with few illusions. Although a great number of those who fought for the Republic were quite comfortable financially, many more among their ranks came from poor areas and had grown up in homes where many of their siblings did not survive, and were familiar with hunger, cold and just about all of the discomforts life could hold. Being a Volunteer meant everything. What little money they had was invested in their weapons and uniforms, which they paid for themselves. The cause they fought for promised them a real chance in life and, in return, commanded a sense of commitment and honour that would not be relinquished easily.

The ranks of the recently arrived British Regiment were gearing themselves up for a fight with truly determined opponents who would rather die than give up. Their hatred of the Crown and all it stood for was not based solely on nationalist ideology, but also on how it affected their daily lives. Death by machine gun or artillery was preferable to the

Republicans than a life lived in constant struggle and humiliation under a system that offered little.

The Volunteers had prepared their positions extremely well. Any weakness in their line had already been exposed by the enemy snipers and remedied accordingly. Commandant Daly had made it his business to reinforce his men, who now waited for what they knew would be an appalling showdown.

As soon as the South Staffordshires took up position, a hail of rifle bullets came from Reilly's Fort. Section Commander Michael Flanagan, who had only just arrived, shouted to his men to open fire from the building's top floor at the first sight of the khaki uniforms now darting around at Bolton Street's junction with the eastern half of North King Street. Section Commander Maurice Collins, meanwhile, manning the south-east-facing windows on the same floor, told his men to stand ready.

Within minutes of his area being secured, Colonel Taylor ordered a single platoon from C Company South Staffordshires to begin its advance westward. Its 50 or so men spread themselves out along the width of the road, and marched with their rifles held diagonally abreast of their bodies. In front of them and about 200 yards to their right was Langan's pub. Its barricade stretched across the road. They scanned the obstruction, expecting to see movement. To their surprise, it appeared undefended so they pressed on.

As their boots clattered on the cobblestones, gruesome scenarios of imminent death or injury played out in the imagination of many of the soldiers. Terrified infantrymen questioned their own ability to hold it together, hoping it would be someone else's day to die, while thoughts of loved ones flashed through the men's minds. Their combat training, coupled with their sturdy and steadfast nature, helped to surmount the terror of advancing into an enemy-held urban battlefield, but it did little to placate the trepidation felt by the men at the front who were now beginning to climb the barricade.

Several fell at the first deafening volley from Langan's, including their lieutenant who died instantly, before another barrage of shot boomed from Reilly's Fort, cutting down more as the shots ripped through them. Langan's fired again. Men were shot to pieces, while order disintegrated all around. It became impossible to fire back. The wounded fell to the ground screaming in agony and clutching at their bloodied uniforms.

Michael Flanagan in Reilly's Fort ordered his men to aim their rifles on North King Street, to the left as they faced it. Their shots tore into the troops, driving them to the opposite side of the road. Additional volleys from Langan's shattered any remaining cohesion the platoon had, and sent its men reeling into the side streets for cover. Their orders compelled them forward regardless, so they pushed their way through the alleys and eventually found themselves on Beresford Street.

This brought them directly into the gunsights of Frank Shouldice and his marksmen, still perched in Jamesons' Distillery tower. They began to cut the troops down one by one. It became impossible for the Englishmen to think straight in the claustrophobic chaos, such was the ferocity of the rebel fire. Several panicked soldiers rushed into Stirrup Lane, seeking shelter in some half-built cottages on the small street, only to be mown down by Section Commander Seán Byrne and his men, whose avalanche of fire decimated them from the very buildings that had presented the illusion of safety.[1] Byrne's men had waited until the hapless infantrymen were at point blank range before opening up. A few traumatised survivors managed to scramble back to their headquarters on Bolton Street eventually, narrowly avoiding death from the shots that whined from the walls and pavements and whipped the air as they ran.

Meanwhile, to coincide with their assault on North King Street, the military intensified their harassment of the seemingly impregnable Republican citadel which faced them from across the River Liffey. The rebels in the Four Courts had little rest. Peadar Clancy's men at the barricade found themselves engaged in a vicious game of cat and mouse with a sniper who was firing from a building on the corner of Cook Street and Lower Bridge Street. For two hours their eyes strained for movement from the building, until a momentary lapse in their enemy's efforts at concealment brought a volley of Mauser and Enfield rounds from the barricade, which finished him.

Almost immediately after the failed first attack on Langan's, Volunteer Thomas Smart was ordered from Clancy's barricade to the Bridewell police station where he and George Flanagan were detailed to reinforce Sergeant Mark Wilson's section manning the building's roof.[2] From there, they had an excellent field of fire along the length of Beresford Street which stretched to their north for about a quarter of a mile, and Church Street, which ran parallel 100 yards or so to the west. Wilson ordered both men to keep their gunsights trained in this particular area. Smart covered the former street, Flanagan the latter. They waited nervously, while Smart surveyed the dead and wounded enemy troops scattered on the ground in Beresford Street.

Roughly an hour later, another two platoons from C Company attacked towards Langan's. Several Lewis guns spewed drum after drum of red-hot rounds at the pub to cover their advance, and the noise was thunderous. In the flats and houses that lined the road, families sought cover from ricochets. The hundred or so troops who moved forward under the umbrella of covering fire were sick with fear. North King Street presented as daunting an objective as any of them had been trained to face. Here their enemy's positions had not been softened up with artillery beforehand and faced them from their front, their side and from above. As the rebel barricade drew ever closer, they saw several wounded young infantrymen from the first attack twisting and jerking on the ground, trying to drag themselves to safety. Mercifully, they were left alone by the Volunteers.

The second attack stalled. The troops were felled once again by another barrage of bullets from Mauser, Enfield and Martini-Henry rifles, each with its own characteristic crack or boom. At the front of the British advance, several men were literally shot to pieces in the repeated carnage. Those just behind were unable to make any progress without suffering a similar fate. It was useless. Reinforcements pushed them forward from their rear, but it was simply impossible to advance. They eventually retreated to Bolton Street to regroup, leaving their wounded and dying where they lay.

The British recognised the additional threat from Reilly's Fort, set about 150 yards to the rear of Langan's, and the rebels there soon felt the increasing wrath of the machine-gunners. They zeroed in on the barricaded sash windows on the east side of the pub. The Volunteers inside scrambled for cover as the plaster in the ceilings and walls around them disintegrated. Soon it became impossible to see anything from inside the position, such was the extent of the dust and plaster in the air. The Volunteers were soon covered from head to toe in fine white dust and found it difficult to breathe. The afternoon warmth did little to comfort them. Curses were added to the chaotic din. A Volunteer swore repeatedly at the lance from which the tricolour fluttered, wedged in the manhole just outside, feeling it was drawing the machine-gunner's attention. Eventually the fire abated, and Lieutenant Jack Shouldice's men readied themselves for the coming onslaught, while his adrenalin-fuelled brother, Frank, did his best to keep the machine-gunners' heads down from the Jameson tower, with his keen eye scanning the streets for targets.

Not far away, the eastern wing of the Four Courts was under constant rifle fire from the increasingly confident Sherwood Foresters, who were filtering into the buildings between the position itself and Capel Street. This area too was heavily populated, and the hard-pressed civilians did their best to stay out of the line of fire.

The South Staffordshires advanced into North King Street for a third time, firing as they went. Windows in the densely populated houses lining the road were shattered in turn as the angry and terrified troops pressed forward, shooting at any potential hiding place for a hated rebel. Rapid fire was aimed by kneeling soldiers at Langan's, causing plumes of dust to fly from its outer wall. Several shots per second hit the structure, and when the machine-gunners zeroed in again, the rate of destruction increased proportionately. The lingering smoke from the smouldering Linenhall Barracks, just behind the pub in Coleraine Street, added to the growing sense of desolation. Some of the troops lying wounded in the street began to quieten, their appalling screams and desperate groans waning with their lives, but relief was unavailable. To move anywhere on the street was to invite a bullet.

The third British assault similarly stalled. An attack was then organised along the rooftops leading towards Langan's. Dislodged slates fell and smashed to the ground below, as the troops made their way awkwardly along the slippery ridges, swearing obscenities as they struggled to maintain their balance. Women and hungry children screamed with fright as machine-gun rounds ripped bizarre patterns of concrete from their homes' outer walls and periodically smashed into their furniture. Some became hysterical.

The infantrymen, however, had not taken into account the rebel positions in Monk's Bakery, just behind Langan's to its north-west, and who now loosed several ferocious volleys on them. The screams from beneath them in the houses and on the streets were now added to by several loud cries from their comrades who fell to the bullets and ricochets that whined through the chimney tops. The frustrated attackers shouted threats and insults. Nothing was working.

One of the flatbed Daimlier trucks used to ferry the Sherwood Foresters across Grattan Bridge, and later on to drive the South Staffordshires into the inferno that was North King Street. MILITARY ARCHIVES

A lull developed. Fighters from both sides drew breath and checked their positions and weapons. The quiet, however, did little to calm the terror felt in many homes in North King Street. Commandant Daly began sending reinforcements towards Reilly's Fort and North Brunswick Street. He knew the tactical importance of both the position and the area, and had been resupplying them since morning. The onset of combat had interrupted his attempts, but he used the lull to compensate. Extra grenades and canister bombs were sent forward with some fresh men, while the wounded were taken to Father Mathew Hall.

Colonel Taylor had no intentions of standing over a bloodbath such as that inflicted on the Sherwood Foresters two days earlier at Mount Street Bridge. When he realised that an unsupported infantry advance along North King Street was futile, he called upon an armoured truck for support. When it arrived, its cargo area was packed to the brim with troops from A Company.

The rebels holding onto Langan's had heard word of the armoured vehicles that had recently appeared on Dublin's streets. They faced one such lumbering giant late on Friday afternoon. Dead and wounded lay in the road to its front, as it noisily shifted its over-stressed gears and advanced towards their positions. They opened fire.

As the vehicle crept forward scores of shots smashed into its steel hull, but to no avail. The men sweating profusely inside its steel cocoon instinctively ducked their heads to the shocking reverberations in the suffocating confined spaces. The heat was dreadful, as was the acidic odour of fear from the 19 petrified men inside. They cursed repeatedly as the truck swerved and jerked violently to avoid the prone bodies, both living and dead, who were at risk of being crushed. It eventually pulled up opposite Langan's. Its driver parked at an angle to cover the disembarking assault troops from both rebel strongholds, but as the men leapt out through the rear door, the surrounding rebels fired with greater ferocity. The first soldier to exit the vehicle was shot dead before his feet touched the ground. His comrades scrambled out and ran for cover, kicking furiously at the nearby front doors while frantically trying to escape the rain of bullets. Civilians screamed and shouted as each of their homes was commandeered by these homicidal strangers with razor-sharp bayonets fixed to their rifles. The South Staffordshires then detailed pairs of men to cover the rear of the houses, before they began firing volley after volley across the road at the rebel post. The truck reversed away from the scene.

It soon returned with another cargo of troops, who then jumped out and charged straight at Langan's, screaming at those inside and firing wildly as they ran. The rebels were now under severe pressure. Fuses were lit on canister bombs and hurled out at the attacking troops, some of which exploded prematurely, adding to the defenders' desperation. The air in the pub stank of gunpowder, human sweat and terror. The fighting was relentless, but still the position held. The troops were driven back into the houses across the road, while the truck retreated once again. Upon its arrival back in Bolton Street, however, the waiting infantrymen paled when they saw that its driver and his co-driver had been hit. As both men lost consciousness, the order was given: 'In you go on foot!' They would have to walk into the maelstrom.

As they marched in roughly 20 troops peeled off to the right and made their way to the rear of Lurgan Street where they came face to face with the charred remains of Linenhall Barracks. From here they attempted to outflank the pub and take it from the rear by advancing along Lisburn Street.

On the far side of Church Street, however, Volunteer Peadar Breslin in Moore's Coachworks was waiting to pounce. As soon as the first British soldier came into view in Lisburn Street, he opened fire. His comrades quickly joined in. The South Staffordshires realised the manoeuvre would be as futile and costly as their failed frontal assaults. As they scanned the nearby houses with suspicion, the roar of artillery in the background was almost constant.

Across Church Street in Father Mathew Hall, things were now desperate. The building was starting to overflow with wounded and its floor was awash with blood. Cumann na mBan members dealt with the increasing number of casualties as best they could. The stench was appalling, as were the cries of the wounded. Both rebel and military casualties were treated alike and died in agony alongside each other, their differences forgotten. British prisoners did their best to help.

Commandant Daly consequently moved his headquarters to the Four Courts. He had all his prisoners either released to fend for themselves, or taken to the Bridewell police station and placed in its basement cells. The ammunition was moved by Vice Commandant Béaslaí with the help of Eamon Morkan to the Four Courts.[3] This proved extremely hazardous. The two men had to make their way onto the street and hope the enemy snipers' aims were off, then clamber across their own barricades. Some of the bombs were accidentally dropped amid the chaos, but to their relief none exploded, and the enemy sniper fire left them unscathed.

As Friday evening drew near, the inevitable British link-up attack, in the form of the 2/5th South Staffordshire Battalion, whose northern flank was supported by two decimated companies of the 2/7th Sherwood Foresters under Major Raynor,[4] was launched from Smithfield against the west wing of the Four Courts. Machine-gun rounds drummed into its stonework and smashed at the inner walls through its shattered windows. Those manning the barricade in Hammond Lane held their heads low as the fire flew over their heads before crashing into the Four Courts, causing showers of bright sparks to burst and cascade to the pavement.

Lieutenant Thomas Allen, from Moyvalley in County Meath, accompanied by Volunteers Seán O'Carroll and Seán Kennedy, positioned in the west wing of the Four Courts, returned their fire. Spent cartridges clattered to the floor at their feet as they aimed and shot their weapons down the length of Hammond Lane, until a British sniper managed to zero in on the three men. O'Carroll's elbow was struck by a .303 bullet, which then ricocheted into 33-year-old Lieutenant Allen's chest.[5] He fell to the floor of the room as the fire intensified again. Those attempting to save him crawled to his aid under the streams of bullets ripping into the walls. Eventually, the father of three was evacuated under fire to Richmond Hospital, where he soon died.

As the attack got under way, the Volunteers caught in its path began putting their well-practised tactic of fire and manoeuvre to good effect. They had spent days linking their vantage points with tunnels and knew the area intimately at this stage. They fired their pistols and shotguns, ideal weapons for such untidy combat, and relocated, leaving the advancing soldiers to storm the buildings, only to find them devoid of fighting men. This vicious game of cat and mouse in the warren of narrow streets was made all the more lethal by the deadly accurate fire of several rebel snipers, who took full advantage of the confusion sown into the ranks of British troops. The attack eventually lost its momentum.

The British now opted to build their own barricade across the top of Queen Street where it meets with North King Street. Several machine-gun posts were moved up before another attempt was made to link up their battalions at the junction of Church Street and North King Street. When this came under fire from Volunteer positions at the top of Red Cow Lane, another armoured truck was called up in support. It made its way into Red Cow Lane only to be stopped by the barricade there. It then reversed in the narrow lane before its rear doors swung open and offered the riflemen inside a chance to engage the insurgents, using the fully open steel doors to protect them. The vehicle then retreated, while its cargo of men jumped out and took position at the lane's southern end.

As the daylight began to wane, so too did the intense shooting, as the South Staffordshires took time to consider their next move. The rebels in Langan's were now running low on ammunition and were badly feeling the strain of the day's fighting. Lookouts watched for any sign of the next attack, while thunderclaps of artillery became louder and more frequent as the GPO, Sackville Street and the surrounding areas were pulverised a mile or so away.

As darkness descended, the firing around the Four Courts eventually ceased. Targets were few and far between for the snipers, despite the flares sent up by the British. The tension was beginning to tell on several Volunteers. A night assault was expected, and nervous sentries scanned the streets to their east. Their comrades quietly took stock of what was happening around them as they tried to rest despite the deafening echoes of artillery and the lightning-like flashes in the night sky that prefigured its many blasts.

At 2 a.m., in the smoky darkness, Section Commander Sheeran ordered the evacuation of Langan's. The worn-out defenders were practically out of ammunition at this stage and made a dash westwards to Reilly's Fort, leaving a single dead man behind. The South Staffordshires wasted no time. They advanced and secured the position, and as soon as this was done, Colonel Taylor rushed in more of his men. He now finally had a small foothold on North King Street.

The fighting in Dublin during Easter Week provided the British Army with many lessons in urban street fighting which are still employed in its training today. In the inferno of North King Street, however, its men were learning the hard way. Taylor's men vented the frustration and anger they felt at dealing with a hidden, embedded and ruthless foe on the civilians in their way. The remaining men of A Company were ordered forward, and as they smashed their way into the terraces of tenement houses as they advanced, troops pumped with adrenalin launched themselves at the inhabitants of the three-storey dwellings, shouting at them, abusing and beating them, while other sections of troops began tunnelling through their walls. They bored holes in the concrete and plaster, fired warning shots through and followed screaming as they made their way towards Beresford Street at the end of the terrace. The civilians cowered before them as the troops yelled 'Sinn Féin bastards!', accompanied by the swinging of fists and rifle butts. Throughout the long night, increasing numbers of soldiers – trigger-happy and highly agitated – filtered through the holes bored between the houses and made their way towards the buildings closest to Reilly's Fort in preparation for a dawn attack.

Across Church Street, Paddy Holohan, who was in charge of the top floor of Clarke's Dairy, ordered a party of men to begin boring through the walls towards Reilly's Fort, with the initial aim of expanding his own positions and with the further intent of making contact with the men there.

Reilly's Fort now contained 15 or so exhausted and dust-covered Volunteers who knew their time was about to come. Sentries kept watch with bloodshot eyes while their comrades grabbed what rest they could. No one really slept: they merely dozed, ready to jump to action at a moment's notice. As Saturday broke they rallied themselves for the expected dawn attack. The sound of English accents from across the junction of North King Street and Church Street prompted them to hasten their preparations.

Those same accents now barked commands and words of encouragement to their men. The British NCOs ordered their sections to keep it together, using their own veneer of steadfastness to bolster each terrified infantryman. 'Just one more push' repeated over and over suggested that this was all it would take to overwhelm their enemies finally.

The more seasoned among them knew the only way out was across the road, and the sooner it was done the better. Some of the less experienced, however, were only able to carry on because of the unambiguous reminders from their sergeants that disobeying orders would present just as brutal a fate as any that could be presented by an enemy. This, combined with loyalty to their comrades and respect for their NCOs, managed to suppress the shuddering anxiety that, unchecked, could render the strongest man among them motionless with terror.

Minutes before sunrise, several doors were slowly opened in the houses along North King Street that led west to Beresford Street. The Volunteers roughly 100 yards away were about to have their vigilance rewarded. Suddenly a whistle blew, and the British charged.

The rebels shot their weapons into the khaki mass of C Company's remnants reinforced by D Company, which poured suddenly from the buildings. Both Companies ran straight into a concentrated wall of fire from several rebel positions, Reilly's to their front, the Malthouse tower to their rear and the Bridewell to their left.

Soldiers fell everywhere, some spun as they collapsed, while others tumbled as their bodies were ripped apart by the deluge of lead, performing an obscene and macabre dance in the half-light. Several threw themselves down instinctively. It was all they could do to avoid the same fate. Conscious thoughts counted for little as the heads of friends and comrades disintegrated close by, having been hit with the type of bullet employed by hunters to take down elephants. Human remains strewn on the ground jerked and flew backward under repeated impacts of concentrated shot. The entire facade of Reilly's Fort was hidden by rifle smoke, such was the weight of fire that flew from its windows.

The troops pinned to the cobblestones shouted confused instructions to each other both to press on and to retreat, while the wounded screamed in pain. Others lay silent as their lives slipped away. A brave few rose to their feet to charge once more, but were quickly driven to the ground again.

The rebels inside Reilly's did not think. They just shot, and shot again. They fired non-stop at the desperate men outside. It was impossible to think such was the level of noise inside the building. Many of the defenders were still covered from head to toe in plaster from the previous day, and the filthy gun-soot that caked itself on their skin gave them a bizarre appearance that reinforced the sense of unreality. Their frantic movements from window to window, or from one vantage point to another, resulted in several accidents as disorientated men slipped on spent shell casings. Men shouted as they fired, cursing the men tumbling before them. Stirring oneself to hatred made it easier to deal with the awful realisation that it was a human being collapsing in agony just yards away.

Soon the hard-pressed troops reeling on the street had to deal with the attentions of Frank Shouldice in the Malthouse tower, who fired his rifle with a mania that belied his usually peaceful nature, trying his best to alleviate the threat to his brother. The situation became impossible. Panicked soldiers stood up to retreat and were cut down as they ran. Their rifles and bayonets clattered to the cobblestones as they fell.

Soon it was over. The firing tapered off when the last of the surviving soldiers had scrambled back to the houses from which they had launched their failed attack. The wide junction was littered with the wounded and dead. The inhabitants of the occupied houses were now confronted with men who had become incandescent with rage. Their earlier aggression paled in comparison to the pure hatred they now exhibited. It was impossible for the civilians to escape, however: anyone who ventured onto the road would be shot down. In any event, their unwelcome guests had no intention of allowing them to leave.

The rebels kept their aim on the road, fully expecting another attack but with greater numbers, and with the aid of their armoured trucks. Jack Shouldice did his rounds, checking to see if there were any wounded or worse. Many of the men were in a state of half-shock, such had been the intensity of the brief firefight.

After a period of relative calm, Shouldice asked for two volunteers to run the gauntlet of North King Street's junction with Church Street in order to procure some much needed ammunition. Edward Delamere and Patrick Flanagan stepped forward. Minutes later, under a barrage of covering fire the two men rushed through the door and raced to Church Street. Upstairs in the building Michael Flanagan breathed a sigh of relief when he saw that his brother had made the crossing safely.

An hour or so later the same men were seen on the return trip climbing over the barricade outside Father Mathew Hall. A thunderclap of covering fire erupted from Reilly's, but it was not enough to silence the machine gun that now followed their path with a ripping stream of bullets. Delamere dashed back inside through the half-open door just as Flanagan, running close behind, was caught by a burst. He collapsed inside the door and fell dead to the floor. His brother upstairs had looked on in horror as the bullets cut him down, while his other brother, George, manning his position on the Bridewell roof some distance away, witnessed the Volunteer's tragic demise, unaware of his identity.

After two hours of a tense stand-off, punctuated by sporadic rifle cracks, Shouldice decided to evacuate Reilly's Fort. His ammunition supply was bordering on critical. They signalled their intention to the rebels manning the barricades on Church Street who lay down covering fire across the junction. This was swiftly added to by volleys from the Bridewell. The rebels opened the front door of the position and bellowed a shout of 'Charge!' This diversion drew a deluge of lead to the building's front, while the insurgents then made a leap from the side windows of their battered fortress before sprinting across the western end of North King Street. One man was wounded in the ankle by a sharpshooter. He was forced to lie as if dead for a time before the enemy infantry turned their attentions elsewhere, and was then carried by two men through a nearby laneway to the relative safety of Father Mathew Hall.

The British wasted no time. They stormed across the junction and rushed into the building from where Shouldice's men had decimated them. Reilly's Fort provided its new conquerors with little in the way of comfort, however, as three Volunteer positions now had it in their rifle sights and opened up with everything they had. The South Staffordshires prepared for a counter-attack, but to their relief it never came.

In taking and holding the position, albeit nearly 24 hours after making their initial assault, the South Staffordshire Regiment had finally succeeded in driving a wedge between North King Street and the Four Courts. B Company was moved up from the rear to consolidate their hold on the eastern flank of Church Street, while their regimental comrades in the 2/5th were also making slow but steady progress from their west. Their planned link-up looked closer.

North Brunswick Street now found itself in the sights of the British planners. They realised the urgent need to provide full support to the men who had captured Reilly's Fort, and accordingly they formed up the men from the 2/5th for an attack along the western axis of North King Street towards the position. Several sections, however, were ordered to North Brunswick Street, running parallel, 50 yards north, where they would launch small-scale probing attacks to ensure the northern flank of their drive to Reilly's was still secure.

The sections initially began their advance into Red Cow Lane. Men crouched in doorways and took shots at the barricade there while others made several rushes forward from one position of cover to another. Garry Holohan was quick to react. He bellowed to his surrounding men for support, and soon the structure was being hotly contested. After a time an impasse developed, with neither side able to gain advantage.

Soon afterwards, the few rebels holding Red Cow Lane were recalled to reinforce the North Brunswick Street positions now under the command of Patrick Holohan. Captain Laffan had been shot in the head in the top floor of Moore's Coachworks while guiding back a reconnaissance patrol, during which Volunteer Phil Walsh had been wounded. With Laffan taken to Richmond Hospital, the garrison found itself leaderless, and so Holohan stepped in.

At this point the British were flooding the area with men. The rebel-held barricade straddling Church Street closest to Reilly's was under constant attack. The scene was one of utter chaos. There was constant fire between the British troops in the streets near the barricade and the Volunteers at Moore's and Clarke's to the north-west, Monk's Bakery to the north-east and, on the roof of the Bridewell, Sergeant Wilson and his men were relentless. Beneath their rooftop position, however, the Bridewell station began to flood with water from a burst main. The prisoners in the basement cells were removed to safety under guard. Just across the road to Wilson's rear, the Four Courts was now under unrelenting sniper and machine-gun fire.

At 1 p.m. the South Staffordshires launched a full-scale attack against the North Brunswick Street positions from the east with all of their reserves. Scores of troops rushed at the barricades both to the north and south of the North King Street/Church Street junction. The barricade across the top of Lower Church Street came under a sustained attack, forcing the insurgents there to retreat to the junction of Mary's Lane and Lower Church Street, situated about halfway along the latter. Another barricade had been placed there in the previous days and it now sheltered the increasingly desperate Volunteers for a time, until the ferocious firing from behind them at the Bridewell swung the pendulum yet again. Sergeant Wilson's men fired mercilessly into the British ranks from the Bridewell, causing their attack in Church Street to falter momentarily.

The enemy's sudden lack of balance was not wasted by the rebels at Mary's Lane and they charged back at the infantrymen, forcing them to retire. The rebels lost two men in the process. The fighting was vicious, and, at this stage, personal. Men screamed and shouted while the wounded collapsed around them. The retreating British turned to fire at their demon-like pursuers while the Volunteers fired as they charged forward. Soon the barricade outside Father Mathew Hall was back in the hands of 1st Battalion, who quickly sent men into the nearby houses and slowly filtered back towards the North King Street junction, desperate to maintain their foothold. Back on the Bridewell roof there was no let-up for Sergeant Wilson's men. Their overheating weapons fired incessantly now into the enemy troops once again fighting for control of Beresford Street.

As the battle for the barricade on the northern side of the North King Street junction intensified, a heavy machine gun pulverised the rebel positions. Then, as it stopped shooting, a Canadian infantryman, on leave in Dublin, leapt across the barricade carrying a satchel of hand grenades which he intended launching at the insurgents. The outcome was inevitable. As he collapsed to the ground having been shot several times, the grenades fell from the satchel and rolled around on the street. Several soldiers rushed once again at the barricade only to be driven back by the unrelenting and murderous fire of the rebels.

A brief lull followed until mid-afternoon when once again the machine gun barked to life. Streams of khaki uniforms now ran forward, but, yet again, to no avail. As two battalions struggled to gain control in the madness, the rebels in the surrounding buildings moved rapidly from window to window, and from position to position, shooting revolver pistols, rifles and shotguns into the mass of Englishmen. Monk's Bakery found itself under enormous pressure and eventually the British gained access to its shop, only to come under intense close-quarter pressure themselves from those in the building's bakery. The rebels refused to give ground without fighting for every inch.

The guns of both sides then fell silent again for a time as a British soldier lying in the middle of the Church Street junction screamed in pain and pleaded for someone to come and help him. His calls went unanswered. No one dared set foot on open ground. A whistle then blew from Moore's Coachworks, followed by a shouted order to 'Cease fire!' This was followed by a loud invitation from Patrick Holohan to: 'Take in that man, we won't fire!'[6] A British NCO shouted a curse back at the Volunteers and ordered his men to open fire. When they did, he rushed forward and attempted to shield himself behind a lamp post. He beckoned his men forward but collapsed suddenly, having been shot by the return fire of the rebels. Holohan blew his whistle again and repeated the ceasefire command. Several soldiers then ran out and carried both the screaming man and their wounded NCO away.

Back in Bolton Street, a private by the name of Davis from the 2/6th South Staffordshires was resting with several of his comrades. The exhausted men were making the most of their reprieve from the firing line, drinking from water canteens and smoking. As they revived, Davis noticed a stretcher being carried from the direction of Great Britain Street by four men in Volunteer uniforms who were accompanied by three enemy officers. The curious party was flanked on both sides by a guard of soldiers. They watched as the group reached the barricaded junction of Capel Street, whereupon the stretcher was manhandled across. Its wounded occupant was then picked up again and carried southwards along the street by the same men and under the same guard of soldiers.

The area to Private Davis' east had been oddly silent since early that morning. As the afternoon turned to evening the warm spring weather was holding. The sun's rays were a welcome distraction from the ominous prospect of having to face once again the unyielding enemy to their west. The men sitting around in clusters spoke with apprehension at the thought of another foray into the cauldron of fire that had claimed so many of their comrades. Some spoke in tones of unbridled hatred towards the Irish for what they had done to them.

Back in the Four Courts, the Bridewell and North Brunswick Street, the deafening silence that followed the previous days and nights' cataclysm of artillery to the east played on the minds of the Republican leaders. Communications with their other garrisons were impossible. In Father Mathew Hall, meanwhile, the nurses carried on, tending to the wounded all around who groaned and cried out in varying degrees of agony. Towards evening, some grew increasingly pale, until their moans abated and their eyes became lifeless.

The rebel fighters took any available opportunity to rest their worn-out limbs, and to placate their hunger and thirst. Exhausted men took rest in shifts, while sentries from both sides kept watch for the ever-present snipers.

10

The General Post Office and Sackville Street: Part 1

'God keep and guard you all, and make your fight successful.'

Shortly after the Citizen Army units had left Liberty Hall on Easter Monday to begin their assaults on City Hall and St Stephen's Green, a larger force of about 150 Volunteers, who had been selected from their various battalions, departed from the same bustling building. After a final check of their weapons and equipment, many among them shook hands and wished each other good luck as they tried their best to contain their excitement and apprehension. They then set off in two columns on their 300-yard march along Lower Abbey Street.

They were led by Commandants Pádraig Pearse, Joseph Plunkett and James Connolly. Their destination was Sackville Street. They planned to take over the imposing GPO, which dated from 1818 and dominated the entire street, and use it as the Irish Volunteer Army headquarters, while establishing there the headquarters of the Irish Republic.

Some of those marching on that sunny morning wore the fern-green uniform of the Irish Volunteers, while several others wore the distinctive bottle green of the Citizen Army. The Cumann na mBan members among them had turned out, impeccably attired in their light-green tunics and long skirts, while many others wore no uniform at all, save for the leather ammunition bandoliers slung across their shoulders which marked them out from ordinary Dublin citizens. Their officers and commandants had made sure to turn out in their very best, in particular 28-year-old Joseph Plunkett who was by far the most flamboyant of the group, adorned with several rings and carrying a sheathed sabre at his side. He was dying of tuberculosis and had recently undergone an operation to try and alleviate the condition. His aide-de-camp, a young Captain Michael Collins, marched beside him, suitably attired in his neatly pressed uniform.

Their choice of weapons was as diverse as their garments. Some carried Mauser rifles, others carried Lee Enfields. A small number had single-shot Martini-Henry rifles and there were also shotguns, a variety of pistols, and pikes.

As the column passed Wynn's Hotel to the left on Abbey Street, they were met with the odd amused shout, but most of the passers-by in the area paid little or no heed to them. Volunteer parades and manoeuvres in Dublin had been quite a common occurrence that spring. Some onlookers nevertheless sniggered quietly. Ironically, several British Army personnel relaxing off duty laughed arrogantly among themselves and turned their backs on what they considered to be an undisciplined bunch of dreamers who were just playing at being soldiers. This indifference worked to the insurgents' benefit. If these troops had kept their gaze on the Volunteers for a moment or two longer, they would have noticed a motor car following behind, stuffed with weapons, ammunition and canister bombs. Such items were not a regular feature on manoeuvre parades, and playing at soldiers was the last thing on the minds of the men and women now marching towards Dublin's main thoroughfare.

When the Volunteers reached Sackville Street two sections of three men each peeled off to the left while the main force turned right. Its ranks then marched for another 200 yards before coming to a halt outside the GPO. Captain George Plunkett ordered the men from the Kimmage Garrison[1] who were placed at the front of the column to: 'Left turn, The GPO ... Charge!' The 22-year-old captain's command was met with a blank stare from the same men. Commandant Connolly's bellowed words – 'Take the Post Office!' – galvanised them into action, and the Volunteers rushed the building.

Those inside were taken completely by surprise. The concept of being in the wrong place at the wrong time dawned rather bluntly on the few British Army and Dublin Metropolitan Police personnel who happened

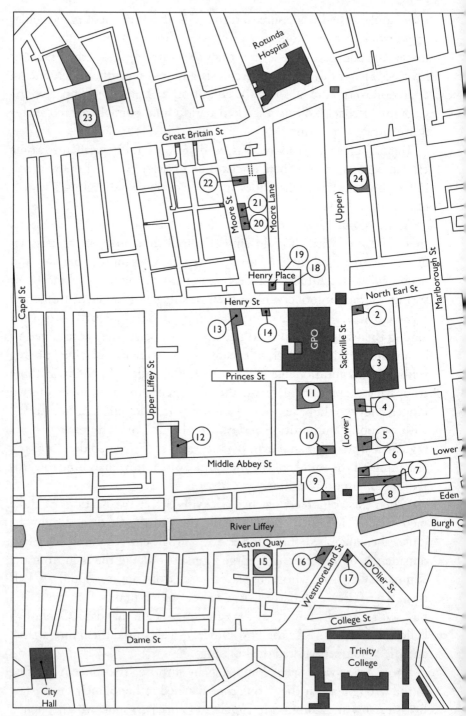

Republican forces General Headquarters (GPO/Sackville Street and Moore Street areas).

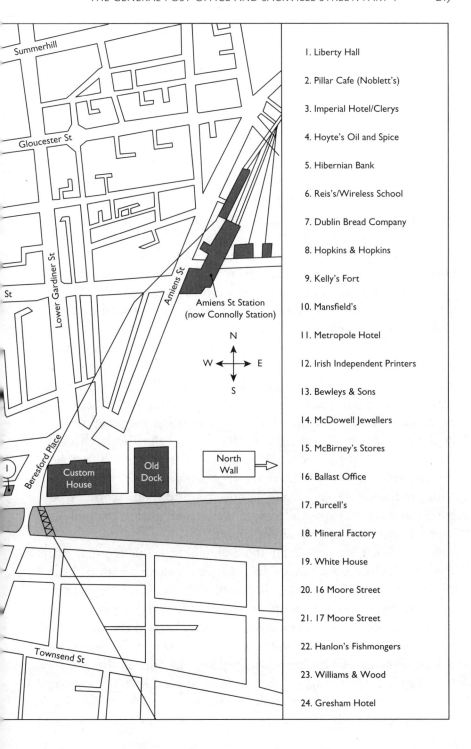

1. Liberty Hall

2. Pillar Cafe (Noblett's)

3. Imperial Hotel/Clerys

4. Hoyte's Oil and Spice

5. Hibernian Bank

6. Reis's/Wireless School

7. Dublin Bread Company

8. Hopkins & Hopkins

9. Kelly's Fort

10. Mansfield's

11. Metropole Hotel

12. Irish Independent Printers

13. Bewleys & Sons

14. McDowell Jewellers

15. McBirney's Stores

16. Ballast Office

17. Purcell's

18. Mineral Factory

19. White House

20. 16 Moore Street

21. 17 Moore Street

22. Hanlon's Fishmongers

23. Williams & Wood

24. Gresham Hotel

to be there, and who were swiftly taken prisoner. The Post Office workers and customers were ordered to leave the building as a shot rang out from Connolly's pistol to convince any stragglers. As these shocked men and women hurried towards the doors, many a jaw dropped at the sight of the Republicans smashing the windows with rifle butts and barricading them with anything that was to hand.

As soon as they had entered the huge interior of the building, a prearranged squad of seven men under the rebel's quartermaster, 31-year-old Mayo native Michael Staines, was sent to seize the Telegraph Office on the second floor. This was to prevent anyone from sending out word to the military of what was happening around them. The squad, armed with handguns, rushed the staircase and came face to face with half a dozen soldiers. The sound of another pistol-shot echoed on the staircase, and a British sergeant collapsed. The rest of the section reached for the ceiling in surrender. A thick Dublin accent shouted out: 'Any more of yiz?' The reply came in an English accent: 'Yeah, the corporal, but he has slipped out for a pint.'

The rebels' haul of ammunition was brought inside. Staines ordered the same squad of his men to use the GPO's mail-sorting pigeonholes for a more imaginative purpose.[2] They separated the different types of ammunition into the pigeonholes, a task carried out with the efficiency of an industrious postmaster. Meanwhile, Cumann na mBan members established a first-aid post in the building's hall. The kitchen and restaurant were commandeered by Desmond Fitzgerald. Throughout the oncoming days their stoves would steadily provide the insurgents with the most uplifting of morale boosters: hot food. Scores of pots, barrels and buckets were filled with water, anticipating the building's supply from the outside becoming cut off.

Several Volunteers made for the building's spacious rooftop, where they smashed into the surrounding slate and concrete with picks and crowbars to allow access to the floor below. As the first hole was bored through, Pearse's aide-de-camp, 33-year-old Dubliner Captain Seán T. O'Kelly, handed two bundles, each containing flags, to the officers who had been ordered by Commandant Connolly to take charge on the roof, Robert Walpole and the ever-energetic Michael Staines. Then, on the building's long white flagpole on the Henry Street side, Staines attached the Irish tricolour, just as Walpole ran across to the Prince's Street side and attached the other flag. Curious civilians on the street below gazed up in wonder, their eyes squinting in the midday sun. As the second flag unfurled in the breeze they noticed something very different and unfamiliar about it: painted on its deep green background were the bright golden letters, 'IRISH REPUBLIC'. A telephone line followed the flags to the rooftop, enabling its section commanders and officers to receive orders from the ground floor.

Shortly afterwards, against the majestic backdrop of the GPO's six huge pillars, Pádraig Pearse read out the Proclamation of the Irish Republic, using his much practised oratorical expertise to its utmost.

Despite the Proclamation's tone and content being somewhat wasted on the half-listening and taunting crowd, Connolly, now standing next to Pearse, shook his hand and thanked God for allowing them to witness such a day. Thomas Clarke conveyed a similar blessing before they retired back inside.

Volunteer Charles Donnelly was approached by Pearse soon afterwards and handed several bundles of the Proclamation to distribute. Donnelly then leaned out one of the windows and called over a newspaper boy. He asked the youngster to hand them out, which he did, before returning a short time later looking for more, now carrying a cap full of coins. 'You were supposed to give them out for free!' was Donnelly's exasperated reaction. The teenager, however, was supporting his mother and siblings. When Donnelly found out, he told him in a more sympathetic tone to take the money home. The boy of about 16 sprinted away, but returned later to join the garrison in the GPO as a Volunteer.

Meanwhile, the crowd outside had begun to disperse. Some of them went home, while others ventured towards either O'Connell Bridge, or to the Parnell Monument at the northern end of the long boulevard. Most were pleasantly excited to find themselves suddenly gifted with front-row seats on an unfolding drama. The prospect of witnessing this historic event was a strong temptation to stay, in spite of the obvious danger from the inevitable military backlash. The warm and balmy early afternoon sunshine only added to the attraction of the bank holiday spectacle; it became referred to afterwards as 'rebellion weather'.

It did not take long for the backlash to manifest itself. For a time, a brief but uneasy calm had descended over Sackville Street. Gunfire, however, could soon be heard from several directions throughout the city, and the growing apprehension felt by many rebels in the GPO intensified with each rifle crack.

POBLACHT NA H EIREANN.

THE PROVISIONAL GOVERNMENT
OF THE
IRISH REPUBLIC
TO THE PEOPLE OF IRELAND.

IRISHMEN AND IRISHWOMEN: In the name of God and of the dead generations from which she receives her old tradition of nationhood, Ireland, through us, summons her children to her flag and strikes for her freedom.

Having organised and trained her manhood through her secret revolutionary organisation, the Irish Republican Brotherhood, and through her open military organisations, the Irish Volunteers and the Irish Citizen Army, having patiently perfected her discipline, having resolutely waited for the right moment to reveal itself, she now seizes that moment, and, supported by her exiled children in America and by gallant allies in Europe, but relying in the first on her own strength, she strikes in full confidence of victory.

We declare the right of the people of Ireland to the ownership of Ireland, and to the unfettered control of Irish destinies, to be sovereign and indefeasible. The long usurpation of that right by a foreign people and government has not extinguished the right, nor can it ever be extinguished except by the destruction of the Irish people. In every generation the Irish people have asserted their right to national freedom and sovereignty; six times during the past three hundred years they have asserted it in arms. Standing on that fundamental right and again asserting it in arms in the face of the world, we hereby proclaim the Irish Republic as a Sovereign Independent State, and we pledge our lives and the lives of our comrades-in-arms to the cause of its freedom, of its welfare, and of its exaltation among the nations.

The Irish Republic is entitled to, and hereby claims, the allegiance of every Irishman and Irishwoman. The Republic guarantees religious and civil liberty, equal rights and equal opportunities to all its citizens, and declares its resolve to pursue the happiness and prosperity of the whole nation and of all its parts, cherishing all the children of the nation equally, and oblivious of the differences carefully fostered by an alien government, which have divided a minority from the majority in the past.

Until our arms have brought the opportune moment for the establishment of a permanent National Government, representative of the whole people of Ireland and elected by the suffrages of all her men and women, the Provisional Government, hereby constituted, will administer the civil and military affairs of the Republic in trust for the people.

We place the cause of the Irish Republic under the protection of the Most High God, Whose blessing we invoke upon our arms, and we pray that no one who serves that cause will dishonour it by cowardice, inhumanity, or rapine. In this supreme hour the Irish nation must, by its valour and discipline and by the readiness of its children to sacrifice themselves for the common good, prove itself worthy of the august destiny to which it is called.

Signed on Behalf of the Provisional Government,

THOMAS J. CLARKE,
SEAN Mac DIARMADA,   THOMAS MacDONAGH,
P. H. PEARSE,   EAMONN CEANNT,
JAMES CONNOLLY.   JOSEPH PLUNKETT.

The Proclamation was read out in front of the General Post Office on Easter Monday, and distributed among hundreds of onlookers, as well as being sold to several dozen by one particularly enterprising youngster, who then threw in his lot with the rebels. NATIONAL LIBRARY OF IRELAND

As the shots rang out, frantic telephone calls were being made throughout the country with demands to send troops to Dublin. 'The Shinners have risen!' was a sentence repeated over and over by half-panicked officers. In Marlborough Barracks on Blackhorse Avenue, Major Wilfred E. Russell-Collis of the 5th Lancers[3] had been left in charge of the 6th Reserve Cavalry Regiment while its commander, Colonel Kirk had left to attend the Fairyhouse Races. He received an urgent call regarding 'disturbances' in the city centre with orders to send men to take a look. He then ordered Captain Wilson to make a reconnaissance patrol with a composite of the 5th and 12th Lancers.

Soon the sound of distant gunshot was added to by a succession of alarming shouts of, 'Lancers! ... Lancers!' which rang out from the direction of the Parnell Monument. The crowds of onlookers scattered as 30 or so British horsemen trotted into view. Inside the GPO, Connolly became aware of the threat to his left flank, and ordered his men to their posts. He told them to hold their fire until he gave the order.

Dozens of rifle barrels began to appear in the building's many barricaded window frames and from its rooftop. After months of training, the rebels' hearts pounded with the daunting prospect of actual combat with a real enemy. The Lancers, meanwhile, lined themselves up by the Parnell Monument, where Captain Wilson took a long look at the two unfamiliar flags fluttering in the breeze above the rebel headquarters. He methodically surveyed Sackville Street. He saw several armed men sprint across the wide boulevard from Lower Abbey Street and into the GPO. The officer ordered his cavalrymen forward.

The horsemen advanced at a slow trot. They made an impressive and intimidating sight in their military finery. Perfectly groomed mounts with confident-looking cavalrymen in the saddle clattered along the cobblestoned street. Lances glinted in the afternoon sunlight. Their presence was an unambiguous display of force, brought forth to strike fear and uncertainty into those who had dared to rise against the Crown in Ireland's capital. On they came.

Lieutenant Michael Boland, of E Company, 4th Battalion,[4] saw the Lancers begin their advance. From his positions in Lower Abbey Street he ordered his men to rush across Sackville Street. When they had gained the far side, a signal came from the windows of the GPO to use the Prince's Street van entrance to get inside. Boland shouted to Lieutenant Eamon Bulfin to find the entrance and ordered the rest of his men to fix bayonets and prepare for an attack. Within seconds, his men had formed two ranks, one kneeling to the front and the other standing behind, both with bayonets fixed to their rifles, now pointing at the approaching Lancers.

The Volunteers inside the GPO let loose just as the head of the Lancers reached Nelson's Pillar. Their shots, fired before Commandant Connolly's command was given, echoed around the surrounding tall buildings and in the narrow side streets nearby. This alerted the horsemen far too soon for his liking. Connolly's subsequent curses at those who had disobeyed his order were quickly drowned in deafening booms as another volley rang out. Captain Wilson shouted at his cavalrymen to turn back. They swung their horses around and drove their spurs into the ribs of the animals and ran for safety. They left three of their comrades dead and one dying on the street, with several horses perishing in agony next to them. A section of Volunteers rushed out to relieve them of their weapons before their bodies were removed to Jervis Street Hospital. Some of the other cavalrymen had received more minor bullet wounds but had managed to remain in their saddles. Scores of civilians who had watched the action unfold from their windows, doorways and nearby street corners and laneways looked on in silence and disbelief.

After this brief skirmish, the GPO garrison returned to the task of fortifying its positions. Morale was sky-high after so readily seeing off the Lancers. Tunnelling into the buildings behind the GPO on Henry Street soon began in earnest, to act as a line of communication or of retreat should the need arise, and the men set to with an enthusiasm bordering on exuberance. The general sense of optimism and excitement was added to by some humorous episodes: one zealous rebel officer convinced himself of the need for urgent dispatches and reports to be handed to his commandant concerning the most trivial of developments, prompting Connolly to quip: 'If that man was standing on his right foot, he would send me a dispatch to inform me that he was shortly going to put down his left foot.'[5] Those around him erupted with laughter.

Volunteer Thomas Devine of E Company 3rd Battalion made his way into the GPO soon after hearing that the rebellion was going ahead. He had just finished a shift in work. When he entered he was pleasantly surprised to see his company commander, Captain Liam Tannam, manning a position at a window. Tannam welcomed him and pointed to the pile of bandoliers and guns recently taken from the Lancers, adding: 'Help yourself.' Devine struggled with the webbing owing to the cumbersome work clothes he wore, so he asked the busy-looking Citizen Army officer next to him to lend a hand. 'Certainly, my son,' was the reply.[6] The man with the Scottish lilt to his accent helped to fit Devine with a bandolier with impressive efficiency before stepping away to deal with another of the countless tasks demanded in what was now a hive of activity. Devine was curious as to why his surrounding comrades were now laughing at him, assuming it was his ridiculous appearance. 'Do you know who that was?' asked one, before he answered them, half-questioningly: 'James Connolly?'

Many people approached the GPO over the ensuing hours to ask the sentries manning its doors and windows if they could take up arms and join them, identifying themselves as comrades from other units, whose plans had been thrown into disarray by the countermand order. During one completely unexpected episode of this nature, Captain Tannam found himself both shocked and amused to add to the garrison's complement two seamen, a Swede and a Finn, who had just arrived in Dublin with their ship, and were keen to take up a cause they felt was close to their own hearts, as their countries were being similarly governed by an empire which had close ties to Great Britain, i.e. Russia. One of these unexpected Volunteers was given a shotgun. During a false alarm, he accidentally fired the weapon and wounded Volunteer James Kenny in the foot. Joseph Plunkett immediately had him transferred to a backroom, where he was assigned tasks that did not involve the use of firearms.

This, however, was not the only case of 'friendly fire' that day: Lieutenant Liam Clarke was nearly killed when a canister bomb exploded in his face. He was blown back several feet, but after regaining some composure refused to have his wounds treated, insisting on staying at his post. He eventually agreed to have his injuries attended to, literally at gunpoint.

Back at Liberty Hall, Irish Citizen Army Quartermaster Jim O'Neill was guarding the huge haul of supplies and ammunition there, accompanied by a large number of men under Captain Frank Thornton.[7] O'Neill had orders to wait until the last stragglers showed up and then barricade the building and create the illusion that it was heavily defended. Thornton busied himself and his men with this while O'Neill saw to it that enough vehicles were commandeered to shift their impressively lethal cargo.

Half a mile to their east, meanwhile, Major Somerville marched at the head of a large column of British troops from the Army School of Musketry in Dollymount to North Wall Quay, where they took over the docks and the North Wall train yards. Their second column, whose task was to occupy Amiens Street Station, were, however, unable to move up in conjunction, having been held up at Annesley Bridge by the Volunteers of 2nd Battalion under Captain Leo Henderson.

Towards late afternoon, a section of men under the command of Fergus O'Kelly was ordered by Joseph Plunkett to cross Sackville Street and take over the Dublin Wireless School of Telegraphy in the block of buildings between Lower Abbey Street and Eden Quay, diagonally across the street from the GPO. The huge rooftop pyramid above the Dublin Bread Company dominated this entire block of buildings. While O'Kelly and his men were labouring away at the aerials on the rooftop the tactical importance of not being overlooked became evident to him. He sent a messenger back to the GPO with a recommendation that the entire block between Lower Abbey Street and Eden Quay be occupied with immediate effect. Commandant Connolly responded without delay, and sent a detachment across with additional orders to construct a barricade across Lower Abbey Street. The latter move was intended to prevent an attack coming from Amiens Street Station. It was feared that the British would use the station as a marshalling area to launch such an attack. Captain Tom Weafer and his 2nd Battalion Volunteers provided the manpower, and 25 of them rushed across the street to reinforce the block. He divided them into two smaller sections: the first, consisting of ten men, was detailed to the Hibernian Bank on the corner of Sackville Street and Lower Abbey Street. The remainder set up their headquarters in the Dublin Bread Company itself. Once their positions were consolidated they set about building the barricade, using several large reels of paper belonging to *The Irish Times* newspaper, and the entire stock of motorcycles and bicycles from both Keating's and Kelly's Cycles Shops on Lower Abbey Street.

The building at the southern end of the block overlooking the river, Hopkins & Hopkins Jewellers, was occupied by Section Commander Séamus Robinson, accompanied by two of the other Volunteers who had peeled off from the main column as they had marched to Sackville Street earlier on. On the opposite side of the road, at the junction of Bachelors Walk and Sackville Street, Kelly's Fishing Tackle Shop was occupied by

Volunteer Peadar Bracken from Tullamore in County Offaly, and the other two men who had left the main force at the same time. These men had honed their marksmanship skills to the point of near perfection with the much lauded Kimmage Garrison. The 'Kimmage Men,' as they had become known over the previous months of preparations, had arrived in the city centre earlier by tram from the Harold's Cross Road, a service which their commander Captain George Plunkett famously insisted on paying for with the words: 'Fifty-two tu'penny fares and don't stop 'till we reach O'Connell Bridge.' The rebels now had two vantage points dominating the bridge: from its north-eastern and north-western flanks.

At Liberty Hall, Frank Thornton received word by messenger from Commandant Connolly that they were now established in the GPO and that he was to evacuate the position and make his way there. Fifteen vehicles of different sizes and descriptions, from horse-drawn wagons to trucks, then set off with approximately 50 Volunteers. Captain Thornton took a last look at Liberty Hall, satisfied that his men had done a good job. The building looked heavily garrisoned. Their short journey was uneventful and soon they were in Prince's Street, where the vehicles were swiftly unloaded.

Roughly 2 miles west, at Kingsbridge railway station, the Mobile Column of the 3rd Reserve Cavalry Brigade under Colonel Portal had now begun to arrive. The brigade consisted of 1,600 troopers, 400 of whom were immediately put on carriages bound for Amiens Street via the Loopline with orders to reinforce Major Somerville at North Wall. Most of the remainder were sent to the relief of Dublin Castle.

Central Dublin contained some of the worst slums in Europe at that time. Many of the tenement houses, inhabited often by 10 to 12 families with one or two rooms apiece, were located close to where this unexpected action was unfolding. As news filtered out of the rebellion and a breakdown in law and order, the inhabitants took to the streets. Initially, there was boorish and drunken behaviour, but it descended into mass looting of shops throughout the Sackville Street area, and eventually resulted in many shops being set on fire.

After repeated appeals to cease the plundering were ignored, Connolly felt compelled to give the order to fire a volley over the heads of the looters. The crowds scattered wildly when they heard the first volley, but quickly gathered again. Another volley was aimed over their heads, but the looting continued unabated. Volunteer Captain William J. Brennan-

Some of the young Volunteer and Citizen Army men who took the GPO. (*L–r*): Desmond O'Reilly, James Mooney, Paddy Byrne, John Doyle, Tom McGrath, Hugh Thornton, John J. Twamly and Bernard Frick. MILITARY ARCHIVES

Whitmore suggested to Connolly that the next volley be fired into the looters,[8] adding that the Volunteers must maintain the rule of law as the rebellion progressed. Mob rule, he claimed, would make a mockery of their entire endeavour. Connolly refused, insisting that such a drastic measure would only be employed in the event of the rebels themselves coming under attack from the increasingly volatile crowds. Frustratingly, every time a section was sent out to deal with the growing numbers of looters, they dispersed, and gathered again as soon as that section returned inside the GPO. The free-for-all continued, gradually tapering off with the approach of evening, when many pillaged the nearby pubs of their wines and spirits.

A strange and ominous type of energy was tangible in the relative silence that accompanied the arrival of nightfall. Thousands of beds were empty in the city centre. The pervading sense of apprehensive excitement forbade much sleep. The situation in Dublin's main street was unprecedented.

At 10 p.m., Commandant Connolly had received word that a large enemy force had positioned itself around the North Wall and was sending patrols to occupy Amiens Street Station. As a countermeasure he ordered 30-year-old Brennan-Whitmore to cross Sackville Street and construct a barricade across its junction with North Earl Street. He was also to occupy the Pillar Café above Noblet's Sweet Shop in the corner building next to the proposed barricade, directly facing the northern wing of the GPO. Next to this was the Imperial Hotel, which was above Clerys Department Store. The captain set off with ten men and dashed across in the darkness before storming into Tyler's Store after forcing its lock. They then broke into Noblet's, ascending its staircase to take position in the Pillar Café. They set up headquarters here and set to constructing the barricade.

As Captain Brennan-Whitmore established himself in his head-quarters, a Volunteer approached bringing word that the owner of a local pub was outside and wanted a word. The curious captain was surprised to find an elderly gentleman suggesting to him the best positions on the roof for his riflemen. The publican explained that in the 'old Fenian days' they had reconnoitred the best vantage points in the event of an uprising. The rebel officer found himself highly impressed with the veteran Republican's choice of tactical firing positions. The publican shook Brennan-Whitmore's hand vigorously and said: 'God keep and guard you all, and make your fight successful,'[9] before handing the captain the keys to his own premises.

The rebels' confidence had risen throughout the day that was now drawing to a close. Communications had steadily come in from runners detailing the general successes enjoyed by all of their garrisons in the city, in spite of some setbacks. In the GPO they settled down for the night to the sounds of the relatively distant battles being fought in City Hall and in St Stephen's Green; 28 men were dispatched to reinforce the former. Hot food was distributed, weapons cleaned and checked, and the rebels grabbed what rest they could. They would soon need it.

At 3.45 a.m. on Tuesday, Brigadier General Lowe arrived at Kingsbridge Station with elements of the 25th Reserve Infantry Brigade. As the troops of the 5th Leinster Battalion and 5th Royal Dublin Fusiliers assembled, Lowe was given a situation report of the state of play in Dublin. He was also informed that reinforcements under Lieutenant-Colonel Meldon of the 4th Dublin Fusiliers Battalion, backed up by

Lieutenant-Colonel McClintock and an Ulster Composite Battalion of the 15th Reserve Infantry Brigade and the 5th Reserve Artillery Brigade under Major Hill were en route. Their estimated arrival time was 2 p.m.

The Volunteers at the Wireless School, having spent a long and nerve-racking night, succeeded in getting its transmitter working (and in doing so, laid claim to the dubious honour of operating the world's first pirate radio station). They were unable to operate its receiver, but nevertheless sent out the repeated message to the world about the birth of the Irish Republic without knowing if anyone could hear them. The British Army and Navy certainly could. Back in the GPO, each passing hour increased the rebels' eagerness for their next encounter. Connolly's morale was as high as on the previous day. At one point in the morning he was heard loudly joking, 'The Citizen Army have captured both the King and Kitchener ... in the Waxworks!'[10] Shortly afterwards, a clearly drunken man was brought before him, having more than likely spent the entire night pillaging a pub. When asked what he wanted, he replied, 'I want to fight for Ireland.' After asking the man if he was sure, Connolly added, 'Will you go home and have a sleep, and when you're sober come back and tell me you want to fight for Ireland and I will give you a rifle.' Whether or not he did return remains a mystery.

On Lower Sackville Street, the men in Hopkins & Hopkins and Reis's Shop had begun tunnelling towards each other. Captain Weafer relocated his headquarters to the Hibernian Bank and ordered a tunnel to be dug through to Hoyte's Oil & Spice building. After they had broken through, Cumann na mBan members set up a field hospital there. Across the street in Kelly's, they were also tunnelling back. Having received five additional men they were loopholing through the buildings towards Middle Abbey Street.

By now the British High Command had revised their plans. They would place a cordon around the rebel stronghold, rather than launch a direct large-scale infantry assault, their aim being to isolate their enemies from their other positions and outposts in the city. With methodical efficiency they selected their strategic positions and began occupying them.

Trinity College's Officer Training Corps, along with its armed porters, found their ranks bolstered by several British soldiers who were on leave in Dublin. Added to this were numerous colonial troops from such far-flung places as South Africa, Canada, Australia and New Zealand, also on leave. Many were seasoned infantrymen and accomplished sharpshooters. In total, about 100 men were available to the military in the 300-year-old College. When the uprising began, the College was like a beacon to loose military units when they realised it had not been taken by the insurgents.

They did not waste any time. Soon the huge rooftop areas of the College's various buildings and their upper floors were teeming with snipers, keen to outdo one another in scoring hits. Some of the more energetic ventured to McBirney's Shop on Burgh Quay where they engaged the positions on the opposite side of the Liffey. Later on, General Lowe ordered Colonel Portal to reinforce Trinity with the 5th Leinsters. As soon as they were in place, extra snipers were dispatched to the southern quays. The battalion brought with it plentiful ammunition, and the energetic riflemen were soon able to avail of the standard 120-round-per-man allowance.

Their sniping skills soon bore fruit, when Captain Tom Weafer was wounded by a rifle shot while checking the positions in the Dublin Bread Company. Captain Liam Tannam was rushed across from the GPO as his replacement. Shortly after he had carefully positioned himself above the bread company's ballroom, he noticed a suspicious-looking mannequin in an upstairs window of McBirney's. A flash suddenly appeared from behind it, and Tannam emptied the five-round magazine of a BSA rifle in its direction. No further gun flashes came from behind the mannequin.

Six miles to the north-west of Dublin city centre, meanwhile, four 18-pounder field guns of the 5th Artillery Reserve Regiment had arrived from Athlone Barracks, accompanied by roughly 160 men. The situation in the Broadstone railway terminus was still unclear at this point to the military, so rather than using it, the guns were disembarked early with their crews and supporting units. Major Hill split the battery into two separate sections, the first of which was transported to Grangegorman, while he travelled with the other to the Royal Hospital in Kilmainham. Once there he was ordered to proceed with haste to Trinity College where he would be placed under the command of Colonel Portal.

In the city's north-eastern suburbs at roughly the same time, the Ulster Composite Battalion marched into Dublin from Fairview. Their train had been unable to reach the city as the line's tracks had been blown up. After marching the 2 miles to the city centre, Lieutenant-

Colonel McClintock split the battalion into two formations. The first was to go to North Wall Quay and the Custom House, while the second was detailed to Amiens Street Station.

Back in the GPO, Frank Thornton received orders to take 20 men and occupy the Imperial Hotel. Once this was accomplished, he had further orders to make contact with Captain Brennan-Whitmore's position on North Earl Street's corner. Before he set off, Commandant Connolly handed him the Citizen Army's 'Plough and Stars' flag to hang outside the landmark building and wished him good luck.

Captain Thornton's section immediately crossed the street to the hotel. Mr Woods, the manager, was summoned and instructed to have all the guests leave. The compliant manager expedited the order with military efficiency and within minutes the building had been left to the rebels. The hotel was then fortified, while tunnelling was soon under way towards North Earl Street. Thornton set to his tasks with enthusiasm but, in his eagerness, neglected to hang the flag given to him by Connolly.

Along the North Circular Road towards evening, the rebel barricade manned by Captain Sullivan of 1st Battalion had been overrun by the 4th Royal Dublin Fusiliers backed up by two of the artillery pieces brought in to the city earlier on. The fall of the position had cleared the way for a strong dismounted force of the 6th Reserve Cavalry Regiment to push in to the city centre where they occupied Rutland Square (now Parnell Square).

At roughly 8 p.m., following another tense, often surreal, but relatively quiet day on Sackville Street, 66 Volunteers from the 2nd Battalion retired from their Fairview positions. Led by Captain Frank Henderson and Lieutenant Oscar Traynor, they fell back to the GPO, bringing with them the first tangible information regarding the military noose being placed around the rebel headquarters. They also brought their prisoners, whose khaki uniforms initially attracted fire from the Imperial Hotel, until James Connolly ran to the street waving his arms wildly and shouting at the men to cease fire, which they did.

After being debriefed, fed and rested, Traynor was ordered to take 22 men and occupy the six-storey Metropole Hotel, next door to the GPO with Prince's Street running between the buildings. They then pressed on to occupy the remainder of the buildings in the same block all the way through to Mansfield's Boot Store on Middle Abbey Street.

Communication tunnels were then bored through the interconnecting walls. Meanwhile the Imperial Hotel's vast quantities of foods were transported to the GPO's kitchens.

Captain Henderson was then ordered to take an additional 22 men and occupy McDowell's Jewellery Shop and Bewley's Provisions Store, both on Henry Street to the left of the GPO's rear. Once these positions were established he received further orders to construct two barricades on Henry Street, on either side of its junction with Moore Street. Following their completion, he proceeded to bore holes in the adjoining walls of the buildings which ran from the GPO to Arnott's Department Store. This would facilitate fully concealed movement all the way from Sackville Street to Liffey Street, a distance of approximately 300 yards. There was to be little rest for either Oscar Traynor or Frank Henderson that night.

Meanwhile, a section of five British snipers crept from Findlater Place to Upper Sackville Street, where they then took up firing positions on the roof of the Gresham Hotel. This afforded them a good angle of fire to the GPO from across the road, approximately 200 yards away. The entire area surrounding the northern end of the street was now infested with the military. After a while a breathless rebel runner informed his leaders in the GPO of a large enemy presence being assembled by the Rotunda Hospital. This news prompted the garrison to prepare for a night attack, but after hours of exhausting suspense it never came. The only distraction in the long hours of darkness was a 'stand to' command to cover an additional 20 Volunteers who were sent across the street to reinforce the Imperial Hotel.

As the sun rose on Wednesday the sniper battles began in earnest. The first item on the British sharpshooters' agenda presented itself shortly before 5 a.m. in the form of Frank Thornton who was now attempting to rectify his mistake of not having hung out the flag the previous day. Over a dozen shots were sent his way as he saw to it that the symbol flew proudly in the early morning breeze, much to the delight of the socialists in the building. The building they now occupied belonged to an individual by the name of William Martin Murphy, a nemesis of both the leaders and the rank and file of the Citizen Army from 1913. They considered him to be a brutal epitome of capitalism.

Both of the relatively small but tactically vital rebel outposts in Lower Sackville Street – Hopkins & Hopkins and Kelly's – were quickly drawn into the increasingly vicious duel with the snipers on the Trinity College roof. The Volunteers' lack of numbers had prevented them capturing Trinity College on Easter Monday. Their enemies now had a well-positioned base of operations in the very heart of the city from where they could effectively cut the Volunteers' lines of communication. College Green, situated just outside Trinity's front gate, already contained the body of an insurgent cyclist, 22-year-old Gerald Keogh, who had attempted to run the gauntlet of fire from its roof with an urgent communiqué from his headquarters, before being shot through the head by an Australian sniper.

The sharpshooters on the Gresham had also opened up with their own dawn chorus. Their enthusiastic malevolence was soon met in equal measure by the return fire of the rebels, glad to be in action after the drawn-out hours of darkness. The British then set up several machine-gun emplacements inside Trinity College, Tara Street fire station, in the Rotunda Hospital and on Amiens Street.

These guns were quick to open fire on the rebel positions on Lower Sackville Street. The Vickers machine gun in Trinity spewed thousands of 3 oz bullets the length of the boulevard. Sporadic bursts came from the other machine-gunners and soon Dublin's main street became a battlefield. The repeated cracks and booms of rifle fire added to the abrasive staccato of the machine guns. Smoky streams of incendiary bullets criss-crossed wildly, setting fire to the few remaining unburnt shop canopies on the street. Huge chunks of concrete and plaster were gouged from the surrounding walls, while dozens of windows were smashed, sending shards of glass flying through the buildings and onto the wide pavements.

At approximately 7.45 a.m., the wrought-iron side gate of Trinity College facing Great Brunswick Street police barracks opened suddenly, and two horse-drawn artillery pieces were rushed out onto the street with their accompanying ammunition transports and crews. Their speed suggested they had an urgent appointment to keep. They immediately made their way onto Townsend Street, skirting the forbidding-looking barracks before making the 90-degree left turn onto Tara Street. Their route had been scouted out earlier and a cordon of riflemen lined the streets and rooftops as they passed to protect the artillery and crews from the nest of riflemen from the Volunteers' 3rd Battalion on the eastern side of Great Brunswick Street.

Six men were assigned to each huge gun, which was quickly uncoupled before its crew worked with the efficiency of beavers to set it up in position. An NCO was in control and selected the target and range. He then chose the ammunition type: high explosive, shrapnel or smoke. Next in line came the gunlayer who sighted the gun on target, and the gunner who waited for the command of 'Fire!' The bombardier determined the propellant charge depending on the range, and ensured each round was properly fused. The next task fell to the rammer, who used a long straight rod to drive home the shell placed in the gun's open breech by the loader who was in turn fed by the bombardier. There were several crews per gun, ensuring that replacements were readily available in the event of casualties. Each member of the battery was highly trained as both a gunner and infantryman, and in Dublin's built-up city centre, where the guns were inevitably separated from one another, one officer was in overall command of each particular gun from the battery. The accompanying tasks of preparing positions, servicing and maintaining the gun and its limber, transportation and logistics fell to each man who was not actually involved in firing the weapon at that particular point.

In spite of their textbook deployment, however, they were unable to anchor the artillery pieces into the rock-solid ground. In any event, they were late. To their right, the grey bow of the *Helga* appeared with its escort ship, the armed trawler *Sealark*. At 8 a.m. the *Helga* opened fire on Liberty Hall, followed by the two field guns. The artillery crews took great care not to be injured by the massive recoils which sent the guns spinning like ice skaters on the cobblestones. They had to be repositioned after each shot. Word of the problem was sent back to Colonel Portal in Trinity College.

Captain Tannam and his men on the rooftop of the Dublin Bread Company strained to pick out targets on board the *Helga*, and several well-aimed shots rang from the metal surrounding its gun. After a couple of dozen shots they came to the attention of the Trinity machine-gunners. A sudden storm of flying lead whipped the air around their crouching bodies as they manoeuvred themselves to reply in kind. The gun fell silent for a time, allowing a brief respite, until Tannam and the others found themselves being assailed again. The gunners had switched the position of their gun.

The fire continued for an hour or so and then stopped suddenly, before several whistles blew in the distance followed by screams of

The interior of Liberty Hall, following its shelling on Wednesday 26 April 1916. NATIONAL LIBRARY OF IRELAND

'Charge!' The machine guns now turned their attentions to Liberty Hall, while the Ulster Composite Battalion launched a bayonet charge across Beresford Place to attack the deserted building, unaware of its earlier abandonment. In doing so they completely sealed off the eastern ends of both Lower Abbey Street and Eden Quay. One of the 18-pounder guns was then returned to Trinity College.

By mid-morning, Tom Weafer, whose wound had been treated successfully, was feeling well enough to resume command of the Dublin Bread Company's block of buildings. He reassured Captain Tannam of his fitness, before the latter made his way to the Hibernian Bank's huge wooden front door, which was at a 45-degree angle to the street junction. Here he waited for a pause in the shooting to make his life-or-death sprint across the street to resume his original command, and to inform Commandant Connolly. The gap eventually came, prompting Tannam to make his frantic dash, but as he traversed a loud cry of 'My Jesus mercy!' rang out from behind, and Captain Weafer collapsed to the floor inside the bank, having been shot through the head by a sniper. Tannam's momentum carried him forward, and despite the bullets that whipped the ground around him, he made it across to headquarters.

In Hopkins & Hopkins, Volunteer Cormac Turner was methodically scanning the south quays opposite with his powerful field glasses. A sniper had been causing serious trouble from one of the buildings there. It turned out to be McBirney's again. Turner frowned as he zeroed in on the source of the enemy fire and pointed out the central top window to Citizen Army man Andy Conroy. Conroy lined up his rifle sights as Turner signalled the same sniper's position across Sackville Street to the men watching from Kelly's. Conroy fired first, followed by a volley from Kelly's. The bricks surrounding the window in McBirney's seemed to explode under the weight of the huge rounds that smashed into them, but more than one shot had met its mark. The enemy sniper was finished.

The general increase in fire convinced the rebel commanders that an attack in force from across O'Connell Bridge was imminent and they gave orders to make ready for such an assault. An ambush was then devised. The rebels set out to create the impression that the Dublin Bread Company and its entire block had been evacuated to lure the enemy across the bridge into what they would assume was uncontested ground, whereupon flanking fire from both sides could be unleashed upon them, catching them in a killing ground with little or no cover.

In the confusion of battle, however, and with no one in the block in overall command, the order, which was carried across the street by an officer, was misinterpreted, and instead of just creating a false impression, the building was actually evacuated, leaving just Kelly's on the opposite side of the road to hold the line at the river. The insurgents retreated under fire in small groups from the entire Dublin Bread Company block back to the GPO. Luckily for their commanders the expected enemy attack never materialised, and a lull developed as the machine-gunners rested.

The snipers all the while continued their contest. Captain Tannam soon claimed three kills among the snipers on the Gresham roof from his new-found perch in the GPO. His first kill had begun as something of a duel between himself and an enemy rifleman who had narrowly missed him as he aimed a high-powered .22 rifle towards the Gresham. The enemy .303 round had smashed into the wooden window frame next to Tannam, but he had reacted with lightning speed and aimed a shot back at the enemy soldier which was both accurate and lethal.

As the church bells throughout the quieter parts of Dublin pealed for noon, the rebel lookouts in Kelly's were met with a most curious vision. Half a dozen navvies had appeared in D'Olier Street not far from Trinity College, dressed in their overalls.[11] Their unexpected appearance suggested that something was not right within the city, apart from the obvious. It seemed to the Volunteers that the gas mains were in need of urgent repairs and they spared the 'emergency workers' their attentions. They began digging up paving slabs.

As the 'navvies' hacked away at the road, Colonel Portal in his field headquarters ordered a number of machine-gun crews to advance to forward positions in Purcell's, a shop at the apex of the triangle of D'Olier Street and Westmoreland Street, which overlooked O'Connell Bridge. Accompanied by 30 or so supporting infantry they clattered their way to their detailed positions and once the machine guns were in place a number of the troops in support moved into McBirney's and its adjoining buildings along the south quays.

As soon as the road was dug up, the artillery piece, which had been returned to Trinity College earlier rushed back out on to the street. It transpired that the 'navvies' had, in fact, been British artillerymen in disguise, and had ripped up the pavement to allow the gun to be 'dug in'. As soon as the rebels realised they had been duped they fired everything they had at the men trying to get it into place. The British deception was successful, nevertheless, and although it was hardly an ideal position for a field gun, its recoil would now be diminished considerably.

At 2 p.m., the 18-pounder and machine guns had been positioned and sighted, and opened fire. The thunderous roar of cannon shattered nearby windows and Kelly's south-facing facade overlooking the river on Bachelors Walk was pulverised under the sustained barrage of shrapnel shells. It simultaneously came under attack from the Vickers gunners in Purcell's as well as the machine-gunners in Tara Street. The noise was deafening. The Volunteers rushed into their tunnels to seek cover from flying debris and bullets, emerging periodically to fire back at their assailants. Peadar Bracken and the others in the position soon realised that the post was now useless. A large crowd of civilians had gathered in the sheltered laneways just off Aston Quay to view the spectacle of the building's exterior and outside pavement being transformed into a mosaic of broken glass and brick. Artillery shells struck roughly every 30 seconds and the building was hosed with bullets. Bracken and the others retreated to reinforce their comrades in Mansfield's Boot Store and the Metropole Hotel.

The earlier evacuation of Hopkins & Hopkins had not gone unnoticed by the British troops, and when the bombardment of Kelly's eventually ceased they became increasingly cocky. The lack of return fire from the now-ruined outpost across the river signalled to them that it was relatively safe to cross O'Connell Bridge. Volleys from the Metropole and Imperial Hotels, however, dissuaded them. In fact, so ferocious was the fire that they were convinced the shots smashing into the bridge wall, the cobblestones and tramlines, and whipping past their heads were actually coming from Hopkins & Hopkins. They regrouped and plastered the same building with lead.

One of the machine-gunners in Trinity College appeared to have developed an intense dislike for the Plough and Stars flag flying outside the Imperial Hotel. He treated it initially to several sporadic doses of Vickers ammunition, until after a time it appeared his distaste got the better of him, leading him to expend several ammunition belts trying to destroy the enemy symbol. The men inside the building cursed the gunner, especially when his bullets began to pepper the vast water tank on the Imperial's roof. The garrison watched as their water supply slowly drained away.

Shortly afterwards, machine-gun bullets began spraying the GPO from the street's northern end. Men rushed to the rooftop, positioning themselves behind the parapet on the Henry Street side, and began shooting back through the balustrades, while trying to keep their heads down. British troops could be seen in the hazy distance darting to and fro, seeking better firing positions. Then a loud and alarming cry of 'Here they come!' sounded out from the roof, quickly followed by the fear-inducing sight of an armoured truck at the Parnell Monument, which began lumbering down Sackville Street towards them.

The rebels on the rooftop opened up with everything they had, barely taking time to breathe between their shots. Their bullets merely ricocheted off the thick metal skin of the improvised mammoth. The insurgents' fire became unsteady and inaccurate in their panic. The British machine guns belched belt after belt of red-hot lead at the Volunteers, trying to cover the advance of the truck.

Amid the melee, however, one particularly calm Volunteer named Joseph Sweeney steadied his Mauser rifle against the parapet of the roof, and fired several ranging shots. When he was satisfied with his aim, he steadied himself again and fired, straight through the driver's slit, killing him instantly. The armoured truck swerved for a few seconds, then stalled abruptly outside the Gresham, where it remained. Its cargo of troops stayed put inside, fearing that to leave the safety of their metal shell would mean certain death, as rebel bullets smashed into the hull. They remained in their claustrophobic shell in the stifling heat for several torturous hours, until another truck arrived to tow them back towards Rutland Square after night fell.

Connolly moved ceaselessly through the GPO, trying to boost morale and encourage the men. His loud and boisterous enthusiasm, alternating with his decisive instructions and orders, could frequently be heard above the frantic shouting throughout the building and the din of the rebel guns, and was a continuing source of reassurance for his fighters.

The Hibernian Bank position was rapidly becoming untenable. The Ballast Office, at the corner of Westmoreland Street and Aston Quay, was now heavily garrisoned and the troops there were concentrating their fire on the beleaguered building. Volunteer Jack Stafford positioned himself on the bank's balcony and fired several shots back across until his rifle stock was shattered by a bullet as he held it. It took several moments for him to realise that his hand had been badly injured by the shot and as he re-entered the building the order was given to evacuate the block. Unfortunately for him, the first-aid position in Hoyte's was the first to leave, meaning his hand would for now go untreated.

As the medics crossed the street waving a Red Cross flag, the enemy ceased fire to allow the stretchers across. The remaining men of the garrison were afforded no such courtesy, however. When they made their break, it seemed that the British Army had reserved their entire arsenal for them. A massive deluge of lead smashed into the walls and windows as they sprinted out and scattered. A few made it to headquarters while others rushed to the Imperial Hotel in the next block. Jack Stafford became lost in the back streets and was forced to hide out in a building, until he eventually escaped and made it back to his home in Drumcondra.

Connolly was now increasingly troubled by the absence of men in the Dublin Bread Company block since it had been abandoned in error earlier. Convinced that the artillery fire battering the lower end of the street was a precursor to a full-on infantry attack, he was anxious to regain the advantage of flanking fire, and now asked for volunteers to cross the fire-swept street to reoccupy the buildings. He handpicked 15 men from the many who stepped forward. Those selected included 26-year-old Belfast-born Séamus Robinson and his two comrades who had originally occupied Hopkins & Hopkins.

They left the GPO using Nelson's Pillar as cover, but as enemy fire was now coming from both ends of the street, casualties were inevitable. The machine-gunners strafed their every move, cutting several of them down. Only ten reached their intended position: the remainder lay dead or wounded in the street. When Robinson and Andy Conroy reclaimed their earlier positions in Hopkins & Hopkins, Conroy said: 'We don't have enough men to hold the position. We will have to go back and get more.' Robinson looked back at him saying: 'What, back out there?' The two men burst out laughing.

Meanwhile, Captain Brennan-Whitmore, having found himself unable to communicate with the GPO, improvised a pulley system whereby the messages were inserted into a tin can attached to a long twine, which was strung across Sackville Street by a daring runner. The improvised communication link worked for a time, until eventually perforated beyond use by a hawk-eyed sniper. The rebels then simply attached pieces of paper with written orders to the same length of string, many of which arrived at their destination containing bullet holes as well as messages.

A short time later, Brennan-Whitmore surveyed the developing carnage from his elevated vantage point in the Pillar Cafe. Machine-gun bullets whizzed and screamed up and down the street, ripping at pavements, windows and walls. He had initially felt very uncomfortable about the strategy employed by Pearse and the other rebel leaders of occupying buildings and simply waiting to be attacked in force by the enemy; having spent several years in the military, he felt a more fluid strategy would have been appropriate. He consulted with Captain Frank Thornton in the Imperial Hotel about a possible breakout into north County Dublin in the event of the tide turning decisively against the rebels, which he felt it inevitably would. If necessary, from there they could join with Thomas Ashe's 5th Battalion, which was engaged in the surrounding countryside. Thornton's response was that the Imperial needed to be held, and could only be evacuated if they were bombed out. The survival of their headquarters depended on their hold being maintained at all costs. Brennan-Whitmore asked him to form an evacuation plan for such an eventuality and to ensure that any men with local knowledge were readily available. The fighting in the area then began to die off slowly as the evening wore on, allowing both sides an unexpectedly restful evening, despite the sporadic interruptions of the snipers and the artillery.

Brennan-Whitmore was not the only one among the Republicans that night with serious reservations about the manner in which the rebellion was being executed. Across the road in the GPO an enigmatic 42-year-old – Michael O'Rahilly from Ballylongford, County Kerry – had spent the better part of the past three days conducting some intense soul-searching and frequently looking upon the apparently naive and occasionally messianic antics of President Pearse with a disillusion that bordered on despair.

The O'Rahilly, as he was more popularly known, had spent the previous weekend travelling the country in his De Dion-Bouton touring car, ensuring that the countermand order was understood and adhered to. He had arrived back at Liberty Hall early on Monday morning, expecting the Irish Volunteers to have been stood down. When he saw that the rebellion was going ahead regardless, he was furious, but famously threw in his lot with the Volunteers saying, 'Well, I've helped wind up the clock – I might as well hear it strike.' His touring car was then filled with weapons, supplies and ammunition, and eventually was used to form part of the barricade in Prince's Street, where it was later destroyed.

Around midnight, in the darkness to the north-west of Sackville Street, an armoured car trundled into Grangegorman and hitched one of the 18-pounders there to its tow bar. Its crewmen jumped into the cargo area as it was towed out to be deployed with the 6th Reserve Cavalry holding Rutland Square.

11

The General Post Office and Sackville Street: Part 2

'Is this the end, Séamus?'

Thursday morning, 27 April 1916, began bright and sunny. The much lauded 'rebellion weather' was holding firm. Many weary Volunteers on the roof of the GPO, having huddled together under a cold moonlit sky, turned their faces towards the warm rays during brief lulls in the fighting.

With a sudden and unholy whistle, an incoming shell smashed into *The Irish Times* printing office on Lower Abbey Street shortly after midday, having been shot from south of the river at Tara Street. Many more followed and the building was soon engulfed in flames. The fire spread at an alarming rate, initially setting the adjacent rebel barricade ablaze, which then spread the fire to both sides of the street. The Hibernian Bank caught fire, and very soon its entire block was at risk. In the Dublin Bread Company block, the Volunteers had no choice but to evacuate. The ten men who had regained this position the previous day rushed for the sanctuary of their headquarters, their every move harassed by bullets and shrapnel from exploding shells. Andy Conroy was hit in the ankle by a machine-gun burst as he ran just behind Séamus Robinson. He managed to raise himself up and limp as far as Oscar Traynor's position across the street, while Robinson and the others reached the GPO. Shrapnel shells now rained down all around. The destruction of Sackville Street was under way.

The ruins of the Hibernian Bank with the bombed-out remains of the block of buildings between Lower Abbey Street and Eden Quay in the background. NATIONAL LIBRARY OF IRELAND

Inside the Imperial Hotel, when the scream of 'Artillery!' was first heard, Frank Thornton rushed to the front of the building to see British gunners trying to position another 18-pounder next to the Parnell Monument. He shouted to his men to open fire. Sensing the great urgency of the captain's orders, a dozen or so riflemen unleashed a frenzy of fire. The enemy artillerymen dashed for cover but the concentration of bullets was such that they were all hit. Their replacements quickly pulled the wounded men out of harm's way before an avalanche of rifle fire flew back at the Imperial Hotel. Its exterior erupted with geysers of flying masonry as scores of bullets struck. Simultaneously the huge gun fired. As it shot its high-explosive round, however, it spun under the recoil and the shell flew into the YMCA building on Upper Sackville Street, which was occupied by British troops.[1] Thinking they were under attack, those inside immediately evacuated the four-storey building.

Realising the danger of having an enemy field gun on Sackville Street, both the GPO and the Imperial Hotel garrisons concentrated everything they had on it and for several seconds the gun was subjected to an overwhelming assault of various calibre bullets. The entire northern end of the street rang out with ricochets before the gun was hastily pulled back to the relative safety of the Rotunda Hospital gardens.

When the bombardment of the Dublin Bread Company's block of buildings finally ceased several hours later, the British command post at Amiens Street Station ordered a company of troops from the Ulster Composite Battalion to advance up Lower Abbey Street, considering it to have been suitably 'softened up' by the shelling. Its mission was to occupy the buildings as far as the junction with Marlborough Street, including Tucks Engineers, Dunlop Rubber and the Abbey Theatre. From there two platoons would advance to Sackville Street, the first of which would then rush across under covering fire from the other, in order to capture and hold the buildings behind Kelly's Fishing Shop, unaware that 'Kelly's Fort', as it was known to the rebels, had been evacuated the previous day. To accomplish this, its troops were to break into the buildings on the block's junction with Middle Abbey Street, and from here they, along with riflemen firing from the Abbey, would cover the second platoon as they rushed across the street in support. They would then attack the position from its rear, clearing the buildings of insurgents one at a time. Once these objectives had been secured, the military could then move their artillery piece across O'Connell Bridge relatively unmolested, and use it to better effect against the rebel headquarters. When their officers fully understood their orders they checked their equipment and set off with their men.

They had a relatively uneventful journey along Lower Abbey Street, where infantrymen set about taking control of their detailed positions which sat to both sides, while their comrades advanced and prepared to cross a destroyed section of the burning barricade.

Vincent Poole, one of three brothers fighting in the Irish Citizen Army, and Tom Leahy, together with Harry Boland of the 4th Battalion Irish Volunteers who was spending his 29th birthday in the growing chaos, prepared themselves in Mansfield's Boot Shop. They coolly held their fire, as did Oscar Traynor and his men at the windows in the nearby Metropole, until the troops slowly came into full view on the Sackville Street side of the barricade, in preparation for crossing the road.

Suddenly, they opened up with volleys so ferocious that their shocked victims were initially unable to pinpoint the source. At least 30 rifles poured their assortment of bullets mercilessly at the troops, several of whom spun around under the impacts of the shots before collapsing. As their comrades cried out in agony next to them, the horrified remainder were forced to retreat. They had no option but to funnel themselves towards the narrow passable section of the burning barricade, beyond which their accompanying platoon was also beginning to take casualties. From here, they bunched up in their frantic attempts to reach safety. Traynor's men and the others could hardly miss. They were decimated.

Volleys of British supporting fire echoed loudly from the Abbey Theatre, and the rebels in Mansfield's found themselves at the epicentre of the clash. They fired like madmen, their volleys accompanied by shouts of encouragement to one another, and streams of verbal abuse towards the enemy. Their gun barrels overheated, rapidly becoming unusable. Water, however, was unavailable to Poole and the others to remedy their alarming predicament. They opened the tins of sardines they had brought with them as rations and which were scattered about on the shop's floor. With shaking hands, they poured the smelly, greasy brine along their smoking barrels. They retched as the overpowering steam blew back at their filthy faces and garments, but their ad-hoc cooling system proved effective, and they were soon shooting again. Oscar Traynor raced into the position with reinforcements, recognising that this building would be pivotal in holding back the inevitable future attacks in increased force from the same direction.

The remaining Ulstermen eventually retreated into the buildings on the eastern side of Lower Abbey Street. The casualties littering the rubble-strewn road outside Wynn's Hotel convinced them that an infantry assault across Sackville Street was impossible for now.

A pair of specialist Citizen Army men were hurried to Mansfield's and the Metropole, weighed down with canister bombs. Volunteer Charles Saurin looked on with concern as the first of them calmly smoked his pipe while laying out several of the improvised bombs in the Metropole. His colleague took up position in an upstairs room in Mansfield's, which allowed him a clear view of both Sackville Street and Abbey Street. Soon the artillery shells began to explode again, and it was not long before Lower Abbey Street was ablaze all the way back to Marlborough Street. The scorching flames licked along Sackville Street as far as its junction with Sackville Place. Dublin's main thoroughfare was now in the grip of a raging inferno for over a quarter of its length, and the air

Mansfield's Boot Store, the epicentre of a vicious battle on Thursday 27 April 1916.
NATIONAL LIBRARY OF IRELAND

stank with acrid smoke. A temporary ceasefire was arranged by both sides to allow the evacuation of civilians from the lower blocks along the eastern section of Eden Quay, which were in imminent danger from the all-consuming flames. The British used the opportunity to remove their dead and wounded from in front of Mansfield's.

As soon as the civilians had been cleared from the area, the artillery piece on D'Olier Street aimed two shots at the GPO, both of which exploded just outside in Prince's Street. The surrounding buildings shook with the detonations. Another two shells quickly followed, exploding on the roof of the Metropole. Oscar Traynor was curious at the debris left in the wake of the shrapnel shells, which looked like molten lead. He discovered that the shrapnel was encased in a type of wax that melted either upon impact or as the lethal shards flew through the air.

The British amended their plan. Following their failed assault on Lower Abbey Street, they decided that any building in the way of their artillery getting a direct shot at the GPO would now be flattened. Unfortunately for those in Mansfield's, the Metropole and the Imperial, this placed them directly in the firing line. The men in the Metropole Hotel soon fell under a sustained barrage of shells. They evacuated its top floors, leaving behind a small handful of Volunteers to deal with the flames, fearful that their position would be engulfed, and that the fires would be blown across to the GPO. Those in Mansfield's were now pounded by the Vickers gun in Purcell's. The Imperial was suffering under the equal wrath of the artillery gunners. Frank Thornton had placed a sniper in one of the Imperial's rear windows. A shell flew through the window next to him and exploded. Thornton and several men ran to his aid, fearing the worst. To their amazement, they found him sitting calmly at his post, stunned, completely deafened, but otherwise uninjured.

Towards evening, the 2/6th Sherwood Foresters began to take control of Capel Street. A runner informed Commandant Connolly of this alarming development. Recognising that his headquarters would soon be completely surrounded, his immediate countermeasure was to order the occupation of several large buildings further back on Henry Street and Liffey Street, which sat on a parallel axis between the rebel headquarters and Capel Street. He then left the GPO to direct the construction of a new barricade just outside on Prince's Street.

Just as he finished at the barricade a stray bullet struck his right arm. He rushed for the medics in the GPO, fearing that his men would see he had been hit, and was promptly attended to. The round had gone straight through and had not shattered any bone. There would be no rest for Connolly, however. Another alarm call sounded from the roof, as another armoured vehicle lumbered up Henry Street from Capel Street. Captain Henderson's men at the rebel positions in Henry Street waited at the ready, hearts pounding at the daunting sight of this monstrosity. As the vehicle drew level, the rebels prepared to light the fuses on their bombs. Suddenly it engaged reverse gear and sped away, drawing a cheer from the roof of the GPO.

Pádraig Pearse was elated with this particular episode. Against all odds the Irish Volunteer Army and Citizen Army were approaching their fifth day of holding out against the might of their occupier, and in doing so were justifying to the eyes of the world their claim to independence.

Suddenly there was a terrific bang. The GPO shook violently as it took its first direct hit. Those on its rooftop scrambled for cover as the shell's explosion tore a gaping hole and horrifically wounded several Volunteers.

Connolly decided that the Middle Abbey Street area needed reinforcing, as he suspected another attack might come from the Capel Street direction. He accordingly selected 30 men to occupy the *Irish Independent* offices, another building owned by his 1913 nemesis, William Martin Murphy. As he was running short of officers he promoted 20-year-old Dubliner Seán McLoughlin to the rank of captain. McLoughlin had been a runner between the GPO garrison and the Mendicity Institute on Usher's Island, about a mile to the south-west, and Connolly had noticed from his several reports that he had a sound grasp of military tactics.

Just after he had dispatched this newly promoted captain, another ricocheted bullet struck his ankle as he stood in an alley near Prince's Street. Connolly fell to the ground grimacing in agony, before trying to drag himself towards the GPO with his unwounded arm. He was spotted by Captain George Plunkett who summoned John Doyle, the garrison's Medical Officer. They carried their commandant inside, where the British Army doctor, George Mahony, who had been captured in the GPO on Easter Monday, examined his wounds and decided to operate, with Doyle's assistance. When the bullet was removed, Connolly was taken to one of the quieter back rooms to rest and placed on a mattress. A kind-hearted comrade gave him a cigarette and a detective novel, to keep his mind off his painful wounds. Connolly would hardly have been in a fit state to absorb a crime drama, no matter how riveting, but he illustrated his legendary gallows humour by referring to his newly acquired comforts as the pleasant by-products of a '*Revolution de-luxe*'.[2] His irrepressible nature was displayed again later: James Kenny, the Volunteer shot by the Finn on Monday and who was on a mattress next to Connolly, heard him say: 'It's a grand thing to be wounded to get all this attention.'[3]

By now another armoured car had arrived in Grangegorman to collect the last remaining artillery piece and its crews. They were transported to Cole's Lane, close to Great Britain Street, where they were deployed with the 2/6th Sherwood Foresters.

As the sky began to darken, the clattering of several dozen horses could be heard coming from Middle Abbey Street and getting closer by the second. In the Imperial Hotel, Frank Thornton screamed orders to his men in alarm. In the *Irish Independent* offices, Captain McLoughlin ordered his men to point all guns towards the same oncoming noise. A hundred yards to his left in Mansfield's, Oscar Traynor and his men also made ready to deal with the expected charge. Suddenly, one of the Citizen Army bombers there sprang to action. He inserted a strap through the handle of a canister bomb and swung it around his head to gain momentum before he prepared to hurl it through the open window in front of him. Then, to his utter shock, the handle fell off. He launched the bomb into a corner while the men shouted and dashed for cover. Luckily, it failed to detonate. The men resumed their firing positions only to witness two dozen or so riderless horses racing wildly by.

At about 10 p.m., Hoyte's Oil & Spice caught fire. Oil drums began exploding, sending others flying through the air. These in turn exploded as they landed or while still airborne, spraying the surrounding buildings with more of the burning fluid. The conflagration on the east side of Lower Sackville Street spread as far as North Earl Street and threatened to engulf the Imperial Hotel which by now was also under constant shell fire.

As the pressure mounted, Captain Brennan-Whitmore sent urgent word to Captain Thornton that the time had come to pull out of the block between North Earl Street and Sackville Place. The intensity of the fire had reached hellish levels. Inner walls began to burn and collapse. The furniture and contents of the various shops and Clerys Department Store had been used to a great degree to fortify the buildings. Now most of it was beginning to smoulder. Wreckage was everywhere and the noise was disorientating. The fittings and stock that had so far been left untouched by the fire and the rebels were strewn about as if a huge whirlwind had raised the entire block from its foundations and dropped it suddenly. Thornton and his men were heavily engaged with aggressive enemy patrols that were filtering into Marlborough Street, making it difficult to plan any sort of coherent disengagement. The pressure was incessant. Ulstermen from the Composite Battalion pressed forward, keen to avenge their earlier treatment from Mansfield's. Their shouted insults and accompanying shots in the narrow streets suggested they were not in the mood for exchanging pleasantries. Capture was unthinkable, as mercy was highly unlikely.

Brennan-Whitmore and his men were the first to leave by the Pillar Café, while Thornton sent his men out of the Imperial Hotel in sections. Volunteer Séamus Daly was positioned at its front windows. He soon ran across the debris-ridden floors to Thornton's position at the back of the huge building, shouting that it was time to pull out. The entire structure was being constantly rocked by deafening explosions. The ceilings repeatedly shook as if they were about to cave in.

Paddy Mahon, who was positioned close to Thornton, shouted back: 'Is this the end, Séamus?' Daly replied: 'Well as far as this building is concerned, it is the end.'[4] Daly's eyes widened in astonishment when Mahon replied: 'I think we should stick it out to the end.'

Thornton and Daly, aided by the building's imminent destruction, convinced Mahon to leave his post. The wind blew violently through the broken windows and created a vortex of supercharged flame, which spread rapidly. When Thornton assured them that he would not be far behind, Mahon and Daly scrambled out through the floors with several others, singing 'A Soldier's Song' to bolster their morale in the chaos.

This left Captain Thornton in the Imperial Hotel accompanied by four others. They fired their weapons like men who had long since shed any veneer of civilised behaviour. Their eyes betrayed no hint of emotion. They stared out from filthy faces along red-hot gun barrels seeking to fell anything in khaki. Their instincts quickened beyond cognitive thought. The noise in the hotel soon reached such a level that their own rifle and pistol shots were barely audible to the five men.

An avalanche-like sound from the roof persuaded them that it was time to go. The building was now completely ablaze. As they ran, their lungs sucked in gulps of filthy oven-hot air while their adrenalin-fuelled limbs propelled them at speed. A burning staircase denied their descent to the building's ground floor. As he scanned the apocalyptic scene for a means of escape, Thornton's watering eyes fell upon a wooden ladder which was beginning to smoulder and burn but it was their only choice. Their uniforms began to catch fire as they descended. They leapt off the ladder at the earliest opportunity, doused the flames and sought relief for their blistering hands and faces.

When the five men reached North Earl Street's junction with Talbot Street, Thornton realised it would be impossible to rush across Sackville Street to the GPO. The road was lit up by huge flames and although the distance across was little more than 100 yards they would be easy targets. They took shelter in a nearby building to draw breath and plan their next move, which was to move out and make contact if possible with Brennan-Whitmore and his men. When the fires again threatened them they made for a large group of tenement houses on the corner of Marlborough Street and Gloucester Street, which provided a safe hiding place for the time being.

Brennan-Whitmore and his men found themselves in the basement of a nearby tenement house on Gloucester Street, having narrowly avoided capture in a chaotic running skirmish along Marlborough Street. With no local knowledge, he decided that they would 'hole-up' where they were for the time being and hope they could link up again at some stage with Thornton's men, whom he assumed were still accompanied by their middle-aged guide from the Imperial. He, however, was long gone.

Their respite was interrupted at first light the following morning with the shout, 'Hands up, in the name of the King!' They were confronted with the sight of scores of troops in the street outside, bearing very fierce expressions. Feeling it was pointless to resist against such odds the captain reluctantly decided to surrender. He and his men were marched out of the building at bayonet point and ordered to line up against its railings, where they were soon joined by about a dozen other men whom they did not recognise and presumed were civilians. A lieutenant then assembled a platoon of troops and positioned them facing the exhausted Volunteers and petrified locals. He ordered them to load and 'present!'

A short, white-haired Major ran up, shouting, 'Stop this play-acting, stop this firing. What the hell is all this about?' This was quickly followed by: 'Put down those damn rifles. Put them down, put them down at once!' The officer was heavily reprimanded and ordered to take the prisoners and march them to the Custom House. Brennan-Whitmore had received an injury to his leg and limped with his men, another of whom, Harry Manning, was more seriously wounded and was carried by two of his comrades. The bewildered but relieved civilians accompanied them, harried all the way by their captors.

At the Custom House, the prisoners were made to lie down on the ground outside its main entrance. After a short time, they were approached by an Australian officer who had just relieved the trigger-happy lieutenant. Brennan-Whitmore enquired as to what was to become of him and his men, to which the reply was: 'You're going to be shot.' Volunteer Kevin McCabe shouted back angrily, 'Well then, you may as well just shoot us here where we lie.'[5] The weary insurgents' fighting spirit seemed to impress the colonial officer, whose unexpected response was to find medics to treat the wounded men, having noticed that Manning's condition was rapidly deteriorating.

Second Battalion Volunteer William Whelan, from County Wicklow, had also escaped from the Imperial Hotel, but in the ensuing chaos, had become separated from the others. Near Great Britain Street he was captured by a British patrol and was kicked and punched before being pushed against a wall. A highly agitated young officer began shouting at him in a language that sounded like German. This continued and Whelan found himself slapped, kicked and punched again, before he was accused of being a German spy. Several references to his long blond hair betrayed the troops' reasoning. An impromptu firing squad was assembled. Whelan nervously began combing his hair with his hands. Suddenly another more senior officer appeared on the scene and immediately ordered the firing squad to cease fire and instead to take the 'German' prisoner. Whelan was placed in an armoured truck for a time, until the officer returned to march him away, asking him: 'Did you get your hair brushed yet?'

Volunteers Harry Colley and Maurice Flanagan had also become separated from Brennan-Whitmore and his men. As they dashed from doorway to doorway northbound along Gloucester Street a machine gun opened up on them with a burst. They sheltered momentarily in the darkness before Colley decided their only chance of escape was to make a run for it. As they did, the gunner fired again from a position at a nearby barricade. Colley had endured more than enough. He charged suddenly at the barricade pointing his bayonet and screaming wildly while Flanagan went to ground with a number of other Volunteers who were following the same escape route. The half-deranged rebel jumped on top of the barricade and lunged at a soldier, who fought back and stabbed Colley in the leg with his own bayonet. Colley collapsed on top of the barricade. He had been hit by several bullets as he charged and now his strength was gone. The same soldier then shot at Flanagan and the others, while using Colley's body as cover. The rebels managed to scurry into some side streets. Several moments later the cries from the badly wounded Volunteer on top of the barricade convinced the troops there to summon an ambulance.

As the scenes of chaos were unfolding on the eastern side of Sackville Street, several small-scale British patrols had ventured up and down Middle Abbey Street into Captain Seán McLoughlin's area of operations, but not in sufficient numbers for him to engage them. He preferred to wait for a similar opportunity to the one presented to Oscar Traynor earlier in the day, involving a much larger force, but his wait was in vain. He climbed onto the roof and used his field glasses to get a better view.

It was not a cheerful one. Sackville Street was turning into an inferno. The air was filled with the constant din of battle. To his north-west, huge flames from the blaze at Linenhall Barracks licked at the night sky. He began to sense how the insurrection mounted by him and his daring comrades would now end: in flames.

As midnight approached, Volunteers from the surrounding smaller outposts, including Captain Henderson's on Henry Street, were filtering into the GPO. The position was now expecting an attack in force. Inside, all was panic and chaos. The headquarters were now in serious peril. Volunteers hurried to the vast basement beneath Henry Street, carrying canister bombs and seeking shelter from the rain of sparks and oily flames now cascading through holes in the roof. Luckily, the wind picked up and changed direction, averting a potential disaster and allowing some relief from the torrential shower of burning embers.

The relief was short-lived. At 3 a.m., a tremendous roar from across the road signalled the end of Clerys and the Imperial Hotel, as the interior collapsed. It had burned with such intensity that the street outside was showered with molten glass. Only the four-storey facade remained stubbornly upright in the 50-foot high inferno. The men in the GPO were awestruck at the sight. There followed a long and exhausting night with no respite as the machine guns and artillery fired relentlessly. The window frames in the GPO were now beginning to smoulder and were repeatedly doused with water. The rebels were forced to move their barricades back from the windows. Just inside the main entrance, another barricade was under construction. An assault seemed imminent.

No such scenes of pandemonium pervaded the ranks of the 3rd Royal Irish Regiment that night, as its infantrymen began methodically deploying on Rutland Square, with the troopers of the 6th Reserve Cavalry in support. When the Royal Irish linked up with the Ulster Composite Battalion to the east and with the 2/6th Sherwood Foresters to the west, the cordon was complete. The net was closing in.

12

The General Post Office and the Battle of Moore Street

'I could see bullets like hailstones.'

Dawn broke in the Sackville Street area on Friday morning to the deafening roars of artillery fire. Each ear-shattering shell burst displaced huge chunks of concrete from the buildings still standing, allowing the British gunners a steadily increasing view of their principal objective. The entire block of buildings that included the Metropole Hotel and Mansfield's still obstructed the line of sight to the GPO from their artillery. The rebels in this battered block were completely spent, but knew they had to hold, and were constantly encouraged by Lieutenant Traynor. Groups of British troops dashed across O'Connell Bridge, 'singly and in two's and three's',[1] taking cover behind the O'Connell Monument. Their number was added to by similarly sized groups approaching from Lower Abbey Street. Several small-scale probing attacks were launched from here, but the weary insurgents held their ground. The bombardment continued. Thick clouds of black smoke drifted across O'Connell Bridge and hung there, obscuring the line of sight for the artillerymen. They were constantly forced to reset their range to the GPO. Mansfield's and the Metropole bore the brunt of the many shells that missed.

James Connolly, unable to walk, was placed on a wheeled hospital bed, and had himself moved to the front of the GPO in order to direct the building's final defence. He still expected a full frontal attack. His enemies, however, had other plans: they would continue closing in on the GPO, insert as many artillery pieces as they could muster, and relentlessly bomb the rebel headquarters into submission. Later in the morning, a British patrol was launched from Capel Street. Two sections from a platoon in C Company, 2/6th Sherwood Forester Regiment, numbering about 20 men, began their advance towards the rear of the GPO along Mary Street and towards Henry Street, intent on scouting out positions from where their commanders could tighten the noose. The young infantrymen moved cautiously forward, bayonets affixed, knowing that just ahead of them somewhere, unseen eyes would be sizing them up along the length of their gun barrels. The civilians still trapped in the nearby buildings waited, petrified, as the dreadful smells of war permeated the smoky air. A soft breeze carried the growing stench from Sackville Street, and it became more repugnant with every step the troops took. Their widened eyes darted from side to side, then upwards to the rooftops. Nothing was more frightening to these young men than advancing into an enemy-held city centre where death could come at any moment: from in front, behind or above. Their NCOs directed them to various positions as they manoeuvred forward. As they crept ever closer, the concealed Volunteers, including Thomas Devine, readied themselves. Oily and sweaty fingers slowly began to squeeze on their triggers, until shots suddenly boomed from all sides, and for several terrible, deafening seconds the patrol was driven back in disarray. With cracks from pistols, shotguns and rifles reverberating in the narrow streets all around, the patrol scrambled backwards in the smoke and chaos, dragging their wounded with them. Not a single shot was returned. Soon afterwards, Volunteer Lieutenant Patrick Shortice pulled his men back to the GPO, following an earlier order he had received.

The British commanders on the ground ordered their own barricades to be built throughout the area. The first of these was placed at Moore Street's junction with Great Britain Street, while another was constructed at the bottom of Henry Street, at its junction with Jervis Street. Any attempt by the rebels to escape down this enclosed, narrow stretch of road, or through nearby Moore St would now be contained.

Seán McLoughlin and his men had also been called back to headquarters from the *Irish Independent* offices. As they entered on

The ruined Metropole Hotel on Sackville Street, abandoned by rebels only moments before the entire structure collapsed. NATIONAL LIBRARY OF IRELAND

Prince's Street their first port of call was for breakfast. McLoughlin led his men into the kitchen where Desmond Fitzgerald informed him of Connolly's injury, little noticing the looks of disgust from his surrounding men at the meagre portions being dealt from what appeared to be a well-stocked facility. After he had eaten, McLoughlin went to see Connolly, while his men positioned themselves defensively with the rest of the exhausted rebels preparing for their last stand.

Back in the Metropole Hotel, word was brought to Oscar Traynor that the top floor of the building was completely ablaze and that nothing could now be done to arrest the flames. Those who had been left there earlier as firefighters were ordered to evacuate to the lower floors. They did so to the sound of sporadic artillery bursts. For a time the intensity of the bombardment dissipated. The gunners seemed to be preoccupied, but every few minutes a report sounded out from the direction of the river, followed by a huge bang. It appeared that the artillerymen were either finding their range, or perhaps just letting the rebels know that they were still there.

At noon, however, the British field guns opened up with intent. Shells now pulverised the GPO roof, while some missed and smashed into the nearby buildings. The streets surrounding the Republican headquarters filled with debris, while raging fires began to spread. The afternoon breeze funnelled itself through the narrow laneways and fanned the flames. It caused the fire in the Metropole to leap across Prince's Street to the GPO roof, setting it alight, just seconds after another shell struck. A fire hose was rushed up from below and the flames were brought under control.

Commandant Pearse now ordered all Cumann na mBan members, with the exception of the nursing staff, to leave the GPO. During a brief lull in the shelling they stepped cautiously out of its Henry Street door carrying both white and Red Cross flags. Several shots came their way initially until a British officer saw the flags through his field glasses and ordered his men to cease fire. The fight for the rebel headquarters would be relentless but honourable. The women marched into Moore Street and up to its barricade. The same officer helped them across before being offered their surrender. To their surprise, however, he told them to keep going. They quickly went on their way, crossing Great Britain Street under the uncomprehending gaze of clusters of British infantry and up the hill of Dominick Street. They were, however, eventually arrested by the Dublin Fusiliers in the Broadstone area.

Pearse ordered any of the remaining sharpshooters still trying to pick out enemy targets in the chaos to take up positions on the top floor of the GPO, while the increasingly worn-out fire crews dealt with the flames. Once again, men rushed to the building's basement with armfuls of canister bombs, to keep them away from the fires. Just after 3 p.m., a shell smashed into the Telegraph Office, having penetrated the roof. The terrific explosion was followed by a huge fire. Extra men rushed up from the ground floor armed with water hoses. The situation was, however, becoming impossible. When they reached the building's second floor they were forced to crawl on their hands and knees to avoid the attention of the machine gun that had been placed in the Gresham. Its incessant fire concentrated on the GPO's gaping windows, making it lethal to stand in spite of the barricades. When they finally managed to get the hoses through the holes in the roof, they were found to be riddled with bullets. The men succeeded, nevertheless, in getting the fire under control for a time.

One of the rooftop firefighters, Jack Plunkett, spotted a British sniper lying prone on a wall in a burnt-out section of the Imperial Hotel. He grabbed his rifle and threw himself into a firing position just behind the roof parapet. He blocked out the surrounding chaos as he focused. He fired, and the rifle recoiled violently into his shoulder. He saw the enemy soldier fall onto rubble on the street beneath with such force that his rifle was split in two with the impact.[2]

Among the many scrambling up to the rooftop were Captain Liam Tannam and Lieutenant Michael Boland. The first thing to catch Tannam's eye was a young Volunteer of about 18 who was wrapping a hosepipe around one of the chimneys. As they approached him to help they could hear the drenched teenager's teeth chattering. The Volunteer spotted them coming, he pulled a handkerchief from his pocket, stuffed it into his mouth and bit down hard. He did not want the officers to mistake his near hypothermia for cowardice. Tannam thought to himself that the young man was 'one of the bravest men' he had ever seen.

The frenzied activity on the GPO's roof was not wasted on the British machine-gunners and snipers, and they fired with abandon. All the while, the incessant shelling rained down destruction on the beleaguered building and fires continued to erupt on its rooftop, which inevitably had to be abandoned. Tannam, Boland, Plunkett, the shivering teenager and the dozens of others on the roof were ordered down to the top floor where their firefighting duties continued. Enemy shots ricocheted from walls now saturated with flames which streamed downward. Soon the entire top floor of the building was on fire.

Towards 6 p.m., Connolly called the Volunteers' Medical Officer, John Doyle, to his side and said, 'You take your line of retreat, with your personnel.'[3] The surrounding bedlam interrupted him momentarily before his attention returned to Doyle. He told him the time had come to move the wounded, along with his deputies and staff, and to commandeer as many Volunteers as he felt necessary. Doyle immediately checked that the way was clear through the many loopholed walls at the rear of the GPO to the Coliseum Theatre. He returned to the GPO and asked Father O'Flanagan, the garrison's 'spiritual administrator', to come with the wounded. He then suggested to Pádraig Pearse that Captain Mahony, the captured British Army doctor, should accompany them. Pearse concurred. Minutes later, 20 women, 23 men and 30 wounded were filtering through the loopholes between the buildings. Another six travelled with them, including Doyle and three of his staff, together with Mahony and the priest. When they reached the theatre, they stopped and waited. An almighty cataclysm thundered behind them: the southern roof section of the GPO had just collapsed.

An avalanche of choking, dusty debris spewed from the windows and doorways of the GPO, leading to complete panic and disorder for a time. Cheers erupted from the ranks of surrounding British Army troops who witnessed the building's apparent demise.

When order was re-established, insofar as the organised chaos in the GPO could be described as 'orderly', the rebellion's leaders – including Connolly, Pearse, McDermott, Clarke and Plunkett – held a brief council of war and concluded that they would have to evacuate their headquarters. They considered their options for a time, and decided that the Williams & Woods Sweet and Soap Factory, located at the junction of Great Britain Street and King's Inns Street, would be suitable as the new general headquarters for the Volunteer army. There would be considerable advantage gained in the securing of this particular building. First, it was both large and close enough to accommodate a garrison of more than 300. Secondly, taking it would involve cutting right into the British line, and would place them at such close range to enemy positions that the further use of artillery would be deemed too risky, in case the gunners hit their own men. This would then leave their foe with two options: a costly infantry assault or a repositioning of their men further away from the Williams & Woods in order to allow their field guns to come into play once again. The latter tactic would allow the Republicans enough of a respite to facilitate a possible breakthrough to the Four Courts.

The Volunteers would leave by the GPO's side doors on Henry Street, before advancing up through Moore Street and filtering through the warren of laneways that led to Great Britain Street. Once there they would fight their way along the wide road for roughly 200 yards and reach the fortress-like factory which would then be on their right. The only drawback was that the manoeuvre would need to take place in darkness in order to keep their casualties to a minimum, but as the remaining

Looking across to the GPO from the ruins of Lower Abbey Street's junction with Sackville Street. NATIONAL LIBRARY OF IRELAND

section of the roof was now completely ablaze and in imminent danger of collapsing in on them, time was not a luxury they had.

Pearse initially mustered a section of 30 Volunteers to advance and secure the factory, pending the arrival of the main force. This perilous assault through no man's land was to be led by The O'Rahilly, who had stepped forward immediately when presented with an opportunity to participate in a manoeuvre that did not involve sitting and waiting for the enemy to strike. His subdued demeanour from the insurrection's earlier days had gradually dissipated and, when presented with an opportunity to lead men whose doggedness had begun to inspire him, he promptly seized it.

At 7.30 p.m., he led his assault force out, dodging the machine-gun bullets which ripped chunks from the broken walls around them. They rushed for the corner of Moore Street and Henry Street, climbing over the shattered remains of the barricade built on Wednesday, before turning right. They then split into two groups, each of which was to advance along the pavements on opposite sides of Moore Street, hugging the doorways for cover until close enough to make a dash for the Williams & Woods factory.

The British were waiting. Their recently built but formidable barricade which now faced the rebels head on was manned by troops from both D Company, 2/6th Sherwood Foresters, and infantrymen from the Royal Irish Regiment, who were not known for their love of 'Sinn Féiners'. Many had seen their close friends being machine-gunned, blown to pieces and gassed to death in Flanders, and considered the insurgents to be nothing more than misguided dreamers. Others among them were completely indifferent to politics, but followed orders from officers who were predominantly diehard loyalists, and had no time for Irish nationalism or those who were willing to kill in its cause.

The Volunteers advanced. The machine guns opened up on them with a deafening crescendo, added to by furious fire from the riflemen, stopping the rebels in their tracks. Within seconds, the bricks of the doorways where they sought cover disintegrated in the hail of bullets. Traumatised civilians huddled together in their homes, shrinking back from their shattering windows, while the rebels accompanying the O'Rahilly now desperately sought to regroup.

Both Thomas Devine and his good friend Lieutenant Patrick Shortice were advancing with the left-hand section. Shortice groaned suddenly as a bullet struck him and then fell wounded onto the street. Devine dragged him back into cover. More men were hit in the doorways as they returned fire while moving forward. Devine made it to Samson's Lane where he noticed that O'Rahilly had been hit but was still on his feet and reorganising the attack. He carried a Mauser pistol in one hand and a sword in the other.

They surged forward once again, joined now by the section on the other side of the road who fired furiously as they advanced from doorway to doorway. The O'Rahilly suddenly sprinted across the road to the sound of whistling rounds that flew by at 700 metres per second. The vicious fire forced him into another doorway. In the meantime, Devine and his section had advanced as far as Riddal's Lane, roughly halfway along the street, when O'Rahilly looked back across the street and shouted, 'Charge!'

The men on both sides rushed towards the barricade, shouting encouragement to one another as they sidestepped the rubble strewn about. The O'Rahilly led from the front and made it as far as Sackville Lane's junction before he fell to the ground, badly wounded. His men some distance back looked on as he dragged himself into the side street

Michael O'Rahilly (The O'Rahilly) who led the initial patrol in force to the Williams & Woods factory. His men charged into the jaws of the machine guns on the evening of Friday 28 April 1916. NATIONAL LIBRARY OF IRELAND

to his right, while bullets smashed into the cobblestones around him. Devine's section then came under murderous fire and was forced back to Riddal's Lane. The opposite section was shot to pieces. Those who escaped the bullets were forced all the way back to Henry Place, towards the southern end of the street. Thirty men had left the GPO to begin the assault. Twenty were now lying dead or wounded in Moore Street.

Just to Devine's rear in the Coliseum Theatre, his garrison's Medical Officer, John Doyle, was increasingly concerned about the rapidly encroaching smoke and flames from the direction of the GPO. When he suggested to Dr Mahony that it was time to find an alternative location for the wounded, the latter agreed. Minutes later, Father O'Flanagan led them all out onto Prince's Street. They made their way through William Street South, a small laneway which took them to Middle Abbey Street. The priest checked to see if the wide road was under fire. Assessing that it was relatively safe to cross, he led them to the southern side of the street. Several ricochets then smashed from the nearby walls. He shouted 'Wounded, Red Cross!' over and over until the firing in their direction ceased.

A section of Sherwood Foresters rushed now to positions near Liffey Street and ordered Father O'Flanagan to approach. An officer ordered him to move the wounded to Jervis Street Hospital. The young officer accompanied them along the short route as the continuous echoes of war reverberated all around. Huge wafts of dust and thick smoke drifted through the narrow road as they went. They finally arrived at the hospital, tremendously relieved. Dr Mahony remained with the wounded as they were brought inside along with the women and the priest. No such welcome was extended to Doyle and the accompanying Volunteers, however. The British officer formed them up and ordered them back towards the barricade, telling them that they were going back to where they had come from to be burnt out or shot with the rest of the rebels. The squad of infantrymen who had accompanied the officer pointed their gun barrels towards them once again as they set off, soon reaching the Liffey Street junction. When the burning ruins of Sackville Street were just 300 yards to their front they were ordered forward. Fear gripped them at every step. Then the officer's voice rang out from behind, 'Those men going out are not to be fired on until out of sight, and out of sight only!'[4] Doyle and the others quickened their footsteps, expecting death at any second, but the troops did not shoot at them. They found temporary refuge in Arnott's Department Store, before hiding out in some nearby buildings.

Just up the road, Seán McDermott sent Frank Henderson to the rapidly disintegrating Metropole Hotel to inform Lieutenant Traynor that both the hotel and the GPO were to be imminently evacuated. The position's men now filtered into the burning headquarters from Prince's Street, accompanied by the men from Mansfield's. All were utterly exhausted. Traynor's men had been relieved when the order came through, as they feared they had been forgotten about and were fully aware that with their own roof and upper floor fully ablaze, there was an immediate danger of the entire structure collapsing in on top of them. Traynor arrived at the GPO only moments before the hotel collapsed in a convulsion of twisted concrete, timber and metal. He was immediately briefed on the pending evacuation of the GPO and ordered his men to line up by the Henry Street exits along with the other Volunteers preparing to make their escape.

Pearse, ever the eloquent speaker, took this opportunity to address his Volunteers. He proclaimed how proud he was to have fought alongside

From Volunteer to Captain to Commandant-General in five days: 20-year-old Sean McLoughlin from North King Street, whose cool head under a cataclysm of fire saved the lives of scores, if not hundreds, of his comrades in Moore Lane and Moore Street. NATIONAL LIBRARY OF IRELAND

such brave men and women. He outlined what they were about to face as they made for their new headquarters. Captain Tannam stood nearby, smoking a cigar in the hope that it would create the illusion of confidence and rub off on his men. Tannam, however, was anything but confident.

Captain Seán McLoughlin's sections of Volunteers were still manning the GPO's windows as best they could, as he barked order after order at them. They were struggling to cope with the intense heat of the surrounding walls. The massive building's exterior had become too hot to touch, while inside, when the rebels turned their hoses onto walls to deal with the invading flames, the water immediately turned to steam. McDermott approached McLoughlin and ordered him to stay close to the garrison's leaders when the time for evacuation came.

McLoughlin went to the Henry Street door of the GPO where he was told of the evacuation plan. He was also told of the mission that had been led out by The O'Rahilly to pave their way. This greatly alarmed the young captain as he knew from his previous vantage point in Middle Abbey Street that Great Britain Street was heavily occupied by the enemy, and that they had also positioned several platoons in the area around Williams & Woods. He rushed out to try and stop the assault party before it was too late, sprinting initially into Henry Place. When he turned the corner he asked the few remaining men sheltering there where The O'Rahilly was. They replied that he was gone.

McLoughlin immediately set about regrouping the leaderless men, assigning each man to positions around Henry Place's junction with Moore Street. The O'Rahilly, meanwhile, was dying slowly of his wounds in a laneway off Moore Street, just yards from the barricade his men had tried to overcome. His last strength was being spent writing a farewell letter to his wife, in which he emphasised, 'it was a good fight.'

Captain Tannam was then sent across from the GPO with two men to cover the junction of Henry Place and Henry Street while the evacuation took place. He ordered the pair to cover the 90-degree left turn in the laneway while he took a look beyond and saw McLoughlin at its far end. He then ordered his men to remain covering the corner while he rushed back across to the GPO to inform Pearse that the way ahead was clear, but that a building referred to as 'the White House' was under heavy enemy fire. The increasingly adrenalin-fuelled captain then re-entered Henry Place and stood by with his men ready to guide the hundreds that were imminently expected.

At the GPO's exit, Pearse gave the officer leading the first evacuation group his final orders. He followed by dropping his upheld sword to the floor repeatedly to signal to each two-to-three-man group that the way ahead was clear, after he had glanced outside each time. As the first few men darted across Henry Street the tension reached unprecedented heights. Volunteer Charles Donnelly, now waiting just inside the doorway, looked around at his fellow rebels: as each man stared and shuffled towards the door, his thoughts darted from hope to sheer terror and from sadness to hate. Their faces were filthy and exhausted. Some of them were visibly shaking, while others paled with the crippling nausea that was only eased by the encouraging words of their comrades, combined with the reassuringly sharp commands from their section commanders. Donnelly's eyes fell upon the young paperboy from Easter Monday. He sent him a reassuring nod as another shell pounded into the front of the building. Time was running out.

As the first section of evacuees turned left at the corner in Henry Place, Captain McLoughlin turned and raised his hand to signal them to stop short of the Moore Lane junction, which was covered by enemy fire. Captain Tannam now beckoned the second group across from the GPO. They were laden down with food supplies as well as weapons.

Some were actually carrying trays of eggs. They were guided into the laneway by Captain Tannam. As another group dashed out of the GPO, a prolonged burst of fire whipped at them and pursued their every step across Henry Street. Feargus de Búrca later commented: 'I could see bullets like hailstones, hopping off the street.'[5]

The first group that ran across Moore Lane was greeted with a vicious burst of fire that tore at the walls of the White House, which faced the laneway to their left. The British gunners at the Rotunda were making the most of this opportunity. Unable to pinpoint the source of the fire in the increasingly chaotic situation, one man shouted that it was coming from the Mineral Water Factory, which was just beyond the bend in the lane. Two sections stormed inside following a shouted order from McLoughlin to attack the building but, having kicked in its doors, opened fire on each other. McLoughlin screamed at them that they were all mad, before he regained control and oversaw a more methodical securing of the building, which they quickly discovered was free of the enemy. Several Volunteers were posted to its roof.

With more and more Volunteers and supplies arriving into the side of the laneway facing the GPO there was a danger of the entire garrison becoming caught like rats in a trap. Every time Pearse dropped his sword another small group sprinted across, harassed all the way by whining .303 bullets. Seán McDermott, suffering from polio, had managed to limp across with a section, but appeared to have run out of ideas. McLoughlin hastily outlined a solution to their predicament. McDermott was quick to agree but not before McLoughlin cleared up an important fact: if his plan was to be effective he had to have full control over its implementation. This was immediately agreed to by McDermott, before a runner was dispatched back to the GPO to inform James Connolly of the developments. The commandant himself was becoming increasingly impressed with the young Dubliner who, on that fateful Friday, was still five weeks shy of his 21st birthday.

The enemy rifles and machine guns continued to take their toll while McLoughlin took command of the situation in Henry Place. He dashed across the fire-swept Moore Lane and ordered the men there to break through the side walls of the buildings on Moore Street from its Henry Place side. Others were detailed into a cordon across its junction with Moore Street to prevent those who were preparing to rush across the laneway from charging blindly onwards into enemy fire on Moore Street itself.

McLoughlin then ran the gauntlet back to the L-bend and saw that the laneway was thronged with half-panicked and apparently leaderless Volunteers. Captain Tannam was struggling to maintain order as the explosions from the enemy artillery rang out ever closer. McLoughlin barked at the men at the bend to form into ranks, while he directed two sections to pull a large van out from the Mineral Water Factory yard. His plan was to block Moore Lane with the vehicle, and once the signal came from the houses currently being bored into, he would send the men across under its cover and begin occupying the buildings in Moore Street.

The van was pushed across the laneway under ferocious fire which wounded several men. They were pulled out of the way and tended to. Soon afterwards the signal came that a small opening had been created into the houses. Orders to advance were sent back. Men began to dash across the mouth of the laneway in similar sized groups to those leaving the GPO. The machine-gunners zeroed in again. An avalanche of bullets whipped at the van and beyond but there was just enough cover for small groups to cross if they sprinted. The White House came under a torrent of fire as the gunners saturated the area.

Captain Tannam was keen to warn the passing Volunteers of the fire being directed at the White House, and shouted at each group to beware when crossing Moore Lane. The warning, however, was misunderstood by one officer who turned the bend and assumed the fire was coming from the building itself. Its facade was so pulverised by now that it appeared that fire was indeed coming from the building. McLoughlin was summoned and an attack was ordered.

Captain McLoughlin's increasingly hoarse voice once again bellowed out above the sounds of collapsing buildings and constant gunfire. He ordered men with bayonets to the front. Some of those ordered to answer that particular call cursed the fact that they had bayonets. McLoughlin then led the attack himself only to find the two-storey building empty. He arranged for a section of men under 25-year-old Captain Michael Collins to hold the building. The energetic Cork man ordered his section to place barricades at the windows and open fire on the Rotunda, but cursed loudly at the lack of material available in the building for such a purpose. His men began sniping back nonetheless. The house's outside walls continued to suffer under the dreadful drumbeat of enemy lead, while the men inside were repeatedly sent scurrying for cover from shots that flew through its smashed windows.

The disorder that had threated the evacuation was now more or less under control, in spite of the attentions of the enemy machine-gunners. Liam Tannam now found himself surprised by the wildly differing attitudes of some of his comrades making the crossing from the GPO. Volunteer Moggy Murtagh strolled out of the beleaguered building holding a huge crucifix across his shoulder and seemed to wander nonchalantly into Henry Place, oblivious to the escalating sense of carnage. Another Volunteer darted across the street wearing a German infantry '*Pickelhaube*' helmet[6] which Tannam presumed had been taken from the nearby waxworks. The same Volunteer grinned broadly at the captain as he passed.

Commandant Connolly was soon carried to the GPO door by Seán Price, Paddy Ryan and several others. James Kenny, the 17-year-old who had been wounded by the Finn on Easter Monday, limped along with several other bodyguards to Henry Place. Joseph Plunkett followed closely behind, as did Thomas Clarke. They were quickly directed to the front of the crowd of Volunteers before being stopped by Seán McDermott just yards short of Moore Lane. They were to wait until given the signal to cross behind the cover of the bullet-ridden van. Suddenly there was another loud thud followed by a groan. A Volunteer collapsed into the stretcher just behind Connolly's head. Unable to turn, Connolly called out, believing Joseph Plunkett had been struck down. He screamed at the surrounding men to get him into the Mineral Water Factory, assuming in the confusion that this was their current objective, and tried to raise himself from his stretcher. An utterly worn-out Joseph Plunkett soon arrived at his side and calmed him. The wounded Volunteer had been shot in the lung, and died slowly nearby, choking on the blood which dribbled from his mouth. His surrounding comrades desperately tried to save him as he gasped and gurgled horrifically.

The daylight was rapidly fading.

Connolly's stretcher party was soon across. Rifles began to bristle outwards like the protruding spines of a porcupine as his men formed a semicircle around him. His stretcher was carefully manhandled through the hole bored into Cogan's Shop, the first building on Moore Street to be occupied by the Volunteers. The men, having bored the hole, began rushing around inside; their frantic manoeuvring had somehow hidden from their view a police constable hiding in a dark corner of an upstairs hallway. When he was eventually discovered and brought to Connolly's attention, he shouted: 'Throw him out to Hell!'[7] The frightened policeman was ejected from Cogan's and disappeared into the surrounding streets.

Pearse re-entered the GPO, having checked at Henry Place how the situation was progressing. Captain Frank Henderson and the others were waiting anxiously to make their move. They were still guarding the prisoners they had taken on Monday and Tuesday. To their astonishment, a door swung open, revealing the barely awake figure of Volunteer Séamus Kavanagh, a namesake of his 3rd Battalion comrade. He had just woken from a deep slumber and his first words to the surprised group were to ask them what was wrong. The 14 men erupted into laughter.

These were the last men to leave the burning headquarters, after the prisoners were set loose to take their chances. Bullets zipped through the air around them as they dashed across to Henry Place, before glancing back momentarily from the shelter it afforded to witness the unearthly roar that signalled the collapse of the GPO's interior. As the building imploded, thick plumes of debris were belched out of its lower windows, covering the entire area with impenetrable clouds of choking dust. The men in the lane froze. When the dust clouds began to disperse only the external shell remained of the landmark building. The flagpole from which the tricolour had fluttered was now on fire, while at the far end of the roof their other flag still flew its golden letters defiantly, until just after 10 p.m., when its pole snapped and it fell into the burning chaos of Sackville Street. The siege of the GPO had come to an end. The fight would continue on Moore Street.

The spent Volunteers began consolidating their new positions on Moore Street and Moore Lane. Their leaders were now established in Cogan's Shop. Captain McLoughlin was proving Connolly's good judgement in promoting him: more than any other individual he was instrumental in maintaining order and cohesion among the hard-pressed Volunteers. His rapid improvisations and clear instructions no doubt saved many lives in the chaos of Moore Street.

The barricade in Moore Lane was added to after darkness closed in and now provided satisfactory cover from the Rotunda gunners. As soon as McLoughlin was happy with it he enlisted the aid of an utterly exhausted Joseph Plunkett and together they organised the building of another barricade across Henry Place itself at its junction with Moore Street, next to Cogan's. Yet more local buildings were relieved of their furniture and contents. The rebels suffered several casualties putting this barricade together, as the background light from the burning GPO presented the machine-gunners at the opposite end of Moore Street with targets of opportunity. Ricochets screamed from the surrounding walls. They pressed on nonetheless.

During this episode, Captain George Plunkett was troubled by the disturbing cries of a wounded man, which mingled with the surrounding sounds of combat, and appeared to come from a sheltered section of Sampson's Lane on the far side of his barricade. He swiftly jumped the fortification and dashed across Moore Street to the side street. Sparks flew from the cobblestones at his feet from the enemy bullets that sought him, but he made it to cover, and discovered a helpless and wounded British soldier appealing for water. He helped the young Tommy to a drink from the soldier's canteen, before hauling him over his shoulder and carrying him back across the street, this time attracting much less fire from the British gunners who appeared to see what he was attempting in spite of the darkness. Once there his rescued foe was carefully manhandled over the barricade by Plunkett's surprised comrades. They were even more taken aback when he said: 'Here take him – I want to get his rifle!'[8] Plunkett then set off to retrieve the weapon, a feat he successfully accomplished under ferocious fire, before turning the same gun against the machine-gunners. The wounded infantryman found himself tended to by Elizabeth O'Farrell, the nurse who was treating James Connolly, who now lay next to him.

The centre of Dublin now resembled the type of hell only previously witnessed by its inhabitants in black-and-white cinema newsreels of the fighting in France and Belgium. Joseph Plunkett had remarked earlier, with apparent pride, that Dublin was the first European city to burn since Moscow in 1812, a comment that would have been met with derision from the thousands of civilians being made homeless, and the hundreds of innocents being killed. His brief and somewhat self-indulgent history lesson was wasted on those around him. They were too busy trying to survive, as machine guns sent belt after belt of bullets whizzing through the half-darkness. Increasingly frequent shell bursts continued to smash metal and concrete all around the half-panicked Volunteers and petrified civilians trapped in the battle zone, sending countless shards of molten shrapnel flying at flesh. Buildings collapsed, filling the air with thick, choking dust, while countless stray bullets ricocheted through the smoky streets. The noxious fumes from the oil works on Sackville Street that now resembled a blast furnace filled the tortured evening air with a horrific stench, matched only in its power to repulse by the nauseating smell of burning human waste, and decaying flesh. At one point, a three-legged dog, having been driven mad by the repeated explosions, scampered across a nearby street, and was unceremoniously mown down by the machine gun. It yelped in agony, its pointless death displaying to all who witnessed its pitiful demise the utter futility of war.

Having supervised the completion of the barricade which now provided excellent cover from the rapacious riflemen and the Vickers gun, Joseph Plunkett returned to Cogan's Shop, where Volunteers worked frenetically around their leaders, busily 'mouse-holing' into the neighbouring buildings, while he and the other leaders held another meeting. Connolly, unable to move from his bed, was clearly unfit to lead them any longer, while Pearse and Plunkett were also suffering terribly from the strain and exhaustion of the previous few days. No other leader among them was of a military mind, so a new one swiftly needed to be found. Connolly stated what everyone else was thinking. 'McLoughlin.' Everyone agreed.

The 20-year-old recently promoted captain was summoned and made Commandant-General of the Moore Street Volunteers, but in place of the yellow shoulder tabs that signified such high office, he was handed a yellow ribbon to tie around his upper arm for recognition. Plunkett added to the occasion by handing him his ceremonial sabre.

Without the time or the inclination to stand on such ceremony, Commandant McLoughlin promptly got back to his tasks. He ordered various sections of Volunteers to begin tunnelling through the houses and buildings along the entire length of Moore Street, and told the remainder of the men to grab what rest they could for the night, leaving lookouts at the ready to alert them of any night attacks. The tunnels were placed in as crooked a line as possible, and on different floors, denying a straight line of sight in the event of one of the houses falling into enemy hands. He then checked the barricades, and the remaining Volunteer positions before pausing to get what meagre rest he could himself.

Commandant Connolly was suffering terribly with his leg wound, which had now become gangrenous. Being stretchered through the various 'mouse-holes' time and time again, in an attempt both to keep up with McLoughlin's advance, and to avoid the artillery that was smashing

Henry Street to pieces, only added to his immense pain. When the rebel leaders reached No. 16 Moore Street, halfway along the eastern side of the road, the decision was made to halt there and use the building as the new headquarters of the Irish Republic. A short time later, Commandant McLoughlin found himself summoned to the position.

Charles Saurin was detailed to the loft at the back of Hanlon's Fish Shop with seven other weary men, including Arthur Shields, who were glad of the opportunity to rest. The sound of artillery and machine gun was unceasing, and the danger constantly imminent. Their current position, however, was peaceful and luxurious compared to the recent nerve-shattering sequence of events. This made Moggy Murtagh's subsequent actions all the more remarkable. As the men sat quietly, smoking and beginning to collect themselves, he stood up and said, 'I think I'll stroll over and see what's happening at the GPO.'[9] He calmly left the room, while the others laughed hysterically.

By the cold light of dawn on Saturday 29 April, the rebel plan to reach the Williams & Woods factory had been amended. The formidable British barricade at the top of Moore Street completely barred their route, so they aimed instead to continue tunnelling through the houses, until close enough to attack and overcome the obstacle with sheer weight of numbers. This tactic also allowed McLoughlin to spread his front line out over a much greater distance, meaning that if the enemy counter-attacked, the defence of the area would be much more manageable. Any advancing force would then have to contend with fire from both its front and side. The rebel leaders had not slept much. Connolly was in severe pain but did his best to maintain the spirits of those all around. McLoughlin had managed to get an hour or so of sleep and now roused himself by sending out for reports from the various positions. After a while he was summoned once again by Pearse, Clarke, McDermott, Connolly and Plunkett, the first of whom asked if he had any ideas regarding their next move. They listened intently as he outlined his hastily but methodically devised plan in his strong Dublin accent.

An assault in force was now to be made against the barricade on Great Britain Street, but only as a diversionary tactic. While the enemy was occupied, the rest of the Volunteer forces would make their escape towards the Four Courts, at this stage thought by the rebels to be an impregnable stronghold. To accomplish this, they would have to fight their way through the Capel Street area.

McLoughlin was unaware, however, that several rebels were already heading in that direction, but that such a plan was the last thing on their minds. Having concealed themselves overnight in the buildings between the ruined GPO and Arnott's Department Store, they were presently emerging from their labyrinth of tunnels, discarding their Volunteer garments and weapons, and helping themselves to less conspicuous looking items of clothing that still hung from the store's partially looted rails. They would then take their chances on the less disputed streets, and hope to fight another day.

A silence briefly fell among the rebel leadership, broken only when Pearse asked McLoughlin for an estimate of how many men they could expect to lose in the breakout attempt. The answer was blunt: 20 to 30 men in the attack against the barricade, and if Capel Street was heavily defended very few could expect to make it to the Four Courts. Civilian casualties could also be expected to be high. As an afterthought he added: 'Where there is life, there is hope.' Eventually the plan was accepted, and McLoughlin set off to prepare the men.

He moved quickly through his positions asking for volunteers for the upcoming death-or-glory attack against the barricade. He soon discovered, however, that the men's morale was polarised. Many seemingly irrepressible rebels stepped forward, but there were several among their exhausted number who looked like they could not take much more. Those who could then checked their weapons and equipment and readied themselves, but their dusty and worn faces betrayed few illusions about surviving the morning.

McLoughlin sent an officer into the loft at the back of Hanlon's where Charles Saurin was stationed, who issued the seven men there with new orders. When the signal came they were to rush from the rear of their building and enter Moore Lane. They would then fire a volley of shots and charge the barricade at its Great Britain Street end, under the noses of the Rotunda machine-gunners. It was hoped that this diversionary attack would distract the enemy while the real assault was made on the Moore Street barricade. As soon as the officer left, an unimpressed Volunteer muttered: 'And seven corpses in Moore Lane.'

A short time later, 30 Volunteers waited next to a back yard opening on to Sackville Lane. Commandant McLoughlin was going out with his men and held a canister bomb in his hand. Behind him stood Séamus Robinson, Sam O'Reilly, Oscar Traynor and Feargus de Búrca. Each man stared intently as a Volunteer slowly pulled back the bolt on the gate through which they would shortly make their charge.

The area surrounding Moore Street had become strangely silent. Millimetre by millimetre the bolt slid across, guided by a shaking hand until a barely audible metallic clink prompted the gathered men to draw in a deep breath and focus themselves on what lay ahead. As their clammy hands held their weapons at the ready their hearts began to beat wildly. McLoughlin had a nearby Volunteer light a match for his bomb while just yards to their rear, Charles Saurin waited apprehensively with his section for the word to go.

McLoughlin then received a sudden message from a runner to return to No. 16. His men were told to stand ready, prolonging their torture. When he returned he was questioned again by a rather shaken-looking Pearse as to whether or not the civilian casualties would be high as a result of their plans. McLoughlin's answer was an unambiguous 'yes' as they would be fighting through a densely populated area. His voice barely disguised his distaste at being asked a question which he had already answered. He set off again to the yard where he picked up his bomb once more and went back to the gate, where several of his men were muttering quiet prayers under their breath. The gate then opened, but yet again the runner returned. When the perplexed young commandant asked him what he wanted this time, the reply was that his plan was to be abandoned, and that he was now to issue the order of ceasefire for one hour. McLoughlin made his way again to No. 16.

Pearse had been overcome with grief when he witnessed a family by the name of Dillon falling victim to the machine gun on Moore Street a short time earlier. This particular family had ventured across the street carrying a white flag, seeking escape from their own burning building, and they were mown down right in front of his exhausted and bloodshot eyes. Pearse had often written and spoken about the glory of battle, even remarking that the blood spilt was the red wine the earth needed to flourish. What he now witnessed was the obscene antithesis of such supposed glory. A look of unimaginable horror had appeared on Dillon's face as his wife and daughter's bodies were pulverised before him, the force of the bullets wrenching them from his arms, before he too was shot. After they had fallen among the debris, they groaned and twitched, as, dying, they struggled to pull themselves to safety. The gunners then realised their mistake, and the area became silent.

A short distance from this dreadful episode, a teenage girl was shot dead in front of her parents, when a stumbling rebel accidentally discharged his rifle after kicking open the back door to their house. It was all too much for Pearse, who was now resting in another room as McLoughlin entered.

Back at the gate, the assembled men who had braced themselves to face certain death seemed too exhausted to betray emotion at the news their commandant-general had for them upon his return. They just stood silently and stared, although more than one gave a sigh of relief. When Charles Saurin and the others realised their appointment with the enemy machine-gunners had been postponed they sat quietly, hugely relieved. They stared blankly at the walls for a time before bowing their heads, utterly wrung out and exhausted.

Silence permeated the red-brick terraces along Moore Street, as the shattered garrison waited for news. And waited.

13

The Surrenders: Part 1

'Five paces forward.'

The ominous silence on Moore Street continued and after a time no movement at all could be detected in the smoky street by riflemen from either side, who strained constantly to seek out the ever-present danger of the enemy.

Lieutenant-Colonel Owens of the Royal Irish Rifles had set up his field headquarters in Thomas Clarke's tobacconist shop on Great Britain Street. This was on its eastern section, just beyond the Rotunda. As he finalised plans for an attack against the rebel positions, the troops to his west crouched behind their barricade at Moore Street with their gun barrels protruding through its many small gaps as they probed for targets of opportunity, which were now few and far between. Owens was convinced that the GPO was still occupied. As he made his plans, he was informed that his ranks would shortly be bolstered by two platoons of Colonel Hodgkin's Sherwood Foresters.

Commandant McLoughlin, meanwhile, was once again summoned back to Pádraig Pearse, whereupon the worn-out President of the Irish Republic informed him that Elizabeth O'Farrell had just been sent to the barricade, with a request to seek terms with the British High Command. McLoughlin asked Pearse, 'Does it mean surrender?' Pearse answered, 'I don't know until we have heard from the British.'[1]

Charles Saurin and Arthur Shields, both still manning the loft of Hanlon's, had begun to wonder what was happening. They had now been ordered not to fire at any soldiers in Moore Lane and it appeared that their suicidal mission was postponed indefinitely. Through their field glasses they could see British soldiers at the barricade. They were standing up and moving about, smoking and chatting.[2] An officer then leaned casually over the top of the barricade, and appeared to be gazing down the length of Moore Lane.

The rebel leadership was becoming dejected. Thomas Clarke, a veteran Fenian activist, and the first man to put his name to their Proclamation, broke down and openly wept at the very idea of surrender. Clarke had spent 15 years in an English prison where he had suffered unimaginable privations and faced them with a stoicism that earned the respect of everyone who knew him. To see the dream of his Republic in tatters was more than he could endure and his grief touched all those around him. The other leaders sat in silence, physically and mentally spent.

McLoughlin left the house for the final time to spread the news, which was met with a stunned silence from the men throughout the block of houses connected by tunnels who had managed to stay awake since the shooting had stopped. Those who had succumbed to their exhaustion were impossible to waken. Their snores were added to by the intermittent cries of the wounded and the crack of continuing distant gunshot. When McLoughlin eventually managed to wake Oscar Traynor, who had only recently fallen into a deep sleep, he informed him of the news. Traynor's lethargy was rapidly replaced by incandescent anger. Elizabeth O'Farrell, a 32-year-old midwife and native of City Quay in Dublin, had during the previous turbulent days acted as a rebel dispatcher, and had remained with the beleaguered garrison as it manoeuvred into Moore Street, where she now helped tend to the many wounded. She was fired at initially as she left No. 16 wearing a red cross and waving a white flag, but the nervous British infantrymen soon realised their mistake and ceased fire as she pressed forward in spite of the danger. She picked her way through the rubble towards the barricade. Moore Street was normally a bustling thoroughfare of market traders on a spring Saturday. Today it was devastated. Its Henry Street end had been blown to pieces during the night, and the carnage of the previous days and nights was visible all around, as were the many victims.

Her 100-yard walk seemed like an eternity, but when she arrived at the British position the infantrymen helped her across. Captain

The ruins of Henry Street, Moore Street and the northern flank of the GPO following a deluge of British 18-pounder artillery shells. NATIONAL LIBRARY OF IRELAND

Tomkins approached and, initially assuming she was a spy, treated her with great disdain before eventually realising his error. He told her to wait while he summoned Lieutenant-Colonel Hodgkin, and handed her over to the commander of 2/6th Sherwood Foresters. She explained that her commandant wished to negotiate terms for surrender. She was subsequently taken to the National Bank, on the north-eastern corner of Upper Sackville Street, while Brigadier-General Lowe, now stationed inside Trinity College, was sent for.

It took General Lowe roughly one hour to arrive at Colonel Owens' headquarters in Clarke's tobacco shop. O'Farrell was soon summoned to meet with him there. When the pair were face to face the general greeted her with a cold stare before instructing her to return to her commandant and inform him that nothing short of unconditional surrender would be accepted.

O'Farrell set off but returned soon afterwards with a written message from Pearse. The general was unimpressed. He repeated the demand, adding that if Pearse himself failed to surrender, followed by James

Connolly 30 minutes later, hostilities would recommence. He offered to drive her back across to Moore Street to deliver his demand. The exhausted nurse accepted the offer.

After some heated and intensely poignant discussion among the Volunteer leaders following her return, unconditional surrender was eventually agreed to. Pearse then stood up and said a final farewell to his men and to the other leaders, knowing it was unlikely that their paths would again converge. He marched slowly towards the barricade with O'Farrell by his side, stared down all the way by the machine-gunners and infantrymen who quietly savoured their approaching victory. He was greeted without any military courtesy by Colonel Hodgkin, and introduced to the general, who was now accompanied by his 18-year-old son, John, a second lieutenant.

As they stood together on Great Britain Street there was much discussion between Commandant Pearse and General Lowe, who appeared to have little time for the former, regarding him as the leader of a motley crew of rebels who did not warrant the military etiquette normally extended to high-ranking enemy officers under such circumstances. An agreement was made nonetheless. O'Farrell was to deliver, under British escort, the surrender order to the other rebel garrisons still holding out in Dublin. These included the Four Courts, Jacob's biscuit factory, the Royal College of Surgeons, Boland's Bakery and the South Dublin Union (the final of surrender of which was subsequently delegated elsewhere).

Gunfire could still be heard throughout the city, but the entire Moore Street/Great Britain Street area had now become noticeably quiet, apart from an occasional sniper round. O'Farrell was detained in the area while Pearse was driven away by car. Exhausted British infantrymen, their bayonets still fixed to their rifles, sat around in clusters on the ground, their faces and hands filthy from gun soot and the dirt that accompanies combat. They rested, fed themselves, drank from their canteens and smoked. The rebels did the same.

Pádraig Pearse was initially driven to the Irish Command Headquarters building on Parkgate Street, next to the Phoenix Park, where he was introduced to General Sir John Maxwell, the 57-year-old Commander-in-Chief of British Forces in Ireland. Maxwell saw to it that the surrender order was appropriately signed before the shattered rebel leader was moved to Arbour Hill Military Prison.

Connolly was now moved, once again by stretcher. Four Volunteers and three of their officers – Michael Staines, Liam Tannam and Diarmuid Lynch – went out with him, the latter of whom led the way. Staines placed a large green flag with a harp emblem across the commandant as he lay on the stretcher. Troops manning the barricade were initially unsure what was happening. A Royal Irish Rifles major by the name of Walsh was summoned to the scene, but he was unaware of the arrangements that the rebels insisted had been made. Major Walsh went to his headquarters for clarification and returned a short time later with a signal for the men to proceed.

As Connolly was carried along Great Britain Street towards Capel Street, Captain Tannam noticed that the surrounding houses were teeming with British troops. At the junction of Cole's Lane he saw one of the 18-pounder artillery pieces that had heaped such devastation upon their short-lived Republic. Its crewmen were still being ordered about by their NCOs until they all paused momentarily to gaze at the curious-looking stretcher party.

Rifle fire was still clearly audible from their west as they approached Capel Street, where they passed Private Davis and his comrades from the 2/6th South Staffordshires who had been pulled out of the line for a much needed break from the recent carnage on North King Street. When they finally reached Capel Street they turned left and walked the half-mile to Dublin Castle. All along their route the expressions on the faces of their enemy varied greatly. Many of them stared menacingly, while a few nodded discreetly and others appeared sympathetic to their predicament.

A sense of the surreal now abounded on Dublin's main street. The silence that followed the days of destruction seemed uncharacteristic and peculiar. Medics treated the wounded, and the dead were collected from the roads and pavements. A different kind of battle was now being waged, that between the increasingly heroic Dublin Fire Brigade and the smouldering buildings throughout Sackville Street and environs, which contained many death traps in the form of unexploded shells, abandoned canister bombs and countless other potential sources of harm. Throughout the week the Fire Brigade's ambulance personnel had equally risked life and limb, rushing the wounded and dying to the city's hospitals, often in the midst of firefights. The firemen's selfless labours were watched now by hundreds of civilian spectators on O'Connell

The often unsung heroes of Easter Week, Dublin's Fire Brigade in the ruins of the shattered city. NATIONAL LIBRARY OF IRELAND

Bridge, eager not to miss a glimpse of the history unfolding before their eyes.

Elizabeth O'Farrell arrived back on Moore Street during the late afternoon with the final instructions for the rebels' collective surrender. They were to come out in batches from Moore Lane onto Moore Street, unarmed. This last point was greatly emphasised. When it was clear to her that their soon-to-be captors' commands were fully understood, she returned to the barricade, where she was subsequently met by a driver and brought to the city's remaining rebel outposts.

When the time came, Volunteer Captain Michael O'Reilly stepped out from the doorway of No. 17 Moore Street waving a white flag. A British Sergeant approached him, followed by an officer. When Reilly told them that the surrender was about to commence the sergeant explained that the British positions around Cole's Lane were still under sniper fire from the direction of Riddal's Lane. Reilly crossed the street and promptly remedied the situation.

The Volunteers began to line up throughout the back yards of the eastern section of Moore Street. Seán McDermott and Seán

McLoughlin each took turns addressing the men in the rear of Hanlon's. They knew what was unfolding, but the news, when it officially came, did not make it any easier to stomach. Their emotions ranged from disgust to inconsolability. Several men spoke up in protest before it was emphasised to them that these were their orders and must be obeyed.

McLoughlin then loudly ordered the assembled men to 'Shoulder Arms!' before he led them out through the yard's Moore Lane gate. They marched to Sackville Lane and then turned left into Moore Street before coming to a halt. As they had marched out McDermott had given the same news to the remaining men of the garrison, and received a similar reaction, before ordering them to follow the same route as McLoughlin.

The Volunteers formed into ranks in Moore Street. As they did, Charles Donnelly scanned his weary-looking comrades looking for the newspaper boy. He wondered to himself if the youngster had made it, and wished he had asked him his name.

As evening slowly drew in, the many rebel wounded had been placed onto rows of makeshift stretchers on the street. Anything that was to hand was used, particularly doors. British medics waited patiently at the barricade to collect their patients.

Volunteer Captain Michael O'Reilly, having returned from Riddal's Lane earlier, was once again detailed to carry the white flag. He would be followed by Joseph Plunkett and an initial section of about 50 Volunteers. McLoughlin, Seán MacDermott and William Pearse would then lead the main body of about 200 men. Their orders stated that those surrendering were to march down Moore Street, turn left into Henry Place, left again on to Henry Street, and then onto Sackville Street where they would take a left at Nelson's Pillar, before finally proceeding to the Parnell Monument. There they would be met by the British forces to accept their surrender.

They followed the instructions and marched along the rubble-strewn route, past the scene of their hectic escape from the burning GPO the previous night, this time untroubled by fire, bullets, flying metal and concrete. As they did, a Volunteer who was positioned just behind Commandant McLoughlin pulled a tricolour from inside his jacket and fixed it to his rifle.

When they stopped for a moment at the junction of Henry Street and Sackville Street, McLoughlin's voice thundered out again, 'Eyes right to the GPO!'³ As the assembled men's heads turned in unison a British sergeant ran towards them, revolver in hand, urging them to hurry up as he feared that the GPO's walls were about to cave in. But McLoughlin was not going to rush his men. They marched on to Sackville Street at the same pace.

The main body of Volunteers eventually reached Sackville Street as per instruction, but were somewhat surprised to find no sign of Captain O'Reilly and his section. As if to lend humour to the tragedy, he had accidentally taken a wrong turn when he reached Sackville Street, and was now heading towards O'Connell Bridge. He was met there by British and colonial troops to whom he offered his surrender. The surrounding crowds pressed in as close as they could to listen to the ensuing conversation. O'Reilly was informed that he was in the wrong place, and after several taunts and surprisingly good-humoured insults had been exchanged between the weary troops from both sides, he turned his men and marched back up Sackville Street, where they joined the ranks of the other Volunteers who had now lined up outside the Gresham Hotel.

The filthy, exhausted, but intensely proud Irish Volunteers and Citizen Army men finally formed into two lines on the eastern side of the tramlines between Findlater Place and Cathedral Street. Behind them was the block of buildings that housed the Gresham Hotel. To both their front and rear there stood a cordon of British infantrymen.

Another command rang out from Commandant McLoughlin: 'Front line five paces forward, rear line two paces back, and deposit arms!' The subsequent metallic clatter of the last rifle hitting the ground signalled to the hundreds now gathering in the area that the battle for Dublin city was all but over. The rear rank then stepped back. Many among them still attempted to goad their adversaries at this point, by pushing their backs up until they were touching the bayonets of the troops standing behind them. The front rank did the same. As they approached closer and closer with every step the pointing bayonets of the men now eyeing them with malevolence, they advanced until their chests began to place pressure on the sharp steel. The tension mounted while in the distance, rifle fire continued to echo sporadically.

General Lowe suddenly ran angrily towards McLoughlin as he bellowed, 'Who the hell gave you the authority to give orders here? I told you to leave your bloody arms in Moore Street. I'll have you damn well shot!'[4]

McLoughlin looked back with contempt. He then drew his sword from his scabbard, before thrusting it to the ground next to the general's immaculately polished boots. Lowe glared back at him.

The surrounding British soldiers now descended on the insurgents and began taking their names and addresses while searching them. A Volunteer named Henry Ridgeway was dragged out of the ranks at one point and questioned by a British officer about the red cross on his arm. Ridgeway explained the obvious answer, i.e. that he was a medic. The officer replied, 'I don't recognise your damn red cross,' and cut off the armlet with a bayonet.

As the fires were slowly dealt with on what was left of Sackville Street, Henry Street, Abbey Street, Eden Quay and Moore Street, the surrendered Volunteers were marched under guard to the Rotunda Hospital, and detained in its grounds facing the north side of Rutland Square. There they found themselves handled with unequal measures of mercy, kindness and utter contempt by their captors. They were detained outside, where several, including Thomas Clarke and Seán McDermott, were treated appallingly by an officer from Gorey in County Wexford named Lee-Wilson. Unfortunately for the officer, the abuse took place in front of the eyes of Captain Michael Collins, who vowed to avenge such ill treatment. The promise was kept three years later.

That same afternoon, outside the Four Courts at about 1 p.m., Father O'Callaghan, the priest who had launched his verbal tirade against the rebels on Hammond Lane soon after the outbreak of fighting the previous Monday, and had generally made a thorough nuisance of himself throughout the week, approached the Church Street barricade, accompanied by a British officer. He was met there by Volunteer Joseph MacDonagh, who separated the officer from the priest, and sent word to Commandant Daly that both wished to speak with him.

Daly soon arrived from the Four Courts, accompanied by Captain Eamon Duggan and another officer. 'On what authority did you bring that officer here?' he asked the cleric. The priest pointed towards Peadar Clancy, suggesting permission had come from the Volunteer who had just returned from a sortie beyond his barricade to deal with a sniper. Knowing this to be a blatant lie, one of the officers lunged at the priest and punched him. His fellow officers dragged him from the screaming priest, and held them apart, while the British officer informed Daly of Pearse's surrender.

Daly sternly told both men to leave immediately, which they did, before he ordered his men back into the Four Courts, expecting an imminent attack in force.

Several hours later, the sombre figure of Elizabeth O'Farrell was seen walking westwards along the north quays under a white flag towards the Four Courts, which was carried by Father Columbus of the Capuchin Friary on Church Street. Commandant Daly met them at the nearby barricade, whereupon O'Farrell handed him the surrender document. It read:

> HQ Moore Street. Believing that the glorious stand which has been made by the soldiers of Irish freedom during the past five days in Dublin has been sufficient to gain recognition of Ireland's national claim at an international peace conference, and desirous of preventing further slaughter of the civilian population, and to save the lives of as many as possible of our followers, the members of the Provisional Government here present have agreed by a majority to open negotiations with the British commander.

It was signed:

> P. H. Pearse
> Commandant General
> Commanding in Chief
> Army of the Irish Republic
> 29 April 1916

Daly handed it back, before speaking to Nurse O'Farrell for a while. He watched them leave before returning inside and gathering his fighting men and women to inform them of the real reason for the cessation in the distant artillery fire. They were both furious and disgusted at the news. One Volunteer commented that the Four Courts could hold out for another month. Others, including Eamon Morkan, stated that they would simply not surrender. They would refuse to hand over their weapons.

After several heated and colourful exchanges of words, they were eventually brought under control. It was decided that since they had mobilised under the authority of their commander-in-chief, his orders

The 32-year-old Nurse Elizabeth
O'Farrell, who stepped out into a
fire-swept street carrying a white
flag, as the insurrection reached
its tragic climax. NATIONAL
LIBRARY OF IRELAND

would be followed, regardless of their distaste at the prospect of surrendering to an enemy whom they felt had not beaten them in battle. Their weapons were another matter. Most were brought outside to the courtyard and smashed.

Commandant Daly's men were to proceed to the small enclosure facing Chancery Place and to hand their weapons through the railings to the waiting Royal Dublin Fusiliers. Daly ordered Lieutenant Liam O'Carroll to round up the garrison.

When the ruined weapons had been presented to the tremendously relieved looking Fusiliers, a major entered the courtyard, accompanied by a section of infantrymen. He looked at the assembled men from 1st Battalion and then turned to Daly asking if his full complement was present. When he confirmed it was, the officer replied: 'If I had known that this was the extent of the garrison here, you would have been out of this by half-past-twelve on Monday morning last.'[5] Daly explained that there were many wounded Volunteers and Cumann na mBan members still inside the building. It was then agreed that Lieutenant O'Carroll would remain with the wounded and Red Cross personnel until the following day.

The Volunteers formed up and marched out through the Four Courts' Chancery Gate where a battalion of Dublin Fusiliers met them. Both sets of fighters had endured hell that week. They were escorted along the quays until they reached Capel Street, where they were instructed to turn left. Eamon Morkan was utterly deflated at his battalion's recent surrender, but loud cries of 'We'll rise again!'[6] from the ranks behind him were heartening. The growing harmonies of rebel songs began to lift his spirits as he and the others marched on, watched all along the way by khaki-clad troops and legions of hungry and weary civilians.

When the surrendered men reached Sackville Street, they came to a halt outside the Richmond Institute for the Blind, directly opposite the Gresham Hotel. General Lowe then bellowed, 'Who is in charge of these men?' Commandant Daly stepped forward. He clicked his heels as he saluted, and answered 'I am. At all events I was.'[7] Lowe gave Daly a contemptuous stare.

A British officer began taking the men's names and addresses in the ranks. He told them that if they had anything on them that they should not have, to drop it at their feet immediately, adding that they were about to be searched. The Fusiliers soon followed the officer's orders. One soldier then approached Vice-Commandant Piaras Béaslaí and pointed at his sword, demanding that he hand it over. Béaslaí refused. Instead, he pulled it from its scabbard and smashed it over his knee, shouting, 'Long live the Irish Republic!'[8]

The secure line of communication from Trinity College enjoyed by the British in the Shelbourne Hotel in St Stephen's Green soon delivered the news that the Volunteer headquarters in Dublin had surrendered. The same information began to filter into the Royal College of Surgeons via the food foragers, who had heard similar rumours of capitulation from the civilians they had encountered as Saturday afternoon wore on. The battle-scarred Green was deathly quiet, save for the spring breeze that rustled through the trees. Shots could still be heard in the distance. The hunt for food now became something of an obsession as supplies were dangerously low.

The remaining handful of rebel trench-fighters were now beginning to starve. They quenched their thirst with what little stale water they could still shake from their canteens, and the growing uncertainty played on their exhausted minds. Many felt relief as evening approached, and some small-scale firing broke out again, anything to take their minds off the dreadful state of limbo that had tortured them for the best part of the day. Others among them found the fighting equally torturous, as it seemed the military were meting out just enough fire to harass them and to deny them any chance of what soldiers in combat inevitably crave: sleep, a luxury that would to their tortured minds have given their foxholes equal status with the most salubrious of hotels.

That same evening on the north side of the Liffey, after a day of almost continuous battle, the Volunteers under Patrick Holohan in Moore's Coachworks and Clarke's Dairy prepared for what they expected would be their final do-or-die defence. Word had not reached them of Commandant Daly's earlier surrender, at least, not on an official level: the news that they were to lay down their arms had been shouted towards them by increasingly cocky enemy troops, but they were not in any way inclined to take instructions from their enemy.

In Father Mathew Hall, Mícheál Ó Foghludha had been dispatched to the Richmond Hospital to find and bring back a doctor. He had, however, failed. Fathers Augustine and Aloysius, two local Capuchin priests, both of whom were at the end of their tether trying to cope with the endless stream of casualties, decided to take matters into their own hands. They left Father Mathew Hall and approached the barricade at the top of Lower Church Street, accompanied by Ó Foghludha who waved a white flag, and asked to speak with the officer in charge. They waited for some time before they were brought to meet Colonel Taylor. They explained their urgent need for doctors but he did not appear overly concerned with their predicament. He turned away and walked off. The pair of priests and the Volunteer remained where they were until Lieutenant John Lowe, the general's son, arrived with a more sympathetic disposition. He sent for Colonel Taylor once again.

In spite of their exhaustion, the rebels in North Brunswick Street still wanted to regain some form of initiative, and planned on mustering their battered men for an attack to recapture Reilly's Fort. Unexpectedly, two doctors and a priest arrived at Clarke's Dairy: Dr Miles, Dr O'Carroll and Father Albert, another local Capuchin, informed them of the surrender order. Holohan replied dismissively that he had not been issued with any such order, and that his men had decided to fight to the finish. He ordered his garrison to carry on with their preparations for the attack. Soon afterwards, the surrounding air resonated to the sound of gunfire yet again.

Fathers Augustine and Aloysius found themselves in Colonel Taylor's company once more as the shots cracked out in the background. Father Augustine asked the battalion commander to agree to a truce. His reply was that he would, on the basis that the enemy also agreed. Mícheál Ó Foghludha was dispatched to his fellow Volunteers with the relevant message. He returned to the continuing sound of gunfire. Taylor now lost what little composure he had and un-holstered his revolver. Placing it against Ó Foghludha's head, he told the terrified Volunteer that if his comrades did not stop firing he would shoot him. Father Augustine rushed towards the dairy shouting that the British had agreed to a truce. Holohan came outside and said he was not in a position to make any terms with the military, but that if the priest felt it necessary, he would agree to a temporary truce. After much consultation it was deemed that the ensuing ceasefire would commence at 7.30 p.m. that evening and last until 10 a.m. the following morning. Lines of demarcation were also agreed upon. Dr O'Carroll was then sent with a joint escort of a single Volunteer and a pair of British soldiers to Broadstone, to brief Colonel Meldon of the truce.

Patrick Holohan re-entered Clarke's Dairy and ordered his brother Garry to organise a guard for their side of the demarcation line. Patrick Kelly was sent out to patrol it. Two British officers simultaneously patrolled the British side. They suddenly overstepped the agreed point and Kelly pulled his revolver on them, warning them to step back. When additional numbers of men rushed out from Moore's Coachworks and Clarke's Dairy, backed up by numerous rifles barrels pointing out of windows at them, they complied.

Fathers Augustine and Aloysius returned to Father Mathew Hall, now accompanied by Volunteer Ó Foghludha and a large number of students from Richmond Hospital. With the help of the Cumann na mBan women they proceeded to move the 27 badly wounded the short distance to the hospital, overcoming the initial resistance offered to them by several soldiers on the way. The Cumann na mBan members then returned to Father Mathew Hall to await the outcome.

On the night of Saturday 29 April 1916, Dublin was in a state of shock. The heart of the vibrant city had been torn out. Almost 3,000 people had become casualties since Easter Monday, and thousands more rendered homeless. For those still living and breathing, there was at least some solace to be found in survival, particularly for those lucky families who had been spared the loss of one or more loved ones. No such comfort, however, was found for those unfortunate civilians who had spent Friday evening and Saturday morning in the custody of an enraged South Staffordshire Regiment.

The houses positioned at the Church Street end of North King Street, and a single house on its opposite side, had witnessed scenes of unimaginable horror. Four innocent civilians – Peter Lawless, James McCartney, James Finnegan and Patrick Hoey – were shot to death in No. 27. In No. 170, Thomas Hickey, his son Christopher and Peter Connolly were shot. Michael Hughes and John Walsh from No. 172 suffered a similar fate, as did Michael Noonan and George Ennis in No. 174. In No. 91, Edward Dunne was killed, while in No. 177, Patrick Bealen and James Healy were shot, before being hastily buried in its basement. The latter victim had been dragged in from the street, before both he and Bealen were subjected to vicious abuse. A man named John Beirnes had been trying to reach Monk's Bakery to help calm and feed its horses only to be shot down on Coleraine Street. William O'Neill saw the body and thought it was his father lying in the road. When he discovered it was not he was shot as he sped away towards Constitution Hill. He was helped into a nearby house where he died in agony five minutes later. In total, 16 innocent civilians were gunned down in North King Street between 6 p.m. on Friday and 10 a.m. on Saturday by the South Staffordshires.

Elsewhere in Dublin, men in British uniform did their best to ensure that the hardships suffered by Dublin's population were eased as quickly as possible. Exhausted Englishmen, Scottish and Welshmen, not to mention colonials, and Irishmen in the uniform of the Crown, went to great pains to see that the young and old alike were given badly needed food and medical supplies, and that aid was swiftly delivered to the stricken.

On Sunday morning at 10 a.m., after a relatively restful night, the official surrender was delivered to the battered and bruised Volunteers in North Brunswick Street by Father Columbus. Patrick Holohan was eventually handed the surrender document by a British officer. In spite of Holohan's initial suspicions to the contrary, his brother Garry subsequently confirmed that the signature it contained was indeed that of Commandant Pearse. Soon afterwards, Patrick Holohan met again with the same officer and made the relevant arrangements. This was followed by a loud shout to fall in.

Fifty-eight shattered but battle-hardened men began vacating the buildings they had occupied for almost a week, to line up on Upper Church Street. The surrounding ranks of British soldiers craned their necks to get a better view of the enemy who had fought so fiercely. Holohan spoke to the men: 'I know you would, like myself, prefer to be with our comrades who have already fallen in the fight – we, too, should rather die in this glorious struggle than submit to the enemy. The treatment you may expect in the future you may judge from the past.'[9]

Lieutenant-Colonel Taylor approached Patrick Holohan and asked where the rest of his men were. He replied that they were all on parade, adding that if the colonel was not convinced, he was welcome to search the surrounding buildings. Taylor swore at him and said, 'This bunch of men and boys held my battalion.' He then stormed away.

Holohan called his Volunteers to order and soon they began their eastbound march along North King Street. The houses on either side of the road were crammed with soldiers, several of whom came out onto the street as they passed. The column was ordered to, 'Halt and ground arms' as soon as they reached the junction of Capel Street. The 1st Battalion's Irish Volunteers then smashed their rifles on the ground. The surrounding troops left them to it. They were then searched for hidden weapons before being marched to Dublin Castle. A sense of desolate shock descended in the uneasy silence that followed in their wake.

14

The Surrenders: Part 2

'From the oldest to the youngest, they don't care a damn.'

On the same Sunday morning, 30 April, 2 miles away from the scene of Patrick Holohan's speech to his men, Lieutenant Joseph O'Byrne, who had managed to get his head down for a few hours in Boland's Mills, was woken by the ringing of church bells in the distance. As he slowly roused himself, his first thoughts were for his positions. Looking around, he saw his men crouching behind windows and other openings, still seeking out the enemy snipers who had now infested the entire length of Lower Mount Street, and were also positioned around the roof of Sir Patrick Dun's Hospital. As the first cracks of their rifles echoed out, he realised they had been fighting for almost a week.

Soon afterwards, Volunteer Seán Byrne, who was cleaning up the mess of blood and bandages from the previous night's casualties in the dispensary of Boland's Bakery, noticed a woman next to the railing outside bearing a white flag. He grabbed his weapon and went out to speak with the woman who introduced herself as Elizabeth O'Farrell. She asked to see Commandant de Valera, adding that she had a message from Pádraig Pearse. Byrne instructed her to go to the dispensary gate on nearby Clarence Street, and went to fetch his commandant.

When de Valera was told of the messenger he was having a much-needed wash. He placed a towel around his neck, before ordering Joe O'Connor to accompany him outside.

When they were face to face, O'Farrell handed de Valera the surrender order, which he then read, before handing it back dismissively, stating that it had not been countersigned by Thomas MacDonagh, the commandant of the Dublin Brigade. O'Farrell left, saying she would return later with the appropriate signature on the document.

A short time later roughly a mile away, she appeared at the top of Grafton Street, again holding aloft a white flag. Many heavy and exhausted eyes darted towards her solitary figure. Rifle sights were trained in her direction as she approached the Royal College of Surgeons, but she was allowed to proceed unhindered. She entered the rebel fortress from York Street.

She was met there by Countess Markievicz, who studied the surrender order with characteristic intensity, before handing it back, and ordering a nearby private to fetch Commandant Mallin, who was now resting in one of the College's back rooms. He too read the document before handing it back to O'Farrell. She then left.

Mallin immediately ordered all officers present to report to him and he soberly informed them of the surrender order. They were aghast. Arguments broke out and many wholeheartedly rejected the idea. They insisted that they were securely entrenched in a very strong position and would be able to carry on the fight. Since Tuesday morning no ground had been surrendered and, indeed, the rebels had only the previous evening been formulating a plan of an offensive nature – the capture of the United Services Club. Some among them doubted it was actually James Connolly's signature on the document. Mallin assured them that it was and insisted sternly that they obey any and all orders given by their commandant. He emphasised that they had entered the fight as an army under his command, and they would remain as such, come what may. His attention was then diverted briefly to a whispered conversation between Lieutenant Bob de Coeur and Thomas O'Donoghue who suggested placing him under arrest and continuing the fight. Mallin smiled at them, saying, 'I know what you are talking about.'[1] He then ordered the entire garrison into the Lecture Hall.

Earlier that morning, Fathers Augustine and Aloysius had been requested by General Lowe to deliver word of Pearse's surrender to Commandant MacDonagh in Jacob's biscuit factory. The general feared that having failed to get the message through to its commandant the previous day, 'he would be obliged to attack and demolish the Factory with a great loss of life.'[2]

When MacDonagh was eventually approached by the pair of priests, he was initially unimpressed, and told them that the surrender order held no weight, having been written by men who were prisoners. He added that he would now assume the role of commander-in-chief, and as such would enter into negotiations, if there were to be any, only with the head of the British military. He conceded that he was prepared to meet their commander at a location of his choosing, should Jacob's be deemed inappropriate.

The priests soon left the biscuit factory and returned to Dublin Castle where they gave General Lowe the message. After a brief consultation with General Maxwell, Lowe said that he was prepared to meet Commandant MacDonagh in the north-eastern section of Saint Patrick's Park, the beautifully landscaped enclosure next to the landmark Cathedral, at noon. As soon as the priests departed with the message, he contacted Colonel Hall of the 2/5th North Staffordshire Battalion with orders to prepare the men to surround and storm the factory should the negotiations be unsuccessful.

Meanwhile, back in the College of Surgeons, as the surrounding Citizen Army outposts fell back on the position, the men and women inside had gathered in its lecture hall. When the surrender order was read out, Sergeant Frank Robbins paled as he muttered 'My God! No! It couldn't be! Anything but that!'[3] Captain Joseph Connolly became animated, shouting that he would not surrender. Captain Bill Partridge eventually succeeded in calming down the fireman, at least momentarily. Many among the exhausted insurgents called for an immediate escape to the Dublin Mountains, where they would form flying columns to carry on the fight. Some began to break down; others continued to protest their determination to escape. A few quietly picked up their rifles and left the College. The surrender was, nonetheless, agreed upon.

Mallin ordered a white flag to be hoisted above the College of Surgeons' York Street entrance, while he and a couple of men made their way to the roof and hauled down the tricolour, replacing the Republican symbol with the white flag. As they did, a couple of enemy rifle rounds clipped the slates nearby. In the Shelbourne Hotel, word was sent to Captain Elliotson to proceed to the top floor. Something appeared to be afoot. When he arrived his attention was directed to the surrender flag fluttering in the breeze 300 yards to his west. He immediately made contact with Dublin Castle.

A short time later, Major Henry de Courcy Wheeler of the Dublin Fusiliers arrived at the top of Grafton Street accompanied by an escort of men from his battalion. He dispatched a runner to the United Services Club and the Shelbourne, with orders for them to hold their fire. He then ordered his escort to remain where they were, with the exception of an NCO who accompanied him as he went to accept the surrender.

When they arrived at the massive front door of the College of Surgeons, behind them St Stephen's Green was completely silent. They knocked, and a shout from behind a broken and barricaded window directed them to York Street. There they were met by Commandant Mallin and Countess Markievicz. Salutes were exchanged before Mallin offered the major his cane as a memento, a gesture accepted by the officer with typical good manners. De Courcy-Wheeler then asked Markievicz to disarm. She removed her Mauser pistol from its holster, kissed it and handed it over. This was all too much for Captain Joseph Connolly, who was overcome with rage. He pulled his own semi-automatic pistol and went to shoot the two enemy soldiers. Luckily for all, he was wrestled under control by his comrades.

The order was given in the College of Surgeons: 'Arms down, three paces backward!' When it had been complied with, the major asked Mallin where the rest of his men were. He answered that they were all present, prompting a brief compliment from de Courcy-Wheeler before he addressed the garrison that consisted of less than half the number he had expected. He told them to collect their stuff and to bring blankets, adding that they would more than likely need them.

A half a mile away, meanwhile, Commandant MacDonagh had met General Lowe at the appointed time. Their parley initially began on the footpath before both men retired to the general's car, watched intently by the two priests and a single Volunteer who had accompanied MacDonagh.

After 20 minutes or so, MacDonagh got out of the car and informed the two priests that he had provisionally agreed to surrender, and that there was to be a truce until 3 p.m. He added that he would need to consult with the men in Jacob's, as well as Commandant Ceannt in the South Dublin Union. General Lowe, whose disposition had improved considerably since the previous day, placed his car and chauffeur at his disposal, after presenting him with a pass to see him through the British lines.

Volunteer Seán Murphy, from his vantage point overlooking the Adelaide Hospital, trained his gun in the direction of the staff car as it pulled up moments later outside the biscuit factory. When his commandant stepped out, Murphy took his finger off the trigger.

MacDonagh stepped inside his fortress and sent word to the officers to assemble for a meeting. While he was waiting he called Elizabeth O'Farrell into his office and countersigned the surrender document for Commandant de Valera. She immediately left for Boland's Bakery.

The gravity of the situation had, however, already sunk in with de Valera in Boland's Bakery. After having deduced some time earlier that the surrender was real, he had summoned Vice-Commandant Joe O'Connor to his side and discussed the uncertain situation. When de Valera asked O'Connor how he felt the men would take the unexpected news, he replied: 'We came out as soldiers under orders and we will carry on as such.'

O'Connor then gathered several men and ordered them to proceed to each Company area and to present each with the immediate order to retire to Boland's Bakery with all arms.

Seán Byrne, in the meantime, had returned to his tasks in the dispensary. He was sitting quietly in its first-aid post when de Valera approached him, saying, 'Byrne, we are about to surrender and you will have to come out with me.'[4] After a moment's pause he added that they would need something that looked like a flag. Byrne tore a piece of nearby tablecloth and tied it to the end of a walking stick he had found. Byrne turned to ask the Commandant what would now become of them, to which de Valera replied, 'I know what will happen to me, but I will do my best for you and the men.'

A Royal Artillery cadet named Mackey, who had been held captive in Boland's Bakery after being taken prisoner as the Volunteers stormed into Westland Row Station the previous Monday, was informed by de Valera that they were leaving. He was then offered the choice of either remaining in the dispensary or going with his captors. Mackey elected to accompany them, fearing that his own people would mistake him for a traitor if he stayed.

The three men then left the dispensary, with Seán Byrne carrying the white flag, and crossed the road to enter Sir Patrick's Dunn's Hospital, where Dr Miles Keogh greeted them. They told him that they wished to surrender. He immediately left but soon returned, accompanied by a British officer carrying a revolver, who led the men to Lower Mount Street, before another officer led de Valera away.

The former prisoner Cadet Mackey was ordered to identify himself and, having explained his situation, was also led away. The officer then led Byrne to a stretch of Lower Mount Street close to its junction with Grattan Street, from where he was instructed to return to Boland's Bakery to muster his surrendered comrades, and in the words of the officer as he pointed towards the same junction, march them into 'yon' street.[5]

Meanwhile, the British military escort had arrived at the College of Surgeons. As the shattered and starving rebels were marched out into York Street, Irish Citizen Army Captain Bill Partridge turned to the women of the garrison and exclaimed: 'Now girls, heads erect!'

They marched to St Stephen's Green West and turned left, passing the front of the College of Surgeons. Many looked up at its bullet-riddled facade and pondered what was in store for themselves and their comrades. The apparent hostility of the crowds gathering near Grafton Street suggested an outlook that was far from bright.

As they marched along Dublin's landmark shopping street they came under a ferocious verbal assault from the civilians. Some struck out at them and some hurled small missiles. Others cheered them, only to find themselves at the receiving end of the same escalating tirade of abuse. Major De Courcy-Wheeler became increasingly concerned and detailed an officer to order his infantryman to 'Present arms!' The measure was immediately effective and the crowd backed off.

Defiance, exhaustion, grief: all these and more were felt by the Irish Citizen Army as they were marched towards Dublin Castle and into captivity. Mallin's men and women were harried by some of their captors as they marched. Some were prodded with bayonets by young British troops unable to contain their anger. Some troops, however, showed the rebels great respect and courtesy, as Commandant Mallin and Countess Markievicz led the column, flanked on both sides by lines of soldiers. The tension, however, was palpable. When several shots rang out from St Stephen's Green many of the captives' instinctively turning heads were met with raised enemy rifles. Apparently there were some who simply refused to surrender. They would fight until their end, which quickly came.

Back across the Liffey, Commandant-General Seán McLoughlin was marching with his hungry, thirsty and worn-out fighters towards

Richmond Barracks in Inchicore from the Rotunda grounds. The men were completely exhausted, having been forced to spend the night huddling and shivering under a cool April sky. A British officer approached McLoughlin and said sharply, 'You are too young to be an officer, you are no longer an officer now.'[6] He pulled the yellow ribbon from McLoughlin's arm. Whether out of kindness or ignorance, this act inadvertently saved him from the fate that soon awaited the rebellion's other leaders.

Back in Jacob's biscuit factory, the officers had assembled as ordered, and as the volume of their collective voices fell to a murmur, Commandant MacDonagh sombrely announced that their surrender had been ordered by Commandants Pearse and Connolly. He then asked the men for their opinion. Many were in favour of fighting on, including newly promoted Captain Dick McKee. But the majority sided with Quartermaster Micheál O'Hanrahan, who in his characteristically reasoned tone advised surrender, emphasising the huge number of civilians who would perish should the British be compelled to bombard the garrison into submission. The quartermaster was tremendously respected by his Volunteers. His meticulous logistical abilities had ensured that few of his men had wanted for even the simplest of things that week, such as food and tobacco, or clean shirts and socks, which for a soldier in combat can have the most profound of influences.

When each man had taken his turn to speak, MacDonagh stood up and said, 'Boys, we must give in. We must leave some to carry on the struggle!'[7] He then ordered the garrison's assembly.

Most among their ranks felt differently when they heard the news. Pandemonium broke out, with men screaming, 'Fight it out, we will fight it out!' while others smashed their guns off the steel sections of flooring. Some stood motionless, as if in shock, while a few seemed relieved, as if having had a great weight lifted from their shoulders.

MacBride was approached by several men evidently keen to carry on the fight with their swaggering major, and asked if they should try to escape or remain there to be captured. He replied, 'Liberty is a sweet thing. If it ever happens again, take my advice and don't get inside four walls.'[8]

Meanwhile, MacDonagh called for order. He gave permission to anyone without a uniform to make their escape, while the others were ordered back to their posts to await the time. He then returned to

General Lowe's car, and was driven the mile or so to the South Dublin Union to make contact with the 4th Battalion.

A short time later, 4th Battalion's commander, Éamonn Ceannt, received the same devastating news of surrender. He, like the other commandants, was appalled at the very idea. His men had thus far held off the military, and he knew his garrison was still well armed, well manned and well supplied. He told Commandant MacDonagh and the pair of accompanying priests that he would need to consult with his garrison before providing his reply.

Ceannt called his men together and told them the news, adding that any man wishing to escape had his permission, considering that the British hold on the surrounding area was tenuous at best. He added, however, 'but that having behaved like soldiers from the beginning, he would like them to behave like soldiers to the end'.[9]

After some time, Ceannt returned to MacDonagh and the two priests, and said to them that Pearse's order would be obeyed. He sent a dispatch to Jameson's Distillery in Marrowbone Lane with orders not to fire on any British Army personnel. When Captain Séamus Murphy received the dispatch he called the position's officers together and informed them of its contents. Although the message did not actually mention surrender, they could read between its lines. When the officers broke up, Robert Holland approached Captain Colbert and asked what was happening. He was told solemnly: 'Their cause will have to be left to a future generation.'

Back in Boland's Bakery, when Vice-Commandant O'Connor informed the assembled men of the garrison's imminent capitulation, several quickly succumbed to rage. One man screamed, 'Why do we want to surrender? We are holding out!' Others shouted themselves hoarse, denouncing anyone who had already done such a thing, while others became despondent and cried, before their anger got the better of them. Some began smashing their rifles, similar to their fellow Volunteers elsewhere. Things for a time looked as if they might get out of control, as factions began to form, the majority of which were unambiguously in favour of carrying on the fight. O'Connor eventually got matters under his command, until finally it was agreed that they would obey the order to surrender.

A short distance away in Boland's Mills, Lieutenant O'Byrne and his men were dumbfounded on hearing the same news. O'Byrne was unable to believe it. The surrender would mean 'the destruction for God knows how long of the movement, built up with such skill and sacrifice in spite of tremendous opposition'.[10] Nevertheless, he sent word to his outposts to assemble at his position. As they made their way to Boland's Bakery, they were under sporadic sniper fire all the while. They cursed furiously amongst themselves.

Meanwhile, in Jacob's biscuit factory, several men made their escape: Vincent Byrne and James Carbury escaped from a window on Bishop Street, having been lowered down by a local priest who had recently been allowed to enter. Covered from head to toe in flour, they could not blend in with the crowd that had gathered, and were pushed at and heckled. One woman, however, grabbed both of them and ushered them into her house where she vigorously brushed their clothes free of the flour before the pair made their escape through the back streets.

The two Olympic cyclists, Michael Walker and his brother John, approached their captain and told him they believed they could get away. McKee looked at them and said: 'More luck, Mick! If you succeed let my mother know I'm safe.'[11] The promise was made and the brothers left Jacob's. Not far away, Séamus Pounch handed his gun to the man next to him, and covered up his Na Fianna uniform with an overcoat before making his escape.

Shortly after 3 p.m., Commandant MacDonagh arrived back in Saint Patrick's Park, having been dropped off by the staff car that subsequently returned to the South Dublin Union with the two priests, Lieutenant Lowe and Major Rotherham. MacDonagh removed his belt, and handed both it and his revolver to General Lowe, who saluted him. Both men agreed that MacDonagh should return straight away to Jacob's to oversee the surrender.

When he arrived back at the stronghold he ordered the garrison's remaining men to parade on the ground floor. He then officially informed them that he had surrendered, and ordered them to leave the factory and form up at attention on Peter Street. The Volunteers of the 2nd Battalion soon began leaving the building. As they did several quietly pleaded with Major MacBride to make his escape. He replied that he could not leave the boys, and that it would be pointless as every G-man in Dublin knew him. When it was then pointed out that there had not been a G-man on the streets since Monday, he simply replied that he would stay.

Once outside, the rebels quickly formed up into fours on Peter Street. Volunteer Jimmy Shields, one of the youngest men in the garrison, accepted the task of taking charge and marching the men to the surrender point.

As they marched towards Bride Street, several Volunteers took the opportunity to slip away into the watching crowds, while the rebel column approached the ranks of British soldiers waiting for them, with General Lowe at their head. Shields then shouted the order to halt, and repeated a similar order to that bellowed out by Commandant McLoughlin the previous evening: 'Five paces forward and deposit arms!' Unlike the preceding day, however, the Volunteers, the British infantrymen, and their general all showed restraint. In the background, rifle shots could still be heard from one of the towers in Jacob's.

As they were marched under escort to Bride Street, Seosamh de Brún watched as a detachment of the Royal Dublin Fusiliers moved into position to occupy the biscuit factory. The ever philosophical Volunteer was struck by the irony of a brother of one of his comrades preparing to march into Jacob's in the uniform of the British Army.

A mile to the west, Commandant Ceannt gave an order for the South Dublin Union's front gates to be opened, before he commanded his men to assemble outside the nurses' home. Moments later, Patrick Smyth, the Union's Ward-master, stood at its gate and admitted Father Augustine and Major Rotherham, the former of whom was covered in flour from his brief visit inside Jacob's. Lieutenant Lowe and Father Aloysius remained in the car, which soon went on its way. Ceannt stepped out of the office closest to the gate and approached the British officer. Rotherham turned to him and said: 'You had a fine position here.'[12] Ceannt replied: 'Yes and we made full use of it. We held your army for six days,' before he led the major to the assembled men of his battalion.

When confronted with the ranks of the 44 remaining men of the Union garrison, the British major asked: 'Mr Ceannt, when will all your men be out?'[13] His eyebrows were raised by the reply: 'They're all here.' Ceannt ordered his men to attention, a command that was swiftly followed by a mass clicking of heels. The men tucked in their chins as their shoulders straightened, while slapping the palms of their hands to the outside of their thighs.

Rotherham appeared highly impressed with the demeanour of Ceannt's Irish Volunteers, and paid them the military compliment of inspecting their ranks, a gesture that signified great respect for a surrendered enemy. The ceremony was succeeded with another order from their leader, to fix bayonets and shoulder arms. This again was done with the efficiency of a well-drilled unit, before they marched out of the Union onto James' Street. A horse-drawn ambulance followed, carrying some wounded, including Captain Douglas fFrench Mullen.

Volunteer Thomas Young had maintained his position on the Marrowbone Lane footbridge since the fighting had died down in the area two days earlier. As the sound of marching boots echoed through the streets and grew louder he signalled to the men in Jameson's Distillery that the Union garrison was approaching from James' Street. Robert Holland raced to where he could see their approach.

Soon afterwards, Commandant Ceannt, Major Rotherham and Father Augustine entered the Distillery through its huge gates where they were met by Captains Con Colbert and Séamus Murphy. A discussion ensued which lasted for about three minutes, and was followed by salutes. The three men who had entered then left, leaving Colbert staring blankly at the ground. Murphy's complexion turned a sickly yellow colour as he walked away. After Colbert had absorbed the magnitude of this turn of events, he blew his whistle and ordered the garrison to fall in and informed them of the surrender. Anyone who wished to escape was given permission, an opportunity that was grasped by quite a few, one of whom shouted, 'Too-ra-loo lads, I'm off!'

Captain Colbert quickly saw to it that the remaining garrison was re-formed, before they were subsequently led out by Captain Murphy. They followed the ambulance at the rear of Ceannt's column while the women marched close behind. Hundreds of curious and relieved local civilians began to emerge from the densely populated houses and flats that lined the route to witness the drama, prompting Ceannt to remark loudly: 'Where were you men when you were wanted!'[14] The same men, women and children watched silently as the 4th Battalion marched eastwards to Bride Road, led by a solitary British officer. As they marched in disciplined formation, with their rifles slung across their shoulders, a local priest remarked on what a fine body of men and women they were.

As if to add light relief to the sombre affair, two drunken men repeatedly tried to join their ranks as they marched. Each time the persistent pair tried to blend in they were swiftly ejected. However, as the eagle-eyed Robert Holland later stated, 'They must have made it into our ranks, as two months later I saw these two men taking their exercise in Knutsford prison.'

Throughout the afternoon, the still air surrounding Dublin's Grand Canal had echoed to sporadic rifle cracks. Their frequency had diminished greatly, however, as Vice-Commandant Joseph O'Connor, having made a stirring address worthy of his new rank, led the 3rd Battalion out from its Boland's Bakery fortress for the final time, with Seán Byrne at his side carrying the white flag. They exited via its Clarence Street gate before proceeding along the short distance to Grand Canal Street, where they turned right and where, to their complete surprise, a great crowd of cheering people had gathered. The men were dumbstruck. Some civilians openly cried as rebels filed past. Others offered sympathetic words, while several more offered to hide their guns. Following this encounter, the men's heads were held a great deal higher as they marched in a disciplined formation of two columns, before turning left onto Grattan Street, where they could see their lanky commandant standing next to a group of British officers waiting for them about a hundred yards away.

When they reached the top of Grattan Street, Joseph O'Connor shouted an order to halt, then stepped forward and handed over his command to his commandant. De Valera responded by ordering the grounding of arms; the subsequent clatter of unloaded weapons being placed in rows on the cobblestones filled many surrendered insurgents with great distaste. O'Connor then carefully placed the sword, which had been presented to him by the men of A Company on Good Friday, at the head of the grounded collection of armaments as a mark of respect to his men.

The 85 remaining Volunteers of the battalion were ordered to put their hands in the air and march to Lower Mount Street where a large number of less sympathetic men waited for them, those being the wearers of British Army uniforms.

After they had been mustered in Mount Street, they were ordered once again to halt and, having been searched for weapons, were permitted to relax a little and lower their hands. Young Andrew McDonnell was standing next to Captain Simon Donnelly when a British officer standing just in front of them looked at the teenager and said, 'Well, sonny, it is all over now and you are all going to be shot.' McDonnell grinned at the officer, who then turned to Dr Keogh and said, 'There you are, they are

A young and apprehensive-looking rebel prisoner is marched across O'Connell Bridge to an uncertain future. NATIONAL LIBRARY OF IRELAND

Irish Volunteers 3rd Battalion, those who 'couldn't care a damn', being marched into captivity on Sunday 30 April 1916. They are pictured here marching along the southern section of Northumberland Road, where the previous Wednesday two British battalions suffered an appalling baptism of fire under their guns. Their commandant, Éamon de Valera, is to their front, with a white X above his head to identify him. DE VALERA PAPERS UCD, COURTESY LA FAYETTE PHOTOGRAPHY all the same – from the oldest to the youngest they don't care a damn.'[15]

Later on, another British officer approached Seán Byrne with instructions that they were to proceed to Ballsbridge. 'Do you know where it is?' he asked. Byrne replied that he did, adding that he would lead the column.

The 3rd Battalion began its southbound march, passing the scorched ruins of Clanwilliam House to the left, before crossing the canal at Mount Street Bridge, and proceeding in columns along Northumberland Road, the scene of such appalling carnage only days earlier.

They eventually arrived at the Ballsbridge showgrounds, where they were to be detained. As they were marched through its Anglesea Road gates, a British private approached Séamus Kavanagh while pointing at the long-striding figure of his commandant, who was several yards ahead of them. He asked Kavanagh, 'Is he your colonel?' Kavanagh eyed the soldier with great suspicion initially, but his demeanour suggested it was a completely innocent question, so he replied, 'Yes it is, but we call him Commandant.'

'What's his name then?' was the soldier's second question, to which Kavanagh replied, 'His name is de Valera.' The private looked at Kavanagh and said, 'Oh! He was a "Devilero" alright.'[16]

As Ireland's shocked capital did its best to come to terms with the magnitude of the week's events, several hundred civilians who had perished in the rebellion were swiftly interred in a mass grave in Glasnevin Cemetery by the authorities who feared an epidemic should they hesitate, due to the late spring warmth. Their number included at least 28 children.

Almost 2,000 rebel prisoners were taken to Richmond Barracks in Inchicore following the fighting. These included the 3rd Battalion, following a brief period of detention in Ballsbridge, where their treatment varied from rough to indifferent.

As soon as the ranks of the captured Republicans were securely under guard, they were separated from their officers. Ships such as cattle boats were assembled to take them across the Irish Sea to camps in Wales and England. Over the next few days, as they marched out from Inchicore for the 4-mile trek that would take them along Dublin's ruined quays to its port, the public reaction varied greatly. In some areas the Volunteers,

Flanked by a guard of troops with bayonets at the ready, Republican prisoners are marched along Dublin's quays into captivity. NATIONAL LIBRARY OF IRELAND

Na Fianna and Citizen Army members received mocking taunts and vociferous abuse, while in others, the sentiment was much more sympathetic. Many civilians confessed that in spite of their revulsion at what they had caused, one could not help but admire their fighting spirit.

The Sherwood Foresters Regiment, whose infantrymen had fought so hard against men like Michael Malone, George Reynolds, Joe O'Connor, Seán McLoughlin and hundreds of others, made up the firing squads of the leaders of the Easter Rising in May 1916. They had suffered appalling casualties in Dublin. Indeed, one of the officers detailed to command such a squad, Captain Arthur Annan Dickson, himself only narrowly survived the fighting on Northumberland Road when his field service manual, placed in his left breast pocket, stopped a bullet. The same booklet and the offending round are today housed in the Imperial War Museum in London.

The ranks of men commanded by Dickson and his fellow officers displayed very little sympathy towards the 14 surrendered men whom they shot at dawn[17] in Kilmainham over a nine-day period in May, some even suggesting at the time that bayonets would be more suitable for the grim purpose than bullets.

With the passage of time, however, military historians from both sides of the Irish Sea have acknowledged the prowess of the rebel fighters who kept thousands at bay for so long, and at such a cost. The British had faced an unflinching foe during the fighting in Easter Week, and the battle had been fought according to the rules of war, albeit with some exceptions. The Crown had engaged an enemy who had fought its forces to a standstill using fundamentally sound military tactics designed to favour a vastly outnumbered and outgunned force, using its intimate knowledge of the landscape and its buildings to compensate for such drawbacks. Their very successful employment of these tactics ironically ended up exerting a great influence on the formation of the British Army's own manual on urban street fighting. With hindsight, it was clear that the execution of such opponents contradicted the very rules they held in such lofty regard. It left many British and Irish with a bad taste in their mouths, and ultimately paved the way for a less conventional and more prolonged conflict, during which the rules of war counted for little.

Many historians have also praised the overall military strategy employed by the British High Command in Dublin during Easter Week. Its swift response and subsequent methodical isolation of the individual Republican garrisons is seen as a prime example of a well-oiled military machine in full flow. Similarly, almost every soldier who fought for the Crown, for whatever reason, fought with both aggression and tenacity. No commander can ask for more from his men.

Some British units were indeed badly led, as were some of those of the Republicans. This is the case in all wars. Atrocities were committed by both sides. This is also true of any armed conflict. Unarmed policemen and several civilians were deliberately shot by Republicans, while the British treatment of Irish civilians in at least three instances amounted to sheer, and in the cases of North King Street and Rathmines, mass murder. It must be remembered, however, that in the killing of innocents in and around Portobello Barracks on Wednesday 26 April the perpetrator spoke with an Irish accent.

In 1917 the same Sherwood Forester Battalions who fought in Ireland's capital were posted to the Western Front, where they joined with the other battalions of the regiment. That regiment remained there until the end of the Great War in November 1918, suffering over 10,000 casualties. Unlike their fallen comrades in Continental Europe, however, those Englishmen who paid the ultimate price in Dublin are not listed as having been 'killed in action'. Instead their deaths are recorded as having 'died on home service'. They lie in well-tended cemeteries, in some cases in graves next to their former enemies. Many descendants of the fallen look forward to the day when their deaths are awarded the same poignant gratitude afforded to those who officially died in combat, such as that displayed annually at London's Cenotaph on Armistice Day, 11 November.

Throughout Ireland's Republican cemetery plots, the Rising's dead are frequently honoured in worthy and moving ceremonies. Similarly, modern regimental associations ensure that the Irishmen who served the Crown as soldiers are remembered as brave men who also fought like lions. Tens of thousands of them joined up to fight in the First World War. Very few imagined themselves engaged in their home town against men who had grown up in the same streets. War, however, is full of such paradoxes. Ironically, when the fighting had finished in Dublin many soldiers in British uniforms, but with Irish accents, expressed their exasperation that the Volunteers had not waited until the Great War had ended before launching their insurrection, saying they would have gladly joined their ranks. As if to prove this, when the fighting they had signed up for in France, Belgium and elsewhere did come to a close, a significant number of these same soldiers employed the skills they had learned in the British Army to bolster the Republican cause. They set themselves against the men of the empire, at whose side they had once stood shoulder to shoulder.

On 26 April each year, a poppy wreath is placed on the railings of No. 25 Northumberland Road by the descendants of the thousands of young Englishmen who marched cheerfully into Dublin on a warm spring morning in 1916, many of whom were never to leave again. Ireland today celebrates those who lived, fought and died during that tumultuous week, each and every Easter Monday, with a variety of events to mark the occasion's annual passing. Many, however, prefer the date of 24 April to mark the actual anniversary of that fateful day in Dublin when the clock struck, and its landscape changed forever.

Epilogue

'Death did not seem to hold any terrors for them.'

VERBATIM WITNESS STATEMENT

Bureau Of Military History, 1913-1921

Statement By Witness

Document Number WS 189

Witness Michael T. Soughley

Identity
Ex D.M.P. Sergeant

I was a Constable in the D.M.P. and attached to Kilmainham Police Station in 1916. On the 24th April when the Rebellion started we were withdrawn from the streets by order of Colonel E. Johnstone, Chief Commissioner, Dublin Metropolitan Police. We had to report to our Barracks in the normal way as if reporting for duty during that week. No one interfered with us. On the 1st of May I went on night duty again. Kilmainham Prison had been closed as a civilian prison about 1904 or thereabouts. At the outbreak of the Great War in 1914 it was reopened as a Military Prison and was used as such when the Rebellion broke out. Towards the end of April 1916 and the end of the Rebellion the Prison was cleared of military prisoners and male and female prisoners were drafted in. Curfew was in force at this time and there were therefore no civilians on the streets.

On the morning of the first executions, at about 2 a.m., there was great activity in Kilmainham Jail. This was the 3rd May 1916. I was at the Police Barracks, Kilmainham, which was situated close to the Jail. Motor cars with staff officers began to arrive in the prison and a party of soldiers came from Richmond Barracks and went into the prison. A short time afterwards a large force of military commanded by an officer also came from Richmond Barracks and also entered the prison. I noticed a Volunteer officer in the centre of the party. They were travelling at a very fast pace. About five minutes after they had entered the prison the first volley of shots rang out. After a lapse of ten minutes a second volley rang out and after a further ten minutes a third volley.

A short time later the military party with the Volunteer officer whom I later ascertained was Comdt. E. Daly, returned to Richmond Barracks. I was told by an N.C.O. who was on the staff of the jail at that time that Tom Clarke had expressed a desire to see Daly before he (Clarke) was executed and as Daly was considered a very important prisoner, being one of the leaders and, in view of the fact that he (Daly) had already been tried and sentenced to death, considerable difficulty was experienced in getting the necessary authority to remove him from the Richmond Barracks to Kilmainham Jail for that purpose. The staff officers withdrew shortly after the executions and the bodies of the three executed men, wrapped in army blankets were removed in a horse-drawn army wagon to Arbour Hill.

This N.C.O. told me that when Comdt. Daly arrived at Kilmainham with his escort he was informed that as Tom Clarke was about to be executed he could not see him. Daly said he would like to see him dead or alive and he was allowed to remain. When the three men were executed their bodies lay in an old shed in which prisoners broke stones in bad weather. Daly went out to this shed - stood to attention and saluted the remains. He then took off his cap, knelt down and prayed for some time. He put on his cap again, saluted again and returned to his escort. Daly stood in the same spot the following morning for his own execution.

This N.C.O., who was a very good Catholic, being Irish and a retired R.I.C. man, told me that some of us should volunteer to go for the priest and relatives of the condemned men who were still to be executed as the soldiers who were driving the cars had a very poor knowledge of the city. He pointed out that there was a possibility that some of these men would go before firing squads without seeing their relatives or having the consolations of their religion. He told me that thirty five blindfolds and white cards had been made in readiness for executions. The white cards were pinned over the condemned men's hearts as aiming marks for the soldiers. I told him I would discuss the matter with the other policemen who were on night duty with me, but I was afraid that they, like me, would not be keen about having anything to do with executions.

When I went on duty that night at 10 p.m. I told the others about the conversation I had with this N.C.O. At first, like myself, they were rather reluctant to have anything to do with the work that was going on in Kilmainham Jail, but after some discussion we decided to go. We reported to the Jail about 11 p.m. that night. This was the 3rd May. We were put in a waiting room and were told that a staff officer had gone up to tell the condemned men that they were to be executed at dawn and to get particulars as to the relatives and clergymen they wished to see. After some time a N.C.O. came down to us. I found that Comdt. E. Daly was on the list and he was anxious to see Father Albert of Church St. as well as his two sisters - Mrs. Tom Clarke and Miss Daly. Miss Daly was staying with her sister, Mrs. Clarke, at Philipsburgh Avenue. I volunteered to bring them to Kilmainham.

The arrangements were that relatives were to be brought first and next we were to take the priest. Then the relatives were to be taken home and finally to take the priest home after the executions were over. We travelled in Army cars driven by soldier drivers.

To make sure that there would be no disappointment about the priest I went to Church St. first where I found Father Albert and told him I would be calling for him later. I went then to Philipsburgh Ave. and got Mrs. T. Clarke and Miss Daly and brought them to Kilmainham. I returned for Father Albert and brought him to the Jail. I brought the two ladies home and after the execution had been carried out I took Father Albert back to Church St. The priest always accompanied the man to his execution and administered the last rites of the Church to him after he was shot. When I arrived at the home of Mrs.

Clarke on the first occasion that night I knocked at the door and Mrs. Clarke opened it. She was in her dressing gown and seemed to be very nervous and was shaking. I later discovered that this was not so, but that it was cold she was I said I was very sorry to hear of her husband's death that morning that I knew him well and never expected he would meet such an untimely end. She replied that there was nothing to be sorry about that he had died as honourably as he had lived.

On the morning of the first executions there was only one firing party for the three men executed and I was told that the soldiers displayed considerable nervousness when the third man was brought out to be executed. On all subsequent mornings there was a different firing party for each man shot.

There was great admiration amongst the staff of the jail for the manner in which the executed leaders met their fate especially Tom Clarke who, notwithstanding his age and frail constitution, expressed his willingness to go before his firing party without a blindfold. I was also told that as far as the others were concerned they did not care whether they were blindfolded or not. Death did not seem to hold any terrors for them.

I had great sympathy for Mrs. Mallin when I brought her home from Kilmainham that morning her husband was executed, because she was in an advanced state of pregnancy at the time and, taking her condition into consideration, was bearing up remarkably well.

On the night prior to the final executions I went to the Jail for what I expected would be the last batch as Asquith, the English Prime Minister, had announced in the British Parliament that they would be the last lot of executions. No relatives of James Connolly were included in the list that we got that night at 11 p.m. He was then lying wounded in a Red Cross Hospital in Dublin Castle. The following morning the executions were completed. The firing parties and staff officers had withdrawn and a mantle of gloom once more hung over Kilmainham Prison. The staff of the Jail, as well as ourselves, were all delighted that the grim work was finished. We went back to our Barracks and about half an hour later were surprised to see a firing party return to the prison as well as staff officers. A four-wheeled General Service wagon drawn by two horses came along the old Kilmainham road at a very fast pace, swung

to the right and went into the Prison. We saw a man
sitting in the wagon surrounded by a number of soldiers
who were sitting around him. As far as I can remember
he was dressed in civilian attire. He did not seem to
be wounded that we could see, but as the soldiers were
sitting very close to him they could be supporting him
with their bodies. A short time after the wagon entered
the Jail a volley rang out and we later learned that
the victim was James Connolly. It would appear as if
Connolly's execution was a rushed affair and squeezed
in at the last moment.

Constable William Barry, 120A, who retired in 1924 and
is now living somewhere in Co. Kerry, saw John McBride
being executed.

Signed: Michael Soughley

Date: 25th Jan 1949

Witness: Matthew Barry
           Comdt

Notes

INTRODUCTION

1. Michael Joseph O'Rahilly, more commonly known as 'the O'Rahilly'. He was a co-founder of the Irish Volunteers in 1913 and also Captain of B company 3rd Battalion, Dublin Brigade. He held the posts of Treasurer and Director of Arms of the Irish Volunteers and was personally involved in the procurement, organisation and landing of arms at Howth on 26 July 1914. He was not a member of the Irish Republican Brotherhood, and was seen as part of Eoin MacNeill's wing of the Volunteers and so was excluded from the secret plans for the Rising.
2. Imelda Kelly (mother of author Darren Kelly), in conversation, 1980.

CHAPTER 1: THE ASSAULT ON THE MAGAZINE FORT, PHOENIX PARK

1. Patrick O'Daly, *Witness Statement* (henceforth *WS*) *220*, p. 3.
2. Na Fianna Éireann, Nationalist boy scout movement, founded in Dublin in 1909 by Countess Markievicz and Bulmer Hobson. They were a highly motivated and trained force pre-dating the Irish Volunteers by nearly four years.

CHAPTER 2: THE BATTLE OF CITY HALL

1. William Oman, *WS 421*, p. 7.
2. The building housed two newspapers which shared offices, the *Daily Express* and *Dublin Evening Mail*. For the purposes of this work, we refer to the building as the *Evening Mail*.
3. Paul O'Brien, *Shootout, The Battle for St Stephen's Green 1916*, p. 11.
4. Francis Sheehy-Skeffington was born in 1878 in County Cavan. He was a member of the Young Ireland branch of the United Irish League, and campaigned for women's rights both in Ireland and Britain. He became vice-chairman of the Irish Citizen Army on its formation during the Dublin Lockout of 1913, in the belief that it would have a purely defensive role, but he resigned when the Citizen Army later took on a militaristic role. On Tuesday 25 April 1916, he attempted to form a Civic Police to prevent the looting of shops in the city centre. This having failed,

he was returning home in the early evening when he was arrested by an officer of the East Surrey Regiment at Portobello Bridge and taken to Portobello Barracks. He was taken out later that night as a hostage by Captain J. C. Bowen-Colthurst of the 3rd Royal Irish Rifles, who was leading a raiding party hunting for 'Shinners'. Having captured some suspects, the captain shot two of the prisoners out of hand and ordered the others to be taken with Sheehy-Skeffington back to Portobello Barracks. There, on the following morning, Wednesday 26 April, Captain Bowen-Colthurst had two of the detainees and Sheehy-Skeffington executed by firing squad. As the firing squad walked away one soldier noticed that Sheehy-Skeffington was still moving and Bowen-Colthurst ordered another volley to be fired into him.

5. Max Caulfield, *The Easter Rebellion*, p. 116.
6. Helena Maloney, *WS 391*, p. 39.
7. Caulfield, *op. cit.*, p. 122.

CHAPTER 3: NORTHUMBERLAND ROAD, MOUNT STREET BRIDGE, BOLAND'S BAKERY AND MILLS: PART 1

1. As it does today, the area has changed little since 1916.
2. Michael Foy & Brian Barton, *The Easter Rising*, p. 117.
3. Mouse-holing was the process of tunnelling between adjoining rooms or buildings' interconnecting walls. This facilitated fully covered movement through a series of positions. The 'mouse-holes' were large enough for one man to fit through at a time. They were placed in a crooked line or on different floors, so that if the enemy penetrated the position he would be denied a straight line of sight throughout the occupied buildings.
4. James Doyle, *WS 309*, p. 5.
5. Séamus Grace, *WS 310*, p. 2. The letter was sent from Richard Balfe and was written in Irish. '*Tá muid ag fanacht leat*' may have been the only words in the letter.
6. W. C. Oates, *The Sherwood Foresters in the Great War, 1914–1918, the 2/8th Battalion*, p. 35.
7. 2/5th, 2/6th, 2/7th and 2/8th refers to the second line 5th, 6th, 7th and 8th Battalions. These were made up primarily of territorials who had enlisted as part of the Home (Reserve) Army and could be deployed anywhere within the United Kingdom. While the first-line battalions, which were made up of professional soldiers of the standing army, were serving in France, the second line would send replacements when needed, but the soldiers had to agree to Imperial Service; by the end of 1914 nearly all reserve battalions had agreed to Imperial Service. The officers were a mixture of territorials and men either wounded or on leave from the front-line battalions. As the war progressed, the second-line battalions were moved to front, and a third-line battalion was formed to send replacements to the first- and second-line battalions.
8. 'C' Company advanced in a box formation, with the lead platoon stretched across the width of the road. The following platoons advanced along the pavements in column, where they could cover side streets and clear houses if necessary.
9. Max Caulfield, *The Easter Rebellion*, p. 192.

10. Dum-dum is the common name given to an expanding bullet and derives from the Dum Dum arsenal near Calcutta in India. The bullet either had a hollow point or a soft point and was designed to expand on impact, which would either limit penetration or produce a large exit wound, resulting in horrific injuries. In 1898, Germany protested against its use, stating that the wounds were excessive and inhumane. In 1899 the Hague Convention prohibited its use in time of war between civilised nations.

11. Paul O'Brien, Blood on the Streets 1916 & The Battle for Mount Street Bridge, p. 58.

12. Oates, *op. cit.*, p. 39.

CHAPTER 4: NORTHUMBERLAND ROAD, MOUNT STREET BRIDGE, BOLAND'S BAKERY AND MILLS: PART 2

1. Captain Gerrard had just returned from the Dardanelles and was stationed with the 5th Reserve Artillery Brigade, based in Athlone.

2. W. C. Oates, *The Sherwood Foresters in the Great War, 1914–1918, the 2/8th Battalion*, pp. 35, 39.

3. Thomas and James Walsh, *WS 198*, p. 19.

4. James Doyle, *WS 309*, p. 11.

5. The term 'shell shock' was widely in use in 1916. Major C. S. Myers wrote an article named 'Contributions to the study of Shell Shock' for *The Lancet* in March 1916. This term was already in use in the trenches, as well as the term 'the thousand-yard stare'.

CHAPTER 5: ST STEPHEN'S GREEN AND THE ROYAL COLLEGE OF SURGEONS

1. Born Constance Georgina Gore-Booth in 1868, elder daughter of Sir Henry Gore-Booth of Lissadell, County Sligo. She married a Polish count, Casimir Markievicz, in 1900.

2. http://irishvolunteers.org

3. Max Caulfield, *The Easter Rebellion*, p. 83.

4. Frank Robbins, *WS 585*, pp. 61–2.

5. James Stephens, *The Insurrection in Dublin*, p. 24.

6. Robbins, *op. cit.*, p. 69.

7. Margaret Skinnider, *Doing My Bit for Ireland*, pp. 134–5. She wore a man's-style uniform in green moleskin, consisting of tunic, knee-breeches and puttees. It is highly unlikely that it displayed any Volunteer or Citizen Army insignia.

CHAPTER 6: THE SOUTH DUBLIN UNION AND MARROWBONE LANE

1. Royal Hospital was the residence of the Commander-in-Chief of the British forces in Ireland.

2. This is not the famous whiskey brand of John Jameson but of his son William Jameson. William went into business with his father-in-law John Stein *c.* 1800 who owned the Marrowbone Lane Distillery. He died soon after and control of his share passed to his brother James, who assumed control of the distillery in 1820 when he purchased John Stein's interest in the business.
3. Peadar Doyle, *WS 155*, p. 11.
4. Paul O'Brien, *Uncommon Valour 1916 and the Battle for the South Dublin Union*, p. 30.
5. Gerald Doyle, *WS 1511*, p. 9.
6. Cumann na mBan (Women's League) was founded in Dublin in April 1914. Although an independent organisation, its Executive Council was subordinate to that of the Irish Volunteers.
7. Thomas Young, *WS 531*, p. 5.

CHAPTER 7: JACOB'S BISCUIT FACTORY

1. A river in north-eastern Italy. No Roman army was allowed to cross the river as it was seen as an act of insurrection. Julius Caesar crossed in 49 BC with the Legion *Legio XIII Gemina* which led to civil war in Rome. A modern equivalent to the term would be 'passing the point of no return'.
2. In the 1912 Olympic Games, Great Britain entered three teams for the road race, one each for England, Scotland and Ireland. All three came under the National Olympic Committee of Great Britain. Michael Walker cycled for Ireland, but under the Olympic banner of Great Britain, and achieved the rank of 67th for the individual road race.
3. Vincent Byrne, *WS 423*, p. 2.
4. Seosamh de Brún, *WS 312*, p. 3.
5. The Separation Allowance was paid to women whose husbands had enlisted in the British Armed Forces for the duration of the First World War. They frequently wore black scarf-type shawls around their heads, hence the nickname.
6. Sceilg (O'Kelly, J. J.), *Dublin's Fighting Story*, p. 79.
7. John MacDonagh, *WS 532*, p. 10.
8. de Brún, *op. cit.*, p. 9.
9. Thomas Slater, *WS 263*, p. 19.

CHAPTER 8: THE FOUR COURTS

1. Nicholas Laffan, *WS 201*, p. 5.
2. Thomas Smart, *WS 255*, p. 2.
3. Michael O'Flanagan, *WS 800*, p. 18.
4. http://irishvolunteers.org
5. McLoughlin acted as forward point, making sure the way was clear. The reinforcements were led by another volunteer whom McLoughlin names as J. J. Scollan. *WS 290*, p. 12.

6. It is interesting to note that some Volunteers used Irish versions of their fore and surnames after 1916: for example, Paddy Daly signed his witness statement 'Patrick O'Daly'. Seán Heuston was already known in Volunteer circles as 'Seán', but had earlier been known to family and friends as 'J.J.'

7. Patrick O'Daly, *WS 220*, p. 9.

CHAPTER 9: NORTH KING STREET AND NORTH BRUNSWICK STREET

1. John Shouldice, *WS 162*, p. 4.
2. Thomas Smart, *WS 255*, p. 3.
3. Piaras Béaslaí, *Dublin's Fighting Story*, p. 105.
4. Lieut.-Col F. Raynor, *'The Robin Hoods' 1/7th, 2/7th & 3/7th Battns. Sherwood Foresters 1914–1918*, p. 290.
5. Seán Kennedy, *WS 842*, p. 13.
6. Seán O'Duffy, *WS 313*, p. 7.

CHAPTER 10: THE GENERAL POST OFFICE AND SACKVILLE STREET: PART 1

1. The Kimmage garrison was made up mainly of men from the Irish Volunteers in Scotland and England. They began to arrive in Dublin in 1915 to avoid conscription into the British Army and were known by the local Dublin Volunteers as 'the Refugees'. They were based at Count Plunkett's Larkfield estate in Kimmage.
2. Michael Staines, *WS 284*, p. 11.
3. Ciaran Byrne, *The Harp and Crown, The History of the 5th (Royal Irish) Lancers 1902–1922*, p. 105.
4. 'E' Company of the 4th Battalion of the Irish Volunteers was known as 'Pearse's own', or the 'Headquarters Company'. The Company was based in the Rathfarnham area with Pearse as the officer in command.
5. Lorcan Collins, *16 Lives, James Connolly*, p. 280.
6. Thomas Devine, *WS 428*, p. 3.
7. Frank Thornton also went under the alias of Frank Drennan.
8. Lorcan Collins, *op. cit.*, p. 280.
9. W. J. Brennan-Whitmore, 'The Occupation of the North Earl Street Area', *An t-Óglác*, p. 4.
10. Desmond Ryan, *WS 428*, p. 11.
11. Max Caulfield, *The Easter Rebellion*, p. 165.

CHAPTER 11: THE GENERAL POST OFFICE AND SACKVILLE STREET: PART 2

1. Frank Thornton, *WS 510*, p. 17.
2. Caulfield, *op. cit.*, p. 245.
3. James Kenny, *WS 141*, p. 6.
4. Séamus Daly, *WS 360*, p. 40.
5. Kevin McCabe, *WS 926*, p. 10.

CHAPTER 12: THE GENERAL POST OFFICE AND THE BATTLE OF MOORE STREET

1. Max Caulfield, *The Easter Rebellion*, p. 243.
2. Jack Plunkett, *WS 488*, p. 28.
3. John J. Doyle, *WS 748*, p. 11.
4. *Ibid.*, p. 13.
5. Feargus de Búrca, *WS 694*, p. 19.
6. The *Pickelhaube* was a spiked helmet worn in the 19th and 20th centuries by German military/police and firefighters. A horsehair plume could be attached, which was common with cavalry regiments.
7. Seán Price, *WS 769*, p. 5.
8. Caulfield, *op. cit.*, p. 263.
9. Charles Saurin, *WS 288*, p. 30.

CHAPTER 13: THE SURRENDERS: PART 1

1. Seán McLoughlin, *WS 290*, p. 29.
2. Charles Saurin, *WS 288*, p. 34.
3. Thomas Leahy, *WS 660*, p. 16.
4. Seán McLoughlin , *WS 290*, p. 32.
5. Liam O'Carroll, *WS 314*, p. 14.
6. Eamon Morkan, *WS 411*, p. 10.
7. Piaras Béaslaí, *Dublin's Fighting Story*, p. 107.
8. Mortimer O'Connell, *WS 804*, p. 26.
9. John J. Reynolds, 'Four Courts and North King Street Area in 1916', *An t-Óglác*, p. 4.

CHAPTER 14: THE SURRENDERS: PART 2

1. Thomas O'Donoghue, *WS 1666*, p. 27.
2. Rev. Fr Aloysius, *WS 200*, p. 6.
3. Frank Robbins, *WS 585*, p. 80.
4. Seán Byrne, *WS 422*, p. 14.
5. *Ibid.*, p. 16.
6. Seán McLoughlin, *WS 290*, p. 34.
7. Eamon Price, *WS 995*, p. 2.
8. Thomas Pugh, *WS 397*, p. 7.
9. James Coughlan, *WS 304*, p. 24.
10. Joseph O'Byrne, *WS 160*, p. 11.
11. Michael Walker, *WS 139*, p. 7.
12. Patrick Smyth, *WS 305*, p. 4.
13. James Foran, *WS 243*, p. 9.
14. Robert Holland, *WS 280*, p. 43.
15. Andrew McDonnell, *WS 1768*, p. 15.

16. Séamus Kavanagh, *WS 208*, p. 13.
17. There is still much confusion over when the executions were carried out. In April 1916 dawn broke at approximately 3 a.m. Daylight saving began in Great Britain on 21 May, so the men executed before that date were shot around 3 a.m., and after 21 May at around 4 a.m. Also, Dublin Mean Time – which was dispensed with after the Rising, on 1 October 1916 – was 25 minutes behind GMT.

Sources

BUREAU OF MILITARY HISTORY, 1913–1921

WITNESS STATEMENTS

Aloysius, Rev. Father. *WS 200*
Archer, Liam. *WS 819*
Augustine, Rev. Father. *WS 920*
Balfe, Richard. *WS 251*
Bean Uí Chonaill, Eilís. *WS 568*
Byrne, Christopher. *WS 167*
Byrne, Seán. *WS 422*
Byrne, Seán. *WS 579*
Byrne, Thomas. *WS 564*
Byrne, Vincent. *WS 423*
Caldwell, Patrick. *WS 638*
Callender, Ignatius. *WS 923*
Christian, William. *WS 646*
Cody, Seán. *WS 1035*
Coghlan, Francis. *WS 1760*
Colley, Harry. *WS 1687*
Collins, Maurice. *WS 550*
Connolly, Matthew. *WS 1746*
Corrigan, William. *WS 250*
Cosgrave, Liam T. *WS 268*
Coughlan, James. *WS 304*
Cremen, Michael. *WS 563*
Crenigan, James. *WS 148*
Curran, Lily. *WS 805*
Daly, Séamus. *WS 360*
De Brún, Seosamh. *WS 312*
De Búrca, Feargus. *WS 694*
Devine, Thomas. *WS 428*
Donnelly, Charles. *WS 824*
Doolan, Joseph. *WS 199*
Dowling, Thomas. *WS 533*

Doyle, Gerald. *WS 1511*
Doyle, James. *WS 127*
Doyle, James. *WS 309*
Doyle, John. *WS 748*
Doyle, P. S. *WS 155*
Doyle, Séamus. *WS 166*
Doyle, Thomas. *WS 186*
Egan, Patrick. *WS 327*
Fitzgerald, Theo. *WS 218*
Folan, Peter. *WS 316*
Foran, James. *WS 243*
Fulham, James. *WS 630*
Furlong, Joseph. *WS 335*
Gay, Thomas B. *WS 780*
Gerrard, E. *WS 348*
Gleeson, Joseph. *WS 367*
Grace, James. *WS 310*
Hackett, Rose. *WS 546*
Hanratty, John. *WS 96*
Hayes, Michael. *WS 215*
Henderson, Captain R. *WS 1686*
Henderson, Frank. *WS 249*
Heron, Áine. *WS 293*
Holland, Robert. *WS 280*
Irvine, George. *WS 265*
Kavanagh, Séamus. *WS 1670*
Kavanagh, Séamus. *WS 208*
Kelly, Patrick. *WS 781*
Kennedy, Seán. *WS 842*
Kenny, James. *WS 141*
Kenny, James. *WS 174*

Kenny, Séamus. *WS 158*
King, Martin. *WS 543*
Knightly, Michael. *WS 833*
Laffan, Nicholas. *WS 201*
Lawless, Michael. *WS 727*
Leahy, Thomas. *WS 660*
Lynch, Michael. *WS 511*
Lynn, Kathleen. *WS 357*
MacCarthy, Dan. *WS 722*
MacCarthy, Thomas. *WS 307*
Mannion, Annie. *WS 297*
Martin, Eamon. *WS 592*
McCabe, Kevin. *WS 926*
McCrea, Patrick. *WS 413*
McDonagh, John. *WS 532*
McDonnell, Andrew. *WS 1768*
McDonnell, Michael. *WS 225*
McDonough, Joseph. *WS 1082*
McLoughlin, Seán. *WS 290*
McMahon, Peadar. *WS 1730*
Molloy, Michael. *WS 716*
Molony, Helena. *WS 391*
Morkan, Eamon. *WS 411*
Mullen, Patrick. *WS 621*
Murphy, Fintan. *WS 370*
Murphy, Seán. *WS 204*
Murphy, William. *WS 352*
Murray, Henry. *WS 300*
Murray, Séamus. *WS 308*
Nicholls, Harry. *WS 296*
Nolan, George. *WS 596*
O'Brien, Annie. *WS 805*
O'Brien, Laurence. *WS 252*
Ó'Buachalla, Domhnall. *WS 194*
O'Byrne, Joseph. *WS 160*
O'Carroll, Liam. *WS 314*
Ó'Ceallaigh, Pádraig. *WS 376*
O'Connell, Mortimer. *WS 804*
O'Connor, Joseph. *WS 157*
O'Daly, Patrick. *WS 220*
O'Dea, Michael. *WS 1152*
O'Donoghue, Father Thomas. *WS 1666*
O'Donovan, Cornelius. *WS 1750*
O'Duffy, Seán. *WS 313*
Ó'Flaithbheartaigh, Liam. *WS 248*
O'Flanagan, George. *WS 131*
O'Flanagan, Michael. *WS 800*

O'Grady, Charles. *WS 282*
O'Keeffe, Seán. *WS 188*
O'Kelly, Fergus. *WS 351*
O'Mara, Peadar. *WS 377*
O'Neill, Edward. *WS 203*
O'Reilly, Eily O'Hanrahan. *WS 270*
O'Reilly, Michael. *WS 866*
O'Rourke, Joseph. *WS 1244*
O'Shea, James. *WS 733*
O'Sullivan, Séamus. *WS 393*
Oman, William. *WS 421*
Peppard, Thomas. *WS 1399*
Plunkett, Jack. *WS 488*
Pounch, Séamus. *WS 267*
Prendergast, Seán. *WS 755*
Price, Eamon. *WS 995*
Price, Seán. *WS 769*
Pugh, Thomas. *WS 397*
Reynolds, Joseph. *WS 191*
Robbins, Frank. *WS 585*
Robinson, Séamus. *WS 156*
Robinson, Séamus. *WS 1721*
Ryan, Desmond. *WS 724*
Saurin, Charles. *WS 288*
Scollan, John. *WS 318*
Shelley, Charles. *WS 870*
Shouldice, John. *WS 162*
Slater, Thomas. *WS 263*
Slattery, James. *WS 445*
Smart, Thomas. *WS 255*
Smyth, Patrick. *WS 305*
Soughley, Michael T. *WS 189*
Stafford, Jack. *WS 818*
Staines, Michael. *WS 284*
Stapleton, James. *WS 822*
Tannam, Liam. *WS 242*
Thornton, Frank. *WS 510*
Traynor, Oscar. *WS 340*
Twamley, John. *WS 629*
Ua Caomhánaigh, Séamus. *WS 889*
Ua h-Uallacháin, Gearóid. *WS 328*
Walker, Michael. *WS 139*
Walpole, R. H. *WS 218*
Walsh, James. *WS 198*
Walsh, Thomas. *WS 198*
Whelan, William. *WS 369*
Young, Thomas. *WS 531*

IMPERIAL WAR MUSEUM, LONDON

Private Papers.
Davis, H. J. Private papers, Catalogue number – *11831*
Dent, R. A. W. Private papers, Catalogue number – *14246*
Hannant, A. C. Private papers, Catalogue number – *7500*
Jameson, A. M. Private papers, Catalogue number – *7072*

Books.
Edmunds, G. J. *The Irish Rebellion: the 2/6th Sherwood Foresters' part in the defeat of the rebels in 1916, their early training.* (Wilfred Edmunds, Chesterfield, 1961) Copy number – *45747.*
Hall, W. G. *The Green triangle, being the history of the 2/5th Battalion, The Sherwood Foresters (Notts. and Derby Regiment) in the Great European War 1914–1918.* (Garden City, Letchworth, 1920) Copy number – *50301*
Meakin, Walter. *The 5th North Staffords and North Midland Territorials (The 46th and 59th Division), 1914–1919.* (Hughes and Harber, Longton, 1920) Copy number – *8216.*
Various. *The War History of the Sixth Battalion, the South Staffordshire Regiment. (T. F.).* (Heinemann, London, 1924) Copy number – *65471.*

JOURNALS

Brennan-Whitmore, W. J., 'The Defence of the North Earl St. Area', *An t-Óglác*, IV, 4 (6 February 1926)
Brennan-Whitmore, W. J., 'The Occupation of the G.P.O.:1916', *An t-Óglác*, IV, 1 (16 January 1926)
Brennan-Whitmore, W. J., 'The Occupation of the North Earl St. Area', *An t-Óglác*, IV, 3 (30 January 1926)
Joyce, J. V., 'The Defence of the South Dublin Union', *An t-Óglác*, IV, 22 (12 June 1926)
Lyons, George A., 'Occupation of Ringsend Area in 1916.' *An t-Óglác*, IV, 13 (10 April 1926)
Lyons, George A., 'Occupation of Ringsend Area in 1916.' *An t-Óglác*, IV, 14 (17 April 1926)
Lyons, George A., 'Occupation of Ringsend Area in 1916.' *An t-Óglác*, IV, 15 (24 April 1926)
O'Daly, Nora, 'The Women of Easter Week', *An t-Óglác*, IV, 12 (3 April 1926)
Reynolds, John J., 'Four Courts and the North King St. Area in 1916', part 1, *An t-Óglác*, IV, 18 (15 May 1926)
Reynolds, John J., 'Four Courts and the North King St. Area in 1916', part 2, *An t-Óglác*, IV, 19 (22 May 1926)
Reynolds, John J., 'Four Courts and the North King St. Area in 1916.' *An t-Óglác*, IV, 20 (29 May 1926)
Saurin, Charles, 'Hotel Metropole Garrison', *An t-Óglác*, IV, 10 (20 March 1926)
Saurin, Charles, 'Hotel Metropole Garrison', *An t-Óglác*, IV, 9 (13 March 1926)
Staines, M. J. and O'Reilly, M. W., 'The Defence of the G.P.O.', *An t-Óglác*, IV, 2 (23 January 1926)

Steinmayer, Charles, 'Evacuation of the G.P.O., 1916.' *An t-Óglác,* IV, 7 (27 February 1926)

Turner, C., 'The Defence of Messrs. Hopkins and Hopkins, O'Connell St.' *An t-Óglác,* IV, 21 (5 June 1926)

SELECTED READING

Books

Bradbridge, E. U., *59th Division 1915–1918* (Chesterfield, Wilfred Edmunds Ltd, 1928)

Byrne, Ciaran, *The Harp and Crown, The History of the 5th (Royal Irish) Lancers 1902–1922* (Self Published, 2008)

Cathasaigh, P. O., *The Story of the Irish Citizen Army* (Honolulu, University Press of The Pacific, 2003)

Caulfield, Max, *The Easter Rebellion* (Dublin, Gill & Macmillan, 1995)

Collins, Lorcan, *James Connolly: 16 Lives* (Dublin, O'Brien Press, 2012)

Coogan, Tim Pat, *1916: The Easter Rising* (London, Phoenix, 2005)

Coogan, Tim Pat, *Michael Collins, A Biography* (London, Arrow Books Ltd, 1991)

Daly, Paul, O'Brien Rónán & Rouse, Paul, *Making the Difference: The Irish Labour Party 1912–2012* (Cork, The Collins Press, 2012)

Foy, Michael & Barton, Brian, *The Easter Rising* (Gloucestershire, Sutton Publishing Ltd, 2004)

Griffith, Lisa Marie, *Stones of Dublin: A History of Dublin in Ten Buildings* (Cork, The Collins Press, 2014)

Hamilton-Norway, Mrs, *The Sinn Féin Rebellion As I Saw It* (London, Smith, Elder & Co., 1916)

Irish Times, Weekly, *Sinn Féin Rebellion Handbook Easter 1916* (Dublin, *Weekly Irish Times,* 1917)

Joy, Maurice, *The Irish Rebellion of 1916 and its Martyrs: Erin's Tragic Easter* (New York, The Devin-Adair Company, 1916)

Kostick, Conor, & Collins, Lorcan, *The Easter Rising: a guide to Dublin in 1916* (Dublin, O'Brien Press, 2000)

McCarthy, Cal, *Cumann na mBan and the Irish Revolution revised ed.* (Cork, The Collins Press, 2014)

McGarry, Fearghal, *Rebel Voices from the Easter Rising* (London, Penguin Books, 2012)

McGuire, Charlie, *Seán McLoughlin, Ireland's Forgotten Revolutionary* (Pontypool, Merlin Press, 2011)

McNally, Michael, *Easter Rising 1916, Birth of the Irish Republic* (Oxford, Osprey Publishing, 2009)

O'Brien, Paul, *Blood on the Streets, 1916 & The Battle for Mount Street Bridge* (Cork, Mercier Press, 2008)

O'Brien, Paul, *Crossfire, The Battle of the Four Courts, 1916* (Dublin, New Island, 2012)

O'Brien, Paul, *Shootout, The Battle for St Stephen's Green, 1916* (Dublin, New Island, 2013)

O'Brien, Paul, *Uncommon Valour, 1916 & The Battle for the South Dublin Union* (Cork, Mercier Press, 2010)

O'Broichain, Honor, *Joseph Plunkett: 16 Lives* (Dublin, O'Brien Press, 2012)

O'Farrell, Mick, *50 Things You Didn't Know About 1916* (Cork, Mercier Press, 2009)

Oates, W. C., *The Sherwood Foresters in the Great War 1914–1918. The 2/8th Battalion* (Nottingham, J. & H. Bell Limited, 1920)

Pearse, Patrick, *The Coming Revolution, The Political Writings and Speeches of Patrick Pearse* (Cork, Mercier Press, 2012)

Redmond-Howard, L. G., *Six Days of the Irish Republic* (London, Maunsel & Co. Ltd, 1916)

Skinnider, Margaret, *Doing My Bit for Ireland* (New York, The Century Co., 1917)

Stephens, James, *The Insurrection in Dublin* (New York, The Macmillan Company, 1917)

Stiles, Dean, *Portrait of a Rebellion, English Press Reporting of the Easter Rising, Dublin, Ireland in 1916* (Self Published, 2012)

Various, *'The Robin Hoods' 1/7th, 2/7th, & 3/7th Battns. Sherwood Foresters 1914–1918* (Nottingham, J. & H. Bell Ltd, 1921)

Various, *Dublin's Fighting Story 1916–21* (Cork, Mercier Press, 2009)

Von Clausewitz, Carl, *On War* (Hertfordshire, Wordsworth Editions Limited, 1997)

Wells, Warre B. & Marlowe, N., *A History of the Irish Rebellion of 1916* (London, Maunsel & Company, Ltd, 1916)

White, G. & O'Shea, B., *Irish Volunteer Soldier 1913–23* (Oxford, Osprey Publishing, 2003)

Booklets

Cumann na mBan, *The Fianna Heroes of 1916* (Dublin, Cumann na mBan, 1931)

Reynolds, John J., *A Fragment of 1916 History* (Dublin, Sinn Féin, 1919)

WEBSITES

www.awm.gov.au
www.blackcountry-territorials.org
www.bureauofmilitaryhistory.ie
www.communistpartyofireland.ie
www.dublin-fusiliers.com
www.grantonline.com
www.inniskillingsmuseum.com
www.irishmedals.org
http://irishvolunteers.org
www.militaryarchives.ie
www.nli.ie
www.thegazette.co.uk
www.westernfrontassociation.com

SPOKEN WORD

CD

RTÉ, *The Story of Easter Week 1916*, RTÉ273CD (RTÉ, 2006)

Acknowledgements

DARREN: to my gorgeous wife, Joanne, no words can describe the gratitude I have for all the help, advice and support you have shown me over the last two years. Also to my children Aaron, Líam and Adele, first for making me laugh when I needed it most and second for just being my lovely kids.

DEREK: the biggest thanks here must go to Lisa, my beautiful wife, and to my equally beautiful daughters, Shannon and Catriona, for all the help and encouragement, and for not collectively disowning me, having been driven demented over the course of several years with this book.

Thanks also so much to our parents and families for their untiring support. The authors would like to thank Commandant Kennedy, Lisa Dolan and all the staff at the Bureau of Military History 1913–1921; Meadhbh Murphy at RSCI Mercer Library; Shahera Begum, Sally Web and staff of the Imperial War Museum; Captain Claire Mortimer, Rob McEvoy and Dermot Gibney of Military Archives, Cathal Brugha Barracks; Orna Somerville and Seamus Helferty at UCD Archives; John O'Sullivan, Berni Metcalfe, Nora Thornton, Glenn Dunne and Keith Murphy, National Library of Ireland; Fergal Connolly, National Museum of Ireland; Mairéad Treanor, Met Éireann; Gwen of La Fayette Photography; and Hugh Beckett, Military Archives.

Thanks to all of the following for help and input: Kevin Brennan, Magda, Thomasz and Kris from Top Floor Hub Photography; Geoff Pye, Terry Cronin, Carolyn Doherty, Axel Meyer, Paul Rumens, Sinclair Dowey, Jim Barrett, Dick Sweetman, Travis Cosgrave, Tom Mates, Las Fallon, John Stritch, Jimmy Sheridan, Ashley Whelan Collins, Jason Sheridan, Petrus Van Hoyden, Majella Kavanagh, Tanith Conway, Thomas

Lawless, Jason Healy, all of whose kind words and comments at this project's genesis made a huge difference. Particular thanks here must go to Theresa Culleton whose tremendous assistance came at a crucial time: her encouragement provided solace when we thought we were mad even to consider that our work would find its way into a bookshop. No less gratitude applies to Pat Rooney for his unflinching critique which was hugely helpful at just the right time.

Thanks to Mick O'Brien of Self-Protection Ireland, for tremendous help and assistance on all things military, owing to which our work has dodged many bullets. His input has enabled us to delve into the depths of the physical, mental and emotional sensations that accompany combat. In this regard he was instrumental in reinforcing to us the huge and often overlooked influence of Non-Commissioned Officers in the military, and the importance of squads and sections when the overall plan breaks down, as it inevitably does. Similar gratitude extends to Patrick Cumiskey of Krav Maga Ireland for introducing Derek to the smell of fear.

Thanks to Paul O'Brien, a hugely respected author of many excellent works on the 1916 Rising, who was always happy to provide valuable advice and encouragement. Similar thanks also to Lorcan Collins, whose unique presentations on the Rising were hugely influential. To Carl Von Clausewitz for the classic book *On War*. Thanks also to Eamon Murphy, Niall Oman and Barry Lyons for their generous permission to use their relatives' photographs, and for providing us with invaluable information with which to cross reference our sources.

Thanks to Byron, Neil and everyone at The Hub Ireland; Jennifer Brookman at the Museum of the Mercian Regiment; Easter Rising Historical Society; War Forces Records and the Western Front Association.

Thanks to all the followers of the Facebook page 'Dublin 1916 Then and Now' whose energetic support helped set us upon this journey. We hope to count on your continuing support in maintaining the memories that bounce from our city walls and place our capital among the most historic in the world. Finally, thanks so much to everybody at The Collins Press for their enthusiasm and tireless support.

Index

Note: Illustrations are indicated by page numbers in **bold**.

Warmington, Alfred 123–4
Warrington Place 79
water towers, Grand Canal Street 46, 76, 79, 80
Watkin's Brewery 118–19, 133, 134
Watling Street 184
Weafer, Tom 147, 151–2, 224, 228, 229, 234–5
Weaver's Square 119
Wellington Barracks 119, 138, 149, 151
Westland Row railway station 6, 46, 86, 162, 295
Westmoreland Street 236, 238
Wexford Street 153, 160
Whelan, Patrick 66, 85, 87
Whelan, Séamus 17

Whelan, William 250–51
White House 264, 265, 266
William Street South 261
Williams & Woods Sweet and Soap Factory 258–9, 263, 271
Wilson, B. 221, 222
Wilson, Mark 199–200, 210–11
Wilson, Peter 186
Wood Quay 187
Wright, H.C. 65–6
Wynn's Hotel 215, 244

YMCA building 242
York Street 100, 106, 163, 292, 293, 294, 296
Young, Thomas 130–31, 132, 134–6, 301